This important collection of essays brings together both established figures and new researchers to offer fresh perspectives on the ever-controversial subject of the history of witchcraft. Using Keith Thomas' *Religion and the Decline of Magic* as a starting point, the contributors explore the changes of the last twenty-five years in the understanding of early modern witchcraft, and suggest new approaches, especially concerning the cultural dimensions of the subject. Witchcraft cases must be understood as power struggles, over gender and ideology as well as social relationships, with a crucial role played by alternative representations. Witchcraft was always a contested idea, never fully established in early modern culture but much harder to dislodge than has usually been assumed. The essays are European in scope, with examples from Germany, France and the Spanish expansion into the New World, as well as a strong core of English material.

Past and Present Publications

Witchcraft in early modern Europe

Past and Present Publications

General Editor: JOANNA INNES, *Somerville College, Oxford*

Past and Present Publications comprise books similar in character to the articles in the journal *Past and Present*. Whether the volumes in the series are collections of essays – some previously published, others new studies – or monographs, they encompass a wide variety of scholarly and original works primarily concerned with social, economic and cultural changes, and their causes and consequences. They will appeal to both specialists and non-specialists and will endeavour to communicate the results of historical and allied research in the most readable and lively form.

For a list of titles in Past and Present Publications, see end of book.

Witchcraft in early modern Europe

Studies in culture and belief

EDITED BY

JONATHAN BARRY
University of Exeter

MARIANNE HESTER
University of Bristol

AND

GARETH ROBERTS
University of Exeter

CAMBRIDGE
UNIVERSITY PRESS

Published by the Press Syndicate of the University of Cambridge
The Pitt Building, Trumpington Street, Cambridge CB2 1RP
40 West 20th Street, New York, NY 10011-4211, USA
10 Stamford Road, Oakleigh, Melbourne 3166, Australia

First published 1996

Printed in Great Britain at the University Press, Cambridge

A catalogue record for this book is available from the British Library

Library of Congress cataloguing in publication data
Witchcraft in early modern Europe: studies in culture and belief /
edited by Jonathan Barry, Marianne Hester, and Gareth Roberts.
    p.   cm. – (Past and Present Publications)
Includes bibliographical references.
ISBN 0 521 55224 9
1. Witchcraft – Europe – History. 2. Witchcraft – England – History.
3. Occultism – Europe. I. Barry, Jonathan, 1956– .
II. Hester, Marianne, 1955– . III. Roberts, Gareth, 1949– .
BF1566.W738 1996
133.4'3'094 – dc20 95–22865 CIP

ISBN 0 521 55224 9 hardback

To Keith Thomas

Contents

Preface

With two exceptions, the essays in this collection arise from papers delivered at a conference on the cultural contexts of the European witch-hunts, held at the University of Exeter in September 1991. The editors are grateful to all those who participated in making that conference a most memorable occasion, and in particular to our co-organiser, Colin Jones, who has also contributed much to making this volume possible. We should also like to thank the organisations whose grants helped fund the conference, namely the British Academy, the Nuffield Foundation, the University of Exeter's Research Fund and the School of English and American Studies at the University.

The editors also wish gratefully to acknowledge *History Workshop Journal* for permission to reprint Lyndal Roper's essay 'Witchcraft and fantasy in early modern Germany', where it first appeared in vol. 32 (Autumn 1991).

The conference was timed to coincide with the twentieth anniversary of the publication of *Religion and the Decline of Magic* by Keith Thomas, and many of the papers sought to re-evaluate the arguments of that work in the light of subsequent research. This collection continues that dialogue, both in its introduction and in the shaping of the essays into five sections reflecting the five chapters on witchcraft in *Religion and the Decline of Magic*. We are very grateful to Keith Thomas for his support for both the conference and this collection; it cannot be easy to be subjected to historiographical dissection while still alive and fully conscious! The editors are very aware of the long period that has elapsed since the conference and would like to thank all the contributors for their patience in awaiting publication of what has become a twenty-fifth anniversary gift, as recorded in our dedication.

Contributors

JONATHAN BARRY is a Senior Lecturer in History at the University of Exeter. He has published widely on the social and cultural history of early modern England, notably on towns. Two monographs are forthcoming on Bristol, based on his Oxford doctoral thesis supervised by Keith Thomas.

WOLFGANG BEHRINGER teaches at the University of Bonn. He has published widely on a variety of subjects including history of communication, prehistory of flight, witchcraft and the social and cultural history of early modern Germany. He is co-editor of the publication series 'Hexenforschung' and editor of *Hexen und Hexenprozesse in Deutschland* (3rd edn 1995). His Ph.D. 'Hexenverfolung in Bayern' is soon to be published in an English translation by Cambridge University Press.

WILLEM DE BLÉCOURT is an historical anthropologist. He is currently attached to the Erasmus University as a NWO post-doctoral research fellow, studying the social history of irregular medical practitioners in the Netherlands and the midwestern United States in the nineteenth and twentieth centuries. He has published extensively on European witchcraft from the fifteenth to the twentieth centuries.

IAN BOSTRIDGE was a British Academy post-doctoral fellow and Junior Research Fellow at Corpus Christi College Oxford, and is now a singer. *Sorcery Shipwrecked: Witchcraft and its Transformations 1650–1750* will be published by Oxford University Press in 1996.

ROBIN BRIGGS is Senior Research Fellow of All Souls College, Oxford and University Lecturer in Modern History. His two more recent books are *Communities of Belief: Cultural and Social Tension in Early Modern France* (Oxford 1989) and *Early Modern France* (Oxford 1977). His book *Witches and Neighbours: The Social and Cultural Context of European Witchcraft* will be published in 1996.

FERNANDO CERVANTES is Lecturer in Hispanic and Latin American Studies at the University of Bristol. He is author of *The Devil in the New World* (Yale 1994) and is currently working on a general history of the Hispanic world, 1450–1700.

PETER ELMER is Staff Tutor, Arts, South West region, for the Open University. He is currently completing a study of the Irish miracle healer, Valentine Greatrakes and is working on a study of the decline of elite belief in witchcraft in early modern England.

MALCOLM GASKILL studied at Cambridge University where, in 1994, he received his doctorate for a thesis on attitudes to crime in early modern England. His current research interests include popular mentalities, and more specifically witchcraft about which he is presently writing a book. He teaches history at Anglia Polytechnic University, Cambridge.

MARIANNE HESTER is Lecturer in the School for Policy Studies at the University of Bristol. Much of her research has been in the area of violence and abuse, with a focus on both contemporary social theory and historical approaches. Her publications include *Lewd Women and Wicked Witches* (Routledge 1992); *Stirring It: Challenges to Feminism* (Taylor and Francis 1994); *Women, Violence and Male Power* (Open University Press 1995).

BRIAN P. LEVACK is John E. Green Regents Professor of History at the University of Texas at Austin. His publications include *The Civil Lawyers in England, 1603–1641* (1973); *The Formation of the British State: England, Scotland and the Union, 1603–1707* (1987); and *The Witch-Hunt in Early Modern Europe* (1987; 2nd edn 1995).

GARETH ROBERTS lectures on Renaissance literature at the University of Exeter. He is the author of *The Open Guide to Spenser's Faerie Queene* (Open University Press 1992) and *The Mirror of Alchemy* (British Library 1994). With Lawrence Normand he is writing *Witch-hunting in Early Modern Scotland* (Exeter University Press 1996), editing *The Comedy of Errors* (Arden 3 Shakespeare), and with Peter Wiseman translating Ovid's *Fasti*. Keith Thomas was the external examiner for his doctoral thesis.

LYNDAL ROPER's most recent book is *Oedipus and the Devil: Witchcraft, Sexuality and Religion in Early Modern Europe* (Routledge 1994). She is currently working on a study of fantasy and witchcraft in Germany. She teaches history at Royal Holloway College, University of London.

JIM SHARPE is Senior Lecturer in History at the University of York. He has published extensively on the history of crime in the early modern period, and is also author of *Early Modern England: a Social History 1550–1760*. He has a major study of witchcraft in England in the press.

1. Introduction: Keith Thomas and the problem of witchcraft

JONATHAN BARRY

Few historical enterprises have been as intensively historiographical and reflexive in character as the study of witchcraft in early modern Europe. Doubts about the very existence, let alone the character, of the object of study, together with the interdisciplinary nature of the subject, have ensured that the explosion of studies in this field since the 1960s has been accompanied by a regular rethinking of its intellectual parameters and conceptual tools. One of the most important moments in this process was the publication in 1971 of *Religion and the Decline of Magic* by Keith Thomas.[1] The essays in this book, arising from a conference held in 1991, examine the developments in witchcraft scholarship in the last two decades or so in the light of Thomas' contribution. In part a review of his influence, it also offers both prescriptions and examples for alternative approaches. This introduction begins this process by re-examining the arguments of *Religion and the Decline of Magic* in the light of subsequent studies (particularly, but not exclusively, in the English-speaking world), as a way of exploring the changing nature of witchcraft research.

Like any reception study, this chapter will chart an uneasy course between analysis of what Thomas himself was arguing and what has been read into his work. *Religion and the Decline of Magic* is a large and complex work, in which witchcraft is only one theme. It could be seen as both a strength and a weakness of the book that it offers a remarkably

---

[1] His approach had been signalled in an earlier article and through the publication in the previous year of Alan Macfarlane's study of Essex witchcraft, based on research supervised by Thomas: K. Thomas, 'The relevance of social anthropology to the historical study of English witchcraft', in M. Douglas, ed., *Witchcraft Confessions and Accusations* (1970), pp. 47–80; A. Macfarlane, *Witchcraft in Tudor and Stuart England* (1970). In this chapter references will be to the revised Penguin edition of *Religion and the Decline of Magic* (Harmondsworth, 1973).

1

multistranded, even eclectic, account, anticipating to some degree almost all subsequent approaches and arguments about witchcraft. At the same time, Thomas, or perhaps one should say 'Thomas–Macfarlane', has been particularly associated with one specific approach, drawing on functionalist anthropology and a specific type of 'village-level' analysis of witchcraft in relation to social tensions. Without adjudicating on the fairness of this encapsulation of Thomas' argument,[2] it is important to note that, like any other historical classic (the obvious parallel would be with E. P. Thompson's *Making of the English Working Class*), *Religion and the Decline of Magic* has become a contested symbol for all kinds of debate about the nature of the historical discipline. However (unlike Thompson's work), the book has not attracted any sustained historiographical analysis since its early reviews.[3] A full analysis of that kind would need to give equal weight to all parts of the volume (for example, the influence on Reformation studies of his view of the magic of the late medieval church and its continued attractiveness), whereas this chapter concentrates on witchcraft.

Like any great work, *Religion and the Decline of Magic* is notable as much for establishing the centrality of its theme as a historical problem as for any specific solution that it offers to that problem. To understand its impact, however, we have to place it alongside a number of other works that, around the same time, were making witchcraft appear a mainstream concern for early modern European history, not just an intriguing side issue. Traditionally, the historiography of witchcraft, itself marginal to historical writing, laid no particular claim to attention as a problem for early modernists. Belief in witchcraft represented the continuation of medieval delusion and superstition, set to be destroyed by the rise of such aspects of modernity as science and legal professionalism. Even those scholars who dissented from this 'whiggish' approach

---

[2] The encapsulation is offered by Thomas himself in 'Relevance of social anthropology'.

[3] T. Ashplant and A. Wilson, 'Present-centred history', *Historical Journal*, 31 (1988), 253–74 (at 257–61) uses the book as an example of the methodological problems besetting 'present-centred history', but does not offer a substantial empirical account of the book. The fullest responses have come from anthropologists and other social scientists, notably in Thomas' exchange with Hildred Geertz: 'An anthropology of religion and magic', *Journal of Interdisciplinary History*, 6 (1975), 71–109. See also: R. Keynes's review in *Journal of the Anthropological Society of Oxford*, 3: 3 (1972), 149–57; M. Crick, *Explorations in Language and Meaning* (1976), pp. 109–26; D. O'Keefe, *Stolen Lightning: The Social Theory of Magic* (Oxford, 1982), pp. 440–9; S. J. Tambiah, *Magic, Science, Religion and the Scope of Rationality* (New York, 1990), pp. 18–24.

did so in a manner which denied witchcraft any problematic status, since they assumed that it really existed, either as diabolical worship (Montague Summers) or as a pagan cult (Margaret Murray).[4] Yet by the 1960s there was mounting empirical evidence that the persecution of witches, at the very least, was growing in intensity in early modern Europe and that this growth could itself be attributed, at least in part, to the forces of modernisation.[5] It was this evidence that Hugh Trevor-Roper so elegantly marshalled in his essay on the European witch-craze.[6] In a world still darkened by Nazism and mortally threatened by the Cold War, Trevor-Roper chronicled the resurgence of what he saw as an elite irrationality, linked in particular to the Reformation's defeat of Erasmian humanism. Yet, for him, as for earlier scholars, witchcraft beliefs amongst the ordinary people were an unproblematic survival of age-old superstitions.

Thomas accepted the challenge posed by Trevor-Roper and the other studies, that is, to explain the greater impact of witchcraft beliefs in the early modern period, and yet dissented from Trevor-Roper's characterisation of both elite and peasant mentalities. Thomas sought to find the 'logical coherence of despised beliefs' (in Macfarlane's words)[7] and how they appealed to those whom Thomas characterised as 'intelligent persons' of the past (p. ix; cf. pp. 105 and 800). As Thomas himself summarised his study's task: 'it has to offer a *psychological* explanation of the motives of the participants in the drama of witchcraft accusation, a *sociological* analysis of the situation in which such accusations tended to occur, and an *intellectual* explanation of the concepts which made such accusations plausible' (p. 559, his italics). It is significant that, despite this ordering of the three tasks, Thomas actually began with the issue of intellectual plausibility.[8]

[4] M. Murray, *The Witch Cult in Western Europe* (1921); M. Summers, *The History of Witchcraft and Demonology* (1926).

[5] Bibliographical surveys of this phase of study and proposals for further research by two of the leading American scholars of European witchcraft can be found in H. C. E. Midelfort, 'Recent witch-hunting research, or where do we go from here', *Papers of the Bibliographical Society of America*, 62 (1968), 373–423 and E. W. Monter, 'The historiography of European witchcraft: progress and prospects', *Journal of Interdisciplinary History*, 2 (1972), 433–51.

[6] H. R. Trevor-Roper, *The European Witch-Craze of the Sixteenth and Seventeenth Centuries* (1967: rev. edn, Harmondsworth, 1969).

[7] In *History Today*, 31 (Apr. 1981), 56–7.

[8] In his response to Geertz, Thomas wrote: 'Neither was my treatment of witchcraft primarily psychological in character. I tried to show that witchcraft *beliefs* were not private delusions, generated by situations of stress, but were anchored in a culturally

This priority is important, given the frequent criticism of *Religion and the Decline of Magic* for its 'functionalist' as opposed to meaning-oriented account of witchcraft.[9] As this introduction will itself question aspects of Thomas' approach, and propose a more cultural model for witchcraft history, it is worth noting that the functionalism to which Thomas himself pleaded guilty is *not* a type of analysis which is content simply to analyse the social utility of a belief or action, regardless of its meaning to the individual actors involved. Thomas himself distinguished a functionalist approach from a 'utilitarian' one, defining the former as studying 'the socially useful consequences of the belief in question, regardless of its intrinsic merits' (pp. 748–50). This may still sound utilitarian, but as frequent passages in *Religion and the Decline of Magic* make clear, these socially useful functions are identified by individuals in relation to their aims and values, not dictated by an abstract social function. Indeed, the 'function' repeatedly identified for magical beliefs, including witch beliefs, is of providing a meaningful explanation for the apparently inexplicable in individual life (e.g. pp. 623, 642, 794). Thomas' explanation of witchcraft in particular, and magic in general, can only be appreciated if it is seen in the context of the close relationship between anxiety, misfortune and guilt which dominates the book (pp. ix, 17–24, 179, 676). The decline of magic, or Weberian 'disenchantment of the world', that Thomas wished to portray is the unravelling of this nexus in personal experience and values. Hence his account of witchcraft accusations hinges on notions of guilt felt by the accuser (as compared to feelings of revenge, envy or rebelliousness, which others in this volume emphasise) and the decline of witchcraft arises, in large part, from the unravelling of this mentality in educated thought, in the minds of 'intelligent persons'.[10] In this sense the criticism

acceptable view of reality . . . part of a much larger corpus of assumptions about the universe.' Thomas, 'Anthropology', 100. However, in an article published in 1985, Thomas regretted that he had not explored further 'the mental assumptions that made [astrology, magic and witchcraft] plausible' (P. Scott, 'Conjuring the Past', *The Times Higher Educational Supplement*, 18 Jan. 1985, 11).

9 Geertz, 'Anthropology', *passim*, especially 79; B. R. Copenhaver's review in *Church History*, 41 (1972), 423; G. Scarre, *Witchcraft and Magic in Sixteenth and Seventeenth-Century Europe* (1987), pp. 41–4.

10 Thomas, 'Anthropology', 98 and 100, emphasises this theme in the book, as does A. Macfarlane, 'Evil' in his *The Culture of Capitalism* (Oxford, 1987), pp. 101–2, where he sees this as the theme linking *Religion and the Decline of Magic* with Thomas' later book, *Man and the Natural World* (1983); for a review of this theme see R. W. Scribner, 'The Reformation, popular magic and the "Disenchantment of the World"', *Journal of Interdisciplinary History*, 23 (1992–3), 475–94. O'Keefe, *Stolen*

of Thomas for having it both ways about whether such guilt served a conservative or radical social *function* (to reinforce norms of neighbourliness about whose breach one feels guilty or to break them) mistakes his main interest (unlike that of Macfarlane), which was not to establish the functionality of witchcraft for society as a whole so much as its plausibility to a specific person faced with an immediate problem (pp. 674–6).[11]

Thomas' functionalism has also been held responsible for his failure to see magic as a system of belief with internal coherence, while granting this privileged status to religion. He has been accused of following Malinowski in treating magic as a pragmatic collection of (ineffective) techniques.[12] It is certainly true that Thomas made this distinction in some crucial passages (pp. 750, 761), and that *Religion and the Decline of Magic* displays his clear preference for what are called 'coherent' (pp. 105, 125, 215, 455, 750) or 'comprehensive' (pp. 384, 391, 760–1) forms of thought over others. But the main thrust of the book as a whole is surely to re-establish for the reader the coherence of magical systems – most clearly in the case of astrology, and least effectively, perhaps, in that of demonology, as we shall see – and also to establish the interconnectedness of both religion and magic as sharing a common meta-belief, namely the anxiety-misfortune-guilt relationship. There are repeated references to magical ideas as 'systems of belief' (e.g. pp. ix, 206, 767) and if one takes the book as a whole it is a study of 'allied beliefs' and 'interconnections' (especially pp. 755–66). *Religion and the Decline of Magic* presents religion and magic, until the late seventeenth century, as part of one cognitive system, at least in relation

---

Lightning, pp. 440–7 emphasises *Religion and the Decline of Magic*'s position as a cognitive intellectual history, while placing it within an 'Oxford' school concerned with social strain.

[11] J. Bossy, 'Early modern magic', *History*, 57 (1972), 399–403 is especially acute on the strains within *Religion and the Decline of Magic*. Peter Burke (in B. Ankarloo and G. Henningsen, eds., *Early Modern European Witchcraft: Centres and Peripheries* (Oxford, 1990), p. 436) sees Thomas emphasising the conservative aspect, compared to Macfarlane, while G. R. Quaife (*Godly Zeal and Furious Rage* (1987), p. 12) sees Thomas as emphasising the radical function.

[12] J. Butler, 'Magic, astrology and the early American religious heritage', *American Historical Review*, 84 (1979), 319; R. A. Horsley, 'Further reflections on witchcraft and European folk religion', *History of Religions*, 19 (1979), 74–6; C. Larner, *Witchcraft and Religion* (Oxford, 1984), p. 145; R. Godbeer, *The Devil's Dominion: Magic and Religion in Early New England* (Cambridge, 1992), pp. 11–13. Thomas, 'Anthropology', 95 claims that such a definition was introduced 'half frivolously', and was alien to his working definition in 'the main body of the book'.

to anxiety, misfortune and guilt (pp. 173, 179, 318, 761–6), although in exploring their connections Thomas stressed magic's debt to religion not vice versa.[13] Thomas' methodological critics have also overlooked the fact that his intended audience was largely one of historians, requiring persuasion to view magic in the same light as religion, who would only be alienated by the implication that religion is just magic.

It is helpful to consider the wider question of Thomas' use of anthropology in this light. Although he clearly valued anthropology, not least for its detached approach, Thomas also deployed it to get historians to take magical beliefs and their analysis seriously. If we look at how anthropology is introduced in *Religion and the Decline of Magic* we find, as E. P. Thompson noted approvingly,[14] that anthropologists are used to suggest hypotheses and provide analogies (e.g. p. 287), but never actually to 'prove' a point that lacks historical evidence. In this respect Thomas is much less anthropological than many subsequent historians who have used models, especially from cultural anthropology, to sustain a historical argument.[15] Indeed one might argue that in *Religion and the Decline of Magic* anthropologists are largely adding credence to approaches and interpretations already suggested by earlier historians and folklorists (especially Kittredge)[16] and, in particular, by Tudor and Stuart writers, above all Reginald Scot (pp. 61–2, 361) and George Gifford (pp. xxi, 257), but also some of the demonologists. If Carlo Ginzburg has proposed the inquisitor as anthropologist[17] (and Lyndal Roper in this collection offers us the inquisitor as psychoanalyst), both Thomas and Macfarlane[18] have shown the roots of modern anthropological analysis in Reformation debates about the categories of religion and magic and their social context (pp. 69, 85). As Thomas himself noted, he has been accused both of importing an alien anthropological vocabulary into the sixteenth and seventeenth centuries, and of restating

---

[13] O'Keefe, *Stolen Lightening*, pp. 445–7 sees Thomas as a Durkheimian whose main conclusion is that witchcraft was created by religion. For a spirited argument that the reverse links should be stressed see A. Kibbey, 'Mutations of the supernatural', *American Quarterly*, 34 (1982), 135.

[14] E. P. Thompson, 'Anthropology and the discipline of historical context', *Midland History*, 1: 3 (1972), 46–7.

[15] An example of Thomas' caution about applying anthropology is his extended discussion of the distinction between witchcraft and sorcery (pp. 551–4).

[16] G. L. Kittredge, *Witchcraft in Old and New England* (New York, 1929).

[17] C. Ginzburg, 'The inquisitor as anthropologist' in his *Myths, Emblems, Clues* (1990), pp. 156–64.

[18] A. Macfarlane, 'A Tudor anthropologist', in S. Anglo, ed., *The Damned Art* (1977), pp. 140–55.

the religion/magic distinction established by interested parties in the period.[19] As he recognised, there are great dangers in privileging an educated and partisan viewpoint of the process being described, but they are not the dangers of anachronism – Scot is far more often used to clinch a case than Evans-Pritchard!

Ironically, the heavy rhetorical use of anthropology has created many problems for the reception of *Religion and the Decline of Magic* (just as Thomas' reverence for statistics could do, as Thompson noted,[20] given that the book is largely non-statistical) because it threw Thomas into the thick of anthropological battles. He not only became identified with an old-fashioned school of British anthropology, but even got caught up in battles over the true legacy of Evans-Pritchard.[21] Most obvious and least defensible of his borrowings from this school is the language of 'primitivism';[22] Willem de Blécourt's essay in this collection offers a sustained critique of the linked language of survivalism. Less obvious, but perhaps even more damaging in 'dating' *Religion and the Decline of Magic*, is Thomas' concentration on African anthropology just when, in 1971, British attention was shifting away from the imperial connection and towards the Continent. Whereas Thompson could argue in 1972 that the more appropriate imperial comparisons would have been with nineteenth-century India, modern readers are more likely to look instinctively for European comparisons. The most extreme example of this is Carlo Ginzburg's reconstruction of a Eurasian shamanistic root for witchcraft, where comparisons with Africa are sidelined as foreign to the European cultural inheritance, but Gaskill's chapter argues a similar case.[23]

However the most immediate objection was to *Religion and the Decline of Magic*'s neglect of what Thomas labelled the 'symbolic' or 'structuralist' approach, in which witchcraft can only be analysed as part

---

[19] Geertz, 'Anthropology', 76 and Thomas, 'Anthropology', 94.

[20] Thompson, 'Anthropology', 48, 55; M. Bowker's review in *Historical Journal*, 15 (1972), 363–6.

[21] Geertz, 'Anthropology', 84; Crick, *Explorations*. For a sympathetic historian's review of this material see M. MacDonald, 'Anthropological perspectives', in P. Corsi and P. Weindling, eds., *Information Sources in History of Science and Medicine* (1983), pp. 63–80.

[22] Thomas, 'Anthropology', 93 notes the 'condescending evolutionary overtones', though he questions whether other preferred terms are more than 'debatable substitutes'.

[23] Thompson, 'Anthropology', 48; E. W. Monter, *Witchcraft in France and Switzerland* (1976), p. 9; R. Rowland, 'Fantasticall and devilishe persons', in Ankarloo and Henningsen, eds., *Early Modern European Witchcraft*, pp. 161–90, especially pp. 172–3; C. Ginzburg, *Ecstasies* (1990), pp. 4, 249, 260.

of a broader system or language of cultural classification.[24] His stated reason for rejecting this model, namely that it can be applied to simple societies but not to a complex one like early modern England (p. 750) seems weak, not least given his own use of African tribal comparisons. But his later response to Geertz, questioning the model of unitary cultural systems in favour of what might be termed cultural 'bricolage', now looks much stronger, not least because most cultural anthropologists have come round to the same approach (for religion as for magic), and Thomas' more pragmatic, situation-centred, model, of culture as a resource rather than a unitary system, seems back in favour, as de Blécourt shows.[25] As will be suggested later, it may be that in the long run Thomas will appear to have accepted too *much* of a symbolic system/ holistic culture model, rather than too little.

Thomas' main debt to anthropologists in the specific analysis of witchcraft was in his focus on the accuser/accused situation (p. 652). He is often assumed to have analysed witchcraft principally as a gauge of social strain, perhaps because this looms large in his 1970 article.[26] In fact this issue is only the subject of one out of five chapters on witchcraft in *Religion and the Decline of Magic* (quite apart from the rest of the book) and there is no sign that it is given priority over the 'making of a witch', the intellectual assumptions behind witchcraft or the history of its rise and decline as a crime – so it seems hardly fair on Thomas (often here bracketed with Macfarlane) to see this as his main preoccupation. Within his analysis of this situation, what has consistently been singled out, first for approval and now increasingly for criticism,[27] is *Religion and the Decline of Magic*'s reliance on the 'charity-refused' model, that is the hypothesis that most accusations of witchcraft arose from situations where the accused was refused charity by the accuser, who then felt guilt

---

[24] Thompson, 'Anthropology', 49–55; Geertz, 'Anthropology'; M. MacDonald, 'Religion, social change and psychological healing in England', in W. J. Sheils, ed., *The Church and Healing* (Studies in Church History 19, Oxford, 1982), pp. 106, 109; Ginzburg, *Ecstasies*, pp. 4–8.

[25] Thomas, 'Anthropology', 104–6. See, for example, D. D. Hall, *Worlds of Wonder, Days of Judgement* (New York, 1989), p. 260 n. 53; R. Sawyer, '"Strangely handled in all her lyms": witchcraft and healing in Jacobean England', *Journal of Social History*, 22 (1989), 485 n. 59; W. de Blécourt, 'Witchdoctors, soothsayers and priests: on cunning folk in European historiographical tradition', *Social History*, 19 (1994), 299.

[26] C. Larner, *Enemies of God* (1981), p. 21; J. P. Demos, *Entertaining Satan* (New York, 1982), p. 483 n. 5.

[27] For approval see, for example, R. Briggs, *Communities of Belief* (Oxford, 1989), pp. 31, 69. For criticism, see Larner's review in *Scottish Historical Review*, 50 (1971), 165–71; Scarre, *Witchcraft*, p. 42; Quaife, *Godly Zeal*, pp. 181, 189–90.

and attributed subsequent misfortune to the malice of the person refused (pp. 660–77). Thomas was rather equivocal on the status of this model, noting many other types of situation and that he had no statistical proof of the dominance of this type (p. 659), and acknowledging the problems posed by the sources in recreating the circumstances behind most accusations (p. 677). He nevertheless concluded firmly that this was the common pattern, *if* one could be deduced at all, referring at one point to 'the overwhelming majority' of fully documented cases (p. 661). But his interest in this type of accusation surely arose largely because of its relationship to his overall theme of misfortune and guilt (pp. 659, 665–7). It is only secondarily, in *Religion and the Decline of Magic* at least, that 'social historians' are invited to view this as a social strain gauge (p. 669). While there have been many criticisms lately of his reliance on this single model, many critics also view accusations in terms of social strain, though they tend to prefer a broader interpretation of the conflicts between neighbourliness and individualism involved than Thomas provided (though see pp. 662, 670).[28] We will return to two key forms of such an interpretation, namely feuding and gender, later in this introduction.

There is however scope for a deeper critique of *Religion and the Decline of Magic*'s focus on the moment of accusation, as revealed in the witchcraft records, as the key to the thinking of the parties involved and especially of its emphasis on the thought patterns of the individual accuser. Despite his own caveats about the stereotyping of reports in indictments and the press (which Gaskill's chapter in this collection shows to be most misleading guides to the nature of the accused and their offences), and the effect of the legal statutes on what was mentioned (namely the concentration on harming of people and animals) (p. 642), Thomas failed to allow sufficiently for the shaping of the evidence we have by its status as legal evidence. Furthermore, he dodged the question of why the particular episodes that got to court did so, compared to the countless other cases of charity refused that cannot have done (pp. 534–5). One problem here is his emphasis on an individual accuser's thinking, rather than the social process that led to a trial. In *Religion and the Decline of Magic*, there is no reconstruction of the complete sequence of events that might turn an individual suspicion into a public case, nor

---

[28] See Demos, *Entertaining Satan*, pp. 298–9; Sawyer, 'Strangely Handled', 461–2; A. Gregory, 'Witchcraft, politics and "good neighbourhood" in early seventeenth-century Rye', *Past and Present*, 133 (1991), 31–66, especially 32–4, 61, 66.

any systematic consideration of the reactions and attitudes of the other participants in this process, though the importance of such matters is implied, though ambiguously, in references to the types of accusation that could be 'plausibly made'.[29]

It is here that one must agree with Thompson that the lack of specific case studies is a crucial weakness.[30] Instead we have a heavy reliance on the (stylised) court material plus contemporary analyses which were themselves generally intended to identify or guide the motives of individual accusers or accused, whether it was in cases of conscience, uncovering of fraud or narrating the 'confession' of the guilty. Much less attention is given to these sources which might recreate the full social dynamics of a witch episode, for example the plays of the period that incorporate witchcraft cases.[31] In this respect Thomas' use of Macfarlane's statistical study of Essex witchcraft is no substitute for a detailed reconstruction of the social relationships of the parties involved in specific cases. Given the evidential problems, such studies are only now emerging in England, one example being Annabel Gregory's study of Rye.[32] Continental legal practices, as Roper's study of Augsburg shows, often give a much fuller picture, while in New England the survival of extraordinarily rich archives of almost every aspect of social life has enabled historians to place witchcraft cases very precisely into their social context, which has often turned out to be rather different, as we shall see, from that predicted by Thomas on the basis of the court records.[33]

---

[29] 'Before a witchcraft accusation could be plausibly made, the suspect had to be in a socially or economically inferior position to her supposed victim. Only then could she be presumed to be likely . . . ' (p. 669). Cf. the slippage from 'Everything thus depended on the prior attitude of those *trying the witch*' (my italics) to 'The basic problem is that of how the initial suspicion came to be formed' (p. 658).

[30] Thompson, 'Anthropology', 50–1.

[31] See P. Corbin and D. Sedge, eds., *Three Jacobean Witchcraft Plays* (Manchester, 1986). This literature is discussed in A. Harris, *Night's Black Agents* (Manchester, 1980).

[32] Gregory, 'Witchcraft'.

[33] The most substantial of many recent American studies are P. Boyer and S. Nissenbaum, *Salem Possessed* (Cambridge, MA, 1974); Demos, *Entertaining Satan*; R. Weisman, *Witchcraft, Magic and Religion in Seventeenth-Century Massachusetts* (Amherst, 1984); C. Karlsen, *The Devil in the Shape of a Woman* (1987; pbk. edn, New York, 1989); B. Rosenthal, *Salem Story* (Cambridge, 1993). European case studies accessible in English include: D. W. Sabean, *Power in the Blood* (Cambridge, 1984), pp. 94–112; M. Kunze, *Highroad to the Stake* (Chicago, 1987); R. W. Scribner, *Popular Culture and Popular Movements in Reformation Germany* (Cambridge, 1987); E. Le Roy Ladurie, *Jasmin's Witch* (1983; translated Brian Pearce, Harmondsworth, 1990); L. Roper, *Oedipus and the Devil* (1994).

In this respect, then, Thomas may stand convicted of unduly neglecting the legal or judicial factors which have attracted so much fruitful attention in recent witchcraft literature.[34] How far such work has invalidated Thomas' account of the broad pattern of legal change and trial practice may be questioned. Although we now know a great deal more about crime and law in early modern England than we did in 1971, most of *Religion and the Decline of Magic*'s observations seem to have held up quite well. One crucial exception may be the assumption that the legal processes were firmly in the hands of the educated classes, reflected in the discussion of the causes of the decline of prosecution in the later seventeenth century. Recent work on participation in the law suggests this is correct only if we define the educated classes very broadly to include many of the middling sort of town and countryside and that a key feature of the early modern period was the new willingness of the middling sort, and perhaps even the poor, to use law for resolving all types of difficulty.[35] This is hinted at in Thomas' remarks on the decline of other types of court and arbitration (p. 672), but now looks much stronger as an explanation of why people turned to the courts to rid themselves of witches. If so, this crucially weakens Thomas' case that we cannot provide a 'supply-side' account of the rise in witchcraft prosecution and must instead look to other aspects of contemporary life to explain a growing popular demand for legal action specifically against witches (pp. 548–51).

At the same time, Thomas' own account of the motives for and benefits of recourse to law by witchcraft accusers looks rather shaky. He suggested that the rise of witch trials in the Elizabethan period reflected the fact that, with the removal of ecclesiastical counter-magic, the trial and execution of witches became the best solution, practically and psychologically, for those frightened of a witch (pp. 315–16, 588–94,

---

[34] For criticism see Larner's 1971 review; R. A. Horsley, 'Who were the witches', *Journal of Interdisciplinary History*, 9 (1978–9), 714; N. Cohn, *Europe's Inner Demons* (1975), p. 160; Gregory, 'Witchcraft', 32. B. P. Levack, *The Witch-Hunt in Early Modern Europe* (1987; 2nd edn 1995) offers the best guide to such work, but see also, in addition to works cited below, C. R. Unsworth, 'Witchcraft beliefs and criminal procedure in early modern England', in T. G. Watkin, ed., *Legal Record and Historical Reality* (1989), pp. 71–98, especially pp. 85–6; R. Briggs, 'Women as victims? Witches, judges and the community', *French History*, 5 (1991), 438–50; J. A. Sharpe, *Witchcraft in Seventeenth-Century Yorkshire: Accusations and Counter-Measures* (University of York, Borthwick Papers no. 81, 1992); A. Soman, *Sorcellerie et justice criminelle (16–18e siècles)* (Guildford, 1992).

[35] J. Sharpe, *Crime in Early Modern England 1550–1750* (1984); C. B. Herrup, *The Common Peace* (Cambridge, 1987).

650).[36] *Religion and the Decline of Magic* describes prosecution's therapeutic (p. 650) and cathartic effects, even suggesting that the absence of witch trials after 1700 would have made witch beliefs decline (pp. 696–7), because of their importance as a practical remedy. So, it is argued, fear of a witch without a magical counter-remedy would 'lead inexorably' to trials as the only sure and legitimate remedy (p. 593). But this poses all sorts of problems. It assumes a populace that has rejected counter-magical remedies, and here Thomas referred the reader back to his discussion of this in earlier sections of *Religion and the Decline of Magic*. However, these passages indicate a distinct reluctance to confirm the view that the Reformation marked a break, either in popular use of counter-magic or in official condemnation of it (pp. 301–13 (esp. 310–11), 324–6, 330–1, 764–5). If any significant change in attitudes towards counter-magic is established, it is only for specific sections of the population, especially the Puritan and more educated, and so one would expect here a discussion of why *these* particular groups now turned to the law. Such an account would help to explain the prominence of 'Puritan' counties like Essex in early cases (p. 536), if this is more than an illusion created by uneven record survival.

However, Thomas could not really develop this argument because *Religion and the Decline of Magic* hardly ever provides an extended social (or indeed religious or political) profile of the accusers, as opposed to the accused, and when it does so it is a very ambiguous one. The emphasis on the 'dependent' status of the accused and the description of prosecution, at one point, as 'class hatred' might suggest antagonism between the middling or elite and the poor, but this remark is immediately qualified by observation that most such cases involve the 'fairly poor' against the poor (p. 673; cf. pp. 669–70). As we shall see, Thomas was reluctant for a number of reasons to present the typical witchcraft accusation as one in which religious belief or superior education encouraged the accuser to take legal action.

Before developing this point, it is worth noting another problem with the emphasis on the law as a remedy preferable to prayer and patience for the godly (pp. 591–3). Thomas failed to explore the pros and cons of taking people to court, both as an individual and as a community. Both in discussing the advantages of a trial and in assuming that it was the

---

[36] 'Ecclesiastical magic crumbled and *society* was *forced* to take legal action . . . ' (p. 594, my italics): a rare personification of 'society', whose exact reference is unclear, since this is not identified as a motive behind the various witchcraft statutes (pp. 549–51).

decision to accuse that was the crucial moment, after which the witch was caught up in a legal process with few chances of escape (pp. 657–8), Thomas ignored his own statistics about the high levels of acquittals, not to mention defamation cases and other ways in which witchcraft accusations could rebound on the accuser (pp. 537, 539, 667–8). There is also clear evidence that most accusations only came after years, often decades, of smouldering distrust of someone as a witch. All of this suggests that a trial was the *last* resort of an accuser and that its success and advantages were far from clear, not least because going to law was itself, for many, an unneighbourly act – one likely to cause guilt as much as it resolved it, and one which risked future reprisals if, as often occurred, the accused was acquitted or, once punished, returned to the same community. Set against the costs and problems of a law case, it may well be that Job-like patience seemed a better bet, psychologically and socially, to many of those who had learned to abjure counter-magic.

This emphasis on the problems associated with a successful witchcraft accusation raises the much wider question of what it is exactly that needs explanation about witchcraft prosecutions. Thomas, as we have seen, sought to make the process comprehensible, but, as Briggs points out in his chapter, one of the dangers of making witchcraft fears seem rational is that we can 'over-explain' what occurred; any satisfactory account of early modern witchcraft must be able to explain its limited and sporadic impact and then the decline of witchcraft prosecution, as well as its incidence. Thomas himself admitted that, given his interpretation, it is the decline of witchcraft that becomes 'baffling' (p. 681), but much of this mystery is removed if we explore the complex legal and social ramifications leading from suspicion to accusation to trial and how many opportunities this offered for a witchcraft prosecution to collapse.

Another consequence of Thomas' effort to see why witchcraft accusations were plausible to intelligent persons was his reluctance to take seriously the notion that factional disputes and the conscious manipulation of false accusations lay behind many cases. John Bossy's penetrating review of *Religion and the Decline of Magic* encapsulated this approach in suggesting a further study entitled 'Religion and the Decline of Feud'![37] Thomas insisted (in what seems a heated passage) that such uses were 'essentially parasitic' on an accepted body of belief

---

[37] Bossy, 'Early modern magic', 403. As Gregory, 'Witchcraft', 36 indicates, Bossy's own work on religion's changing role in concepts of good neighbourhood has been of crucial importance.

and honest accusation (p. 646).[38] There is a danger here of too polarised a contrast – between conscious manipulation and 'honest' belief. Many of the later case studies of accusations have convincingly accounted for them precisely in terms of such factionalism, noting that those targeted as witches, though particularly vulnerable as individuals (or perhaps presented as such in the stereotyped indictments or trial tracts) were representatives of a rival group in a local power struggle. However, as these studies also show, in these power struggles the accusation of witchcraft was not *merely* a rhetorical tool, because it often expressed a genuine belief by the accusers that their opponents stood for a dangerous principle threatening the community – which might indeed make them 'witch-like' in their threat to social harmony.[39] In this respect, at least, witchcraft cases, like many other criminal offences, offer an invaluable means of penetrating the social strains and rival values of early modern communities, but in such investigations notions such as charity, neighbourliness, malice and nonconformity have to be approached not as descriptions of social behaviour so much as complex vocabularies, whose applications to specific people and acts are subject to constant contestation and change.

Again, it is easier to understand why Thomas sought to distance himself from the 'feuding' approach when we bear in mind his historiographical context. His emphasis on the genuineness of individual fears of witchcraft was a response both to rationalistic accounts of witchcraft (as simply the product of manipulative conspiracies) and, more particularly, the existing scholarship which presented witches as one of a number of interchangeable scapegoats sacrificed to partisan rivalry – a position particularly identified at that point with Trevor Davies' work on England and Trevor-Roper's European study.[40] Unable to find much evidence in the English case for their sweeping identification of rival sides

---

38 Thomas' argument that feuding or fraud explanations fail because they cannot explain 'how such beliefs came to exist in the first place', is, though true, hardly appropriate, since his own discussion in the chapter in question is about the way in which people applied accepted beliefs to specific situations. As *Religion and the Decline of Magic* argues later (p. 689), transparently self-interested manipulations of witchcraft accusations might, in the long term, discredit witchcraft accusations altogether, but, while the belief existed, they supplied, as Gaskill shows, a resource available for the vengeful as well as the guilt-ridden: only empirical analysis can show which was more common.

39 This is particularly clear in Boyer and Nissenbaum, *Salem Possessed.*

40 R. Trevor Davies, *Four Centuries of Witch Beliefs* (1947); Trevor-Roper, *European Witch-Craze.*

manipulating witchcraft (pp. 595–8), Thomas may have neglected the possibility that more localised factionalism might be involved, even if nationwide sectarian struggles were not. As Briggs notes, elite objections to witchcraft prosecutions often rested on the belief that they were simply the pursuit of local vendettas.

Whatever the reason, Thomas' rejection of the model of witches as rebels or 'enemies of society' has put him at variance with a wave of studies, notably the work of Christina Larner, which have strongly restated the need to see witchcraft as a product of the ideological struggles and elite concerns of the sixteenth and seventeenth centuries, when states or rulers under threat identified themselves with divine right and their opponents, internal and external, with diabolic wrong.[41] Again, we should note that Thomas recognised the potential applicability of this approach, both to the Continent and to England. *Religion and the Decline of Magic* argues for its relevance to continental demonology, and assumes that such scapegoating of 'enemies within' was indeed widespread in England, but in the shape of anti-Catholicism not the persecution of witches (pp. 647, 667–8). The chapters by Peter Elmer and Ian Bostridge in this collection both indicate that Thomas may have underestimated the potential of the witch stereotype in the minds of those who saw England, too, as a godly state under threat, especially in the mid and late seventeenth centuries. Thomas' emphasis on the witch as a threat to specific individuals, not society at large, reinforces, and is reinforced by, his emphasis on the individual accuser not the social process of prosecution.

Only in one subset of witchcraft cases was Thomas prepared to look in detail at the ideological manipulation and implications of witchcraft, namely in the case of possession (pp. 572–88). Here the account is extremely thorough – as later studies have testified[42] – and brings out the

---

[41] Larner, *Enemies of God* and *Witchcraft and Religion*; S. Clark, 'Inversion, misrule and meaning of witchcraft', *Past and Present*, 87 (1980), 98–127; R. Walinski-Kiehl, '"Godly State": confessional conflict and witchhunting in early modern Germany', *Mentalities*, 5: 2 (1988), 13–24.

[42] See M. MacDonald, *Witchcraft and Hysteria in Elizabethan London* (1991), p. lvii n. 18, which also gives due credit to the other fundamental study for England, D. P. Walker, *Unclean Spirits* (1981). Other excellent recent studies are D. Harley, 'Mental illness, magical medicine and the devil in northern England, 1650–1700', in R. French and A. Wear, eds., *The Medical Revolution of the Seventeenth Century* (Cambridge, 1989), pp. 114–44; C. Holmes, 'Women, witnesses and witches', *Past and Present*, 140 (1993), 45–78; F. N. Brownlow, *Shakespeare, Harsnett and the Devils of Denham* (Newark and London, 1993).

political and religious context of accusations and trials very clearly. Yet possession cases are discussed, not in the chapters on witches and their accusers, but in that on intellectual preconditions, so that this particular subset of cases is never fully integrated into the rest. This is a pity, not least because Thomas himself noted their vital role in fuelling legal doubts about witchcraft (p. 689): recent work on England and New England has stressed their disproportionate prominence in the literature of witchcraft and in debate about it, and there were a growing proportion of trials involving possession in the period leading up to the decline of prosecution. English possession cases led more often to specific witchcraft accusations than continental ones, so intensifying the link (pp. 583–4). Possession cases are also usually the most fully documented – much more so than those of charity refused (with which they can overlap, of course). If, as recent studies have suggested, possession cases were of particular importance to the educated groups who wanted to see the clear hand of the devil in witchcraft accusations, and yet were also cases in which the age, gender and social stereotypes of the witch were likely to break down, then they begin to take on a much more central place in the history of witchcraft than *Religion and the Decline of Magic*'s presentation implies.[43]

One conclusion that emerges forcefully from possession cases, but which may also apply more widely, is the metaphorical, symbolic and linguistic slippage that occurs between accusations of witchcraft and other labels, such as papist, or puritan, or rebel, explored by Roberts and Elmer in their chapters. Again, Thomas noted this usage of witchcraft vocabulary (see pp. 568–9, 580–1), but declared it outside his brief to explore (pp. 679–80). Once again this is comprehensible in terms of his primary intention to render individual belief in witches plausible, not to explore its place in the cultural classifications of the day. One of the paradoxes of *Religion and the Decline of Magic*, given that it is often identified as primarily 'about' witchcraft beliefs, is that, of all the magical ideas discussed, the only one whose intellectual status is largely taken for granted, and whose metaphorical linkages with other systems of thought is not explored (though see pp. 567–9), is demonology itself. Compared to the pioneering accounts of the nature of, and connections between, astrology, providence, prophecy etc., very little effort is made to place demonology contextually.

In part this may be because a much fuller literature already existed on

---

[43] See Karlsen, *Devil*, pp. 254, 342 n. 5 and Holmes, 'Women'.

demonology than on the other systems of belief Thomas was studying.[44] But it also reflects his position on the vital question of England's relationship to continental demonology, to which we must turn. One of the standard criticisms of *Religion and the Decline of Magic* has been that its account of English witchcraft, by emphasising the contrast between the English and continental experience, rendered it, at best, irrelevant to continental studies and, at worst, flawed by its inability to explain both the similarities and contrasts between English history and that of the rest of Europe.[45] It is striking how rarely *Religion and the Decline of Magic* is cited by historians of continental witchcraft, particularly in France (with the exception of scholars from an Anglophone background, such as Soman or Briggs);[46] it has only recently been translated into Dutch and never into French or German.[47] No review of *Religion and the Decline of Magic* appeared in *Annales ESC* and *Annales* historians of witchcraft, such as Ladurie and Muchembled, rarely cite Thomas, although they do use Macfarlane.[48] American scholars such as Monter and Midelfort appear to have been much more influential, together with Norman Cohn, whose pioneering work on the origins of the diabolic witchcraft stereotype directed scholarly attention onto issues very different from those highlighted by Thomas.[49] As historians focused on the specific formulation of witchcraft as a diabolic crime, and the history of this notion, both within educated writings and in relation to legal and cultural practice, *Religion and the Decline of Magic*, for all its prestige in the historical world in general, was placed rather on the

---

[44] Notably, for England, W. Notestein, *A History of Witchcraft in England* (Crowell, NY, 1911).

[45] See, for example, Larner, *Enemies of God*, p. 22 and *Witchcraft and Religion*, pp. 52–3.

[46] Soman, *Sorcellerie* and Briggs, *Communities of Belief.*

[47] *Man and the Natural World* appeared in French translation as early as 1985; only the chapter on 'witchcraft and its social environment' has appeared in German (in C. Honneger, ed., *Die Hexen der Neuzeit* (Stuttgart, 1978), pp. 256–308). I owe this last reference to Willem de Blécourt, who has also pointed out, quite correctly, that such translations indicate 'popular interest' rather than academic influence, given that most academics on the Continent would expect to use the English original.

[48] See, for example, the works referred to (or not) in Ladurie, *Jasmin's Witch*; R. Muchembled, 'L'autre côté du miroir', *Annales ESC*, 40 (1985), 288–306; Muchembled, *Les derniers bûchers* (Paris, 1981). In M. D. DuPont-Bouchet et al., eds., *Prophets et sorciers dans les Pays Bas XVI–XVIIIe siècle* (Paris, 1978), pp. 29, 38, 252 Thomas' work is praised but assimilated to Macfarlane's (as history from below) and cited only for the loss of ecclesiastical counter-magic at the Reformation.

[49] H. C. E. Midelfort, *Witch Hunting in South-Western Germany 1562–1684* (Stanford, 1972); Monter, *Witchcraft in France and Switzerland*; Cohn, *Europe's Inner Demons.*

sidelines.[50] However, there are important exceptions: the book was translated into Italian, with a foreword by Carlo Ginzburg, and it was also highly influential on Hungarian witchcraft studies.[51]

Yet a close reading of *Religion and the Decline of Magic* shows that, although his emphases were different, Thomas was well aware of the trends in continental scholarship. His brief but highly perceptive comments on the medieval origins of the learned stereotype of the witch, and on the imposition of this stereotype through clerical and legal means, especially through inquisitorial methods, still provide a perfectly respectable summary of the subject (pp. 521–2). Thomas' concern, however, was to refute the attempt, above all by Robbins,[52] to explain the rise in *English* witchcraft persecutions through a fusion of popular *maleficia* fears and the learned stereotype (pp. 542–5). This Thomas found chronologically unconvincing, since neither the translation of demonological ideas into English, nor their further translation into statute law, occurred until the very end of the Elizabethan period, while most trial cases never invoked these aspects (pp. 522–34).[53] *Religion and the Decline of Magic* is fully in keeping with later scholarship in recognising the impact of England's different legal system in this respect; its accusatorial mode and lack of thorough torture prevented any systematic eliciting of diabolical witchcraft confessions (pp. 617–18, 687). As we shall see, it is possible, as Briggs and Sharpe argue, that Thomas overstated the contrast between a diabolical interpretation imposed from above and a maleficial concern felt from below (pp. 534, 594–5), but if so he was very much in tune with many of his 'continental' critics.

Indeed, Thomas may be said to have had the last laugh. One of his positive observations about links between English and continental witchcraft was to suggest that endemic maleficial fears, and the model of charity refused, might be found to apply widely across the Continent, underlying the more spectacular outbreak of witch hunts (pp. 534, 677). Recent scholarship, as Briggs and Behringer stress, has very much

---

[50] R. Kieckhefer, *European Witchcraft Trials* (1976); E. Peters, *The Magician, the Witch and the Law* (Hassocks, 1978); J. Obelkevich, ed., *Religion and the People 800–1700* (Chapel Hill, 1978); J. B. Russell, *A History of Witchcraft* (1980).

[51] I owe this information to Gabor Klaniczay. Another Oxford historian to have applied Thomas fruitfully to central Europe is R. J. W. Evans, *Making of the Hapsburg Monarchy 1550–1700* (Oxford, 1979), pp. 381–418.

[52] R. H. Robbins, *The Encyclopaedia of Witchcraft and Demonology* (New York, 1959).

[53] Here Thomas was restating the central claim of Kittredge, *Witchcraft*.

vindicated this view, even for the French and German heartland. Furthermore, recent attention to the European 'periphery', such as the Baltic area and Eastern Europe, has produced a picture of persecution which is in many ways more akin to Thomas' England than to what was long taken to be the 'continental' norm from which England had deviated.[54] Perhaps most interesting of all has been the work on southern Europe, and especially Italy, where, despite the intellectual currency of demonological views of witchcraft, recent work (often citing Thomas for comparisons) has seen the process of persecution largely in terms of *maleficia* and illicit magic.[55]

It might be thought that this very similar pattern of concern in the strongly Catholic countries of Spain and Italy poses a challenge to *Religion and the Decline of Magic*'s analysis of the interplay of religion and magic, which inevitably centres on the impact of the Reformation and Protestantism. However, a close reading of *Religion and the Decline of Magic* does *not* reveal any attempt to identify a strong Protestant/ Catholic dichotomy on matters of witchcraft and magic. Two issues are crucial here. The first concerns the hostility of the clergy both towards rival magical practitioners and to popular use of remedies outside the church's control. *Religion and the Decline of Magic* repeatedly argues that the church's concern about these problems, and its efforts to use both courts and preaching to weaken its rivals, was a common thread linking the medieval and Reformation period[56] and typical of both Catholic and Protestant churches, with no provable pattern of change that could account for the rise of witchcraft accusations, at least in England

---

[54] Many earlier studies can now be conveniently explored in English in Ankarloo and Henningsen, eds., *Early Modern European Witchcraft*. Peter Burke makes the point about Thomas' work on pp. 338–40.

[55] See, for example, M. P. O'Neil, 'Sacerdote overro Strione', in S. Kaplan, ed., *Understanding Popular Culture* (Berlin, New York and Amsterdam, 1984), pp. 53–83; R. Martin, *Witchcraft and the Inquisition in Venice* (Oxford, 1989), especially p. 240; D. Gentilcore, *From Bishop to Witch* (Manchester, 1992); G. Ruggiero, *Binding Passions* (New York, 1993). An extremely important exception to this picture is C. Ginzburg, *The Night Battles* (1983), dealing with the *benandanti* of the Friuli, though even here the authorities appear initially to have been expecting to suppress illicit magic, not a collective cult. The reliance of Italian (and Spanish) historians on ecclesiastical sources may have reinforced this impression; the history of witchcraft prosecutions in Italian secular courts remains to be written.

[56] The criticisms (notably in V. Flint, *The Rise of Magic in Early Medieval Europe* (Princeton, 1991), pp. 393–6) of *Religion and the Decline of Magic* for portraying the medieval church as shamelessly exploiting popular magical beliefs thus seem hardly fair, though many have certainly read Thomas as implying this (e.g. Godbeer, *Devil's Dominion*, p. 25).

(pp. 301–10, 313, 325–6, 331). The decisive change in this respect, it is argued, came in the late seventeenth century, when, at least in England, the church stopped worrying about its rivals (pp. 309–10, 313, 764–6) (unlike, one might note, the Catholic church in Southern Europe, where as a consequence court cases involving magic continued much later). Secondly, *Religion and the Decline of Magic* makes it very clear that the abandonment of ecclesiastical counter-magic, which is of course vital to its explanation of witchcraft accusations, was not simply a Protestant phenomenon, but a common tendency across Europe. Indeed, late medieval demonology is explained in part as a result of the early rejection of such counter-magic by various continental churchmen, a reforming impulse that passed England by until the Reformation (pp. 588, 594–5).[57] Marian bishops such as Bonner were as hot against magic as their exiled Protestant opponents (pp. 595–6), while the Puritan demonologists of the Elizabethan and Jacobean period drew their ideas from Catholic sources (pp. 521–5).

This stress on the shared features of Reformation and Counter-Reformation, pioneering in its day, has perhaps been obscured by *Religion and the Decline of Magic*'s emphasis, within the discussion of possession, on the continuing exploitation, by the recusant priests of the English mission, of the power of exorcism (pp. 582–8). More work might be done on the relationship between this particular aspect of ecclesiastical counter-magic and broader attitudes to witchcraft and magic. It may well be that, while exorcism (and hence witchcraft) was also important to the Catholic church in other countries, such as France, where they faced strong Protestant competition, it lacked the same credibility in the more securely Catholic churches of Spain and Italy.[58] The need to see exorcism in the context of religious pluralism is underlined by Thomas' elaborate documentation of the way in which Puritans in England developed their own ritual of exorcism by prayer and fasting, so boosting their own clerical claims, and how firmly this was challenged and suppressed by

---

[57] Though on p. 598 the lack of 'any effective ecclesiastical defence' is seen as a Protestant problem. The one area in which a really distinctive Protestant position is stressed is in relation to ghosts, following the rejection of purgatory (pp. 702–3). On the possible relation of this to witchcraft in England see G. Bennett, 'Ghost and witch in the sixteenth and seventeenth centuries', *Folklore*, 97 (1986), 3–14.

[58] See Walker, *Unclean Spirits*; G. Levi, *Inheriting Power* (Chicago and London, 1988); C. Zika, ed., *No Other God Except Me* (Melbourne, 1991), pp. 59–113; D. Gentilcore, 'The church, the devil and the healing activities of living saints in the Kingdom of Naples after the Council of Trent', in O. P. Grell and A. Cunningham, eds., *Medicine and the Reformation* (1993), pp. 134–55.

the Anglican establishment (pp. 574–80). Another illustration of how missionary work might generate very different perspectives on the magical powers of religion is provided by recent studies of the New World, exemplified by Fernando Cervantes' chapter in this collection.[59]

Thomas' determination to stress the parallels between Protestant and Catholic thought may have prevented him from exploring the different priorities within Protestant and Catholic demonology, in particular the emphasis on the covenant image within Protestant thought, compared to the inversion of the mass in Catholic witchcraft imagery. Stuart Clark, in particular, has illuminated the broader links between theological and pastoral ideas and witchcraft.[60] As Cervantes' essay shows, however, many of the theological distinctions thrown up in these debates had long ancestries, underlining Thomas' emphasis on continuity.

At the heart of such work has been the perception of the churches, whether in Europe or overseas, as engaged in a missionary or evangelical role, namely to change the minds of the ordinary people. Our understanding of witchcraft has thus become bound up with our view on this process of 'acculturation' or, as it is sometimes called, the 'reform of popular culture'. Since the publication of Peter Burke's pathbreaking synthesis, *Popular Culture in Early Modern Europe* (1978), studies of the nature of popular beliefs have generally been conceived within this framework, or at least in reaction against it. Given *Religion and the Decline of Magic*'s subtitle, 'studies in popular beliefs', it is hard now not to apply the same interpretative framework, retrospectively, to its account.[61] And there are aspects of Thomas' analysis which suggest such an outlook, not least his tendency, at certain points, to contrast the views

---

[59] See also F. Cervantes, 'The devils of Querereto', *Past and Present*, 131 (1991), 51–60; Cervantes, *The Devil in the New World: The Impact of Diabolism in New Spain* (New Haven and London, 1994); I. Silverblatt, 'Andean witches and virgins', in M. Hendricks and P. Parker, eds., *Women, 'Race' and Writing in the Early Modern Period* (1993), pp. 259–71, 362–5; A. Megged, 'Magic, popular medicine and gender in seventeenth-century Mexico', *The Seventeenth Century*, 8 (1993), 217–43.

[60] S. Clark, 'Protestant demonology' in Ankarloo and Henningsen, eds., *Early Modern European Witchcraft*, pp. 45–81.

[61] Thomas' work is seen as part of this approach in G. Klaniczay, *The Uses of Supernatural Power* (Cambridge and Oxford, 1990), p. 192 n. 16 and Karlsen, *Devil*, pp. 268–9 n. 10. Burke himself reviews the debate in 'Revolution in popular culture', in R. Porter and M. Teich, eds., *Revolution in History* (Cambridge, 1986), pp. 206–25. The most direct application of witchcraft to this debate has been in the work of R. Muchembled: for his general approach see *Culture populaire et culture des élites* (Paris, 1978). An excellent critique of historical uses of 'popular culture' is provided by M. Shiach, *Discourse on Popular Culture* (Cambridge, 1989).

of the 'educated classes' (e.g. pp. 538–40, 681, 694, 697) with those held at 'village' (pp. 533, 697–8), 'grass-roots' (p. 595) or 'local' (pp. 598, 698) 'level' (his favourite term) and his distinction between demonological ideas 'imposed from above' and pressures about *maleficia* emanating 'from below' (pp. 534, 543–4, 548, 595, 598).

However, an overall balance-sheet of *Religion and the Decline of Magic* indicates very wide differences from the 'Burkean' position, save in one crucial respect. In the first place, the term 'popular' is usually used in *Religion and the Decline of Magic* in the 'inclusive' sense, of widely or even universally held, rather than in the 'exclusive' sense which sets it sharply against 'elite'. Although this is never theorised (itself an indication that Thomas was not thinking within this perspective), it is evident in the types of authority to which Thomas turned to discover the 'popular belief'. Frequently these are highly educated people, who are not being cited for what they think ordinary people believe, but for their own beliefs (e.g. pp. 275, 318–24). Indeed, even Acts of Parliament can be cited quite unconcernedly as an indication of popular belief (p. 525)! If there is any 'exclusion' process here, then the contrast appears to be between lay and clerical (or perhaps theological) (e.g. p. 602). After all, Thomas' aim, as we have seen, was to recreate the magical thinking of the 'intelligent' early modern person, and while this need not imply education or high status, most of his intelligent commentators are in fact of that type (many are clergymen).

What is spectacularly absent from *Religion and the Decline of Magic*, for those returning of it in post-Burkean days, is any sustained account of 'the reform of popular culture' as a new movement in the sixteenth and seventeenth centuries. Throughout the book, as we have seen, Thomas played down any notion of the Reformation marking a break in clerical or elite attitudes towards popular beliefs; rather he stressed continued ambivalence. This is true both of the general account of magical practices and also of the specific discussions of witchcraft beliefs. Unlike later studies, no priority is given to analysis of how far, if at all, those who accepted the diabolical view of witchcraft sought either to impose or teach this belief to the ordinary people, nor how far they might have used fears of witches to impose a broader programme of social and ideological control on the people. Indeed, reacting to the early versions of such ideas, which are portrayed as conspiracy theories, Thomas systematically exonerated the clergy and judiciary from responsibility for any such campaign (pp. 544–7, 598, 797).

Over the last twenty years this has rendered Thomas' account rather marginal to the body of research, notably that of Muchembled and Larner, which has restated such acculturation models in their 'strong' form (that is, that fears of witchcraft were deliberately used as part of an elite imposition of discipline).[62] However, as both Levack and Behringer's chapters in this collection suggest, Thomas' view of the judiciary and state authorities is now being reasserted, even by those interested in the relationship of witchcraft to state formation across Europe. Their doubts arise less from a dislike of conspiratorial models than from close empirical study of the place of the state apparatus in witchcraft persecution, even in the continental heartlands of witch hunting. Once again, England has come to seem more 'normal', and indeed Thomas' own assumptions about the ruthless inquisitorial methods of the Continent (pp. 534–4, 687) now seem overstated, in the light of recent revisionist accounts, especially of the ecclesiastical inquisitions.[63] However Levack's chapter, like other work of this type, with its emphasis on how the central legal authorities eventually brought local witch trials under the discipline of strict legal and theological principles, leaves open the argument that, in an earlier stage of state formation, the judicial and clerical elites may have provided (to some degree unintentionally), through witchcraft statutes and preaching, a mechanism for other groups to employ. In the short term, the strengthening of legal mechanisms may have encouraged witchcraft prosecutions, while in the longer term it rendered them increasingly unsustainable. In the English case, where the legal and religious establishment was already strong in 1500, such contradictions were manifested in divisions of attitude amongst the legal authorities, leading (as Thomas identified) to cycles of success and failure for witchcraft prosecutions, obscuring any long-term chronological changes before the late seventeenth century (pp. 535–8). Behringer's summary of recent German work shows similar complexities in different jurisdictions. Once again, the short-term

---

[62] Larner, *Enemies of God*; R. Muchembled, 'The witches of the Cambrésis', in Obelkevich, ed., *Religion*, pp. 221–76; Muchembled, 'Satanic myths and cultural reality', in Ankarloo and Henningsen, eds., *Early Modern European Witchcraft*, pp. 139–60.

[63] See G. Henningsen, *The Witches' Advocate* (Reno, 1980); S. Haliczer, ed., *Inquisition and Society in Early Modern Europe* (Totoja, NJ, 1987); J. Tedeschi, 'Inquisitorial law and the witch', in Ankarloo and Henningsen, eds., *Early Modern European Witchcraft*, pp. 83–118; E. W. Monter, *Frontiers of Heresy* (Cambridge, 1990); M. Perry and A. Cruz, eds., *Cultural Encounters* (1991); J. Tedeschi, *The Prosecution of Heresy: Collected Studies on Inquisition in Early Modern Italy* (Binghampton, NY, 1991), especially chs. 6–7.

advantages of harnessing popular hostility to witches into campaigns of persecution were generally shown to be outweighed by the dangers, both to legal stability and to elite control, when witch hunting got out of hand.

The more lasting objection to Thomas' lack of concern for 'acculturation' is that, while one may not wish to portray ideas as simply being 'imposed from above', it is equally naive to imagine them simply rising up 'from below'. As studies of 'acculturation' have grown more sophisticated, they have led to highly illuminating analysis of the interaction between, for example, demonological and *maleficial* ideas. This has been explored for England with great subtlety by Clive Holmes, who has shown the need for close analysis of how, through legal proceedings, clerical preaching, casuistry and press accounts, a dialectic emerged between what we may loosely call popular and learned views of witchcraft, so that each modified the other.[64] It is from this perspective that Sharpe calls in his chapter here for a closer analysis of the popular image of the devil found in witchcraft cases, in particular in the Hopkins cases. As he (like Ginzburg before him)[65] points out, if *any* references to the diabolic in popular accounts are to be automatically labelled the product of learned interference with a non-diabolic popular tradition, then we have a tautological position (similar to the self-confirming nature of magical theories Thomas so painstakingly demonstrated! (pp. 95, 137, 409, 654, 732, 767–9)). On the other hand, as Dutch historians have noted, popular belief in the devil and his relationships with people, even pacts with them, did not automatically translate into accusations of witchcraft.[66]

Although Sharpe includes Thomas in his criticisms, this seems unjust. There are, after all, telling if brief discussions in *Religion and the Decline of Magic* of both marks and familiars, and what they imply about popular devil beliefs, to which Sharpe draws fresh attention (pp. 530–1, 618–19, 680). Once again, Thomas' restraint on these subjects must be considered in the light of the historiography he was building on: the work of Kittredge and of subsequent folklore and literary scholars, especially K. M. Briggs, had opened up all these themes.[67] Moreover, *Religion and*

[64] C. Holmes, 'Popular culture? Witches, magistrates and divines', in Kaplan, ed., *Understanding Popular Culture*, pp. 85–111; Holmes, 'Women' (the latter lays noticeably greater emphasis on elite control than the former).

[65] Ginzburg, *Ecstasies*, pp. 4–11.

[66] M. Gijswijt-Hofstra, 'Recent witchcraft research in the Low Countries', in N. van Sas and E. Witte, eds., *Historical Research in the Low Countries* (The Hague, 1992), p. 31.

[67] Kittredge, *Witchcraft*; K. M. Briggs, *Pale Hecate's Team* (1962).

the Decline of Magic's accounts of the devil figure and then of the possible temptations that the devil might have been thought to offer a witch contain, at least by implication, a strong case for expecting a powerful role for the diabolic in popular thinking (pp. 560–7, 621–6). What this does not imply, in *Religion and the Decline of Magic*, is an authentic place for the continental stereotype of the devil-worshipping witchcraft sect within English (or indeed European) popular belief (p. 627). Evidence that this may underestimate the extent to which, by the seventeenth century at least, popular diabolism had developed, is strengthened by Elmer's chapter, which presents a mid-seventeenth-century England in which even Sabbath-like gatherings can be imputed to hated groups like the Quakers, though some of these accusations were dreamed up by educated people.

Nevertheless, there remains a fundamental gap in *Religion and the Decline of Magic*'s analysis of witchcraft. This can be summarised briefly as a lack of concern for the processes of cultural transmission, compared to the intellectual plausibility and social/psychological usefulness of given ideas. There is no extended discussion, for example, of the role of education, the press, sermons, customary events or story-telling practices in the transmission of beliefs, nor of the impact that changes in or conflicts between these rival methods of transmission had on the survival, transformation or varied prestige and acceptance of these ideas. We are informed in passing that 'the continental concept' failed to take root in England although 'it was disseminated in many vernacular treatises and reports of leading trials, published with the deliberate intention of stimulating more prosecutions' (p. 533). Yet we learn nothing more about the nature of this campaign, or why it might have failed.[68] Again, the fascinating and crucial observation that, in many areas of early modern life, such as business, administration and the like, witchcraft beliefs were almost completely absent, is not followed up (p. 693). Quite apart from its implications for the 'decline' of witchcraft, to which we shall return, this comment surely raises fundamental issues about the cultural contexts in which witchcraft, or magical ideas more broadly, might become part of the individual's way of understanding and those other areas of life where it would not. As cultural historians have

---

[68] Translations and 'frequently published accounts of European witch-trials' are also noted on pp. 524–5, but the discussion there concludes, somewhat contradictorily, that 'most demonological treatises remained locked up in Latin or some other alien language'.

increasingly argued, not only is a particular cultural vocabulary only comprehensible within a broader language, but also all complex cultures (certainly early modern Europe) contain a wide variety of different languages. One of the most crucial and potentially most volatile aspects of a culture is precisely how these different languages coexist, often in tension, and what happens when two, potentially conflicting ways of understanding the world come to overlap in people's understanding of a particular situation.[69] The chapters by Elmer and Bostridge both offer valuable interpretations of the decline of witchcraft in terms of such 'discourses'.

Such a criticism may seem paradoxical, even ungrateful, given that *Religion and the Decline of Magic* has done more than almost any other study to open up the interconnectedness of apparently different intellectual traditions within the worlds of magic and religion. To ask for more must be seen as a tribute, not a reproach, but more is surely needed, especially in relation to witchcraft. One of the major contributions of *Religion and the Decline of Magic* to witchcraft historiography was its insistence that witchcraft be seen within the broader context of magic and religion, yet, though many have praised this, few have taken up the challenge. Indeed, it can be claimed that *Religion and the Decline of Magic* itself fails to bring out, within its witchcraft chapters, the range of themes raised in other sections of the book. For instance, the account of the intellectual foundations of witchcraft (though not of many of the other magical ideas) focuses solely on the religious (that is, Christian) background (p. 559). As Roberts' chapter suggests, this is to neglect the potentially crucial role played by classical witch figures, such as Circe, in early modern thought. Thomas' discussion of the neo-Platonic or hermetic notions of nature and their equivocal impact on witchcraft could well be extended into other areas (pp. 265–8, 691–2). The same could be said of the role of folklore and romance in creating and transmitting images of the devil, magic and the witch in this period.[70]

Before pursuing this point further in relation to Thomas' work, it is

---

[69] An excellent introduction to such ideas, which also applies them in a highly relevant context, namely the varied legal discourses of early Stuart England, is G. Burgess, *The Politics of the Ancient Constitution* (1992).

[70] The classical background is emphasised, by contrast, in J. C. Baroja, *The World of the Witches* (1964) and again in his 'Witchcraft and Catholic theology', in Ankarloo and Henningsen, eds., *Early Modern European Witchcraft*, pp. 19–43. On the possible links of hermeticism and witchcraft see I. Merkel and A. Debus, eds., *Hermeticism and the Renaissance* (1988).

worth noting that this question of cultural transmission applies with equal force to many other recent accounts of witchcraft. It poses a particular challenge to those models which emphasise the late medieval establishment of a diabolic witch stereotype, produced from a fusion of popular and learned fears of heretical and anti-social sects, which, once formed, is then believed to have been carried intact through several centuries, finally reaping its harvest in witch trials in the late sixteenth and seventeenth centuries as it travelled round Europe.[71] The central problem with this account, as with any diffusionist model, is that it posits a once-and-for-all fusion of ideas into a set stereotype, when it would be equally plausible, on *a priori* grounds, to suggest that, given the cultural resources available from biblical, classical and folklore traditions, each generation and group reconstructed the witch stereotype for themselves (as Thomas may have implied on pp. 522 and 540). More plausible still, of course, is that *both* processes occurred, but we shall never be sure until close studies of the cultural transmission and transformation of the 'stereotype' have been done. From the evidence currently available, for example of the sheer variety of demonological ideas and the way in which different aspects came to the fore in different cultures, there would seem to be more support for the 're-creationist' than the diffusionist model.

Such issues of cultural transmission were clearly not on Keith Thomas' agenda. In *Religion and the Decline of Magic* such questions are raised (with commendable regularity) only to be sidelined, by emphasis that the task at hand is 'to determine the social consequences of such belief, *as it was thus inherited*' (p. 730). But this formulation contains a number of weaknesses. Beliefs are not inherited, but must be reproduced socially. Moreover, their chances of reproduction, and their status in each generation, depend crucially on the agencies to whom their transmission is entrusted. As Thomas himself noted, for example, about magical beliefs and practices, these were very hard to define in terms of any inherent characteristics or purposes, but were considered magical because they were not authorised by the established authorities (p. 227). As he also observed, 'most of those millions of persons who today would laugh at the idea of magic or miracles would have difficulty explaining why. They are the victims of society's constant pressure towards intellectual conformity' (p. 774). Yet even this formulation is

---

[71] A convenient synthesis of the work on this 'cumulative concept of witchcraft' is provided by Levack, *Witch-Hunt*, pp. 27–67.

problematic, since societies may differ widely over time and place in their concern for (and ability to enforce) intellectual conformity.

The implications (and perhaps the cause?) of Thomas' view of the cultural transmission of witchcraft beliefs (during their heyday) as a matter of inheritance become clear when we examine more closely his account of the decline of magic and witchcraft. It is regarding this period[72] that *Religion and the Decline of Magic* strongly supports the Burkean model of cultural change. Though Thomas offered no strong support for an 'acculturation' phase in the relationship between elite and popular culture during the sixteenth and seventeenth centuries, he firmly endorsed the notion that this later period saw the dissociation of 'educated' (his preferred term, rather than 'elite') and 'popular' (or often 'village') culture (pp. 797–8). To understand what he sees this as involving, we need to look beyond the witchcraft section of the book and consider his discussion of prophecy and of 'allied beliefs'. Here, in explaining the breaking of the hold of these ideas on educated opinion, Thomas paid particular attention to the loosening grip of tradition as a source of authority (pp. 509–14, 719–24, 689–92, 771–4, 793–4). At one point he concludes 'eighteenth-century England was not a traditional society in the sense that fifteenth-century England had been' (p. 724).

A number of different cultural changes appear to be involved in this process, concealed to some extent by that ambiguous word 'tradition'. In part, Thomas is discussing the declining power of the authority of the past, of ancestral wisdom and practice, to establish norms of behaviour. But he also appears to be referring to the declining weight of 'tradition' as a means of cultural transmission. This in turn may be subdivided into two related points. The first is a shift away from an image of education or culture as the 'handing-down' of received wisdom as a given, and the second is the declining prestige of those institutions whose rationale and social prestige rested on their fitness for such handing-down. Caught up in both these processes was the emergence of new forms of thinking that could not be transmitted by tradition, indeed that could only be legitimated by the rejection of tradition and the acceptance of newness, of change, as a good thing. To Thomas this was exemplified by the scientific revolution and the new orderly cosmos of Newtonian mechanical philosophy (pp. 512–13, 719, 751, 771–4, 791–2).

---

[72] The dates suggested in *Religion and the Decline of Magic* vary between c. 1650, c. 1700, the late seventeenth and the early eighteenth century (e.g. pp. 268, 310, 382, 693, 697, 797).

If one may apply Thomas' general ideas here to his discussion of witchcraft, one can perhaps understand better his notion of decline, which has often been criticised as unconvincing in its reliance on a change of attitude (an optimism about future discoveries) as sufficient to explain the loosening of educated beliefs in witchcraft (pp. 689–92, 788, 790–2).[73] Thomas was surely relying for much of the force of his argument here on the long-established view within intellectual history that sees in the late seventeenth century a break with the intellectual conformity and reverence for tradition which had held people, by and large, within the mindset that made magic and witchcraft plausible. In this case the nature of cultural transmission becomes *the* crucial question in explaining decline, yet *Religion and the Decline of Magic* does not pursue it thoroughly. Maybe this reflects a residual sense that the decline of such beliefs in the face of 'science' is natural (e.g. pp. 772–4, 793); such lingering rationalism is criticised by de Blécourt and Bostridge. But Thomas also rejected a purely cultural explanation, arguing that 'what is most necessary to produce a sense of change is the fact of change' (p. 510). Such change, though never clearly defined, appears to be largely socio-economic in nature and might perhaps be labelled 'modernisation'. The spectre of the breakdown of traditional life in favour of new, impersonal, perhaps urban forms of living, which changed the psychological and intellectual needs of society and individuals, looms large here (pp. 509–10, 723–4, 795–7). In the face of change, however, a crucial intellectual distinction is reintroduced: magic could not adapt to new needs and innovate, whereas science could (pp. 772, 793). As Thomas himself noted: 'This brings us to the essential problem. Why was it that magic did not keep pace with changing social circumstances?' (p. 786). No answer is given to this question, as attention is instead directed to showing that technology had not yet supplied the answers to the problems magic had helped to assuage.

At this point it is worth considering further E. P. Thompson's critique of Thomas for his failure to recreate the meaning of magic and witchcraft in the popular culture of eighteenth-century England.[74] The force of Thompson's critique was in large part due to his commitment to the study of tradition and custom as a mode of cultural transmission, and his

---

[73] See Monter's review in *Journal of Modern History*, 44 (1972), 264; Butler, 'Magic', 339; R. Attfield, 'Balthasar Bekker and the decline of the witchcraze', *Annals of Science*, 42 (1985), 395.
[74] Thompson, 'Anthropology', 51–5.

distrust of the bland notion of modernisation. His emphasis on the changing meanings of witchcraft to rural people, as their social circumstances changed and as their relations with the clerical and other authorities shifted, reminds us of the potential for a 'history' of popular beliefs which is not really taken up in *Religion and the Decline of Magic*, where it is educated rather than popular beliefs that change, although the circumstances of village life alter. However, Thompson's own eighteenth-century concern with magic as a class-specific oppositional ideology would not apply, if the dissociation model is correct, to the earlier period when respect for custom and shared intellectual assumptions were, according to Thomas, the norm. *Religion and the Decline of Magic*'s observations on the role of witchcraft and magic in later village life can only be regarded as suggestive.

Given the respect accorded his observations, however, one can understand the feelings of scholars of later periods that Thomas' account is unsatisfactory as a model.[75] As de Blécourt shows, the study of popular beliefs after the end of witchcraft prosecutions requires a more complex model than that provided by the 'survivalist' language used by Thomas (a most un-'functionalist' language, one might note) (pp. 129, 794–800). He also notes the problems involved in his rural or village model for such survival (pp. 540, 798). The bias of evidence towards rural beliefs may simply reflect the assumption of folklorists that such beliefs only survived in the countryside,[76] and no real effort is made to explore the potential functions of such ideas in alternative contexts. Within *Religion and the Decline of Magic*'s model of witchcraft accusation, the growth in Poor Law provision, together with the supposed 'impersonality' of urban life, left villages with close personal relationships the only suitable sites for the appropriate social relationship between accuser and accused (pp. 695–7). Yet much recent work on urban society, both in the early modern period and later, has emphasised the continued centrality of personal, kin and neighbourhood contact, even in London. Significantly, the only reference given in *Religion and the Decline of Magic* to prove the impersonal character of urban life is the (surprised) observation of an

---

[75] See, for example, M. Gijswijt-Hofstra and W. Frijhoff, eds., *Witchcraft in the Netherlands from the Fourteenth to the Twentieth Centuries* (Rotterdam, 1991); J. Barry, 'Piety and the patient', in R. Porter, ed., *Patients and Practitioners* (Cambridge, 1985), pp. 145–75.

[76] See G. Bennett, 'Folklore studies and the English rural myth', *Rural History*, 4 (1993), 77–91; Levack, *Witch-Hunt*, pp. 129–33. Thomas himself noted his reliance on the rural studies of the Folklore Society (p. 540 n. 56).

Englishman at life in Venice (p. 629), while the example of Englishmen as prying neighbours refers to citizens and hence to town life (p. 630). As for the confused feelings of guilt and hostility caused by poverty, one might well argue that these remained more salient in pre-industrial towns and pastoral areas, with their more fluid class relations, than they did in the increasingly polarised villages of arable England.[77]

One can, therefore, question key aspects of Thomas' social history of decline, just as many historians (including, latterly, Alan Macfarlane) have questioned the linkage between the growth in witchcraft fears and the social pressures of the sixteenth century.[78] Once again, however, it is only fair to note how tentative and relatively minor such socio-economic explanations are in *Religion and the Decline of Magic*'s argument. Thomas was very cautious about attaching any overarching class or group label to beliefs, such as, for example, associating the self-help and self-confidence themes with artisan or bourgeois attitudes (pp. 670–3, 796–7). He was similarly critical of any efforts to identify professional groups or specific religious or political factions as collective actors with a clear position on witchcraft (with the exception, as we have seen, of possession cases). Indeed, his position on witchcraft was rather different from his repeated willingness in other areas of magic to define a characteristically 'radical' or 'sectarian' stance, set against a more establishment one (pp. 146, 763–4).

Arguably such caution prevented him from offering an explanation of decline which others, building on his work on magic in general, have subsequently developed. They have argued that the decline in elite acceptance of magic, including witchcraft, owed much to the association of such beliefs with sectarian and enthusiastic religion during the Civil War period.[79] They have offered a much more ideological reading of the process of dissociation from popular ideas, seeing it less as the result of a new confidence, as Thomas argued (pp. 691, 777–8, 790, 792), but rather as a response to a new *fear* of radical, or potentially radical, ideas, following the Civil War. Such ideas are consonant with the new,

---

[77] See, for example, K. Snell, *Annals of the Labouring Poor* (Cambridge, 1985); J. Barry, ed., *The Tudor and Stuart Town* (1990).

[78] A. Macfarlane, *Origins of English Individualism* (Oxford, 1978), pp. 1–2, 59–60; Horsley, 'Further reflections', 94.

[79] See, for example, B. Easlea, *Witch-Hunting, Magic and the New Philosophy* (Brighton, 1980), pp. 198, 201, 218; M. MacDonald, *Mystical Bedlam* (Cambridge, 1981), pp. 198–231; MacDonald, 'Religion, social change and psychological healing'; R. Porter, 'Was there a medical enlightenment in eighteenth-century England?', *British Journal of Eighteenth-Century Studies*, 5 (1982), 49–64.

politicised readings of the scientific revolution, and in particular of the triumph of mechanical philosophy, which historians of science such as Margaret and James Jacob, Simon Schaffer and Steven Shapin have offered, building on the pioneering work of Charles Webster.[80] Similar analyses have been offered of the growth of the social sciences, an area which Thomas himself rightly stressed as vital in studying the displacement of astrology and prophecy (pp. 783–5, 791).[81] Such studies have made it increasingly clear that the establishment of these new modes of thought was to a large extent about policing the boundaries, social, religious and intellectual, of acceptable belief, and that many magical ideas came under sceptical attack precisely because of their dubious credentials when so examined. This provides a powerful answer to the question which Thomas so honestly posed, namely why, when the arguments against witchcraft in the late seventeenth century were still, to all intents and purposes, those advanced by Scot a century before, and others before him, they now suddenly carried so much more weight (pp. 681–5, 692–3, 773). Just as Scot's scepticism was born out of profound fear and dislike of Catholic superstition,[82] so in the late seventeenth century scepticism about witchcraft often arose from hostility to other known and feared enemies, who, as Elmer and Bostridge both show, now seemed much more threatening to educated culture than witches or even demons.

Many of these new interpretations can be integrated fairly easily into Thomas' analysis, although they throw doubt on his emphasis on the optimistic and self-confident nature of the new world order in the late seventeenth century. However this emphasis on self-confidence itself arises out of a more deep-seated assumption in *Religion and the Decline of Magic*, which is less easily maintained in the light of subsequent scholarship. When Thomas falls back on the notion that there was more optimism about explaining the world in the late seventeenth century

---

[80] C. Webster, *The Great Instauration* (1975); Webster, *From Paracelsus to Newton* (Cambridge, 1982); M. C. Jacob and J. R. Jacob, 'The Anglican origins of modern science', *Isis*, 71 (1980), 251–67; S. Shapin and S. Schaffer, *Leviathan and the Air Pump* (Princeton, 1985).

[81] P. Buck, 'Seventeenth-century political arithmetic', *Isis*, 68 (1977), 67–84; Buck, 'People who counted', *Isis*, 73 (1982), 28–45; J. Appleby, *Economic Thought and Ideology in Seventeenth-Century England* (Princeton, 1978); J. G. A. Pocock, *Virtue, Commerce and History* (Cambridge, 1985).

[82] L. L. Estes, 'Reginald Scot and his discovery of witchcraft', *Church History*, 52 (1983), 44–56. Cf. MacDonald, *Witchcraft and Hysteria*, pp. xxxix–lv, on the issues of power behind disputes in Jacobean London.

(even if that optimism had still not borne fruit in the technological control which, according to Malinowski, should have been needed to weaken the hold of magic) (pp. 785–8), he was developing a point implicit in his understanding of the Reformation. He argued that this involved a new commitment to intellectual 'self-help' and the diffusion, in the long term, of an attitude that spurned the 'cheap' solutions offered by magic in favour of the harder methods, both of personal faith and of natural science (pp. 331–2, 785, 787–9). As Geertz observes, this explanation is problematic;[83] it is unclear why resort to magic was any less self-reliant than resort to more established remedies, and Thomas himself noted that self-help and trust in, for example, providence coexisted (p. 789).[84] Unfortunately these ideas are not developed, in large part because of Thomas' commitment, as we have seen, to exploring intellectual change at the level of individual experience rather than broader movements. Yet this in itself reflects his vision of the Reformation as primarily working at the level of the individual believer, now forced onto his own resources of faith and Bible study. The unacceptable psychological pressures that Thomas sees this as putting on individuals are crucial to his explanation of how so many forms of magic continued to flourish in the post-Reformation world (pp. 87–9, 315–16, 593, 648).

This emphasis on the individualistic legacy of the Reformation now seems old-fashioned, since recent scholarship has stressed the continued emphasis on collective forms of religious life in the Protestant church, at least until the cataclysm of Civil War. Ironically, proponents of a 'slow Reformation' and of the continuity within the Church of England of many old Catholic practices (who often cite Thomas as evidence for the functionality and vitality of medieval Catholicism) are threatening to undermine his major contention about the Reformation, namely that it

---

[83] See Bossy's review and Geertz, 'Anthropology', 81–3. In response to her criticism of this emphasis on an attitudinal shift, Thomas explained that 'when I wrote of a shift from reliance on magic to *sturdy* self-help, I had in mind not a psychological change so much as a doctrinal one . . . The crucial shift was "attitudinal" in that it reflected a changing attitude to the relationship of God and man' ('Anthropology', 100, my italics). The continued reference to sturdiness suggests, however, Thomas's uncertainty on this point, though he explicitly distances himself from the psychological reading of his text offered in R. A. LeVine, *Culture, Behaviour and Personality* (Chicago, 1973), pp. 254–70.

[84] R. Porter, 'Medicine and the decline of magic', *Strawberry Fayre* (Autumn 1986), 88–94 suggests that the replacement of 'magical' self-help by commercial services and products was crucial here.

involved a sweeping reform that robbed people of the old consolations and protective remedies that the medieval church had offered.[85] It is now argued that, within Protestantism, individual self-help was always seen as dependent on, and subordinate to, the collective good of the church community. Indeed, many have seen the Reformation as a catalyst, not for self-help, but for tighter pressures for conformity to established authority. David Harley argues, for example, that the Protestant doctrine of providence and the attack on unauthorised magical practitioners should be seen together. The doctrine of providence required the individual to accept the judgement of God, which was interpreted as meaning turning in need only to those professions, such as the clergy, medical or legal men, authorised by society (and the church) to provide a remedy, and not to illicit practitioners.[86] As Thomas himself stressed about village society (pp. 628–32), and as Elmer explores in this collection, the vision of social harmony and consensus, in which self-help and individualism were a threat unless properly channelled, was intensely powerful up to, and arguably well beyond, the Civil War.

Yet during and after the Civil War the possibility of harmony and consensus was shattered irrevocably, with consequences for witchcraft that Elmer and Bostridge explore. In the more divided society that ensued the fundamental association between guilt and misfortune, on which *Religion and the Decline of Magic*'s arguments depend, was transformed, at least in public debate. In part, as Elmer shows, this was because, with every sect or party in the ensuing struggles stridently identifying itself with good and its opponents with evil, the whole notion of a polarised world became tarnished: a grey world seemed both more plausible and less divisive. In part it arose from a new willingness to tolerate individual vices for public benefits, together perhaps with a more general tolerance of diversity, as this came to seem inevitable.[87] But

---

[85] See, for example, C. Haigh, 'The recent historiography of the English Reformation', *Historical Journal*, 25 (1982), 1000. *Religion and the Decline of Magic* itself offers considerable evidence of continuity, not least by citing Puritan critics of the Church's continued 'magical' dimension (pp. 79–84, 328–30).

[86] P. Collinson, *The Religion of Protestants* (Oxford, 1982); D. Harley, 'Spiritual physic, providence and English medicine 1560–1640', in Grell and Cunningham, eds., *Medicine and the Reformation*, pp. 101–17.

[87] Bowker's review highlighted this issue. W. J. Sheils, ed., *Persecution and Toleration*, Studies in Church History 22 (Oxford, 1984) and O. Grell, J. I. Israel and N. Tyacke, eds., *From Persecution to Toleration: The Glorious Revolution and Religion in England* (Oxford, 1991) explore this theme for England. For Europe in general see W. Monter, *Ritual, Myth and Magic in Early Modern Europe* (Brighton, 1983).

it was also the result of the blunting and discrediting of the legal mechanisms for suppressing witches, as they were directed at other targets, ones that seemed to contemporaries even more questionable. Thus the church courts' abandonment of the campaign against illicit magic after 1660 (pp. 309–10, 313) may be explained not by a sudden change of view about magic, but by their preoccupation with chasing religious dissenters, a campaign which, in the long run, left them with little power over anybody after 1689. Instead, unorthodox views and nonconformist behaviour came to be controlled by the subtler tactics of ridicule and neglect. In particular, in educated society at least, the links that individuals made between guilt and misfortune became the subject for private meditation rather than for public action or discussion. As Bostridge argues, it is vital to distinguish between three different levels of witchcraft's history: prosecution, the public discourse of witchcraft, and private beliefs, and, although all three will certainly have inter-related, we cannot pre-judge the nature of such relationships.

Although these observations about 'decline' have been based on the English experience, many of the points can be applied to the continental situation. Dutch historians, in particular, have developed similar explanations. As Hans de Waardt has argued, a crucial dimension in understanding the history of witchcraft prosecutions and beliefs is establishing the shifting boundary between the public and private spheres, which in turn depends on the changing position of the church and state in enforcing intellectual and moral conformity within divided societies. It is unfortunate, as noted before, that *Religion and the Decline of Magic*'s preoccupation with the personal plausibility of a witchcraft accusation prevents the systematic exploration of the circumstances in which this would enter the public sphere, and those in which it would not. Dutch historians have suggested, furthermore, that this issue is very closely tied up with gender, with witch prosecutions flowing from cases where male concerns and interests were threatened. The removal of witchcraft from the public sphere resulted from and further intensified the 'feminisation' of witchcraft, although it would be dangerous to set up public and private as new polarities, let alone to identify them straight-forwardly with a male public and female private sphere.[88]

---

[88] M. Gijswijt-Hofstra, 'The European witchcraft debate', *Social History*, 15 (1990), 181–94; H. de Waardt, *Toverij en Sameleving. Holland 1500–1800* (The Hague, 1991), pp. 337–9 (English summary); Gijswijt-Hofstra and Frijhoff, eds., *Witchcraft in the Netherlands*. See also Geertz, 'Anthropology', 82 on the public-private distinction and Holmes, 'Women', for a subtle analysis of how women were used within a

This brings us on to the whole question of gender. It is a considerable irony that someone whose early articles on gender history were so influential and unusual for a male historian of the time is often now accused of blindness to gender issues in his greatest work.[89] The problem is not that Thomas failed to recognise the predominance of women amongst those accused (pp. 519, 620–1, 678) nor that he ignored the issue, though such an accusation could be levelled at his account of possession cases, which plays down any significance to age or gender (p. 572). But the account of 'standard' witchcraft cases in *Religion and the Decline of Magic* explains gender variations in terms of a more basic factor, namely dependence (pp. 607–8, 611, 620–1, 623, 669–73, 678). Again, it is worth remembering the historiographical background. Not only was Thomas writing at a time when the subordination of gender to class considerations was routine, but he was very clearly reacting to the influence of Margaret Murray's theories about witchcraft prosecution as the persecution of a female religious cult. This predisposed Thomas to favour an account which stressed the individual, even solitary, female experience, rather than the collective, and to distrust anti-female conspiracy theories as a mode of explanation (pp. 614–17, 626–7, 632–4). Instead, as we have seen, all the attention in terms of accusation is placed on the individual relationship of accuser and accused. It is interesting, however, to note that this relationship is gendered in the text as that between male accuser and female accused (pp. 646, 652–3, 657–8, 665, though see p. 670 for the accused as 'a poor man');[90] this despite Thomas' claim, unsubstantiated elsewhere in his text, that 'the idea that witch-prosecutions reflected a war between the sexes must be discounted, not least because the *victims* and witnesses were themselves as likely to be women as men' (p. 679, my italics). As is noted in the same paragraph, the image of the female witch cult in continental demonology

male-dominated public process of prosecution. For cautionary words on the relation of polarised representations to social realities see S. Clark, 'The "gendering" of witchcraft in French demonology: misogyny or polarity?', *French History*, 5 (1991), 426–37.

[89] See Scott, 'Conjuring'; K. V. Thomas, 'Women and the Civil War sects', *Past and Present*, 13 (1958); Thomas, 'The double standard', *Journal of the History of Ideas*, 20 (1959), 195–216. For a convenient summary of recent work on this subject see M. Wiesner, *Women and Gender in Early Modern Europe* (Cambridge, 1993), ch. 7.

[90] During the earlier discussion of 'cunning *men* and popular magic', where they are mostly assumed to be men, we are then told that '*she* [the "cunning woman" or "wise woman"] was always perched precariously on the brink of social isolation' (p. 291, my italics).

contained many overt elements of mysogynistic feeling which *Religion and the Decline of Magic* argues were absent from the typical English case, which revolved around feelings of guilt towards dependent women, not hatred or fear of women's power (pp. 678–9).

Two main critiques have been offered of this telescoping of gender issues into those of dependence. The first, explored by several chapters in this collection, is that this depends on exaggerating the typicality of the model of charity refused. For example, the Dutch and German studies in this collection show that a whole range of other anxieties, both of and about women, are of great importance, in particular issues relating to motherhood and infancy. Thomas himself allowed for this by noting that different social contexts might well bring different sources of guilt and anxiety to the fore (p. 677). More directly challenging, since it relates to the English experience, is the claim of both Gaskill and, in particular, Hester that Thomas has missed the many occasions where what is at stake is women's power, not their weakness, and that accusations are often part of a competition for resources, in which women's claims are undercut by the identification of female power with dangerous sexuality and hence with diabolic power.[91] Here *Religion and the Decline of Magic*'s argument that, in England at least, the devil was associated with failure not success (pp. 621–4, 644), appears vulnerable, not least because many of the tales cited of the devil *failing* to satisfy the wishes of those he tempts, might best be seen as cautionary tales designed to limit women's ambitions for success, or to reinforce men's fears about women's desires, not as true stories of witches as failures. As Roberts' chapter on the Circe figure shows, male writers were all too conscious of the threat posed to male potency and virtue by the seductions of witchcraft.

This leads to the second, and arguably more powerful objection, since it would apply even if the 'charity refused' model is accepted. This is that Thomas neglected what Hester calls the 'gendering of expectations and meanings' involved even in that situation, and in particular the way in which curses and 'malignity' were perceived by those involved. Hester offers telling examples where it is the person refused, not the refuser, who becomes the accuser, suggesting that gender roles may have pre-

---

[91] Karlsen, *Devil*; M. Hester, *Lewd Women and Wicked Witches* (1992); M. Gaskill, 'Witchcraft and power in early modern England: the case of Margaret Moore', in J. Kermode and G. Walker, eds., *Women, Crime and the Courts in Early Modern England* (1994), pp. 125–45.

dominated over social relationships. *Religion and the Decline of Magic*'s discussion of cursing is dominated by the theme of guilt, and so revolves around the notion of a 'justifiable' curse, one which the accuser could fear, feel guilty about, and yet seek to turn against its perpetrator by the charge of witchcraft (pp. 599–611, 659–65). What is not explored here, despite its appearance in several of the key quotations cited (e.g. pp. 610–11, 677–8), is the contemporary assumption that such cursing was a basically female prerogative, and that, however justifiable a curse might be, the tongue that uttered it was a female tongue, that unruly member on which so much evil was blamed and which was so much distrusted. It was around the figure of the tongue (together with images of sexuality, of course) that the paradox of female power/powerlessness revolved, and it is as important to consider how accusers constructed and presented the curser as malignant as to understand their feelings of guilt, particularly if we are to understand how they persuaded others to accept such a characterisation. When cases came to court, it was this question of character that became decisive, while the courts were also full of defamation cases in which it was the slanderous naming of someone else as a witch that showed the malignity of the unruly female tongue involved.[92]

Religion and the Decline of Magic contains a discussion of women as scolds (pp. 632–3), but within a separate section dealing with women as nonconformists. These arguments surely deserve Carol Karlsen's general rebuke that, in trying to find out what made witches vulnerable to accusation, historians have strayed over the line into making witches appear culpable.[93] It is hard to know how else to read the comparison with arsonists (which is also equally disturbing for its apparent acceptance of social panics about arson attacks as an accurate record of

---

[92] P. Tyler, 'The church courts at York and witchcraft prosecutions 1567–1640', *Northern History*, 4 (1969), 84–109; P. Rushton, 'Women, witchcraft and slander in early modern England', *Northern History*, 18 (1982), 116–32; J. Sharpe, 'Witchcraft and women in seventeenth-century England', *Continuity and Change*, 6 (1991), 179–200; M. Ortega, 'Women as the source of evil in Counter-Reformation Spain', in A. Cruz and M. Perry, eds., *Culture and Control in Counter-Reformation Spain* (Minneapolis, 1992), pp. 196–215; J. Sharpe, 'Women, witchcraft and the legal process', in Kermode and Walker, eds., *Women, Crime and the Courts*, pp. 106–24. On the general theme see D. Underdown, 'The taming of the scold', in A. Fletcher and J. Stevenson, eds., *Order and Disorder in Early Modern England* (Cambridge, 1985), pp. 116–36 and J. Wiltenburg, *Disorderly Women and Female Power in the Street Literature of Early Modern England and Germany* (Charlottesville and London, 1992), especially ch. 9.

[93] Karlsen, *Devil*, pp. 118–19, 131–2, 310 n. 3 (where Demos is named) and 313 n. 50.

the roots of arsonism) (pp. 634–7). But even more revealing is the observation, after a paragraph of describing the horrific assaults conducted by men on suspected witches, that 'sanctions of this kind inevitably constituted a check upon *outbursts of temper,* swearing or cursing, or similar *expressions of malignity . . .* could thus inhibit the expression of *vicious feelings,* and help to reinforce the prevailing ethic of neighbourliness and communal solidarity. But they increased the sense of isolation experienced by the person who had become estranged from her neighbours, and they enhanced *her desire for revenge'* (p. 634, my italics). Whose malignity or desire for revenge, one might ask, needs the most emphasis and exploration in this passage?[94]

Similar concerns arise about the previous section in this chapter, on 'the temptation to witchcraft' (pp. 620–8). Here Thomas, perhaps because of the legacy of Murray's positive answer to the question, 'were there really witches?', inquired, largely using confessions, whether any women might have believed themselves to be practising *maleficium* or even diabolic witchcraft, and if so why. This is, of course, a perfectly legitimate question, and in some ways a brave one to ask. Over the last two decades few historians have wanted to ask it, not least because the focus on the elite demonological stereotype and its dissemination has, as Ginzburg complained, led to neglect of the extent of supernaturalism, even anti-Christian beliefs, in popular thought and practice.[95] But one must question both the balance and the methodology of *Religion and the Decline of Magic*'s discussion of 'those who thus mentally allied themselves with Satan' (pp. 626, 638). As is noted, we are dealing here with a 'tiny proportion' (p. 618) of those accused, namely those whose confessions survive in any detail, and at most only 'a few' (p. 626), who may have believed that the devil had 'granted their wishes'.[96]

---

[94] Note that 'the desire for revenge' and 'malevolence' of witches are emphasised here (pp. 623–4, 638), though in the discussion of accusations we are firmly told that it is 'not necessary for the suspected witch to have given evidence of her malevolence. The victim's guilty conscience could alone be sufficient' (p. 665). The guilt feelings of the accusers appear to protect them from the charge of feeling malice or vengefulness, whereas the 'justifiable' resentment of the accused does not prevent her feelings being 'malevolent'. Levack, *Witch-Hunt,* p. 152 reads Thomas as emphasising these behavioural characteristics of the witch.

[95] Ginzburg, *Ecstasies,* pp. 2–11. But see H. C. E. Midelfort, 'Were there really witches?' in R. Kingdon, ed., *Transition and Revolution* (1974), pp. 189–205; Horsley, 'Who were the witches?'; Levack, *Witch-Hunt,* pp. 11–20.

[96] A 'substantial proportion' had malevolent thoughts and 'many' issued curses (p. 624), but, as *Religion and the Decline of Magic* itself shows, this could be done from a perfectly orthodox religious stance (pp. 599–611). N. Spanos, 'Witchcraft in histories

Furthermore, the discussion depends on the assumption that there is *anything* in the confession that reflects the motives and beliefs of the accused, not at the time when the confession was made, but when the supposed temptation or offence took place. Here there is a crucial distinction between the way in which Roper, in her chapter here, uses evidence elicited by torture, and how Thomas used his material. *Religion and the Decline of Magic* acknowledges that such confessions depended on leading questions (pp. 617–19) plus the attempts of witches to convince themselves, *retrospectively*, that they were guilty (p. 628). In studying how they did this, we can learn much of interest, as Thomas himself puts it, about 'the motives and temptation to which both interrogator and accused [should that be either/or?] assumed that witches were liable to be subject' (p. 620), and this is how Roper uses her Augsburg material. But in *Religion and the Decline of Magic* we slip from such analysis of what was plausible in the construction of witch-craft narratives, to the supposed reconstruction of witches' thoughts prior to the period of accusation.[97] No convincing example is given (except Scot's opinion) before we are told that, though 'it would be wrong to suggest that all persons accused of witchcraft had had malevolent thoughts about their neighbours . . . a substantial proportion of them certainly had, for it was the witch's malignity which gave the charge plausibility in popular eyes, and, *though that malignity could be inferred from the witch's social situation*, it was often evidenced by her actual behaviour'. As the passage I have emphasised here suggests, it is at points like this that the lack of an elaborated discussion of the social, and especially gender, expectations that underlay such inferences creates problems. For Thomas, a gender explanation would involve 'psycho-logical or psychoanalytic' understanding of the possible motivations of individual women, but such explanations need surely be deployed if, and only if, the evidence they seek to explain is not more easily and reliably

of psychiatry', *Psychological Bulletin*, 85 (1978), 429–31 and Levack, *Witch-Hunt*, p. 18, both use Thomas to construct an account of the women who might have seen themselves as witches.

[97] 'Her curses and imprecations thus *symbolised* the accused witch's relationship to society' and 'How can we today separate the allegations which had at least *some symbolic truth* from those which were in every sense false' (pp. 625, 627, my italics) both seem to imply, though somewhat ambiguously, such an approach. For the further development of Roper's approach see *Oedipus and the Devil*, where, in her essay of the same title, she follows the same route as Thomas does here, using confession material as an accurate guide to motivations, albeit perhaps unconscious ones, in past actions, which the accused learns to recognise through interrogation.

accounted for by the social attitudes that brought them to trial. It is hard to see anything discussed in this section of *Religion and the Decline of Magic* that would fall into this category, and much that could have been more profitably considered under the heading of gendered expectations about likely witch behaviour. The process involved here, and the primary responsibility of the community for the 'making of a witch' is so brilliantly and poignantly conveyed in the passage from *The Witch of Edmonton* that ends the section (p. 628) that one cannot help wishing such a literary source had been given more attention.

Furthermore, lack of interest in this labelling process prevented Thomas from developing his analysis of female nonconformity more widely to consider the use of the 'witch label' in the broader language of gender relations. Here his very determination to get at the 'reality' of the social situation in witchcraft trials produced a very different balance of detail from that of a historian concerned to establish how, for example, fear of being called a witch or, indeed, the power conveyed by being able to call another a witch, helped to determine the behaviour of many women well beyond the dependent groups singled out by Thomas.[98] Characteristically, however, Thomas threw into the end of his discussion of gender an observation which is now seen as of crucial relevance to this whole theme, namely the notion that accusations against women of witchcraft depended on the prevalent view of female sexuality as naturally active and lascivious, and that a new emphasis (after about 1700) on women as passive and less sexual than men may have changed the whole linguistic context for witchcraft, and in particular its suitability as a public topos by which to discuss and regulate female behaviour (p. 679).[99]

Thomas follows up this spectacular insight into the public/private and linguistic dimension of witchcraft by observing 'there is still much about the fantasy side of witch beliefs which cries out for explanation. The concept of witchcraft provided a way of looking at the world and an imaginative vocabulary for many individuals who were not themselves directly involved in witchcraft accusations' (pp. 679–80). As many of the chapters here indicate, it is precisely this 'cultural' dimension of the

---

[98] Hester, *Lewd Women*, especially pp. 200–1.

[99] Karlsen, *Devil*, pp. 255–7; Hester, *Lewd Women*, pp. 156–7. Typically, Lawrence Stone suggested a diametrically opposite perspective, noting provocatively 'Is it more than a coincidence that witches vanish just at the time when *Fanny Hill* appears?' ('Magic, religion and reason' [a revised version of his 1971 review of *Religion and the Decline of Magic*] in his *The Past and the Present* (1981), p. 165).

subject which is now being explored. I wish to conclude this introduction by considering further some of the implications this work may have for the task which Thomas claimed for himself, with characteristic modesty: 'All that has been advanced here is a social explanation of the context in which accusations were made and an outline of the intellectual assumptions which made them plausible'(p. 680).

It was suggested earlier that the gap between intellectual assumptions and the social context of accusations could be bridged, at least in part, by a fuller analysis of cultural transmission, following Thomas' own observations elsewhere in *Religion and the Decline of Magic*. We need to establish the politics of witchcraft beliefs, as a way of understanding both the conjunction of circumstances which affected the outcome, always precarious, of a specific incident where witchcraft was involved, and in explaining the 'structural transformation', as Hans De Waardt has put it, which affected the prestige and plausibility of witchcraft.[100] This will involve the detailed reconstruction of individual cases and of shifting interest groups. But at the same time, it must also allow for the dimension of 'fantasy' and 'imagination', in Thomas' words, in cultural history.

Religion and the Decline of Magic is a supreme effort of sympathy, to make rational (to the rational) that which could so easily be dismissed as irrational, and throughout the text the rational writer intervenes to lead us, as readers, through the wild thickets of his subject. The book is, in many ways, a triumph of storytelling, of the selection of topics and evidence to guide the reader to the mental reconstruction of an alien world which, in travelling through, we learn to understand in its own terms. Yet, as the language used in this paragraph deliberately suggests, that process is as much literary as 'rational' – it involves the imagination and, if not fantasy, then certainly storytelling. Precisely because of the irrational, fantastic nature of its subject-matter, not to mention the Gothic quality of earlier accounts of its subject, the tone must, to carry conviction, be as realistic and plausible to the rational reader, as, to take a pertinent example, Defoe's historical novels.

What happens if we apply this parallel to the written evidence on which *Religion and the Decline of Magic* itself depends? Thomas was of course, as a great historian, conscious of the nature of his sources, although his tendency to break down such sources into countless short quotations produced the danger that the reader, if not the author, would

[100] De Waardt, *Toverij*, p. 339.

fail to grasp the setting for each statement. Generally, however, he used his sources as statements of fact or feeling, not as examples of rhetoric or storytelling. Yet there are a number of reasons for thinking that any history of witchcraft (and *Religion and the Decline of Magic* is not only that, of course) needs a more reflexive attitude to the nature of history and storytelling than *Religion and the Decline of Magic* displays. One reason is that the contemporary debate about witchcraft was itself so resolutely historical, culminating in Francis Hutchinson's *Historical Essay concerning Witchcraft* (1718) and so much of our evidence has come down in the writings of such histories, whether scholarly studies or the popular trial narratives so often labelled 'the history' of a particular witch. As this suggests, many of these accounts are shaped by contemporary conventions about what would or would not carry conviction as a truthful and entertaining account. There was, in the sixteenth and seventeenth centuries, no clearcut borderline between story and history, as historians of the novel have emphasised.[101] At the same time, many of the other sources are equally structured by rhetorical assumptions and by the need to provide a verisimilitudinous narrative, whether they be the accounts of witnesses at a trial or a witch's confession or even, in the continental context, an inquisitorial report. The obvious need for the historian in this context is to take account of the likely problems of bias and selectivity created by this, which Thomas nearly always does. But the more creative challenge, which historians are now taking up, is to explore the positive dimension of past evidence as storytelling, by considering the meaning of the story itself, and its significance in shaping the very history it is recording.[102] Thus, for example, it has become clear that reports of witch trials were themselves of fundamental importance in shaping the behaviour of the parties in subsequent trials. Thomas himself suggested that in possession cases those possessed, and the way in which their possessions were reported, were influenced in 'language and style' by earlier cases (pp. 572, 574). Studies like Roper's chapter suggest ways in which the very process of trial and interrogation, the requirement to tell a story about witchcraft, could radically affect the people involved, not just in terms of whether they believed in witchcraft, but in their attitudes to many other aspects of life. Again, Roberts'

---

[101] L. J. Davis, *Factual Fictions* (New York, 1983); M. McKeon, *Origins of the English Novel 1600–1740* (Baltimore, 1987); J. Hunter, *Before Novels* (New York, 1990).

[102] For a recent account of the Salem episode which employs this approach to great effect see Rosenthal, *Salem Story*.

chapter suggests the need to see witchcraft as constituted, in considerable part, by the reiteration and transformation of literary images and texts as these were constantly reworked in the writings of the time.

In such circumstances, the line between fact and fiction, historytelling and storytelling, will be blurred, not just for the subsequent historian but also for the contemporary participant, above all when dealing with as elusive a subject as witchcraft. This very circumstance is itself of crucial importance to an understanding of witchcraft's history. Cases of witchcraft always occupied the borderlines between what seemed possible and impossible. Indeed, the notion of a devil seemed necessary to many demonologists precisely to retain the boundary, by providing a naturalistic explanation of how the apparently incredible could come to pass.[103] Yet, as Roper's discussion of the slippage between poisoning and witchcraft reveals, the boundaries we draw between natural and supernatural methods are not timeless ones. As an intellectual theory, or even as a source of cautionary or illuminating tales, this borderline status was perhaps a strength, giving society an 'imaginative vocabulary'. Yet witchcraft was also a crime and one imputed to specific individuals. This meant the need to come down firmly on one side of the fact–fiction borderline – to establish what had actually happened. As *Religion and the Decline of Magic* argues, the decline of witchcraft owed much to the dilemmas that it had always posed to those concerned for proof (pp. 685–8, 694). Set against this was the unbearable prospect to many that, if witchcraft was pronounced an illusion, both earlier legal processes and many of the cultural authorities, above all the Bible, that declared it to exist, were themselves wrong (pp. 550, 567). Hence the great attraction of the compromise that declared witchcraft a possibility, but each specific case impossible to prove (pp. 686–8).

Recent work on seventeenth-century culture has identified a growing concern at that period to separate fact from fiction more firmly or, if this was impossible, to declare discourses where the two overlapped to be beyond the realm of acceptable public knowledge. For reasons which appear to centre on the clash of competing ideologies, thinkers (across Europe and in many fields) sought to regulate both language and ideas to demarcate areas of certainty from those of mere conjecture or fantasy and

---

[103] See S. Clark, 'The scientific status of demonology', in B. Vickers, ed., *Occult and Scientific Mentalities in the Renaissance* (Oxford, 1984), pp. 351–74; Clark, 'The rational witch-finder', in S. Pumfrey et al., eds., *Science, Culture and Popular Belief in Renaissance Europe* (Manchester, 1991), pp. 222–48.

to reconstitute public life on the basis only of that which could be presented as realistic and verifiable fact, or assented to as probable conjecture. One of the undoubted victims of this process, as Barbara Shapiro has noted, was witchcraft, which, despite the efforts of various leading members of the Royal Society to establish its empirical character, defied such categorisation. But, as Shapiro suggests, changing attitudes to witchcraft were not merely the outcome of a cultural process decided elsewhere, for the problems they raised so acutely may well have forced a resolution of the wider issues.[104]

Thus we return once again to the ironic possibility that, in its very success in making witchcraft beliefs seem plausible and rational, Keith Thomas may have underplayed the fictive aspect so central to his subject. But even this outcome is anticipated by the sceptical rationalist of *Religion and the Decline of Magic.* In 1971, as Thomas noted, historians rewrote 'the history of their dead ancestors to show that they too suffered from the problems of sex, class or money' which obsessed the historians (p. 505), but by the 1990s their anxieties have altered. As storytellers (or journeyers into the world of the dead, to use Ginzburg's characteristic reformulation), historians are more in demand for reports of Balkan shamanism or gender labelling than of village poverty.[105] Yet *Religion and the Decline of Magic* still weaves its spell over successive generations of readers, not least for its unforgettable impression of a great historical imagination at work. It would, however, be less than true to Thomas' own wishes for us to remain under the magician's spell: sturdy self-help in developing and amending the account he provided is required. This collection is offered in that spirit.

---

[104] B. Shapiro, *Probability and Certainty in Seventeenth-Century England* (Princeton, 1983), pp. 194–226.

[105] Ginzburg, *Ecstasies*, p. 24. I have received great assistance in the preparation of this essay from my fellow-editors and from Stuart Clark, Colin Jones and, in particular, Willem de Blécourt. Its subject himself read and commented on it with characteristic generosity and encouragement.

Part 1

The crime and its history

2. 'Many reasons why': witchcraft and the problem of multiple explanation

ROBIN BRIGGS

It is a familiar paradox to claim that the more we know about any subject, the harder it becomes to generalise about it. The last twenty-five years have been a golden period for the historical study of witchcraft, transforming the subject from an esoteric byway into a regular concern of social, religious and intellectual historians. Valuable research has been carried out in virtually every country in Europe, and in the New World, enhancing our knowledge enormously in both depth and breadth. Hugh Trevor-Roper's pioneering essay, which did much to stimulate this interest, also reminds us how far we have travelled.[1] The information available for a modern synthesis is greater by several orders of magnitude than that available to him around 1960. A wide range of interpretative strategies, drawing on virtually every kind of theoretical and interdisciplinary approach, has been brought to bear on the phenomenon. We certainly understand far more about the inner logic of both beliefs and persecution than our predecessors. Yet it is apparent that no kind of definitive interpretation has emerged; if in some ways this is comforting for those still working on witchcraft, it is also somewhat daunting. Whatever the attractions of knowing that a mystery remains unsolved, one would prefer to have something more than ever-increasing complexity to claim as a result of one's efforts. It does seem at least possible that the strongly empirical bias of most historians has contributed to this situation, and that the wood is at times being lost for the trees. At the same time the social anthropologists, to whom historians have often looked for guidance at the theoretical level, appear to have largely abandoned witchcraft studies in recent years, perhaps because the

---

[1] H. R. Trevor-Roper, *The European Witch-Craze of the Sixteenth and Seventeenth Centuries* (Harmondsworth, 1969), first published in *Religion, the Reformation and Social Change* (London, 1967), pp. 90–192.

structuralist explanation of the phenomenon is too facile to be very interesting.

One of the reasons for studying witchcraft has been that it illuminates many other subjects, and can help us to reconstruct the distinctive social and intellectual character of a past age. Few topics remind us more vividly that the past is a foreign country, whose assumptions were often very different from our own. In trying to explain the 'other', historians are indeed very close to social anthropologists; so close that it may be necessary to borrow an important principle from these disciplinary neighbours. This is that social practices can only be fully understood in the context of society as a whole. Causation and meanings should never be expected to be simple, even in societies much smaller and less varied than that of early modern Europe. As I shall try to show, the range of viable explanations for the multifaceted nexus we call witchcraft now available bears out this general claim. In consequence, the subject continues to pose a major challenge to the rather minimalist theories historians commonly employ in describing both social structures and social change. To put it another way, this is such a rich and exciting topic that it should encourage us to improve, refine and rethink our own procedures.

At this point the fashionable move would be an appeal to some aspect of post-modernist theory, perhaps to demonstrate how overlapping discourses of witchcraft across time have determined both the nature of the phenomenon and our reactions to it. Such approaches do have the great virtue of disturbing our complacency, but I have yet to find them of much help in accounting for change. They also tend to seem remote from the relatively banal details of the trials themselves, even coming close to that 'enormous condescension of posterity' rightly deplored by E. P. Thompson.[2] I shall operate on the more traditional assumption that there was a past reality, never fully recoverable, which historians are best able to cope with in a relatively artisanal fashion. My arguments, which fall into the general category of middle-range generalisations, are in part variations on the old *question mal posée* theme; they suggest that we already have very reasonable explanations for what we need to explain. We know most of the answers, if we can just get our own thinking straight. Certainly there is not much hope that new evidence will transform the situation in some dramatic fashion. Having spent many years working on one of the richest archives in Europe I feel reasonably

---

[2] E. P. Thompson, *The Making of the English Working Class* (London, 1963), p. 12.

confident in making this assertion. The systematic study of hundreds of witchcraft trials does enable one to thicken the texture in helpful ways, and to test various hypotheses in a reasonably searching fashion. These documents also provide much information about the lives and thoughts of ordinary people, but they have severe limitations, to which I shall refer in passing. What should emerge from such studies is a more finely grained picture, one of whose features will inevitably be greater diversity at local level. Since this is precisely what my own approach would predict, I naturally feel quite comfortable with the prospect.

Most of us, I assume, would agree that any serious interpretation of European witchcraft must be multifactorial, relating it to a number of discrete, or at least separable, causes. Any attempt to suggest that there is a single cause, or even a dominant one, a hidden key to the mystery, should be treated with the greatest suspicion. There has been no shortage of heroic attempts in this direction, of course. Some have thought witches really existed, whether as devil worshippers (Summers), heretics (J. B. Russell), pagans (Margaret Murray), or social rebels (Michelet, the early Le Roy Ladurie).[3] Others have seen the conspiracy as lying among the persecutors, whether benighted clerics or avaricious judges (Lecky, Lea, Robbins).[4] Even Trevor-Roper's sophisticated analysis has a strong anti-clerical tinge.[5] There has been a rash of medical pseudo-explanations, invoking syphilis, ergotism and magic mushrooms.[6] A feminist myth has come into existence, usually accompanied by wild inflation of the numbers, in which women were the real target, particularly in their role as healers.[7] In many cases it is easy to see how personal convictions have

[3] M. Summers, *The History of Witchcraft and Demonology* (London, 1926); J. B. Russell, *Witchcraft in the Middle Ages* (Ithaca and London, 1972); M. Murray, *The Witch-Cult in Western Europe* (Oxford, 1921); J. Michelet, *La sorcière* (Paris, 1862); E. Le Roy Ladurie, *Les paysans de Languedoc* (Paris, 1966), pp. 407–14.

[4] W. E. H. Lecky, *History of the Rise and Influence of the Spirit of Rationalism in Europe* (London, 1865); H. C. Lea, *A History of the Inquisition in the Middle Ages* (New York and London, 1888), III, pp. 492–549; R. H. Robbins, *The Encyclopedia of Witchcraft and Demonology* (London, 1959).

[5] Trevor-Roper, *The European Witch-Craze*, p. 116, 'It seems incontestable that the cause of this revival (of the witch-craze) was the intellectual regression of Reformation and Counter-Reformation, and the renewed evangelism of the rival Churches'.

[6] Examples include: S. Andreski, *Syphilis, Puritanism and Witch Hunts: Historical Explanations with a Forecast about AIDS* (London, 1989); L. R. Caporael, 'Ergotism: the Satan loosed in Salem?', *Science*, 192 (1976), 121–6; M. J. Harner, ed., *Hallucinogens and Shamanism* (New York, 1973).

[7] For a fuller discussion see R. Briggs, 'Women as victims? Witches, judges, and the community', *French History*, 5 (1991), 438–50. As I make clear there, I do not regard gender explanations as irrelevant, but they need to be treated with proper critical care.

shaped the interpretations; in others I am tempted to invoke historians' tendency to omnipotence at the expense of the past. One of the most tiresome forms of this, often found in writings on witchcraft, is to treat our ancestors as if they were little better than mental defectives. There may also, in some cases, be a wish to explain away a peculiarly unpleasant part of the European past as an aberration, or blame it on a specific group.

Many of these explanations do have some validity, of course; the objection is to giving them an exclusive or dominant role. Rather similar objections can ultimately be made to the more elaborate theories advanced by Robert Muchembled and Christina Larner.[8] Despite their awareness of the complexities, both end up with an overemphasis on the part played by the state; they put witchcraft in a political or sociological framework which proves to be a misfit. Larner's work in particular is so attractive, evidently shrewd and full of good things, that one needs a strong critical sense to catch her overstretching her case (and breaking her own rules). With both historians a detailed examination of particular cases ends up reducing allegedly strong causes to weak or partial ones, which only operate in a minority of instances. Muchembled's crude use of the concept of acculturation (which he appears to have foresworn in his most recent work) has also done much to muddy the waters.[9] This inappropriate model leads to such unsatisfactory results as a simple binary division between popular and elite culture, and a claim that lay judges 'belonged to the shock troops charged with inculcating a new definition of the sacred in the polytheist and animist masses'.[10] When Larner described the witch hunt as 'the pursuit of ideological crime in the

---

The reasons for persecuting witches cannot be simply equated with those for the predominance of women among the suspects. To treat trials as if they were primarily motivated by a desire to assert masculine dominance seems to me as absurd as it is to deny that this was a common secondary feature. For female healers the most influential text has been B. Ehrenreich and D. English, *Witches, Midwives, and Nurses: A History of Women Healers* (New York, 1973). For a powerful refutation of many of their claims see D. Harley, 'Historians as demonologists: the myth of the midwife-witch', *Social History of Medicine*, 3 (1990), 1–26.

[8] R. Muchembled's general theories are most easily found in the convenient collection *Sorcières, justice et société aux xvie et xviie siècles* (Paris, 1987), those of C. Larner in *Witchcraft and Religion: The Politics of Popular Belief* (Oxford, 1984).

[9] In R. Muchembled, *L'invention de l'homme moderne: sensibilités, moeurs et comportements collectifs sous l'Ancien Régime* (Paris, 1988), Muchembled clearly renounces much of his earlier position, and avoids the term 'acculturation' completely.

[10] R. Muchembled, 'Lay judges and the acculturation of the masses (France and the Southern Low Countries, sixteenth to eighteenth centuries), in K. von Greyerz, ed., *Religion and Society in Early Modern Europe, 1500–1800* (London, 1984), p. 65.

process of legitimizing new regimes', or wrote of 'the conspicuous and unequivocal way in which the ruling elite controlled and manipulated the demand for and supply of witchcraft suspects', she seems to me to have been hardly less wrong than Margaret Murray.[11]

It is not just that monothematic explanations have so far failed to work in practice for the specific instance of witchcraft. I have been unable to think of any comparable social phenomenon which can be usefully treated in this way. Although it may not be capable of formal expression, I suspect there is an explanatory law which dictates that complex problems of this type never have simple or precisely identifiable causes. Careful analysis usually reveals overlapping levels and strands of both causation and meaning, which are extremely hard to rank against one another even in individual cases. Once we start aggregating, the variables multiply so fast that chaos theory, with its patterns of unpredictability, is the scientific model which best fits the case. This is not a counsel of despair, however; I would argue that it liberates us from the impossible demands created by a heavily mechanistic conception of human society. Too many theories resemble the work of Cartesian natural philosophers, wanting the world to cling in tight patterns sustained by a kind of cosmic velcro, when the reality is much more flexible and less tangible.

Witchcraft is itself a reification, an imposed category whose boundaries are anything but clear. It's not just that witchcraft and the legal persecution of witches need to be distinguished, as they certainly do. The persecution also needs to be broken down into its components, not treated as if it obeyed a single set of laws. Perhaps the most crucial distinction is that between the endemic trials of individual witches and more concentrated episodes of witch hunting. These latter in their turn differ sharply when conducted by members of the ruling elite from outbreaks whose main inspiration lay among the people; and possession cases form another distinct category. In any detailed study it is desirable to multiply these divisions further, classifying accusations and accusers as narrowly as possible. To give one simple example, the sharp distinction commonly drawn between English and continental witchcraft does not compare like with like, since it sets endemic local trials against witch hunts.[12] In fact individual English cases are much more like their

---

[11] Larner, *Witchcraft and Religion*, pp. 139, 52.

[12] It should be said that the various comparisons drawn by Keith Thomas, in *Religion and the Decline of Magic* (London, 1971), pp. 435–583, are typically nuanced; it would be hard to claim that any of them were seriously wrong. Nevertheless, the overall effect does tend to overstate the contrast to some degree, as when he writes: 'On the

analogues over the Channel than either are to large-scale hunts, while the Hopkins episode has a decidedly continental feel. If English witches said little about the pact, and less about the sabbat, this is readily explained by the peculiarities of the legal system under which they were tried. The conclusion to which one is repeatedly driven is that while there is a common group of causal elements behind all types of witchcraft persecution, they operate with variable force in specific cases. There is no such thing as a 'typical' witchcraft case, although the vast majority do conform to a limited range of patterns.

In this context the idea of the witchcraze, even the more moderate one of the witch hunt, can easily mislead. A very high proportion of the known European witchcraft trials were clearly instigated from below, although this was only possible with the aid of a legal machinery established by the elites, and some degree of interaction between local law enforcers and the general population was commonplace.[13] Detailed research almost invariably produces dramatic reductions in the numbers associated with local waves of persecution; a map showing these would emphasise their scattered quality across both time and space. Terrifying though such episodes were, they never gave any sign of coalescing into some more general movement. Over most of Western Europe the steady flow of cases which marks the period from the 1570s to the 1630s was made up of people accused of *maleficium* by their immediate neighbours, with only occasional encouragement from above. This is one important way in which this specific form of persecution seems to differ from most others. Persecution in the wider sense does obviously follow certain general patterns, yet here too it is vital not to aggregate them crudely. R. I. Moore's brilliant account of *The Formation of a Persecuting Society*, which draws many suggestive parallels, is also admirable for his reluctance to systematise them.[14] As Moore shows, the original targets for persecution were a triad of heretics, Jews and lepers, all of whom were at times accused of fantastic behaviour later attributed to witches. Such persecution was only possible in the context of linked changes in the political, social and intellectual character of Europe; it helped to

Continent the persecution of witches as a sect of devil-worshippers inevitably started from above. But in England the initial driving force was the fear of *maleficium*. It therefore emanated from below' (p. 499).

13 For a particularly helpful discussion on this point, see C. Holmes, 'Popular culture? Witches, magistrates, and divines in early modern England', in S. L. Kaplan, ed., *Understanding Popular Culture* (Berlin, 1984), pp. 85–111.

14 R. I. Moore, *The Formation of a Persecuting Society* (Oxford, 1987).

redefine boundaries and defend the interests of dominant groups. At the same time there were independent reasons for attacking these specific targets, so that each was different, and we can never say whether persecution was somehow a necessary part of the new social order, or merely resulted from an unfortunate combination of circumstances. Understanding *how* persecution worked limits the range of plausible explanations for *why* it happened, and is the vital first stage of any serious analysis, but does not necessarily supply an answer to the broader causal questions.

It is a striking fact that the first targets for persecution in medieval Europe did not include witches, although there must have been plenty available. Nevertheless, one conclusion I find irresistible is that these early persecutions of heretics and others linked into the treatment of witchcraft, in terms of both ideas and legal mechanisms. Most early witchcraft cases involved leading members of the elites, revealing the same cynical manipulation for political and financial ends as had been common in the other instances. Only very slowly and intermittently did these exceptional occurrences blend into a wider attack on everyday witches. My contention is that this attack never developed anything like its full potential, and that the subject becomes easier to understand if we concentrate on the limitations of the campaign against witchcraft. To employ a metaphor in rather bad taste, this was a bonfire which never got properly alight, although there were occasional spurts of flame at points across its surface. This may sound rather surprising, and there is no denying the horrors which took place on a wide scale. For all this, we need to remind ourselves constantly that there was a virtually endless supply of ready-made suspects, of whom only a small proportion were tried and convicted, while on the theoretical level the crime summed up just about every known form of deviance, yet never persuaded most members of the elites to give it high priority. If one took the more lurid imaginings of the demonologists seriously, then the devil's power to cause harm through his servants was the deadliest threat Christendom had ever faced. The point was picked up by Weyer, who asked ironically why rulers bothered with armies, when a group of witches would be an invincible secret weapon if they could do what they claimed.[15] Paranoia

---

[15] Weyer's work is now conveniently available in an excellent English edition, G. Mora, ed., and J. Shea, trans., *Witches, Devils and Doctors in the Renaissance: Johann Weyer, De praestigiis daemonum*, Medieval & Renaissance texts and studies, LXXIII (Binghampton, NY, 1991). The passage cited is on pp. 217–18.

about witches seems to have been relatively rare; most of the determined witch hunting can be traced back to a small number of known individuals, who were not much more typical of the elites as a whole than zealous searchers out of ritual satanism are today.

At a deeper level witchcraft trials clearly had numerous functional characteristics. They drew communities together to purge themselves of the evil within, and used the idea of pollution to reinforce threatened boundaries. The more general drives of both the state and the churches to impose tighter moral and social controls on the population could attract widespread popular support on this particular issue, while serving the ends of the ruling classes. In a much more ambiguous way clerics, lawyers and doctors could all find opportunities to display their expertise and increase their prestige. In an age of sharply increasing social and economic divisions, the projection of evil on to the resentful poor had many attractions for their superiors. The imaginative and prurient appeal of the subject helped to make it a staple of the early trade in printed books – although not to the extent that it dominates children's books today. The impact of print and growing literacy also helped to bring to a head some deep epistemological issues, which focused attention on witchcraft, occult power and the possibilities of deception. As a form of fantasy, expressing the inner worlds of early modern Europeans, witchcraft belief mixed up a potent cocktail of forbidden libidinal and social desires; the process of extracting confessions helped to merge these with popular notions of a more folkloric kind. At all levels of society gender clearly played a part, with masculine insecurities and aggression liable to find ready expression in both theory and practice. One should add the point that unlike several other types of offenders against society, witches also had specific victims, who had positive motives for accusing them. The fundamental popular belief in the effective power of malevolence, and its location in certain individuals, was one element we can safely say was indispensable to the persecution.

On the basis of the research done to date, these are the broad categories within which we should seek to construct an interpretation of the witchcraft trials. This cannot be done by simple aggregation, however, because even in isolation these factors have an awkward tendency to explain too much. If we put them all together, we seem to have constructed a juggernaut capable of sweeping all before it; witchcraft appears so wonderfully functional and central to early modern Europe that it is the relative moderation and brevity of the persecution which needs explaining. At this point it is the fine-grained approach which becomes essential, with close attention to all the links through which these multiple causes interacted, and to the various types of friction, slippage and resistance which limited their effects. What we end up with is a complex model of social interaction, full of checks and balances, which allows considerable scope for the merely contingent. A range of general factors derived from the data is collected, then reassembled into a structure whose likely outcome is strikingly similar to what actually happened – which is the most we are entitled to expect. This may be the Heath Robinson rather than the hi-tech style of historical explanation, but I think it conforms remarkably well to the untidiness of all complex societies. If we take it seriously, it enables us to escape from the crude primary colours of an interpretation such as that by Muchembled, in which persecution is little more than an epiphenomenon of political and religious change, an aspect of the penetration of the countryside by the early modern state and church. There is a genuine relationship here, but it is no more fundamental than many other elements; to exaggerate it is to lose the subtleties essential to any truly satisfying historical analysis.

Witchcraft has proved so malleable, as both an active problem and a historical one, because it is in a very special sense a 'transparent' crime, in which there is a hole at the centre. Witches simply did not perform most of the acts alleged against them, and usually confessed by them. This is not the same as claiming they were wholly innocent persons, but it does create special difficulties of interpretation. In a particular case we may think we see a husband wanting to get rid of his wife, a neighbour convinced her child is bewitched and hoping for a cure, an old enemy seeking revenge, and a ruined peasant trying to explain calamitous losses of animals and property; all these themes can be present in a single case. Just as the witnesses imputed motivation to the witch, so the historian makes rational guesses about their own motives, often based on the merest scraps of dialogue or veiled hints in the testimony. When so much is going on in the mind, and so little in the external world, there must be a tentative quality to every interpretation. At this point one really is thrown back on intuition, with the only checks being a scrupulous refusal to push the evidence too hard, and the use of as many cases as possible to give some sense of relative frequency. The most difficult problem of all, to my my mind, is that of detecting behind-the-scenes manipulation by persons who may never appear at all, or attacks on substitutes for the real targets. Boyer and Nissenbaum's analysis of the hidden subtext of the Salem Village trials convinces me, because so much consequential detail seems to fit, but it is hard to see how it could ever be thought proven.[16] Muchembled's rather similar attempt for Bouvignies, on the other hand, relies almost wholly on hypotheses framed to support his prior assumptions, rather than anything that can be called evidence. He could be right in this case, even so, but I don't accept the general argument developed from the example, because I have examined a large number of similar trials nearby. These provide only a handful of cases which could possibly support his thesis, and none which definitely do so.[17] This doesn't stop his claims being worthwhile, because it is only by the painstaking formulation and testing of such hypotheses that we will make further progress.

What I have left out so far is the well-known story of the development of a coherent theory of witchcraft, which brought together the everyday witch, the devil and the night-witch. While this complex process had its own vital part to play, and deserves much more attention than it can receive here, there is a great deal it cannot explain. Quite apart from the vexed question of how far such intellectual processes reflect social pressures, early fifteenth-century trials already show the essential elements of the pact and the sabbat in place. The time-lag before really extensive persecution began is far too great to be disregarded. Whether we can ever explain the chronology adequately is another matter, particularly because our information about the crucial period from the late fifteenth to the late sixteenth century is so scanty. At present it looks as if there was curiously little persecution in the first half of the sixteenth century, which also saw a lull in the production and publication of works of demonology. Nevertheless it is significant that witchcraft does have a reasonably clear chronological pattern, which renders it rather different from many other topics in social history. In consequence there has been a dangerous tendency to build interpretations around the principle of simultaneity, supposing that temporal connections are also causal ones as soon as they have any kind of plausibility. This was the basis for the idea that the Inquisition turned on witches as it ran out of heretics, whose flimsiness was revealed when it collapsed on the identification of a group of forgeries.[18]

---

[16] P. Boyer and S. Nissenbaum, *Salem Possessed: The Social Origins of Witchcraft* (Cambridge, MA, 1974).

[17] R. Muchembled, *Les derniers bûchers* (Paris, 1981). For a fuller critique, see R. Briggs, *Communities of Belief* (Oxford, 1989), pp. 53–7.

[18] N. Cohn, *Europe's Inner Demons* (London, 1975) and R. Kieckhefer, *European Witch Trials: Their Foundations in Popular and Learned Culture, 1300–1500* (London, 1976), exposed the forgeries concerned.

As the numbers of trials rise after 1560, and the records improve dramatically, we can begin to look at the relationship between the different elements as they interacted in practice. The English case demonstrates that quite extensive legal action against witches could develop without an important role for the pact, still less the sabbat. This was probably only possible within a peculiar legal system which did not follow inquisitorial practice, so that confessions owed more to folk belief than to prompting from judges, but it is still a very important limiting case. One might even argue that the more elaborate theories of the demonologists were more of an outgrowth from the system than a central part of it. As already suggested, endemic persecution on the Continent was strikingly similar to that in England in most respects. Accusers were overwhelmingly concerned with *maleficium*, to which the judges also paid a great deal of attention. When they could tell stories which suggested some kind of diabolical presence, or return from suspicious places, however, they did so with some enthusiasm. At the same time it is evident that suspects had little difficulty in producing accounts of both the pact and the sabbat, in response to very simple questions; genuine leading questions are exceptionally rare in all the trials I have ever seen. Early trials do not differ noticeably from later ones in these respects, so that both the differences and the supposed fusion between popular and learned notions of witchcraft are strangely elusive at this level; it looks much more like a shared belief system. The whole complex of beliefs was obviously reinforced by widespread practices of reading out material from the trials at the time of executions, but this cannot explain its creation. Although I think Ginzburg's investigation of the sabbat has turned up a blind alley, he is surely right to protest that it did not just involve the superimposition on local sorcerers of standard charges against deviants.[19] The demonologists may have proceeded in this way, in line with the scholarly conventions of their time, without having much relevance to the routines of persecution or the material supplied by confessions.

The striking variations in local versions of the sabbat rather emphasise the extent to which it meshed in with folklore. We are in danger of falling victims to the same syncretist fallacies as the demonologists here, for the full-blown diabolical festival in the de Lancre style is an extreme case. It is very misleading to write as if there was a mature version of the beliefs

---

[19] C. Ginzburg, *Ecstasies: Deciphering the Witches' Sabbath* (London, 1990). Like most critics, I find the methodology employed in this book unsatisfactory.

which included night-flying, infant murder, cannibalism, sexual orgies and parodies of Christian ritual, and formed the basis for the great witch hunts. Most accounts are relatively drab by comparison; having read around 300 confessions from Lorraine, I can say that most of the elements listed above are either very rare or wholly absent. Even sexual activity is mentioned by only a small minority. The commonest notion is that witches travelled to the sabbat by air; some of them did indeed mount broomsticks and fly up the chimney. Yet I find it hard to accept Cohn's view of the significance of this element, for most of the journeys were relatively short, so that participants quite often said they had returned on foot.[20] Grandiose meetings of hundreds of witches had no functional purpose in local persecution, unless it was to furnish a convenient excuse for those who preferred not to denounce their neighbours. Most of the intense witch hunts, as well, took place in very restricted areas, so that night-flying appears just another elaboration pointing up the exceptional nature of the occasion. As many of us have pointed out for different localities, stories about the sabbat function on the principle of inversion, in a thoroughly folkloric fashion.[21] In the case of Lorraine, what resulted was essentially an anti-fertility rite, where reluctant participants had a miserable time, usually ending with the ancient ritual of beating water to create hailstorms to their own detriment.

What seems to have occurred in most of Europe was a limited and uneasy coalescence between longstanding popular beliefs and the agencies for enforcing social and religious conformity. It was fortunate that these latter almost never functioned with the kind of ideological enthusiasm which a minority of reforming clerics and lawyers espoused, in arguments we need to treat with suitable caution as guides to the thinking of the day. Such ambitions ran far ahead of practical realities as well as general opinion. Rulers were eager to appropriate legal authority as a way of increasing their power and status, much less willing to contemplate the enormous financial implications of creating efficient agencies of law enforcement. Most convicted witches were so poor that the confiscation of their goods met only a fraction of the cost of their trial. Many such factors combined to restrain persecution, while among the elites there was a whole range of more fundamental doubts, such as

---

[20] N. Cohn, *Europe's Inner Demons*, pp. 228–9, where it is treated as a very important elite addition to the stereotype of the witch.

[21] For a particularly clear exposition, S. Clark, 'Inversion, misrule and the meaning of witchcraft', *Past and Present*, 87 (1980), 98–127.

the question of manipulation of local courts through influence and perjury, to pursue local vendettas. This was a key enemy of the new legal systems, and among French lawyers at least the practical scepticism about witchcraft accusations gave great weight to just this point.[22] There was grave concern about the prospect that the people might use a crime which raised such severe problems about proof as a way of settling private scores. This useful worry may in fact have been something of a misconception, for where – as in the case of Lorraine – the courts readily convicted, the rate of accusations nevertheless stabilised at a relatively modest level. Those with reputations as witches might seem easy targets, yet many never went to court at all, and most of those who did had been under threat for years, even decades.

At the popular level the problem is not to explain why witchcraft beliefs exist – very few known cultures lack something of the kind. The reasons for this are presumably a mixture of the social and the psychological; the need to explain misfortune as more than the result of chance or incompetence, the projection of hostile feelings on to others, the resentment of demands made by dependent neighbours. 'Scapegoating' appears to be a natural tendency in human society, which combines easily with beliefs in supernatural powers. Why are these invoked in particular cases? This seems to depend on a combination of (1) the nature of the misfortune; (2) recent hostile contact with the suspect; and (3) the level of general concern about witchcraft. Suspicions created in these ways are reinforced by communal activity, especially gossip. There is a whole process of developing reputations, so that each community should have its witches. The healers and cunning folk play an important part here, possibly using witchcraft as a standard explanation, and offering various forms of counter-magic. We can perceive a vision of the world in which the community is surrounded by hostile forces, only held out by a magical and spiritual carapace. This last is sustained by religious practice in general, but expressed most clearly in such rituals as ringing bells against storms and beating the bounds. Individuals can protect themselves and their animals by a range of more personal acts; if they believe themselves bewitched, they can try to force or bribe the suspect into healing them. For long periods this has probably functioned as a closed system, with occasional crises seeing suspects lynched or driven into exile. Over most of Europe the official agencies for prosecuting

---

[22] A. Soman, 'La décriminalisation de la sorcellerie en France', *Histoire, économie et société*, 4 (1985), 179–203, esp. 200–2.

offenders never really latched into it effectively; the reasons for this reticence may be as complex as those which underlie the more obvious phenomenon of persecution. They certainly seem to me to call for more sophisticated interpretative practices than most historians of the subject have employed to date.

There is nothing surprising in the fact that most European countries experienced periods of witchcraft persecution, since there were so many ways in which the various layers of popular and elite attitudes could interact. It is quite hard to construct scenarios in which so pervasive a set of beliefs would not have generated such results for some period, although nothing should be regarded as inevitable. In many respects the startling feature is the brevity of the period of severe persecution, when witchcraft beliefs have such a long and vigorous independent history. Numerous problems become easier to understand if we think in terms of a longstanding elite scepticism, which was partly breached in the sixteenth and seventeenth centuries. As an example, masculine concern to maintain or reinforce patriarchal relations is much more plausible as an indirect cause, which helped in creating a temporary receptivity to popular pressure. This was just one of the reasons why some members of the ruling groups became concerned with the problems raised by witch-craft accusations, and wanted to take them more seriously. The resulting arguments were readily incorporated into struggles for legitimacy in the political and religious spheres. This did not require extensive trials, and indeed small numbers of show trials were ideal, especially if they took the supremely dramatic form of possession cases. In theory the witch may have been the ultimate deviant, combining virtually every negative quality that could be imagined; in practice even those who helped build this elaborate fiction often expressed serious caution over legal proceedings against real-life suspects. In most instances the experience of persecution did more to create doubts about its wisdom than to encourage intensification. The Counter-Reformation Bavaria of Maximilian I looked ideal territory for an ideologically motivated witch hunt, which did attract some support from some well-placed ducal councillors, but aroused widespread hostility from a range of local power holders. This was so effective that despite a trickle of cases well into the eighteenth century the overall numbers for the region are notably low.[23]

Many other areas had analogous experiences, which emphasise just

---

[23] W. Behringer, *Hexenverfolgung in Bayern: Volksmagie, Glaubenseifer und Staats-räson in der frühen Neuzeit* (Munich, 1987).

how patchy and unpredictable witchcraft persecutions really were across Europe. This is true even at the microscopic level; Macfarlane could supply no satisfactory explanation for the absence of trials in parts of Essex, nor can I for large variations within the duchy of Lorraine.[24] Our difficulty in such cases is understandable, for there is no evidence for non-events, but it seems unlikely that elite attitudes can be the relevant variable. It is important to recognise that popular belief in supernatural power did not exclude practical scepticism; people were well aware of the ways in which accusations could be the vehicles for other antagonisms. The network of personal and familial relationships often inhibited recourse to outside authority, while communities tended to close ranks against outsiders. All this forms part of an extraordinarily complex picture, which defies simple explanation. What we are looking at is a hotly disputed boundary zone where categories, practices and beliefs either clashed or failed to work properly. There is a sense in which all the issues involve power – political, religious, economic, sexual, psychological – but this is more a commentary on human relationships in general than on witchcraft in particular. If this seems frustrating to the historian who merely wants to account for 'the witch-craze', that is primarily because such an ambition is misconceived, most crucially in supposing that there is a single phenomenon to be explained. On the other hand, there are still enormous possibilities for those who see the material as a way into both the social world and the mental structures of early modern Europe. Once we concentrate on the processes which shaped individual episodes, distinguishing between categories with proper care, repeating patterns do become evident, even if they are never quite identical. It is at these middle and lower levels that interpretation can become more precise, provided we allow the general scheme to remain properly fluid. If the result is a mosaic of small overlapping narratives, I suggest that is what social life really comprises, and that historians should accept the fact with good grace.

[24] A. Macfarlane, *Witchcraft in Tudor and Stuart England: A Regional and Comparative Study* (London, 1970), esp. pp. 147–56.

3. Witchcraft studies in Austria, Germany and Switzerland

WOLFGANG BEHRINGER

The field of witchcraft studies appears to be holding pace with innovations in scholarly communications just as well as other academic pursuits. The number of international conferences has grown considerably since the 1980s.[1] Their conference volumes offer excellent reference points for acquainting oneself with the latest developments and research in progress throughout Europe and the rest of the world.[2] However, a glance at the catalogue of the Pisan exhibit *Bibliotheca Lamiarum* or the internationally renowned journal *Past and Present* give the impression that nationalistic tendencies in scholarship still linger on, indeed may have even hardened in the age of 'European Unity'.[3]

A closer examination of witchcraft studies and their historiography

[1] Kiel (1980): Stockholm (1984); Vienna (1986); Bayreuth (1987); Wolfenbüttel (1987); Budapest (1988); Weingarten (1989); Exeter (1991); Weingarten (1992); Paris (1992); Pisa (1994); Amsterdam (1994); Karlsruhe (1994); Lausanne (1994); Weingarten (1995).

[2] Kiel (1980); Christian Degn, Hartmut Lehmann and Dagmar Unverhau, eds., *Hexenprozesse. Deutsche und skandinavische Beiträge* (Neumünster, 1983); Stockholm (1984): Bengt Ankarloo and Gustav Henningsen, eds., *Häxornas Europa 1400–1700. Historiska och antropologiska studier* (Lund, 1987), translated as *Early Modern European Witchcraft. Centres and Peripheries* (Oxford, 1990); Weingarten (1986): Sönke Lorenz and Dieter Bauer, eds., *Hexenverfolgung. Beiträge zur Forschung* (Würzburg, 1995); Bayreuth (1987): Peter Segl, ed., *Der Hexenhammer. Entstehung und Umfeld des Malleus maleficarum von 1487* (Cologne/Berlin, 1988); Wolfenbüttel (1987): Hartmut Lehmann and Otto Ulbricht, eds., *Vom Unfug des Hexen-Processes. Gegner der Hexenverfolgung von Johann Weyer bis Friedrich Spee* (Wiesbaden, 1992); Budapest (1988): Gábor Klaniczay and Eva Pocs, eds., *Witch-Beliefs and Witch-Hunting in Central and Eastern Europe* (*Acta Ethnographica Hungarica. An International Journal of Ethnography*, 37 (1991/2), nrs. 1–4) (Budapest, 1994); Paris (1992): Nicole Jacques-Chaquin and Maxime Préaud, eds., *Le sabbat des sorciers* (Grenoble, 1993). See also p. 72.

[3] Clive Holmes, 'Women: witnesses and witches', *Past and Present*, 140 (1993), 45–78; *Bibliotheca Lamiarum. Documenti e immagini della stregoneria dal Medioeva all' Età Moderna* (Pisa, 1994).

reveals that this was not always the case. Long before the onset of modern conference tourism, an international forum of witchcraft studies thrived and communicated in the former language of learned discourse, Latin.[4] For this traditional intelligentsia, it was a matter of course that Christian Thomasius (1655–1728) analysed a pan-European array of documents for his *Dissertatio de origine ac progressu processus inquisitorii contra sagas.* Pierre Bayle (1647–1765) constantly referred back to Thomasius' text and John Wagstaff published a commentary on Thomasius, the *De crimine magiae*, in 1701. And the cosmopolitan character of witchcraft studies did not end with the use of Latin as the lingua franca. Thomasius himself authorised the translation of several of his English treatises into German. That Eberhard David Hauber (1695–1765), the Lutheran superintendent of the County Schaumburg-Lippe and later a pastor in the Danish capital of Copenhagen, analysed English and French literature in the 1730s as part of his *Bibliotheca acta et scripta magica* went without question. Scipio Maffei (1675–1755) acknowledged the writings of Thomasius, Malebranche and Hauber in his attack on the tract *Del Congresso notturno delle lammie* by Abbot Girolamo Tartarotti (1702–61). Celebrating the so-called 'Bavarian War on Witchcraft Beliefs' in 1767, the Viennese scholar Konstantin von Kautz (1735–97) reviewed a wide variety of early Enlightenment debates on European witchcraft. The German researcher Johann Moritz Schwager translated Bekker's *De Betooverde Wereld.* The bibliography of the Saxon crown librarian, Johann Georg Theodor Grässe (1814–72), the *Bibliotheca magica et pneumatica*, also made unhesitating reference to the pan-European literature.[5]

The same rings true for the *History of Witchcraft Trials* by the liberal theologian Wilhelm Gottlieb Soldan (1803–69), who was elected by the progressive party to the Chamber of Representatives in Hessen-Darmstadt. Soldan's political opponent was Jacob Grimm (1785–1863), a polyglot who, in his own time, was cited by Jules Michelet (1798–1874). The liberal historian, Joseph Hansen (1862–1943), undertook extensive research forays after studying in Rome and he cultivated numerous international contacts. He advised the American witchcraft scholar, George Lincoln Burr (1857–1938), during his stay in Germany

---

4 Peter Burke, *Küchenlatein. Sprache und Umgangssprache in der frühen Neuzeit* (Berlin, 1990).
5 Wolfgang Behringer, 'Zur Geschichte der Hexenforschung', in Sönke Lorenz, ed., *Hexen und Hexenverfolgung im deutschen Südwesten* (Ostfildern, 1994), pp. 93–146.

and translated Henry Charles Lea's *History of the Inquisition in the Middle Ages* (1887) into his native German.[6]

Henry Charles Lea's (1825–1909) own engagement, just before his death at age eighty-four, with the third volume of Hauber's *Bibliotheca acta et scripta magica*, a depiction of witchcraft persecutions in France, was no mere coincidence.[7] Conversant in witchcraft literature as no other, Lea certainly knew where to direct his attention. Hauber had edited extensive sources: Thomasius, that jurist from the Reformed Prussian University of Halle, who originally founded witchcraft studies; Grässe, who published the first collective bibliography; Soldan, author of an early paradigmatic account of the subject; and the Cologne archivist, Hansen, who unquestionably delivered the consummate synthesis of previous witchcraft studies. Together, these works comprised the legacy of the Enlightenment, and their authors were all heroes of liberalism and major representatives of the 'Soldan paradigm', a term coined by William Monter.[8] Soldan's *History of Witchcraft Trials* and Hansen's *Sources and Examinations into the History of the Witchcraze* provided the very foundations for today's witchcraft studies, a fact substantiated by lexical entries in older encyclopaedias into the 1930s.[9] However, the very nature of these studies confronted anyone interested in the history of witchcraft with a language barrier. This was obvious to Lea and Burr, as it later was for Malinowski and Febvre. Of course, there are very good reasons why German dominated the early discourse on witchcraft studies. The international reputation of German scholars before the First World War is of less significance than the fact that by far the majority of persecutions occurred within the boundaries of the Holy Roman Empire and, therefore, the greatest number of source documents originate from that region.[10]

Margaret Murray's article, 'Witchcraft', appeared in the 1929 *Encyclopedia Britannica* and was probably the first lexical entry

---

[6] Henry Charles Lea, *Geschichte der Inquisition im Mittelalter*, 3 vols. (Bonn, 1905).

[7] Henry Charles Lea, *Notes for a History of Witchcraft* (1909), published by Arthur C. Howland as *Materials Toward a History of Witchcraft*, 3 vols. (Philadelphia, 1939).

[8] William Monter, 'The historiography of European witchcraft: progress and prospects', *Journal of Interdisciplinary History*, 2 (1971/2), 435–53.

[9] *La Grande Encyclopédie. Inventaire raisonné des sciences, des lettres et des arts*, XXX (Paris, c. 1899), pp. 288–9; *Enciclopedia Italiana di scienze, lettere ed arti*, XV (Rome, 1936), pp. 841ff.

[10] Wolfgang Behringer, 'Allemagne, Mère de tant des sorcières. Au coeur des persécutions', in Robert Muchembled, ed., *Magie et sorcellerie en Europe du Moyen Age à nos jours* (Paris, 1994), pp. 59–98.

internationally published, although it displayed a genuine lack of engagement with early modern Latin and German witchcraft studies. Unhindered by a knowledge of primary sources, she painted a fantastic portrait of the European witch-craze that might have been envied by romantic authors like Jacob Grimm or Jules Michelet, themselves not without a penchant for fantasy. The elegant lady, whose training in Egyptology was interrupted by the First World War, pushed the 'romantic paradigm' to its limits.[11] However, not until the 1960s did the editorial staff of *Britannica* discover that her entry represented a serious *faux pas*. As a consequence, rather than attempting to correct the mishap, they aspired to a second attempt at 'modernisation'. Ultimately, *Britannica* did awkwardly excuse themselves for the previous Murray entry. Nonetheless, in its place they incorporated new entries which were also radically one-sided: first, one, by Evans-Pritchard (along with Malinowski, Clyde Kluckhohn's study of Navaho witchcraft and several other ethnologists), followed by another from Keith Thomas and Alan Macfarlane. Thomasius, Grimm, Soldan and Hansen passed into oblivion without mention. The 1974 entry 'Witchcraft' in *Britannica* made plain the attempt to eject all unnecessary ballast.[12]

We should refrain from pinning the entire blame for the ignorance exuded by the 1974 entry on the editorial staff alone, since it reflected a general paradigm-shift in contemporary historiography, one especially conspicuous in witchcraft studies. In the 1960s, Keith Thomas played a seminal role in this paradigm-shift by suggesting a rapprochement of social history and social anthropology. His *Religion and the Decline of Magic*[13] was certainly the most impressive announcement of the paradigm-shift, even if Alan Macfarlane's *Witchcraft in Tudor and Stuart England* (1970) was initially cited far more often and Julio Caro Baroja's *Las Brujas y su mundo* was a harbinger of the shift a decade earlier. *Religion and the Decline of Magic* characterised itself – apart from its many other renowned accomplishments – as a study based exclusively on English sources and almost solely on English literature. Here, we express two important caveats on our critique. First, that it is entirely possible to compose a good book on the basis of a limited analysis of the available literature and, second, that there is a world of

[11] Margaret Alice Murray, 'Witchcraft', *Encyclopedia Britannica*, XXIII (Chicago/London/Toronto, 1959), pp. 59–98.

[12] 'Witchcraft', *New Encyclopedia Britannica*, XIX (1974), pp. 895–900.

[13] Keith Thomas, *Religion and the Decline of Magic. Studies in Popular Beliefs in Sixteenth and Seventeenth Century England* (London, 1971).

difference between present studies and those of the late 1960s. Today, no serious university instructor would allow doctoral candidates under their charge to limit themselves to witchcraft historiography solely in their native language, at least, one would hope that this is now the case.

Even a good book contains errors. Let this example serve as a case in point: 'On the Continent, the persecution of witches as a sect of devil-worshippers inevitably started from above. But in England the initial driving force was the fear of *maleficium*. It therefore emanated from below.'[14] Today, this sounds almost like a parody of that same famous article by Trevor-Roper, then so bitterly opposed by the protagonists of the paradigm-shift,[15] but Keith Thomas was serious, basing his claim on the Soldan paradigm. Even before the paradigm shift, anyone with an intimate knowledge of the early German-speaking witchcraft scholars – the Swiss ethnologist, Eduard Hoffmann-Krayer, the Lüneburg psychologist, Otto Snell, the Austrian Jurist, Fritz Byloff, the Zurich theologian, Oskar Pfister, or the Göttingen ethnologist and historian, Will-Erich Peuckert,[16] for example – would have known that such statements were hardly even half-truths. I will presently demonstrate how recent research has considerably modified earlier perceptions. For, beyond their potential to reveal previous perceptions as mere clichés, present witchcraft studies from Central Europe offer international scholars a vast array of new and interesting results in methodologies.

II

At the end of the Nazi dictatorship, witchcraft studies in Austria and Germany were in a difficult dilemma. The contamination of anthropology, social history and sociology through the ideals of National Socialism motivated a knee-jerk reaction and a withdrawal to a rationalist paradigm which tacitly associated the irrationality of racism and the

---

14 Ibid., p. 499.
15 Alan Macfarlane, *Witchcraft in Tudor and Stuart England. A Regional and Comparative Study* (London, 1970), p. 9; Lawrence Stone, 'The disenchantment of the world', *The New York Review of Books*, 2 (Dec. 1971), 17–25.
16 Otto Snell, *Hexenprozesse und Geistesstörungen. Psychiatrische Untersuchungen* (Munich, 1891); Eduard Hoffman-Krayer, ed., 'Luzerner Akten zum Hexen- und Zauberwesen', *Schweizerisches Archiv für Volkskunde*, 3 (1899), 22–40, 81–122, 189–224, 291–329; Fritz Byloff, *Hexenglaube und Hexenverfolgung in den österreichischen Alpenländern* (Berlin/Leipzig, 1934); Will-Erich Peuckert, *Pansophie. Ein Versuch zur Geschichte der weissen und schwarzen Magie* (Berlin, 1935; 2nd edn 1956, 3rd edn 1976).

Germanic myths with the 'witch-craze'.[17] Numerous law dissertations in the 1950s and 1960s wrestled with the past in a head-on confrontation with legal injustice during the era of witchcraft persecutions. *Emigré-*scholars played an important role, like the jurist Hans von Hentig (1887–1974), founder of American 'victimology' studies, who eventually returned to Bonn,[18] or Kurt Baschwitz (1886–1968), founder of newspaper studies in the Netherlands and editor of the first synthetic history of witchcraft persecutions after the Second World War; the latter employed modern theories of crowd psychology simultaneously in use for an explanation of fascism.[19]

Although a noteworthy study occasionally appeared in German during the 1960s and 1970s,[20] and even after Will-Erich Peuckert translated Baroja's *Las brujas* as early as 1967,[21] the paradigm shift of witchcraft studies went without much notice in Germany. Incredibly, the path-breaking studies of H. C. Erik Midelfort (*Witch-Hunting in Southwestern Germany*) and William Monter (*Witchcraft in France and Switzerland*) met with only hesitant acceptance.[22] The discrepancy between the social historical methods of Scandinavian witchcraft scholars and those of their German hosts became clear at an international conference held in Schleswig in 1980: Bengt Ankarloo and Gustav Henningsen identified themselves with English social anthropologists, among them Bronislaw Malinowski, E. E. Evans-Pritchard, Keith Thomas and Alan Macfarlane. In contrast, German participants were fixed on older witchcraft studies and the ghost of Joseph Hansen loomed heavily over the proceedings.[23]

---

[17] Barbara Schier, 'Hexenwahn und Hexenverfolgung. Rezeption und politische Zurichtung eines kulturwissenschaftlichen Themas im Dritten Reich', *Bayerische Jahrbuch für Volkskunde* (1990), 43–115.

[18] Herbert A. Strauss and Werner Röder, eds., *International Biographical Dictionary of Central European Emigrés 1933–45*, II (Munich/New York/London/Paris, 1983), pp. 492–3.

[19] Kurt Baschwitz, *Hexen und Hexenprozesse. Die Geschichte eines Massenwahns und seiner Bekämpfung* (Munich, 1963).

[20] Herbert Schwarzwälder, 'Die Geschichte des Zauber- und Hexenglaubens in Bremen', *Bremisches Jahrbuch*, 46 (1959), 156–233; Hartmut Heinrich Kunstmann, *Zauberwahn und Hexenprozess in der Reichsstadt Nürnberg*, Diss. Jur. Mainz (Nuremberg, 1970).

[21] Julio Caro Baroja, *Las Brujas y su mundo* (Madrid, 1961), translated as *The World of the Witches* (London, 1964).

[22] H. C. Erik Midelfort, *Witch-Hunting in Southwestern Germany, 1582–1684. The Social and Intellectual Foundations* (Stanford, 1972); William Monter, *Witchcraft in France and Switzerland. The Borderlands during the Reformation* (Ithaca/London, 1976).

[23] Degn et al., eds., *Hexenprozesse*.

In the 1970s, rare seminars on the social history of witchcraft persecutions held in Germany met with an enthusiastic response. Two early organisers were Hartmut Lehmann in Kiel and Richard van Dülmen in Munich and, later, Saarbrücken. In Hamburg, a first, albeit voyeuristic, exhibit on witches took place. Although the claim is often heard, the feminist movement cannot be held entirely responsible for these developments. This factor did lead to a number of sympathetic publications,[24] but, lest we forget, the rising sensibility for human rights and the movement against political repression also played important parts. Particularly in Germany, student unrest, the generational change, a shift in political power and the beginnings of international tourism all added to the impetus. Numerous translations of classics, like Marcel Mauss' 'General Theory of Magic' and the texts of Mircea Eliade, as well as an edition of Malinowski's works by the German ethnologist, Fritz Kramer (b. 1941), witnessed the broad intellectual interest of Germans in non-European cultures.[25] Among publishers, Suhrkamp in Frankfurt was particularly helpful in providing teachers and students with theoretical materials, but the leftist alternative, Syndikat press (also Frankfurt), and even the more traditional houses of Klett-Cota (Stuttgart) and Hanser (Munich) made significant contributions: the Swiss sociologist, Claudia Honegger (b. 1947), who already fostered the spread of French annalist historiography, moved quickly to translate important passages from Hugh Trevor-Roper, Jeffrey Burton Russell, Keith Thomas, Alan Macfarlane, Robert Mandrou and Jeanne Favret into German.[26] In the same year, the Viennese ethnologist, Brigitte Luchesi (b. 1943), also translated Evans-Pritchard's *Witchcraft, Oracles and Magic among the Azande.*[27]

The paradigm-shift made great headway among German-speaking researchers in the 1980s. Nevertheless, this reception did not literally follow the lines drawn out in translations. Excellent studies translated

---

[24] Gabriele Becker, Silvia Bovenschen and Hartmut Brackert, eds., *Aus der Zeit der Verzweiflung. Zur Genese und Aktualität des Hexenbildes* (Frankfurt am Main, 1977).

[25] Marcel Mauss, *Sociologie et anthropologie précédé d'une Introduction à l'oevre de Marcel Mauss par Claude Lévi-Strauss* (Paris, 1950); Mircea Eliade, *Le chamanisme et les techniques archaiques de l'extase* (Paris, 1951); Bronislaw Malinowski, *Schriften in vier Bänden* (Frankfurt am Main, 1979–86).

[26] Claudia Honegger, ed., *Die Hexen der Neuzeit. Studien zur Sozialgeschichte eines kulturellen Deutungsmusters* (Frankfurt am Main, 1978).

[27] E. E. Evans-Pritchard, *Witchcraft, Oracles and Magic among the Azande* (Oxford, 1937); trans., Brigitte Luchesi, *Hexerei, Orakel und Magie bei den Zande* (Frankfurt am Main, 1978).

years earlier, like those of Claude Lévi-Strauss or Kai Erikson[28] were ignored, while the untranslated standard works of Keith Thomas and Erik Midelfort enjoyed intense and continued popularity. Apart from two microhistorical studies – David Meili's anthropological dissertation 'Witches in Wasterkingen' (directed by Arnold Niederer in Basel) and Michael Kunze's juridical dissertation 'The Pappenheim Trial' (directed by Sten Gagnér in Munich)[29] – the majority of new German witchcraft studies joined in to an implicit dialogue with English scholarship, broadened somewhat later by an engagement with the works of Carlo Ginzburg and Robert Muchembled.[30] In the course of this dialogue, it soon became clear that the collision of new theoretical offerings with the imposing findings of older German witchcraft studies would ultimately form the basis of a prolonged debate.

Even before a massive onslaught of dissertations, two *habilitations* appeared on the historiographic fringes in 1978 and 1979, which encompassed the entire range of the debate to follow in coming years. The avant-garde work of the ethnologist, Hans Peter Duerr (b. 1943), *Dreamtime: On the Boundaries between the Wild and Civilization*, compared shamanist experiences among non-European cultures and the European demonological discussion in its entirety, in an attempt to call the very basis of European rationality into question.[31] The stringency of Dieter Harmening's anthropological-philosophical method succeeded in tracing the lineage of European literature on the supernatural. His thesis begins with a rather obscure introduction, suggesting that an explication of the existence of magic in the Middle Ages is impossible, because contemporary texts represented mere tropes with little basis in reality; otherwise, though, his work is an outstanding depiction of the transmission of ideas at the level of text.[32]

To organise the rapidly proliferating field of research, Stuttgart

---

[28] Claude Lévi-Strauss, *Anthropologie Structurale* (Paris, 1958); Kai T. Erikson, *Wayward Puritans. A Study in the Sociology of Deviance* (New York, 1966).

[29] David Meili, *Hexen in Wasterkingen. Magie und Lebensform in einem Dorf des frühen 18. Jahrhunderts* (Basle, 1980); Michael Kunze, *Highroad to the Stake. A Tale of Witchcraft* (Chicago/London, 1987).

[30] Carlo Ginzburg, *The Night Battles* (Baltimore, 1983); Robert Muchembled, *Culture populaire et culture des élites dans la France moderns (XVe–XVIIIe siècles)* (Paris, 1978).

[31] Hans Peter Duerr, *Traumzeit. Über die Grenze zwischen Wildnis und Zivilisation* (Frankfurt am Main, 1978).

[32] Dieter Harmening, *Superstitio. Überlieferungs- und theoriegeschichtliche Untersuchungen zur kirchlich-theologischen Aberglaubensliteratur des Mittelalters* (Berlin, 1979).

historians Sönke Lorenz and Dieter Bauer announced the first national conference on witchcraft studies in 1985, when a Research Group for Interdisciplinary Witchcraft Studies (the Arbeitskreis Interdisziplinäre Hexenforschung or AKIH) was set up to informally organise the field.[33] The AKIH proceeded to summon a major conference in the following year. Since then, annual meetings have been held to provide young scholars with a public forum to present and discuss their latest findings. Subsequently, the Stuttgart Academy arranged four major international conferences in Weingarten: Witchcraft Persecutions. Recent Research on Southwest German Trials (1986); The End of Witchcraft Persecutions (1989); Major Witchcraft Persecutions in the West: Centers and Driving Forces (1992); Women and Witchcraft Persecutions (1995). The conference volumes are set to appear in a special series on witchcraft studies by the Franz-Steiner Press beginning in 1995.[34] In 1994, the AKIH presented the public with a catalogue from the exhibition on witchcraft held in Karlsruhe that year, which concentrated on recent findings for Southwest Germany. To a certain extent, Midelfort's research was subjected to revisions, some verifying the foundations of his research, others suggesting the path-breaking potential of micro-historical interpretations.[35] The Stuttgart-based AKIH has since become the backbone of German witchcraft studies, indeed, it offers an international forum for researchers from Germany, Austria, Switzerland, Luxembourg, France, England, Holland, Denmark, Poland, Hungary, the United States and Australia.

In accordance with the laws of cultural production, conferences and exhibits organised independently of the AKIH reached their highpoint during the anniversary celebrations of the *Malleus Maleficarum* in 1987: major exhibits were organised in Germany (Saarbrücken in Saarland) and Austria (Riegersburg near Graz in Steiermark),[36] and several

---

[33] On the goals of the AKIH, see 'Hexenforschung. Eine Einfürung zur Reihe' in *Hexenforschung*, eds., Dieter R. Bauer, Wolfgang Behringer, Heide Dienst, Sönke Lorenz, H. C. Erik Midelfort, and Wolfgang Schild, *vol. I: Das Ende der Hexenverfolgung*, eds., Sönke Lorenz and Dieter R. Bauer (Stuttgart, 1995), pp. ix–xvi.

[34] Conferences of the AKIH: ibid., pp. xvii–xxvii.

[35] Lorenz, ed., *Hexen und Hexenverfolgung*.

[36] Richard van Dülmen, ed., *Hexenwelten. Magie und Imagination vom. 16.–20. Jahrhundert* (Frankfurt am Main, 1987); Helfried Valentinisch, ed., *Hexen und Zauberer. Die grosse Verfolgung – ein europäisches Phänomen in der Steiermark* (Graz/Vienna, 1987); for an accounting, see Valentinisch, 'Die steirische Landesausstellung 1987 "Hexen und Zauberer". Erfahrungen, Ergebnisse und Überlegungen', *Mitteilungen des Instituts für österreichische Geschichtsforschung*, 98 (1990), 381–93.

conferences on witches and witchcraft trials took place, most importantly a major Viennese meeting on the role of magic (1986), one in Bayreuth (1987) on the *Malleus* and another in Wolfenbüttel (1987) on the opponents of persecutions.[37] Smaller conferences occupied themselves with topics such as the relationship of witchcraft persecutions to medicine (Stuttgart, 1987), 'witchcraft today' (Weingarten, 1988), Friedrich Spee (Düsseldorf and Trier, 1991), the witches' sabbath (Stuttgart, 1991), witchcraft persecutions and regional history (Lemgo, 1992), and the history of witchcraft studies (Karlsruhe, 1994). Apart from these findings, partially published in conference volumes,[38] so many minor conferences and exhibitions on the subject took place, that their recollection would simply be redundant.

III

Owing to the political and juridical diversity of the Holy Roman Empire, which consisted of hundreds of independent territories and presents a confusing puzzle even for an initiated historian,[39] German-speaking researchers sought, at first, to analyse comparatively regional sources and developments, and to establish a chronology of witchcraft trials, their spatial distribution and their connection to over-arching theories. In addition to older witchcraft studies, Midelfort's initial forays into Southwest German trials in Baden-Wurttemberg provided them with a concrete point of departure. His work was supplemented by similar territorial studies, such as Gerhard Schormann's 1977 analysis of the fragmented German Northwest (Saxony),[40] my own 1987 work on Southeast Germany (Bavaria),[41] and Eva Labouvie's 1991 study of the

---

[37] Peter Segl, ed., *Der Hexenhammer. Entstehung und Umfeld des Malleus maleficarum von 1487* (Cologne/Berlin, 1988); Lehmann and Ulbricht, eds., *Von Unfug des Hexen-Processes.*

[38] Dieter Harmening, 'Himmlers Hexenkartei. Ein Lagebericht zu ihrer Erforschung', *Jahrbuch für Volkskunde*, 12 (1989), 99–112; Harmening, ed., *Hexen Heute. Magische Traditionen und neue Zutaten* (Würzburg, 1991); Gunter Franz, ed., *Friedrich Spee. Dichter, Seelsorger, Bekämpfer des Hexenwahns (1591–1635)* (Trier, 1991); Gisela Wilbertz, Gerd Schwerhoff and Jürgen Scheffler, eds., *Hexenvergolgung und Regionalgeschichte. Die Grafschaft Lippe im Vergleich* (Bielefeld, 1994).

[39] Gerhard Köbler, *Historisches Lexikon der deutschen Länder* (Munich, 1989).

[40] Gerhard Schormann, *Hexenprozesse in Nordwestdeutschland* (Hildesheim, 1977).

[41] Wolfgang Behringer, *Hexenverfolgung in Bayern. Volksmagie, Glaubenseifer und Staatsräson in der frühen Neuzeit* (Munich, 1987), English translation in preparation with Cambridge University Press.

splintered jurisdictions of the Western German Saarland.[42] Austria offered an intensive examination of the Steiermark by Helfried Valentinitsch, as well as Manfred Tschaikner's comparative analysis of the Vorarlberg.[43] In these cases, research was oriented along modern political boundaries to establish a comparative overview from the perspective of politically, structurally and confessionally heterogeneous regions. Since Monter, there has been a conspicuous lack of comparable regional studies for Switzerland; only portions of Peter Kamber's examination of the Waadtland (Canton Vaud) appeared in print.[44]

Examinations of persecutions within the contemporary boundaries of ecclesiastic and secular territories are largely limited to dissertations and master's theses, which, to their credit, take account of more recent developments in the field.[45] Three detailed studies of ecclesiastical territories with track records of intense persecution are particularly noteworthy: the studies of Herbert Pohl and Horst Heinrich Gebhardt on the electorate of Mainz;[46] Rainer Decker and Gerhard Schormann on the electorate of Cologne;[47] and the work of Walter Rummel and several

---

[42] Eva Labouvie, *Zauberei und Hexenwerk. Ländlicher Aberglaube in der frühen Neuzeit* (Frankfurt am Main, 1991); Labouvie, *Verbotene Künste. Volksmagie und ländlicher Aberglaube in den Dorfgemeinden des Saarraumes (16.–19. Jahrhundert)* (St Ingbert, 1992).

[43] Helfried Valentinitsch, 'Die Verfolgung von Hexen und Zauberern im Herzogtum Steiermark – eine Zwischenbilanz', in Valentinitsch, ed., *Hexen und Zauberer*, 297–317; Manfred Tschaikner, *'Damit das Böse ausgerottet werde'. Hexenverfolgungen in Vorarlberg im 16. und 17. Jahrhundert* (Bregenz, 1992).

[44] Peter Kamber, 'La chasse aux sorciers et aux sorcières dans le pay de Vaud. Aspects quantitatifs (1581–1620)', *Revue historique vaudoise*, 90 (1982), 21–33.

[45] Herbert Breiden, 'Die Hexenprozesse in der Grafschaft Blankenheim von 1589 bis 1643', Diss. Jur. Bonn (1954); Herbert Klein, 'Die älteren Hexenprozesse im Lande Salzburg', *Mitteilungen der Gesellschaft für Salzburger Landeskunde*, 97 (1957), 17–50; Otto Seger, 'Der letzte Akt im Drama der Hexenprozesse in der Grafschaft Vaduz und Herrschaft Schellenberg', *Jahrbuch des Historischen Vereins des Fürstentums Liechtenstein*, 57 (1957), 137–227, 59 (1959), 331–49; Rainer Decker, 'Die Hexenverfolgung im Hochstift Paderborn', *Westfälische Zeitschrift*, 128 (1978), 314–56; Gisela Wilbertz, 'Hexenprozesse und Zauberglaube im Hochstift Osnabrück', *Osnabrücker Mitteilungen*, 84 (1978), 33–50; Wilbertz, 'Die Hexenprozesse in Stadt und Hochstift Osnabrück', in Degn et al., eds., *Hexenprozesse*, pp. 218–21; Walter Niess, *Hexenprozesse in der Grafschaft Büdingen. Protokolle, Ursachen, Hintergründe* (Büdingen, 1982).

[46] Herbert Pohl, *Hexenglaube und Hexenverfolgung im Kurfürstentum Mainz. Ein Beitrag zur Hexenfrage im 16. und beginnenden 17. Jahrhundert* (Wiesbaden, 1988); Horst Heinrich Gebhardt, *Hexenprozesse im Kurfürstentum Mainz des 17. Jahrhunderts* (Aschaffenburg, 1989).

[47] Rainer Decker, 'Die Hexenverfolgung im Herzogtum Westfalen', *Westfälische Zeitschrift*, 131/2 (1981/2), 339–86; Alfred Bruns, ed., *Hexen – Gerichtsbarkeit im kurkölnischen Sauerland* (Schmallenberg-Holthusen, 1984); Gerhard Schormann, *Der*

other authors on electoral Trier.[48] Thus far, only one of four secular electorates has received adequate attention, the Calvinist Palatine of the Rhine. The results were stunning: the works of Bernd Thieser and Jürgen Michael Schmidt have demonstrated conclusively that – as in the case of many other centralised territories – few trials were conducted in the Palatine, and also that, for reasons of principle, absolutely no witches were executed. Contrary to the intensive prosecutions of its smaller neighbours, indeed perhaps because of their experiences, the ruling elite developed official methods intended to nip any attempts at prosecution in the bud, refusing to admit accusations of witchcraft in their law courts.[49]

It is highly likely that many persons were involved in this conscious effort, especially the members of the court, the central administration, the territorial university in Heidelberg, the intermediate bureaucracy, the magistrates of larger cities and towns, jurists in county courts, and the clergy. In Catholic territories, in Bavaria for example, elevated to an eighth electorate during the Thirty Years War, a variety of monastic orders (Jesuits, Franciscans, Capuchins, etc.) – with their attendant internal complexities – can be added to this list of opinionated participants. Is it possible to attribute the revulsion toward executions in the Electoral Palatinate to religion, thereby confirming Max Weber's theory on Calvinism? Unfortunately not, since large persecutions occurred only miles away in the similarly Calvinist counties of Nassau, Isenburg-Büdingen and Hanau. In the County of Büdingen alone, over 200 persons were burned as witches within several years during a series of persecutions initiated by a 'witch-doctor', used for this purpose by the local authorities, as the study by Walter Niess shows.[50]

These examples prove that monocausal theories based on confession or other singular factors simply do not work. For, even if Erik Midelfort could demonstrate that, in the largely Protestant Southwest of Germany,

Krieg gegen die Hexen. Das Ausrottungsprogramm des Kurfürsten von Köln (Göttingen, 1991).

[48] Walter Rummel, *Bauern, Herren und Hexen. Studien zur Sozialgeschichte sponheimischer und kurtrierischer Hexenprozesse, 1574–1664* (Göttingen, 1991); Gunter Franz and Franz Irsigler, eds., *Hexenglaube und Hexenprozesse im Raum Rhein-Mosel Saar* (Trier, 1995).

[49] Bernd Thieser, *Die Oberpfalz im Zusammenhang des Hexenprozessgeschehens im süddeutschen Raum während des 16. und 17. Jahrhunderts* (Bayreuth, 1987); Jürgen Michael Schmidt, 'Die Kurpfalz', in Lorenz, *Hexen und Hexenverfolgung*, pp. 207–18.

[50] Walter Niess, *Hexenprozesse in der Grafschaft Büdingen. Protokolle, Ursachen, Hintergründe* (Büdingen, 1982).

the will to persecute after 1600 was limited to Catholic rulers, my own complementary regional study of Southeast Germany demonstrated just the opposite. After initial persecutions around 1590, the political elite there recognised the growing danger and fought vehemently against such a domestic policy. Since the Catholic bishoprics of Augsburg and Eichstätt did continue to persecute, they threatened neighbouring territories both by denunciations and by acting as models for zealots, so that it was sometimes necessary to achieve an active consensus, limited by confessional, political or socio-structural boundaries: when the Prince-Abbot of Kempten decided against participating with the Bishop of Augsburg in a joint persecution, military measures had to be undertaken to defend his subjects against arrest. The multiconfessional, but Catholic controlled imperial city of Augsburg conscientiously checked each accusation of witchcraft, but, much to the chagrin of the bishop, also decided against prosecutions. The tiny Lutheran imperial city of Kaufbeuren initiated a persecution, but then realised their mistake, stopped the hunt and produced legislation forbidding any further accusations against witches. The most interesting case was the duchy of Bavaria, one of the largest territories in the empire, the leader of the Counter-Reformation and a gathering place for ideological hard-liners. A discussion of domestic policy which included all elements of the ruling elite (the whole government, the regional university, and civic magistrates) began around 1590, polarising factions in the regime. In the coming factional conflicts, the moderate party always managed to triumph. They developed a political line of argumentation which, though not questioning the actual existence of witches, did succeed in complicating the procedure for prosecution to such a degree as to render it virtually impossible. This faction focused on the Chancellor of the Bavarian Estates, Johann Georg Herwarth, famous for his correspondence with Johannes Kepler, and he allied himself with the Jesuit, Adam Tanner, in 1602. This influential moral theologian published a formal critique of prosecutions for witchcraft, later championed by none other than that radical and influential opponent of witchcraft, Friedrich Spee.[51]

Examples of centralised states organised along early absolutist lines

---

[51] Wolfgang Behringer, 'Von Adam Tanner zu Friedrich Spee. Die Entwicklung einer Argumentationsstrategie (1590–1630) vor dem Hintergrund zeitgenössischer gesellschaftlicher Konflikte', in Theo G. M. van Oorschot, ed., *Friedrich Spee (1591–1635). Düsseldorfer Symposium zum 400. Geburtstag. Neue Ergebnisse der Spee-Forschung* (Bielefeld, 1993), pp. 154–75.

such as Bavaria, the Palatine, the duchy of Württemberg or the small territory of Vorarlberg ruled tight-fistedly from Innsbruck all demonstrate the role of political decisiveness on the part of rulers in the matter of witchcraft, as well as demonstrating the supra-regional and supra-confessional construction of political ideals. Indirectly, they validate the 1977 hypothesis of Gerhard Schormann, made in his regional study of the northwest and expanded in 1981 to all of Germany: generally, large territories with stable, successfully centralised states tended to avoid persecutions or stepped in quickly to retard them, regardless of confession. This is as true of Bavaria and Austria as of Bohemia, Saxony or Prussia, which made up the greater part of the eastern German-speaking areas. In the west, apart from Württemberg, the Electoral Palatinate and Jülich-Kleve-Berg, persecutions were far more prevalent. Scrutiny modifies this picture somewhat: some small territories conducted intensive persecutions, while neighbours exercised caution or forbade them outright. The legal historian, Günther Jerouschek, has shown in his habilitation on the imperial city of Esslingen, that excessive persecutions even exercised a crucially moderating influence on the developing judicial system.[52] Nevertheless, we can generalise that the countless tiny baronies, counties and ecclesiastical territories faced a greater danger of persecutions, being more dependent on the whims of their rulers and the mood of the populace. Levack correctly follows the Schormann thesis, recognising that the particularism of the German West and Southwest were major contributors to the high rate of executions in these regions.[53]

IV

Because of the volume of research in recent years, allow me to synopsise developments in several areas. Let us begin at the level of popular perceptions. By addressing the question of popular fantasies, we can access the 'structures of the *longue durée*' (Braudel) particular to the entire arena of magical beliefs and their operation, just as present in German-speaking regions as in other parts of Europe.[54] Muchembled's

---

[52] Günther Jerouschek, *Die Hexen und ihr Prozess. Die Hexenverfolgung in der Reichsstadt Esslingen* (Sigmaringen, 1992).

[53] G. Schormann, *Hexenprozesse in Deutschland* (Göttingen, 1981).

[54] Achim B. Baumgarten, *Hexenwahn und Hexenverfolgung im Naheraum. Ein Beitrag zur Sozial- und Kulturgeschichte* (Frankfurt am Main, 1987), pp. 366–96; Pohl, *Hexenglaube*, pp. 236–92; Labouvie, *Zauberei und Hexenwerk*, pp. 219–26; Christa

complete repertoire of popular culture in France is applicable to Germany. Literacy played an important role as a structural element of magical folk-culture, but illiterates displayed a remarkable capacity for memory, pushing the vital essence of popular magic to its conceivable limits and producing magical incantations of great poetic power.[55] Inquisitorial protocols frequently contain inventories of suspicious objects present in ordinary households, especially among the possessions of local 'specialists ' – a rich array of devices for use in both black and white magic.[56] Mimes, gestures, appearances and behaviour all played an important role in the conduct of magical activities (as well as in the identification of witches).[57] We should always keep in mind that magical power and abilities of the 'chosen' were still proudly paraded in the popular culture of Central Europe in the sixteenth century. Of course, popular conjurers seldom enjoyed high rank in the social hierarchy, but they continued to maintain an intermediary position in popular cultures, evoking awe and fear.[58]

Independent of Christian demonology, indeed often in open opposition to it, the greater portion of the population believed in the material efficacy of magic. Although theologians maintained that no one other than the devil could cause 'unnatural' phenomena, and then only with God's tacit consent, the populace believed in the direct efficacy of magical operations and did not necessarily view them as illegal.[59] In this regard, magic was not a crime, but an instrument, often referred to quite neutrally in testimony as the 'Art'.[60] This 'Art' was seldom challenged by the authorities, giving the impression that 'magical folk-culture' was relatively unaffected by ecclesiastical visitations and witchcraft

Habiger-Tuczay, *Magie und Magier im Mittelalter* (Munich, 1992); Eva Labouvie, 'Wissenschaftliche Theorien – rituelle Praxis. Annäherungen an die populäre Magie der frühe Neuzeit im Kontext der Magie- und Aberglaubensforschung', *Historische Anthropologie*, 2 (1994), 287–307.

55 Pohl, *Hexenglaube*, pp. 283–9; Wolfgang Behringer, *Mit dem Feuer vom Leben zum Tod. Hexengesetzgebung in Bayern* (Munich, 1988), pp. 193–212.

56 Behringer, *Hexenverfolgung in Bayern*, pp. 184–8; Behringer, ed., *Hexen und Hexenprozesse in Deutschland* (3rd edn Munich, 1995), pp. 20–72.

57 Behringer, *Hexenverfolgung in Bayern*, pp. 171ff., 179ff.

58 Labouvie, *Zauberei und Hexenwerk*; Tschaikner, *Damit das Böse ausgerottet wurde*, p. 175.

59 Labouvie, *Zauberei und Hexenwerk*, pp. 57–154.

60 Dagmar Unverhau, *Von Toverschen und Kunstfruhwen in Schleswig, 1548–1557. Quellen und Interpretationen zur Geschichte des Zauber- und Hexenwesens* (Schleswig, 1980); Tschaikner, *Damit das Böse ausgerottet wurde*, pp. 55, 62.

persecutions.[61] Understandably, fears focused primarily on maleficent magic directed against crops, especially grain and vineyards, followed by attacks on the health of humans and animals, and then activities such as the theft of milk, etc.[62] Magic and anti-magic were an integral part of daily life, just like other supernatural occurrences, for example miracles.[63] Within the framework of 'magical folk-culture', maleficent magic was fought with the aid of fortune-tellers and other specialists in anti-magic.[64] They conducted the fight with special rituals aimed at forcing witches to recant their *maleficium*.[65] In the sixteenth century, even the authorities resorted to the advice of sooth-sayers to track down witches; on occasion, these augurs – themselves central characters in the folk-culture of magical beliefs – sometimes unintentionally unleashed a volley of accusations culminating in major persecutions that targeted them among the first victims.[66]

By now, it is obvious that Keith Thomas could just as easily have conducted his investigations on the basis of German documentation. In all of Europe, the belief in magic represented a 'normal part of village life, widespread and regular'. More extravagant popular perceptions, like those presented for Krsniki in Slovenia[67] or for Ginzburg's *Benandanti* in Italy, are more difficult to confirm in early modern Germany, where only rare exceptions like the *Nachtschar* have been identified.[68] Nevertheless, there are several local variants of the belief in fairies,[69] widespread in Europe, and, against the backdrop of Christian demonology, we occasionally encounter archaic beliefs in fantastic creatures that needed

---

[61] Baumgarten, *Hexenwahn*, pp. 375–6; Pohl, *Hexenglaube*, pp. 275–88; Labouvie, *Verbotene Künste*.

[62] Pohl, *Hexenglaube*, pp. 271-4.

[63] Rebekka Habermas, *Wallfahrt und Aufruhr. Zur Geschichte des Wunderglaubens in der frühen Neuzeit* (Frankfurt am Main, 1991).

[64] Labouvie, *Zauberei und Hexenwerk*, pp. 238–50.

[65] Behringer, *Hexenverfolgung in Bayern*, p. 93; Tschaikner, *Damit das Böse ausgerottet wurde*, p. 195. See also Alfred Soman, 'The Parlement of Paris and the great witch hunt (1565–1640)', *16th Century Journal*, 9 (1978), 31–44, esp. 43.

[66] Schormann, *Hexenprozesse*, pp. 59–60; Behringer, *Hexenverfolgung in Bayern*, pp. 181–4; Tschaikner, *Damit das Böse ausgerottet wurde*, pp. 61–2, 91–2.

[67] Maja Boskovic-Stulli, 'Kresnik-krsnik, ein Wesen aus der kroatischen und slowenischen Volksüberlieferung', *Fabula*, 3 (1959/60), 275–98.

[68] Wolfgang Behringer, *Conrad Stoeckhlin und die Nachtschar. Eine Geschichte aus der frühen Neuzeit* (Munich, 1994).

[69] Eva Pocs, *Fairies and Witches at the Boundary of South-Eastern and Central Europe* (Helsinki, 1989).

to be expunged by ritual means.[70] Other archaic survivals include beliefs in the congenital inheritance of magical abilities,[71] ecstatic experiences of flight in unconscious states,[72] or, reminiscent of shamanist perceptions of lycanthropy, the ability to fly magically,[73] in the form of a cat, a hare, a fox, a dog, a raven or a butterfly, as well as Ginzburg's werewolf complex,[74] and finally, the Eurasian transmigratory 'bone-wonder', the literal reincarnation of an animal after its consumption, through the preservation of its bones and skin.[75]

The well-known advantage of regional and local studies lies in the fact that variations and peculiarities are brought to the fore. The results are hardly surprising; witches ostensibly caused storms along the North Sea coast or mud-slides and avalanches in the mountains.[76] Other regionally specific patterns are more difficult to explain, such as the irregularity of werewolf beliefs.[77] Interestingly, in Germany there were only two places intimated in connection with 'witches' dances': the older 'Witches Mountain' is the Heuberg in Southwest Germany, already mentioned in the fifteenth century, while the Blocksberg in Saxony, appearing with frequency in the literature of the seventeenth century, achieved prominence after Goethe integrated it into his *Faust*.[78]

The connection of women to magic had already appeared in Tacitus' *Germania*, in early medieval sources on *maleficium*, in hagiographies like the *Vita Corbiniani*, in Germanic law codes, such as the *Pactus Alamanorum*, or in penitentials, for example, the influential *Correctur* of

[70] Baumgarten, *Hexehwahn*, pp. 386–7; Behringer, *Hexen und Hexenprozesse*, pp. 13–14, 27ff., 37–8, 43–4, 52–3, 71.

[71] Pohl, *Hexenglaube*, pp. 248ff.

[72] Tschaikner, *Damit das Böse ausgerottet wurde*, pp. 75–6.

[73] Mircea Eliade, 'Der magische Flug', *Antaios*, 1 (1958), 1–12; Wolfgang Behringer and Constance Ott-Koptschalijski, *Der Traum vom Fliegen. Zwischen Mythos und Technik* (Frankfurt am Main, 1991); Wolfgang Behringer and Dieter R. Bauer, eds., *Fliegen und Schweben. Interdisziplinäre Annäherung an eine menschliche Sensation* (Munich, 1995).

[74] Pohl, *Hexenglaube*, pp. 270–1; Carlo Ginzburg, *Ecstasies: Deciphering the Witches' Sabbath* (London, 1990), pp. 153ff.

[75] Maurizio Bertolotti, 'Le ossa e la pelle dei buoi. Un mito pupolare tra agiografia e stregonaria', *Quaderni Storici*, 41 (1973), 477ff; Behringer, *Chonrad Stoecklin*, pp. 45–52.

[76] Tschaikner, *Damit das Böse ausgerottet wurde*, pp. 174–5.

[77] Alfred Bruns, 'Die Oberkirchner Protokolle', in Bruns. ed., *Hexen-Gerichtsbarkeit*, pp. 11–90; Valentinitsch, 'Die Verfolgung'; Carlo Ginzburg, 'Freud, der Wolfsmann und die Werwölfe', *Zeitschrift für Volkskunde*, 82 (1986), 189–99; Ginzburg, *Ecstasies*, pp. 154–61.

[78] Behringer, *Hexen und Hexenprozesse*, pp. 187, 234, 248, 250, 345, 409.

Burchard of Worms[79] which addresses the issue of nocturnal flight. Germanic tribes can be regarded as 'Germans' to the same extent that the Gauls were French, but the enormous degree of continuity in a geographic area still provides for interesting analyses. Philologists have generally held Christian demonology or the *Malleus* wholly responsible for the targeting of women as witches.[80] However, reports of executions of women for witchcraft are spread throughout the Middle Ages. Sources from the eleventh and thirteenth centuries indicate that women were occasionally held collectively culpable for weather magic[81] and that the term *striga* was surely appropriated from antiquity, as Claude Lecouteux reveals. He has connected the term *Unhold* to the older derivative *striga holda* employed by Burchard in the *Corrector*, and he attributes its demonisation to Christian missionaries, who applied the negative prefix '*un*'. According to Lecouteux's observations, this regrouping of semantic context had already occurred in the thirteenth century, as in the case of the witch's pact.[82] Three points of inquisitorial terminology were innovative: a belief in the necessity of a composite picture as a unifying influence on regional peculiarities; the view of an international demonic conspiracy; and the belief in a radically systematic persecution. In German, the term *Hexerei*, a linguistic innovation, was simply the popularisation of a provincial Swiss word for magic. It appeared for the first time in a trial for magic in Lucerne in 1419, still carrying its original meaning.[83] Only thereafter was *Hexerei* identified with a new crime, invented by the inquisition. In this context, it quickly spread throughout the remaining German-speaking lands.[84]

In the fifteenth century, it was by no means inevitable that Germany would soon become the centre of witchcraft persecutions in Europe. Italy, France or even Spain might have been more likely candidates. The origins of witchcraft conceptions, as Andreas Blauert has recently pointed out, can be precisely worked out relative to place and time, first

[79] Edith Ennen, 'Zauberinnen und fromme Frauen – Ketzerinnen und Hexen', in Segl, *Der Hexenhammer*, pp. 7–22.

[80] Joseph Hansen, 'Die Zuspitzung auf das weibliche Geschlecht', in Hansen, *Quellen und Untersuchungen zur Geschichte dex Hexenwahns und der Hexenverfolgung im Mittelalter* (Bonn, 1901), pp. 416–44.

[81] Monica Blöcker, 'Frauenzauber-Zauberfrauen', *Zeitschrift für schweizerische Kirchengeschichte*, 76 (1982), 1–39.

[82] Claude Lecouteux, 'Hagazussa – Striga – Hexe', *Hessische Blätter für Volks- und Kulturforschung*, 18 (1985), 57–70.

[83] Monter, *Witchcraft*, p. 23.

[84] Johannes Franck, 'Geschichte des Wortes "Hexe"', in Hansen, *Quellen*, pp. 614–71.

appearing in the region near Geneva around 1435.[85] In his *Formicarius*, composed during the Council of Basel, Johannes Nider gave no reports of witchcraft trials in Germany.[86] It can be shown with relative precision that newly elaborated witchcraft beliefs slowly evolved in German-speaking regions of Switzerland before spreading. Blauert suggests that the older tradition of Waldensian persecutions and trials for magic were only later interpreted as witchcraft trials, as in the famous Lucerne chronicle of Hans Fründ.[87] At the time of the *Malleus*, the limited acceptance of inquisitorial witchcraft beliefs had little impact in Germany. For that very reason, the papal bull *Summis desiderantes affectibus* of 1484 was of paramount importance.[88] It is noteworthy that the agitation of preachers in the trade centres of the Rhine in the 1480s met with remarkable resonance, as Walter Rummel, Willem de Blécourt and Hans de Waardt have shown.[89] Blauert attributes a major wave of witchcraft trials in Switzerland in the years 1477–86 to an agrarian crisis, during which time an elaborated concept of witchcraft replaced older perceptions of magic as a means to fathom concrete situations of social malaise.[90]

The first ascertainable major persecution within the modern boundaries of Germany, which illuminates a whole spectrum of recurring themes, was the Ravensburger persecution of 1484.[91] Based upon this incident, the inquisitor Heinrich Institoris, who signed his name in German as 'Kremer', composed the infamous *Malleus Maleficarum*.[92]

---

[85] Andreas Blauert, *Frühe Hexenverfolgungen. Ketzer-, Zauberei- und Hexenprozesse des 15. Jahrhunderts* (Hamburg, 1989); Blauert, ed., *Ketzer, Zauberer, Hexen. Die Anfänge der europäischen Hexenverfolgungen* (Frankfurt am Main, 1990).

[86] Blauert, *Frühe Hexenverfolgungen*, pp. 56–60.

[87] Ibid., pp. 67ff.

[88] On the classifiation of Papal decrees: Ernst Pitz, 'Diplomatische Studien zu den päpstlichen Erlassen über das Zauber- und Hexenwesen', in Segl, *Der Hexenhammer*, pp. 23–70; André Schnyder, 'Der "Malleus maleficarum". Fragen und Beobachtungen zu seiner Druckgeschichte sowie zur Rezeption bei Bodin, Binsfield und Delrio', *AfK*, 74 (1992), 323–64.

[89] Walter Rummel, 'Gutenberg, der Teufel und die Muttergottes von Eberhardshausen. Erste Hexenverfolgungen im Trier Land', in Blauert, *Ketzer, Zauberer, Hexen*, pp. 91–117; Willem de Blécourt and Hans de Waardt, 'Das Vordringen der Zaubereiverfolgungen in die Niederlande. Rhein, Maas und Schelde entlang', in Blauert, *Ketzer, Zauberer, Hexen*, pp. 182–216.

[90] Blauert, *Frühe Hexenverfolgungen*, pp. 75–8.

[91] Rudolf Endres, 'Hexenhammer und der Nürnberger Rat', in Segl, *Der Hexenhammer*, pp. 195–216.

[92] Peter Segl, 'Heinrich Institoris. Persönlichkeit und literarisches Werk', in Segl, *Der Hexenhammer*, pp. 103–26.

In reality, the *Malleus* was occasioned by the failure of his activities in neighbouring Tyrol. As in the case of his predecessor, Nicolaus Cusanus,[93] the new Bishop of Brixen, Georg Golser, rebuked this elaboration of witchcraft beliefs, indeed he called the inquisitor Kramer a senile old man (*propter senium gantz chindisch*). In fact, his evaluation seems to have hit the mark, if one compares the testimony of the women of Innsbruck with the interpretations of the inquisitor in the *Malleus*, as has Heide Dienst.[94] On behalf of the bishop, the estates of Tyrol and the citizenry of Innsbruck, Kramer was thrown out of the county in 1485, and all the women he arrested were set free. This incident justified his publication of the *Malleus*, which appeared in print for the first time in Strasbourg in 1487.[95] In view of these facts, it is obvious that papal inquisitors were outsiders in fifteenth-century Germany and were handled as such. Nevertheless, the resonance of their ideas promoted agitations in the Rhineland in the 1490s.[96] Therefore, the extent of witchcraft trials during the decades of ferment before the Reformation is in definite need of re-examination. In a letter to the city council of the Imperial City of Nuremberg, Heinrich Kramer mentioned that his accomplishments included the execution of over 200 witches.[97]

A witchcraft persecution in the small Lutheran territory of Wiesensteig in the Swabian Alb, in the year 1563, claiming the lives of some sixty-three women was, as far as we know, the largest hunt in Germany up to that time, pre-Reformation persecutions included.[98] In the following years, trials accumulated in the German West, provoked by a famine at the onset of the 1570s, more than likely the cause of intensified anti-witchcraft legislation in electoral Saxony.[99] In the second half of

---

[93] Wilhelm Baum, *Nikolaus Cusanus in Tirol. Das Wirken des Philosophen und Reformators als Fürstbischof von Brizen* (Brixen, 1983), pp. 246–8.

[94] Heide Dienst, 'Lebensbewältigung durch Magie. Alltägliche Zauberei in Innsbruck gegen Ende des 15. Jahrhunderts', in Alfred Kohler and Heinrich Lutz, eds., *Alltag im 16. Jahrhundert. Studien zu Lebensformen in mitteleuropäischen Städten* (Munich, 1987), pp. 80–116.

[95] Segl, *Der Hexenhammer*, pp. 108–9; Heide Dienst, 'Magische Vorstellungen und Hexenverfolgungen in den österreichischen Ländern (15.–18. Jahrhundert)', in Erich Zöllner, ed., *Wellen der Verfolgung in der österreichischen Geschichte* (Vienna, 1986), pp. 70–4, esp. 78–9.

[96] Rummel, 'Gutenberg', pp. 91–117.

[97] Endres, 'Hexenhammer', p. 207.

[98] *Wahrhafftige und erschreckenliche Thatten und Handlungend der 63 Hexen und Unholden, so zu Wiesensteig mit dem Brand gerichtet worden* (*s.l.*, 1563), reprinted in Behringer, *Hexen und Hexenprozesse*, pp. 137ff.

[99] Behringer, *Hexen und Hexenprozesse*, pp. 148–58.

the 1580s, witchcraft persecutions in Germany reached their first conjunctural high-point,[100] coincidentally paralleling an increased attention to magic throughout Europe in general, familiar to us in the analysis of serial documents, such as the files of the Holy Inquisition in Spain[101] and Venice,[102] as well as the court records examined by Macfarlane for Essex,[103] and Gábor Klaniczay for Hungary.[104] The beginning of major persecutions in France, Switzerland, Germany and Scotland arose in this context.[105] Ripples of these persecutions penetrated into the Baltic region.[106] Up to that point, the worst persecutions in Germany occurred in the electorate of Trier, where 368 persons were executed as witches.[107] This persecution exceeded all former dimensions, even if it had not reached the extent of those in the neighbouring, mostly French-speaking Duchy of Lorraine, where, according to the figures of Nicolas Remy, 800 witches were burned within a ten-year period.[108]

V

From the beginning of the seventeenth century, Germany set out on a peculiar path, in so far as a number of smaller territories conducted persecutions and the simultaneous acceptance of witchcraft trials progressed rapidly. The implementation of witchcraft persecutions spread contagiously, but any politically coordinated effort with that direct intent was conspicuously lacking. There was, to use the terminology of Christina Larner, no 'national witch-hunt' in Germany.

---

[100] Schormann, *Hexenprozesse*, pp. 55–6; Decker, 'Die Hexenverfolgung'; Behringer, *Hexenverfolgung in Bayern*, pp. 122–223.

[101] Jean-Pierre Dedieu, 'The Inquisition and Popular Culture in New Castile', in Stephen Haliczer, ed., *Inquisition and Society in Early Modern Europe* (London, 1987), pp. 129–46, esp. 140ff.

[102] Ruth Martin, *Witchcraft and the Inquisition in Venice, 1550–1650* (Oxford/New York, 1989), pp. 259ff.

[103] Macfarlane, *Witchcraft in Tudor and Stuart England*.

[104] Gábor Klaniczay, 'Witch-hunting in Hungary: Social or Cultural Tensions?', in Klaniczay, *The Uses of Supernatural Power* (Cambridge, 1990), pp. 151–67.

[105] Schormann, *Hexenprozesse*; Monter, *Ritual, Myth and Magic in Early Modern Europe* (1983); Christina Larner, *Enemies of God. The Witch-Hunt in Scotland* (London, 1981).

[106] Maia Madar, 'Estonia I: Werewolves and Poisoners', in Ankarloo and Henningsen, *Early Modern European Witchcraft*, pp. 257–72, esp. 260–1.

[107] On the associated demonology: Peter Binsfeld, *Tractatus de confessionibus maleficiorum et sagarum* (Trier, 1589) – further material on this subject forthcoming in Gunter Franz and Franz Irsigler, eds., *Hexenglaube und Hexenprozesse im Raum Rhein-Mosel Saar* (Trier, 1995).

[108] Nicolas Remy, *Daemonolatria* (Lyon, 1595), preface.

'Germany', *per se*, did not even exist as a nation, and the empire lacked any central agency for the promotion of witchcraft trials. When imperial institutions (e.g. the Chamber Court or the Imperial Court Council) intervened, they tended to present a deterrent factor. Even in those instances where the empire did not possess necessary jurisdiction, cautious hindering still occurred.[109] The proclivity to intervene in Germany, indeed in international terms, peaked in the years 1625–35.[110] For, although only a relatively small number of territories were occupied with the persecution of witches at that time, those that did so conducted their persecutions with an unforeseen vehemence. For example, a contemporary pamphlet reported the burning of 600 witches in the small Franconian bishopric of Bamberg.[111] However, can one trust this report in light of the fact that events of a similar order magnitude have since been unmasked (by Norman Cohn and William Monter) as fabrications?[112] Henry Kamen's doubts regarding numbers of executions are already well known, for Germany as for elsewhere.[113] However, in this case, they are unjustifiable: it has become clear that, in addition to the aforementioned 600 burnings by the bishop of Bamberg, another 600 seem plausible there. Yet another 300 fell victim to a subsequent bishop of Bamberg. There were also some 1,200 victims from the persecutions of two Würzburg bishops, 1,800 victims from those of three bishops of Mainz, and, probably, 2,000 victims of one bishop of Cologne. All together, these figures from the territories most intensively beset with persecutions total almost 6,000 burnings.[114] The fact that neither the clergy nor the nobility were spared as victims attests to the radical nature of these persecutions.[115]

[109] Behringer, *Hexenverfolgung in Bayern*, pp. 141, 160, 193, 208, 254, 288, 329–30, 346; Sönke Lorenz, 'Das Reichskammergericht', *Zeitschrift für Württembergische Landesgeschichte*, 43 (1984), 175–203.

[110] Schormann, *Hexenprozesse*, p. 55; Levack, *The Witch-Hunt in Early Modern Europe* (1987), pp. 174–5.

[111] *Kurzer und warhafftiger Bericht und erschreckhliche Neue zeitung Von sechshundert Hexen, zauberern und Teufelsbannern, welche der Bischof zu Bamberg hat verbrennen lassen . . .* (Bamberg, 1659), reprinted in Behringer, *Hexen und Hexenprozesse*, pp. 260ff.

[112] Norman Cohn, *Europe's Inner Demons: An Enquiry inspired by the Great Witch-Hunt* (London, 1975), pp. 130ff.; Monter, *Witchcraft*.

[113] Henry Kamen, *The Iron Century. Social Change in Europe, 1550–1650* (London, 1971), p. 236.

[114] Pohl, *Hexenglaube und Hexenverfolgung*; Gebhardt, *Hexenprozesse*; Schormann, *Der Krieg gegen die Hexen*.

[115] Harald Schwillus, *Kleriker im Hexenprozess. Geistliche als Opfer der Hexenprozesse des 16. und 17. Jahrhunderts in Deutschland* (Würzburg, 1992).

The worst persecution of witches, in Germany as well as in European context, is generally considered that of the Cologne archbishop, Ferdinand of Bavaria.[116] Ferdinand was born the son of Duke Wilhelm V of Bavaria (ruled from 1579 to 1597) and Renata of Lorraine. He was the younger brother of Duke (later Elector) Maximilian I of Bavaria (ruled 1597–1651) and the cousin of Bishop Franz Wilhelm of Wartenburg. In 1594, Ferdinand left Bavaria to take the post of the coadjuture of Cologne from his uncle, Archbishop Ernst of Bavaria, who assumed the rulership there in 1595. In 1612, Ferdinand succeeded his uncle to the archbishopric and the electoral title, a position he held until his death in 1650. Contemporary reactions to the extraordinary nature of Ferdinand's persecutions provide us with some clues to their extent. However, Ferdinand of Bavaria was not only archbishop and elector of Cologne, but in an accumulation of offices surely unprecedented for the post-Tridentine Church, he was also prince-bishop of Hildesheim, Munster, Lüttich and Paderborn – territorial sovereign over lands stretching from Northern Germany to the Spanish Netherlands and the borders of France. The Paderborn witchcraft persecution is of particular interest, because Friedrich Spee wrote a work of fundamental importance there, his *Cautio Criminalis*,[117] which, as we now know, essentially transformed conceptions of witchcraft persecutions among many ecclesiastics and jurists. By the mid-seventeenth century, its radical and plausible argumentation led many ecclesiastic princes in the empire to completely prohibit the execution of witches in their territories, among them the bishop of Trier, Carl Caspar of Leyen (1652–76), and the archbishop of Mainz and bishop of Würzburg, Johann Philipp of Schönborn (1647–73).[118]

Contemporaries were especially concerned about the reasons behind the proclivity for major persecutions in Germany. When one compares Friedrich Spee, Matthäus Meyfart (1590–1642),[119] and Hermann Löher (1595–1678)[120] with previous opponents of persecutions like Johann Weyer, it is obvious that their arguments assumed a different tone.

[116] Decker, 'Die Hexenverfolgung', p. 375; Schormann, *Der Krief gegen die Hexen*.
[117] Decker, 'Die Hexenverfolgung', pp. 315–35.
[118] W. Rummel, 'Friedrich Spee und das Ende der Kurtrierischen Hexenverfolgungen', *Jahrbuch für Westdeutsche Landesgeschichte*, 1989, pp. 105–16.
[119] Christian Hallier, *Johann Matthäus Meyfart. Ein Schriftsteller, Pädagoge und Theologe des 17. Jahrhunderts* (Neumünster, 1982).
[120] Hans de Waardt, *Toverij en Samenleving. Holland 1500–1800* (Rotterdam, 1991), pp. 150–1.

Surely, gullibility, self-enrichment and other motives were factors behind persecutions. However, there is an innovative element, one that Spee perceives as the primary motivation behind witchcraft persecutions: 'This is all the fatal consequence of Germany's pious zealotry.'[121] All of the aforementioned bishops are regarded by confessional historiography as fanatical protagonists of the Counter-Reformation.[122] In his biography of the reforming bishop, Julius Echter, Götz von Pölnitz concluded, not without a degree of psychological finesse: 'The whole generation was overcome by an exceedingly tenacious spirit of struggle, directed partly against their heterodox opponents and partly against miscreants in their own camp, but most severely of all against the individual ego and everything sinful associated with it.'[123] It should not be forgotten that the bishops who figured among the generation of witch hunters were also the first generation seriously confronted with enforced sexual segregation and celibacy. Rather than viewing witchcraft persecutions as an instrument of religious conflict, as earlier authors and Trevor-Roper still did,[124] we should locate the proclivity for radical solutions among the first generation of bishops in the development of new personality traits, the spirit of fanatical severity with which they were brought up to treat themselves and others. The basis of this severity was formed by a radical 'gloomy world view', occasionally assuming an apocalyptic tenor and a subjective awareness of an imminent state of emergency, thereby justifying exceptional measures, at least in the case of the exceptional crimes behind this situation.[125]

'Gloom' worked its way into life at court: gone are the days of a renaissance zest for life – unrestrained celebration was a thing of the past. Princes like the Cologne Archbishop Ferdinand of Bavaria spent their lives bound in a rigid moral corset. They imagined themselves constantly threatened by the devil's temptation and the assaults of his minions, they spent nightly vigils in prayer and took a personal role in public

---

[121] F. von Spee, *Cautio Criminalis* in German translation by J. F. Ritter (Munich, 1982), p. 286. [In 1971 Frankfurt reproduction of the original Latin edition (no editor given), the passage occurs in Latin on p. 388.]

[122] Behringer, *Hexenverfolgung in Bayern*, pp. 237–41, 330–1; Gebhardt, *Hexenprozesse*, pp. 317–27.

[123] Götz von Pölnitz, *Julius Echter von Mespelbrunn, Fürstbischof von Würzburg und Herzog von Franken (1573–1617)* (Munich, 1934), pp. 303–4.

[124] Hugh R. Trevor-Roper, *The European Witchcraze of the 16th and 17th Centuries* (Harmondsworth, 1969).

[125] Behringer, *Hexenverfolgungen in Bayern*, pp. 112–21.

penitential processions: Ferdinand processed barefoot in penitential garb, a heavy crucifix slung over his shoulder in imitation of the saviour. This was no simple demonstration intended to create an impression on the public; the spirit of gloom and severity affected princes as well as their subjects. In private, they wore hair-shirts, heavy penitential belts and practised self-flagellation.[126] One need not be a strict Freudian to understand how this accentuated consciousness of one's sinfulness might arouse self-deprecation, neurosis and projection complexes. Their elite functionaries, those jurists and theologians who fulfilled the duties of educators, father confessors and councillors, and accepted decisive posts at court and the universities, necessarily suffered other pressures than did the potentates. Status neurosis had risen greatly since the fifteenth century, when the estates could still invoke the privileges of nobility (*Indigenatsprinzip*) to win public office. Individuals now faced difficulties arising from what Norbert Elias identified as a 'social coercion to self-coercion' that fell on the nobility in courtly society,[127] as well as from a rigid normative code in education, professions of faith, work ethics and expected forms of behaviour upon which their social status depended.[128] It has thus been argued that the striving for the ideal 'Christian' state fanned the fires of witchcraft persecutions.[129]

VI

Let us proceed to the conditions motivating charges of witchcraft, or to put it crudely, the role of the people. The major shift in German witchcraft studies in recent years has been the recognition of a massive desire for persecution stemming from the general population. One apparent peculiarity of Central Europe is the role of communities, the self-

---

[126] Edith Ennen, 'Die kurkölnische Residenz Bonn und ihr Umland in einem Jahrhundert der Kriege', in Dietrich Höroldt, ed., *Bonn als kurkölnische Haupt- und Residenzstadt 1597–1794* (Bonn, 1989), pp. 15–204, esp. 93–4.

[127] Norbert Elias, *Über den Prozess der Zivilisation. Soziogenetische und psychogenetische Untersuchungen*, 2 vols. (Basle, 1939), translated as *The Civilizing Process*, 2 vols. (Oxford, 1982).

[128] Wolfgang Behringer, 'Gegenreformation als Generationenkonflikt, oder: Verhörsprotokolle und andere administrative Quellen und Mentalitätsgeschichte', in Winfried Schulze, ed., *Ego-Dokumente* (Berlin, 1995). For a specific example of the mental strains of university education on the nobility, see a recent American dissertation: David Lederer, 'Reforming the spirit: society, madness and suicide in Central Europe, 1517–1809' (New York University, 1995), pp. 250–9.

[129] Bernd Roeck, 'Christlicher Idealstaat und Hexenwahn. Zum Ende der europäischen Hexenverfolgungen', *Historisches Jahrbuch*, 108 (1988), 379–405.

appointed protagonists of witchcraft persecutions who placed their superiors under massive pressure to conduct them. This unexpected connection between the formation of states and witchcraft persecutions has been a primary subject of discussion for some time. Whereas it was previously held that the introduction of a comprehensive judicial system led to an increase in persecutions along the lines of well-known, fundamental, early modern processes ('social disciplining' for example) the opposite argument now holds sway. Successful and early state-formation in large states like France, Austria, Bavaria, Saxony or Brandenburg promoted a specific type of rationality, a *raison d'état*, that could check the irrational desires for persecution stemming from the general populace with the aid of efficient administrations. Medium and small territories, where most major witchcraft persecutions occurred, often had poorly functioning systems of administration, so that communities could exercise much greater local autonomy. During major persecutions in electoral Trier,[130] electoral Mainz,[131] the Franconian bishoprics, and in the valleys of the Main, Rhine, Nahe, Saar and Mosel, segments of the population pushed so actively for the persecution of alleged witches that the authorities feared open revolt. Therefore, and with good reason, Gerhard Schormann's thesis of a decisive programme of extermination pursued by the ruling authorities in electoral Cologne has been thoroughly contradicted.[132] The complete helplessness of state authorities in several small territories is illustrated by events in the bishopric of Trier, where over the course of many years, as Walter Rummel and Eva Labouvie have shown, the authorities proved unable to disarm village witch-hunting committees. These wrested control from the official courts and only turned persons considered guilty of witchcraft over to the authorities for legal execution.[133]

As our recognition of popular modes of action increases, the background to *all* major witchcraft persecutions becomes more apparent. Even well-organised states faced these problems: the County of Tyrol confronted similar communal uprisings aimed at initiating witch hunts

---

[130] Rummel, *Bauern, Herren und Hexen*; Labouvie, *Zauberei und Hexenwerk*.

[131] Pohl, *Hexenglaube*, pp. 6, 148ff.; Gebhardt, *Hexenprozesse*.

[132] Schormann, *Der Krieg gegen die Hexen*; Thomas Becker, 'Hexenverfolgung in Kurköln. Kritische Anmerkungen zu Gerhard Schormanns "Krieg gegen die Hexen"', *Annalen des historischen Vereins für den Niederrhein*, 195 (1992), 202–14; Walter Rummel, '"Der Krieg gegen die Hexen" – Ein Krieg fanatischer Kirchenfürsten oder ein Angebot zur Realisierung sozialer Chancen? Sozialgeschichtliche Anmerkungen zu zwei neuen Büchern', *Rheinische Vierteljahresblätter*, 56 (1992), 311–24.

[133] Rummel, *Bauern, Herren und Hexen*; Labouvie, *Zauberei und Hexenwerk*.

on its outskirts, as Manfred Tschaikner demonstrated in the case of Vorarlberg.[134] Tschaikner emphasises that stereotypes in the older literature blaming the government in Innsbruck for persecutions are poor explanations. Court records reveal precisely the contrary: the central government restricted local enthusiasm for persecutions with drastic measures and imposed heavy sanctions against the leaders of pogroms in an attempt to nip witchcraft persecutions in the bud.[135] We know of similar occurrences in other well-functioning early absolutist territories, such as Bavaria and Württemberg,[136] and conditions were probably not much different in the Austrian crown lands, the electorates of the Palatine, Saxony and Brandenburg.[137] An old depiction of a consensus between subjects and rulers has been confirmed in an unexpected fashion: anarchy in small states requires authorities to conform to popular demands for persecutions. The population connected the witch hunt with individual welfare, as well as an eschatological hope of salvation that might or might not cloak its motives in theological justifications. Why did peasant witch hunters need Roman law or inquisitorial demonology in the fight for their subsistence? Indeed, did they need their rulers at all? Communally organised populations had their own rituals with which to identify witches, test them informally and isolate them socially. The official witchcraft trial often manifested the terminal point after a prelude panning out over decades. And the identification of witches has much more to do with things we have learned from Evans-Pritchard[138] than with Roman law – an inference that could topple a few fundamental assumptions of recent international witchcraft studies, not least of all the centre-periphery model of Christina Larner, which posits a direct connection between intensity of persecution and Roman law, inquisitorial procedure and a developed demonology.[139]

The historical-anthropological work of Rainer Walz explores the internal viciousness of village interactions, the treatment of suspects and ritual conflict in everyday situations on the basis of trial records from the

[134] Manfred Tschaikner, 'Hexenverfolgungen in Dornbirn', *Dornbirner Schriften*, 8 (1990), 53–79, esp. 60ff.
[135] Ibid., pp. 71–2.
[136] Behringer, *Hexenverfolgung in Bayern*; Midelfort, *Witches*.
[137] Schormann, *Der Krieg gegen die Hexen*, pp. 142ff.
[138] E. E. Evants-Pritchard, *Hexerei, Orakel und Magie bei den Zande* (Frankfurt am Main, 1978).
[139] Larner, *Enemies of God*, p. 197.

county of Lippe. He examines the important role of defamation, the lack of sympathy and the brutality of interpersonal conflict within the context of honour as a central category of early modern identity formation. Walz traces the importance of accusations of witchcraft in internal village relations to their seriousness on a fictive scale of defamation and to a logical reduction of contingencies, a simplification of coincidences, that employed magic as an explanation for all manner of misfortunes.[140] Frictions arising from social intercourse cannot be reduced, as Thomas and Macfarlane suggest, to any one dominant modality, such as the refusal to give alms. After an initial wave of enthusiastic attempts to broadly apply the 'Thomas–Macfarlane model' (Peter Burke),[141] it has become clear that it depicts only one of many possible scenarios and that every form of conflict lends itself in principle to a transference onto the level of witchcraft. Walz refutes the view of persecutions as a means of modernisation or disciplining on the part of the authorities in the sense of an acculturation of village communities[142] on account of their dysfunctionality.[143] In the region under consideration, Walter Rummel demonstrates, in his social-historical analysis of patterns of accusations by village committees, that village outsiders and deviants were less affected, that the vast majority of accusations were raised against community members with high local status by members of middling status, who instrumentalised the accusations for use in internal village rivalries.[144]

Neighbourhood conflicts described by Evans-Pritchard for Africa, and Macfarlane in England, and which, in all probability, spanned the entire late Middle Ages and early modern period,[145] surely played an important role in trials for magic and witchcraft. While individual suffering satisfied itself with individual accusations, this is not the case for those

---

[140] Rainer Walz, *Hexenglaube und magische Kommunikation im Dorf der frühen Neuzeit. Der Verfolgungen in der Grafschaft Lippe* (Paderborn, 1993).

[141] Peter Burke, 'The comparative approach to European witchcraft', in Ankarloo and Henningsen, *Early Modern European Witchcraft*, pp. 435–41, esp. 438.

[142] Robert Muchembled, 'The witches of the Cambrésis. The acculturation of the rural world in the sixteenth century', in John Obelkevich, ed., *Religion and the People, 800–1700* (Chapel Hill, 1979), pp. 221–76, 315–23.

[143] Rainer Walz, 'Der Hexenwahn im Alltag. Der Umgang mit verdächtigen Frauen', *Geschichte in Wissenschaft und Unterricht*, 43 (1992), 157–68.

[144] Walter Rummel, 'Hexenprozess als Karrieremöglichkeit. Ein Beispiel aus der Epoche des konfessionellen Konfliktes am Mittelrhein, 1629–1631', *Kurtrierisches Jahrbuch*, 25 (1985), 181–90; Rummel, *Bauern, Herren und Hexen*, pp. 319–20.

[145] Macfarlane, *Witchcraft in Tudor and Stuart England*, p. 30; Thomas, *Religion and the Decline of Magic*, p. 564.

popular movements of unrest which form the background to major persecutions. These movements can be traced to collective, rather than private misfortunes, such as crop failures or livestock and human epidemics attributed to weather magic. In such situations, accusations were collective rather than individual and were formally raised by household representatives, i.e. by men in the forum of village politics. There is no evidence substantiating the opposition of women to their representation in matters of collective interest by men. In all major witchcraft persecutions involving action by entire communities, weather magic played at least a catalytic role, as in Trier, Mainz, Cologne, Bamberg, Würzburg, Eichstätt, and others.[146]

VII

Engagement with contemporary statements reveals that the subjective expression of an emergency situation was always employed to justify exceptional measures. The problem remains whether a subjective impression of a world out-of-order can actually be related to objectively measurable conditions.[147] The complex interaction of socio-historical and climatic factors might have acted as a 'Malthusian trap' during the sixteenth century. Climatic deterioration, the so-called 'Little Ice Age', disrupted long-standing demographic growth[148] in the second half of the century. Damp summers and cold winters significantly worsened conditions in the agricultural sector between 1560 and 1630s, bringing famine and increased susceptibility to disease in their wake. Since Christian Pfister's paradigmatic study of the history of climate in Switzerland, we have access to accurate figures for climatic change during individual years and we can identify those years with damp, cool summers and cold, long winters as those during which witchcraft persecutions occurred, coinciding with years which were unfavourable for agriculture, particularly in the grain and viticultural sectors.[149]

In the foreground of the major witchcraft persecutions of the 1560s, the late 1580s and the 1620s, we discover unusual climatic conditions,

[146] Behringer, *Hexen und Hexenprozesse*, pp. 148–54, 195–6, 217ff., 249.
[147] Wolfgang Behringer, 'Weather, hunger and fear. The origins of the European witch persecutions in climate, society and mentality', *German History*, 13 (1995), 1–27.
[148] See Tschaikner, *Witches*, pp. 806–7.
[149] Christian Pfister, *Klimageschichte der Schweiz 1525–1860. Das Klima der Schweiz von 1525–1860 und seine Bedeutung in der Geschichte von Bevölkerung und Landwirtschaft* (Bern/Stuttgart, 1988), pp. 116–29.

so-called 'cumulative cold sequences'.[150] However, weather reports, glacial studies and dendro-chronology are not the only aids to our comprehension of witchcraft persecutions: with the help of Moritz John Elsas' price series, we can gauge the effects of climatic conditions on the price of consumables[151] and, as Wilhelm Abel pointed out long ago, their relationship to famine and plague years.[152] The general deterioration of ecological circumstances must have been particularly severe for a society with relatively primitive technology and inadequate social welfare. Time and again, we hear the same arguments from contemporaries given at the start of major persecutions: peasant communities march off to the castle of their feudal overlord, demanding under threat that the vermin be exterminated. Traces of any religious, indeed any counter-reformatory motivation are conspicuously lacking. Efforts were directed against users of weather magic, just as in tales from the early and high middle ages, such as those appearing in the writings of Agobard of Lyon or the annals of the cloister Weihenstephan. The question of why women were held responsible for weather magic in Central Europe is an interesting one, especially from the standpoint of mythology, though not in terms of what William Monter calls a 'romantic approach';[153] instead they offer a task for folklore scholars like Andreas Blauert.[154]

Apart from the specific charge of weather magic, the question of the high proportion of women charged with witchcraft in general needs to be considered in specific contexts. In Germany, like other areas, some 80 per cent of the accused and victims were women, even with regional variations. Only in present-day Austria do we find some regions (Vorarlberg) where women were persecuted exclusively, as well as others where all (Upper Austria) or at least most of the victims (Salzburg, Carinthia) were men.[155] There are also drastic diachronic variations: generally, the widespread cliché of the old crone as a witch persisted only

---

[150] Ibid., p. 150.

[151] Moritz John Elsas, *Umriss einer Geschichte der Preise und Löhne vom ausgehenden Mittelalter bis zum Beginn des 19. Jahrhunderts*, 2 vols. (Leiden, 1936/49).

[152] Wilhelm Abel, *Agrarkrisen und Agrarkonjunkturen in Mitteleuropa vom 13. bis zum 19. Jahrhundert* (Berlin, 1935); Abel, *Massenarmut und Hungerkrisen im vorindustriellen Deutschland* (Göttingen, 1972); A. B. Appleby, 'Epidemics and famine in the Little Ice Age', *Journal of Interdisciplinary History*, 10 (1980), 643–63.

[153] Monter, 'Historiography'.

[154] Monter, 'Historiography'; A. Blauert, 'Hexenverfolgung in einer Spätmittelalterlichen Gemeinde: der Beispiel Kriens/Luzern um 1500', *Geschichte und Gesellschaft*, 16: 1 (1990), 8–25.

[155] Valentinisch, *Hexen und Zauberet*, p. 290.

during the first decades of persecutions. Since persecutions were also much worse during these years, the overall statistics on victims are slanted. In the course of the seventeenth century, the percentage of men and children rose steadily. During the infamous 'Zauberer-Jackl' persecution in the archbishopric of Salzburg around 1680, the vast majority of victims were young men, the 'sorcerer boys'.[156] Furthermore, accusations against women were often raised by other women, not men. This was no clever trick of a society based on a patriarchal ideal, but instead resulted from rigid gender segregation in traditional societies. Private misfortune was often associated with female areas of responsibility, such as the household economy or the health of children. As Heide Wunder, Ingrid Batori and, most recently, Eva Labouvie all point out, people affected by misfortune usually sought the guilty party in the area of responsibility where the misfortune occurred.[157] Additionally, the specifics of female discourse revolved around interpersonal relationships rather than things or objects. This explains why communications among women, so-called gossip, were more explosive and antagonistic than those among men, who engaged in more object-oriented and distanced discourses.[158] Nonetheless, one should consider the question of the *longue durée* of mentalities here as well, because women were held more responsible for public forms of magic than men during the Middle Ages.[159] This is as true of witches as of other charismatic women since the thirteenth century, and one has to consider the related question of gender-specific changes in social structure in late medieval society.[160]

---

[156] Norbert Schindler, 'Die Entstehung der Unbarmherzigkeit. Zur Kultur und Lebensweise der Salzburger Bettler am Ende des 17. Jahrhunderts', *Bayerisches Jahrbuch für Volkskunde* (1988), pp. 61–130; see also his *Widerspenstige Leute. Studien zur Volkskultur in der frühen Neuzeit* (Frankfurt am Main, 1992).

[157] Heide Wunder, 'Hexenprozesse im Herzogtum Preussen während des 16. Jahrhunderts', in Degn, *Hexenprozesse*, pp. 197–203; Wunder, 'Frauen in der Gesellschaft Mitteleuropas im späten Mittelalter und in der Frühen Neuzeit (15.–18. Jahrhundert)', in Valentinitsch, *Hexen und Zauberer*, pp. 123–54; Ingrid Batori, 'Die Rhenser Hexenprozesse der Jahre 1628 bis 1630', *Landeskundliche Vierteljahresblätter*, 33 (1987), pp. 135–55.

[158] Heide Wunder, *'Er ist die Sonn, sie ist der Mond'. Frauen in der Frühen Neuzeit* (Munich, 1992), pp. 199ff.

[159] Edith Ennen, 'Zauberinnen und fromme Frauen – Ketzerinnen und Hexen', in Segl, *Der Hexenhammer*, pp. 7–22.

[160] Susanna Burghartz, 'Hexenverfolgung als Frauenverfolgung? Zur Gleichsetzung von Hexen und Frauen am Beispiel Luzerner und Lausanner Hexenprozesse des 15. und 16. Jahrhunderts', in Lisa Berrisch, et al., eds., *3. Schweizer Historikerinnen-Tagung. Beiträge* (Zürich, 1986), pp. 86–105; Peter Dinzelbacher, *Heilige oder Hexen. Schicksale auffälliger Frauen in Mittelalter und Frühneuzeit* (Zürich, 1995).

VIII

At this point, I wish to break off my attempt to introduce some of the results of witchcraft studies in German-speaking areas into the present discussion. I hope that this presentation has demonstrated how the present state of research in German-speaking regions has changed over the last two decades. The sources are rich and the wealth of materials offers continued opportunities for innovative historical studies in the areas of popular culture, gender and mentalities, as well as for more traditional ones, such as church, social and legal history. Not least of all, there are great possibilities for research in experimental fields of research, such as historical anthropology, epistemology or the history of psychology. Therefore, it seems likely that historical witchcraft studies will expand in the future. And, even if witches never actually did fly to the great diabolical meetings, as attributed to them by contemporaries, it certainly appears likely that modern researchers will continue to do so for some time.[161]

---

[161] For information on the Research Group for Interdisciplinary Witchcraft Studies (AKIH), see footnote 33 or contact Prof. Dr Sönke Lorenz, Historisches Seminar der Universität Tübingen, Wilhelmstr. 36, 72074 Tübingen; or Dieter R. Bauer, Direktor der Katholischen Akademie der Diözese Rottenburg-Stuttgart, Im Schellenkönig 61, 70184 Stuttgart, both in the Federal Republic of Germany.
This chapter was translated by David Lederer.

4. State-building and witch hunting in early modern Europe

BRIAN P. LEVACK

During the last two decades a number of historians have attempted to establish a causal relationship between the great European witch hunt of the sixteenth and seventeenth centuries and the development of the modern state. These scholars have claimed that 'the rise of the nation-state' is at the very least one of the secondary causes of the witch hunt;[1] that the hunt resulted from the centralisation of royal power;[2] that it is one reflection of the advance of public authority against 'particularism';[3] that it is integrally related to the assertion of reason of state;[4] and that it proceeds from an impulse towards both absolutism and state sovereignty.[5] The general impression one gets from this line of argument is that witches were in a certain sense victims of the advance of that emerging leviathan, the centralised, bureaucratised, secularised modern state. The purpose of this chapter is to examine this line of argument and to suggest some limitations to it. It will also test some of these theories about the connection between state-building and witch hunting with reference to one country in which it is alleged that they are especially apparent, the kingdom of Scotland.

The argument consists of four separate but related strands. The first deals with judicial and administrative centralisation, which is incontestably one of the most salient features of state development. Here the

---

[1] Christina Larner, *Enemies of God: The Witch Hunt in Scotland* (London, 1981), p. 193.
[2] Joseph Klaits, *Servants of Satan: The Age of the Witch Hunts* (Bloomington, IN, 1985), pp. 131–47.
[3] Robert Muchembled, 'Satanic myths and cultural reality', in B. Ankarloo and G. Henningsen, eds., *Early Modern European Witchcraft* (Oxford, 1990), p. 139.
[4] Wolfgang Behringer, *Hexenverfolgung in Bayern: Volksmagie, Glaubenseifer und Staatsräson in der Frühen Neuzeit* (Munich, 1987), p. viii.
[5] Hilde de Ridder-Symoens, 'Intellectual and political backgrounds of the witch-craze in Europe', in *La sorcellerie dans les Pays-Bas sous l'ancien régime (anciens pays et assemblées d'états)*, 86 (1987), 37–64.

argument is that the growth of the state involved the advance of central, i.e. royal, jurisdiction, as a result of which areas which had enjoyed a large measure of autonomy, especially those on the geographical periphery of royal domains, came within the ambit of central government control. The ideal after which rulers strove was 'a centralized authority with a perfect bureaucracy, consisting of local official bodies that were merely executive powers'.[6] This attack on localism and particularism, so it is claimed, led to an increase in the prosecution of witches, as the state enforced witchcraft edicts from the central government and instructed local authorities about a crime they were ill prepared to prosecute. No matter where prosecutions occurred, they reflected the inexorable process by which the juggernaut of the state imposed its authority on subordinate units.

The second strand of the argument deals with both the officialisation of judicial power and its enhancement through new methods of repression, especially judicial torture. The rise of large-scale witch hunting was facilitated by the adoption of inquisitorial procedure, according to which governmental officials conducted the entire legal process by themselves and used physical force to compel men suspected of secret crimes to confess. Inquisitorial procedure was improved during the fifteenth and sixteenth centuries, mainly by involving the state more and more in the initiation of cases,[7] and by the seventeenth century it had become one of the main features of the absolutist state.[8] When witches were subjected to this procedure they became entrapped in what is referred to as the state machine, from which, so it is argued, there was little hope of escape. It is interesting to note in this connection that the justification given for the exercise of these new judicial powers was the doctrine of 'reason of state', which itself reflected the 'secular rationality' of the early modern period.[9]

The third strand of the argument deals with the efforts of the state to reform society and transform it into a godly community. This involved the disciplining of the population or the 'acculturation of the rural world' that Robert Muchembled sees as one of the main characteristics of the

---

6 Ibid., p. 43. See also R. Muchembled, *Popular Culture and Elite Culture in France, 1400–1750* (Baton Rouge, 1985), p. 261.

7 Laura I. Stern, 'Inquisition procedure and crime in early fifteenth-century Florence', *Law and History Review*, 8 (1990), 300.

8 R. C. van Caenegem, 'Slotwoord', in *La sorcellerie dans le Pays-Bas sous l'ancien régime*, pp. 206–8 links witch hunting with absolutism in this context.

9 Behringer, *Hexenverfolgung*, p. viii.

absolutist state. This enterprise was undertaken by an entire hierarchy of officials, from the king down to the local judges and parish priests, all of whose authority the state was promoting.[10] The prosecution of witches, according to this thesis, was just one part of this process of acculturation, one in which the state, usually with the assistance of the church, pursued the ultimate objective of destroying superstition, producing a more godly and homogeneous population, and promoting obedience to the 'absolute king and to God'.[11]

The fourth part of the argument concerns the relationship between church and state. One of the main indications of the growing power of the state during the early modern period was that it effectively gained control over, or at least secured the support of, the church. In terms of jurisdiction, this meant either the assumption of control by secular authorities over matters previously entrusted to the church, or the use of ecclesiastical courts to provide effective support for secular tribunals. These changes, which took place throughout Europe in the sixteenth century, greatly facilitated the prosecution of witches. The state, with its almost unlimited judicial resources, was much more capable of conducting these prosecutions than the church had ever been. Even more important was the cooperation that developed between church and state, which was especially apparent in a crime of mixed jurisdiction like witchcraft. As that cooperation became more common, the crime of witchcraft was often viewed as treason against God on the one hand and an act of rebellion against the state on the other.[12] The identification of secular and religious crime was deliberate: the state prosecuted witches, so it is argued, in order to legitimise new regimes through the pursuit of religious deviants.[13]

It is not the purpose of this chapter to challenge all these propositions. There is much of value in the historical work that has just been

---

[10] Muchembled, *Popular Culture*, esp. pp. 224–30.

[11] Ibid., pp. 235–78; R. Muchembled, 'The witches of the Cambrésis: the acculturation of the rural world in the sixteenth and seventeenth centuries', in *Religion and the People, 800–1700*, ed. J. Obelkevich (Durham, NC, 1979). On the concept of acculturation and its applicability to early modern Europe see Peter Burke, 'A question of acculturation?', in *Scienze, credenze, occulte livelli di cultura: convegno internazionale di studi Firenze, 26–30 giugno 1980*, Istituto Nazionale di Studi sul Rinascimento (Florence, 1982), pp. 197–204.

[12] Christina Larner, *Witchcraft and Religion: The Politics of Popular Belief* (Oxford, 1984), p. 128, argues that when Christianity became a political ideology in the sixteenth century, religious crimes like heresy and witchcraft became political crimes.

[13] Larner, *Witchcraft and Religion*, p. 139.

summarised, and historians of witchcraft have used it to deepen our understanding of the phenomenon we are studying. It is, for example, incontestable that the secularisation of witchcraft prosecutions had a dramatic impact on the intensity of prosecutions and the number of executions.[14] It is also incontestable that the use of inquisitorial procedure by temporal authorities facilitated numerous prosecutions that otherwise might have been unsuccessful. There is, however, a danger inherent in this line of thought that we shall view the state, and especially the monarchy and the central authorities that most clearly embodied and represented it,[15] as the dynamic force in witchcraft prosecutions. Nothing could be further from the truth. The active, the dynamic force in most witchcraft prosecutions were local authorities, members of local elites who did whatever they could to gain the sanction of central authorities but who did not serve as their direct agents. The central officers of the state, moreover, did much more to restrain these local authorities than to abet them in their efforts to prosecute witches.[16]

In order to illustrate this point, let us look closely at the Scottish situation. In many ways Scotland serves as the ideal test case for the process we are studying. The witch hunt in that country has been referred to as one of the major witch hunts in Europe, and the intensity of prosecutions was quite high, perhaps twelve times as great as in England, although it did not reach the level of some German states.[17] While by

[14] B. P. Levack, *The Witch-Hunt in Early Modern Europe* (London, 1987), pp. 77–84; Larner, *Enemies of God*, p. 66.
[15] The definition of the state used throughout this chapter is a formal and autonomous political organisation under one sovereign and final authority, the officers of which have the legally sanctioned authority to require obedience from the inhabitants of a large and usually contiguous territory over an extended period of time. The state is not coterminous with the central government. See Michael Braddick, 'State formation and social change in early modern England', *Social History*, 16 (1990), 1–17, esp. 4–5. One of its most salient characteristics, however, is that its officials owe their primary allegiance to a set of political institutions under a sovereign authority and serve as the agents of that authority. See John Brewer, *The Sinews of Power* (Cambridge, MA, 1990), p. 252 n. 1. It is the central authority that gives unity to the state.
[16] For a briefer and more qualified statement of this thesis see Levack, *Witch-Hunt*, pp. 85–90. For a different approach to the same problem which reaches similar conclusions see Alfred Soman, 'Decriminalizing witchcraft: does the French experience furnish a European model?', *Criminal Justice History*, 19 (1989), 1–22. Soman does not study Scotland in his article but cites it as an example of a poorly developed state which consequently had a large number of prosecutions.
[17] Scotland, with a population of less than 1 million people, executed somewhere between 1,000 and 1,500 witches, whereas England, with four times the population executed no more than 1,000 and probably no more than 500. Larner, *Enemies of God*, pp. 63, 65; C. L. Ewen, *Witch Hunting and Witch Trials* (London, 1929), p. 112. A. Macfarlane,

no means one of the most powerful states of Europe, Scotland made sustained efforts throughout the sixteenth and seventeenth centuries to increase the power of the central government, and it is precisely this attempt to strengthen the state that lies at the centre of the argument that has been outlined above. The Scottish parliament proclaimed the imperial status of its monarchy even earlier than did England, and from the fifteenth century onwards its rulers aspired towards absolute power.[18] Scotland also experienced a reception of Roman law and adopted at least some aspects of inquisitorial procedure. Torture was used as part of an effort to repress political dissent and to assist the state in prosecuting crime.

The links between this process of state development and witch hunting appear to be stronger in Scotland than in other European states. The prosecution of witches was secularised in Scotland at a fairly early date, and there was considerable cooperation between church and state in prosecuting the crime. James VI, the king of Scotland during one of the country's most intense periods of witch hunting, not only was a royal absolutist but also wrote a treatise that encouraged the prosecution of witches.[19] There were many efforts made throughout this period to associate witchcraft with political dissent.[20] Finally, and most important, the crime of witchcraft was, according to Christina Larner, centrally managed. It seems therefore that Scottish witchcraft prosecutions can easily be placed within a framework of political development. According to Larner, 'The Scottish witch hunt spanned a period which began with the rise of the doctrine of the divine right of kings and ended with the decline of the doctrine of the godly state.'[21]

Our inquiry must begin with the passage of the Scottish witchcraft statute of 1563, the law upon which all secular prosecutions were based until its repeal in 1736.[22] On the face of it, this, like other European witchcraft statutes, proclamations or edicts, was an attempt by the state to assume control of a crime that was prosecuted, if at all, under the jurisdiction of relatively impotent church courts. But the statute does not

---

Witchcraft in Tudor and Stuart England (London, 1970), p. 62, estimates the number of English executions at 300.

[18] Acts of the Parliaments of Scotland (hereafter APS), II, p. 95.

[19] Stuart Clark, 'King James's Daemonologie: witchcraft and kingship', in S. Anglo, ed., The Damned Art (London, 1977), pp. 156–81.

[20] See, for example, Brian P. Levack, 'The great Scottish witch hunt of 1661–62', Journal of British Studies, n.s. 20 (1980), 107–8.

[21] Larner, Enemies of God, p. 192.

[22] APS, II, p. 539.

represent any such secular initiative. The witchcraft statute was adopted by a parliament that was under considerable pressure from the church to inaugurate a campaign of moral reform and establish a godly discipline.[23] This pressure marked the beginning of a long campaign by the clergy to encourage secular Scottish authorities to prosecute witches.[24] This pattern is worth noting; the history of witchcraft prosecutions in Scotland is much more the story of a reluctant central government responding to pressure from subordinate authorities, in this case the clergy, than the attempt of a developing state to discipline the population.

Far more important than the 1560s, at least for our purposes, are the 1590s, when intense witch hunting began, apparently under the supervision of the central government. Regarding the crisis of 1590–1 and the subsequent orgy of witchcraft prosecutions much has been written, and there is no question that James VI, who became convinced that he, a divine right monarch who was the chief enemy of Satan, was the target of the witches' activities, played a significant role in it.[25] At one point he personally interrogated the North Berwick witches, who together with the earl of Bothwell were believed to have been involved in treason as well as witchcraft. But it would be misleading to see the government as the inspiration of the large rash of witchcraft trials that took place between 1591 and 1597, much less those that occurred after 1597. It is true that between 1591 and 1597 the privy council issued standing commissions to local authorities to seek out and punish witches in their towns and parishes.[26] These commissions, however, represented responses to local pressures for prosecution, not initiatives taken by the king or privy council. Moreover, the government, having responded to

---

[23] J. Gilmore, 'Witchcraft and the Church in Scotland subsequent to the Reformation', Ph.D. thesis, University of Glasgow, 1948, p. 24. Larner, *Enemies of God*, p. 66, shows that the pressure from the Church was not specifically for a witchcraft statute, but that the parliament included one in its legislation. It remains uncertain exactly who was responsible for the passage of a separate witchcraft act.

[24] Two years after the act was passed the General Assembly complained to the queen that a number of horrible crimes, including witchcraft, were not being suppressed. Gilmore, 'Witchcraft and the Church of Scotland', p. 24. The pressure became particularly strong in the 1640s, when covenanters increased their efforts to make Scotland a godly state. See *APS*, V, p. 646.

[25] Clark, 'King James VI's *Daemonologie*'; Larner, *Witchcraft and Religion*, pp. 3–23; Helen Stafford, 'Notes on Scottish witchcraft cases, 1590–91', in *Essays in Honour of Conyers Read* (Chicago, 1953), pp. 96–118.

[26] See, for example, *Register of the Privy Council of Scotland* (hereafter *RPCS*), IV, p. 680; V, pp. 296–7. For the operation of such a commission in Burntisland see *RPCS*, V, p. 405.

the crisis in this way, discovered that the situation had become out of control, and in 1597 the privy council withdrew the standing commissions.[27] In order to prevent such miscarriages of justice from ever occurring again, it insisted that henceforth all witchcraft trials receive authorisation from the privy council or the parliament. It was this decision that made Scottish witchcraft, in Larner's words, a centrally managed crime, and it was this central management that allegedly allowed large witch hunts to develop in Scotland at a later date.[28]

But how much 'management' did the central officers of the Scottish state exercise over witchcraft prosecutions, and what was the effect of that management? Secular witchcraft prosecutions in Scotland took three different forms. The first was a prosecution in the central criminal court, the court of justiciary, a process that was often initiated by the lord advocate before royal judges. The second was in a circuit court, presided over by a judge from the central courts. The third was by a commission of justiciary, a warrant granted by either parliament or privy council that allowed members of local elites, such as elders and magistrates, to prosecute and execute witches. There was much more central management of the crime in the first two situations than the last. Although the government approved all three types of prosecutions, and to that extent exercised some control over the judicial process, it actually *supervised* the process only in the central and the circuit courts, in which officials of the central government conducted, or at the very least presided over, the trials. When commissions of justiciary were granted, however, the government virtually abdicated its control, allowing the local authorities to proceed as they wished, without any guidance or supervision from the state.

This failure of the government effectively to 'manage' prosecutions in the localities assumes enormous significance when we learn that a solid majority of Scottish witchcraft prosecutions originated in parliamentary or conciliar commissions of justiciary, while less than one-third took place in the justiciary court or in the circuit courts.[29] Even more significant are the outcomes of those commissioned trials which, on the basis of admittedly limited evidence, resulted in the astonishingly high

[27] Ibid., 409–10.
[28] Larner, *Enemies of God*, p. 71; *Witchcraft and Religion*, p. 78. Larner argues that the council could serve as a central 'switchboard' for local prosecutions, thereby stimulating national panics. There is no evidence that it ever served such a function.
[29] C. Larner, C. H. Lee and H. V. McLachlan, *Source-Book of Scottish Witchcraft* (Glasgow, 1977), p. 237, Table 2.

conviction rate of 95 per cent. By contrast the conviction rate in the central courts was 57 per cent, while in the circuit courts, which did not function effectively until the late seventeenth century, the conviction rate dropped to an even lower 45 per cent.[30] What these figures suggest is that central authorities tended to exercise a restraining influence over Scottish witchcraft prosecutions while the members of local elites took the lead in demanding and obtaining their prosecution and conviction.

It is important to emphasise that the activities of local elites which are reflected in these statistics are not those of private individuals, much less vigilantes. These men were acting by properly delegated authority, and the fact that they went to great lengths to obtain it, sending an agent to Edinburgh and producing sufficient documentation to the proper authorities, suggests that the rule of law was perhaps more firmly established throughout the kingdom than is usually conceded. What we are witnessing, however, is much more the local elite's use of the judicial authority of the state for its own ends than the central government's imposition of its will on subordinate authorities in the localities. The initiative is coming from the periphery, not the centre. The elders and magistrates who conducted these local trials were acting as the rulers of their towns and villages, not as agents of the central government or as executors of a central governmental policy. The role that central state authorities played in the process was minimal. They ensured that there was a basis for the commission, but did virtually nothing after that. They had neither the money nor the personnel effectively to manage these prosecutions, and it is possible that they did not really care that much about tying local justice more closely to the centre, at least during James VI's reign.[31] Nor did central state authorities do anything to facilitate the spread of witch hunts from one area to another, even though they had a mechanism for achieving that effect.

Once we recognise the essentially local dynamic of Scottish witchcraft

---

[30] Ibid. In each calculation I have considered only those cases whose outcomes are known. I have also excluded those cases classified as 'miscellaneous', since they were never fully tried, the accused having escaped from jail. The conviction rate for the circuit courts is especially low, since those courts heard cases only very late in this period, by which time the hunt was declining. The statistics for the trials authorised by commission receive confirmation from Sir George Mackenzie, who claimed that 'scarce ever any who were accused before a Country Assize of Neighbours did escape that trial'. *The Laws and Customs of Scotland in Matters Criminal* (Edinburgh, 1678), p. 88.

[31] Jenny Wormald, 'Static periphery, shifting center: royal power in Scotland in the reign of James VI and I', forthcoming.

prosecutions, the role of the central government as a moderating influence, sometimes even as a sceptical influence, on the prosecution of witches becomes clearer. It was the central government, for example, that resisted the demands of the local presbyteries to issue standing commissions again during the 1640s, a time when witch hunting became more intense than it had ever been before.[32] It was the central government that exposed the famous prickers, John Kincaid and John Dick, as frauds in 1662.[33] And it was central justices like Sir George Mackenzie who were most responsible for the decline in Scottish witchcraft prosecutions in the late seventeenth century.

But what about the procedures that were used to try those witches who were successfully prosecuted? Part of the argument that links witch-hunting to the growth of state power is the employment of inquisitorial procedure and the use of torture in the prosecution of witches. Both of these developments mark the officialisation and bureaucratisation of the judicial power as well as the replacement of private by public authority. With inquisitorial procedure the state assumes control over, if it does not also initiate, prosecutions, and through methods like torture it acquires the information that it needs successfully to prosecute dissenters and other enemies of the government. In many ways the advent of inquisitorial procedure is the quintessential expression of the new power of the state.

Now it is important to recognise that Scottish criminal procedure was only partially inquisitorial. Scotland never did away with the petty trial jury, for example, an institution that vanished in those countries where the state gained full control of the judicial process. Nevertheless, Scottish courts did employ many features of continental criminal procedure, such as the initiation of cases by information and the creation of a legal dossier, and therefore it is worthwhile to inquire whether those features of Scottish justice contributed to the intensification of witch hunting.[34] A strong case can be made for the fact that they did not.

---

[32] *Acts of the General Assembly of the Kirk of Scotland* (Edinburgh, 1845), p. 27; *APS*, VI, pt. 1, p. 197.

[33] *RPCS*, 3rd ser., I, pp. 187, 210.

[34] On Scottish criminal procedure see generally J. I. Smith, 'Criminal procedure', in *An Introduction to Scottish Criminal Procedure* (Edinburgh, Stair Society, 1958), pp. 426–48. Scotland did not have a presenting jury. Although it did have a mechanism whereby prominent individuals from a locality could present criminals to the justice clerk, the system did not always work effectively. Even when it did, all Scottish criminal judges retained the right to charge criminals on the basis of information they had obtained themselves. Regarding the trial itself, Smith claims that 'the tribunals

The main consideration here is that anything resembling inquisitorial procedure was utilised only in the court of justiciary and on circuit, where trained judges could oversee the judicial process, and it was precisely in these tribunals that witch hunting was greatly restrained. The lord advocate, to be sure, did initiate cases that might not have otherwise reached the courtroom. But once the case began, the officialisation of the Scottish criminal process worked to the advantage of the witch, resulting in a surprisingly high percentage of acquittals, almost as high as in England. One reason for this was the fact that in these central trials the witch was often granted a defence counsel, a luxury denied to her southern English neighbour.

The relative moderation of central Scottish witchcraft trials can also be explained by the infrequency of the administration of judicial torture. Here we come to one of the great misconceptions in the history of Scottish witchcraft, one which also helps to explain the severity of local prosecutions. Contrary to widely held assumptions, Scottish courts did not have authority to use torture as an ordinary instrument of criminal prosecution. The Scottish law of torture was in fact almost the same as its English counterpart. Torture could be administered only by a warrant from the privy council or parliament and only when the members of those bodies considered information from the accused to be vital to the state. For this reason, the great majority of English and Scottish torture warrants dealt with crimes of a political nature: treason, rebellion, sedition, attacks on prominent statesmen and religious subversion.[35]

Considering the large amount of information we have regarding the use of torture in Scottish witchcraft cases, one would expect to find a large number of warrants dealing with that crime. This is not the case. Between 1590 and 1689 the Scottish privy council issued only two warrants to torture suspected witches: the famous trials of 1591 in which

were concerned with ascertaining the facts, not providing rules whereby two sides might, more or less decorously, sublimate a trial by combat and words'. *Selected Justiciary Cases*, II (Edinburgh, Stair Society, 1972), p. x.

[35] The English torture warrants for the period 1540–1640, which number eighty-one, are listed in John Langbein, *Torture and the Law of Proof* (Chicago, 1976), pp. 94–123. A total of thirty-four Scottish warrants for the years 1590–1689 appear in *RPCS*. An additional five warrants were granted by parliament. See *APS*, IV, p. 108; V, pp. 396, 706; VI, pt. 11, p. 390 ('any uther forme of probatioun'); IX, pp. 30b, 102a, 191b. Mackenzie was correct therefore when he claimed that torture was 'seldom used' in Scotland. See *Laws and Customs of Scotland*, p. 543. In general see R. D. Melville, 'The use and form of judicial torture in Scotland', *Scottish Historical Review*, 2 (1905), 225–48.

James VI was the intended victim, and the trial of six men for murder by poison, witchcraft or some other 'develische' practice in 1610.[36]

If the official authorisation of torture in Scottish witchcraft cases occurred so infrequently, how then do we account for its reported use in numerous other witchcraft prosecutions? How, for example, do we account for the report published in England in 1652 that six Scottish witches had been whipped and their feet and heads burned by lighted candles while hanging by their thumbs with their hands tied behind their backs?[37] The answer is that local magistrates were using torture illegally, a practice that central Scottish authorities only periodically tried to curb.[38] In the case just cited, officials of the kirk were accused of having applied the torture before referring the case to the civil magistrate. In fact, almost all the evidence we have regarding the use of torture in Scottish witchcraft cases indicates that local magistrates or clergy, not central judges or councillors, were administering it without warrant, usually during the interrogations that took place shortly after apprehension.[39] Even the well-known torture of Alison Balfour, who was tried before the court of justiciary in 1594 after having been kept in the caspieclaw for forty-eight hours, appears to have been conducted by local authorities without warrant.[40]

In many instances the torture took the form of pricking the witch with

---

[36] *RPCS*, IV, p. 680; IX, p. 83. In one sense the warrant of 1591 authorised an 'indiscriminate witch-hunt', as Larner has argued, since the commissioners were given the power to examine and torture 'all and sindrie persons' who had been, or would be, accused. The warrant did not, however, authorise indiscriminate witch hunting in the localities. It did not delegate the authority to torture to any other individuals besides the six commissioners, and it specifically reserved to the Council the decision whether to put the interrogated suspects to the knowledge of an assize. In Scots law, the word 'assize' denotes a jury, not a local circuit court. The document did not authorise the commissioners to 'send them for trial at a local assize'. Larner, *Enemies of God*, p. 70.

[37] *Two Terrible Sea-Fights . . . likewise The Tryal of six Witches at Edenbourgh* (London, 1652), p. 4.

[38] The clearest examples of attempts to prohibit judicial torture appear in *APS*, VI, pt. ii, p. 538 and *RPCS*, 3rd ser., I, 188–9. For other conciliar action against the unauthorised use of torture see *RPCS*, III, pp. 40–1; IV, pp. 290–1.

[39] See for example the report of locally administered torture in 1652 in B. Whitelocke, *Memorials of the English Affairs* (London, 1652), p. 522. One of the main reasons for the use of torture at the local level is that the Council required a confession before granting an *ad hoc* commission to try the suspect. See Mackenzie, *Laws and Customes*, p. 88.

[40] The case is known only through the use of testimony from it in the justiciary court two years later. R. Pitcairn, *Ancient Criminal Trials in Scotland* (Edinburgh, 1829–33), III, pp. 374–7. For the illegal torture of the witches of Pittenweem in 1704 see Folger Shakespeare Library, MX x.d. 436 (58), letter of Mr Miller, 19 Nov. 1704.

a needle or 'the boodles' in order to discover the Devil's Mark, which according to demonological theory was insensitive to pain and could not bleed. This task, which was often entrusted to a professional pricker and which was technically legal, could easily develop into a form of torture, in which a suspect could be pricked repeatedly until she confessed. It appears that many of the confessions elicited during the great Scottish witch hunts of 1649 and 1661–2 were the result of torture administered under this pretext.[41]

It appears therefore that the growth of state power and the official-isation of the judicial process did very little to intensify witchcraft prosecutions in Scotland. Indeed, it was the *failure* of the state to control local authorities and to supervise local justice, that led to the great prosecutions of the seventeenth century. These local authorities figured how to use the power of the state to their advantage, mainly by obtaining commissions that entitled them to proceed. Once they started that procedure, however, they virtually ignored the rules regulating the administration of justice that the state had established, and illegally used one of the most terrifying instruments of state power, judicial torture, to secure convictions. No wonder that Sir George Mackenzie, one of the most ardent royal absolutists in Scottish history, a lawyer who struggled for the elimination of juries and the implementation of a fully inquisi-torial system of criminal procedure, should have deplored the actions of these ignorant 'country men' in the provinces.[42] It is also important to note that Mackenzie, who had participated in some of the witch trials of 1661 in Midlothian on special assignment by parliament, distinguished himself as the greatest critic of witchcraft prosecutions in his country, one whose brilliant defence of the witch Maevia has a prominent place among his published pleadings.[43]

The attitude of Mackenzie also suggests two other conclusions. The first, certainly not new among witchcraft historians, is that scepticism developed more quickly at the centre, especially among members of the ruling elite, than in the localities. That argument can even be extended to James VI, whose scepticism, which allegedly originated in England, can

---

[41] W. Stephen, *The History of Inverkeithing and Rosyth* (Aberdeen, 1921); William Ross, *Aberdour and Inchcolme* (Edinburgh, 1885), p. 331; *RPCS*, 3rd ser. VI, p. 13. In 1662 the privy council took action to stop the pricking, torture and abuse of accused witches. Ibid., 3rd ser. VI, p. 198.

[42] Mackenzie, *Laws and Customes*, pp. 88–90.

[43] Sir George Mackenzie, *Pleadings in Some Remarkable Cases* (Edinburgh, 1673), pp. 185–97.

actually be backdated to his days in Scotland.[44] Whether the scepticism of central authorities can be explained by their uninvolvement in the hysteria that often surrounded local witch hunts or by their commitment to high standards of judicial impartiality is uncertain, but the pattern is clear. The second conclusion is that the process of decriminalising witchcraft, in which Mackenzie took an active part, always began in the centre, not on the periphery.

Leaving Scotland for the moment, let us ask whether we can extend this argument regarding state power to other European countries. It would seem that England, the country with which Scotland in most frequently compared, would completely destroy the argument and provide strong negative support for those who see links between absolutism and state power on the one hand and intense witch hunting on the other. The low number of witchcraft convictions in England is widely known, and it is tempting to attribute this, at least in part, to the country's low level of 'stateness'.[45] It should stand to reason that a country with such limited central power, the great hold-out against the inexorable tide of absolutism in Europe, the home of the common law which had resisted the officialisation of the judicial process and prohibited the use of torture, should have had a relatively mild and short-lived witch hunt. The problem here is that we tend to confuse what Michael Mann has referred to as despotic and infrastructural state power.[46] England may have resisted the impulse towards absolutism, and its central government may have been both small and constitutionally restricted, but its judicial system was highly centralised, and the central government was able to run the country quite effectively. Indeed, if we measure stateness by the *effective* judicial power of the central government, England, a country with a common law and a national circuit court system, was one of the most powerful states in Europe. There is no better illustration of the effects of this strength than in the prosecution of witches, which was undertaken locally and without central governmental initiation but which was supervised quite closely and effectively by central judges at the semi-annual assizes. It was this supervision, which was almost absent in local Scottish trials until the late seventeenth century, which ensured that

---

[44] Clark, 'King James's *Daemonologie*', pp. 161–4. See also H. N. Paul, *The Royal Play of Macbeth* (New York, 1950), pp. 90–130.

[45] Kenneth F. Dyson, *The State Tradition in Western Europe* (Oxford, 1980), pp. 36–44 for the argument that England is a 'stateless society'.

[46] Michael Mann, 'The autonomous power of the state: its origins, mechanisms and results', in John A. Hall, ed., *States in History* (Oxford, 1986), p. 114.

the English prohibition of judicial torture would be enforced and the rules of evidence applied. The process did not, of course, prevent convictions and executions, especially when a witch-hanging judge like Sir Edmund Anderson was presiding, or when the judge failed to instruct the jury properly, as in Exeter in 1682.[47] But the overall effect of central supervision on the intensity of prosecutions and the rate of convictions and executions was negative.[48]

The importance of central supervision in English witchcraft prosecutions can be illustrated by the effects of its failure in the 1640s, when England experienced the largest witch-hunt in its history. Between 1645 and 1647 the self-defined witch-finders Matthew Hopkins and John Stearne, acting with considerable support and encouragement from towns and villages in the southeastern part of the country, discovered and assisted in the prosecution of large numbers of witches. In their work of detection they used procedures of highly questionable legality, including the torture of forced sleeplessness. Under normal circumstances the justices of the assize would have prevented the use of such evidence at the trials. At the Essex assizes in the summer of 1645, however, where most of the early convictions in this witch hunt took place, the circuit judges from Westminster were not in attendance. Instead, the court was convened under the presidency of the earl of Warwick, a legally untrained nobleman who represented military authority.[49] Without the participation of judges from the central court, the justices of the peace who prosecuted the cases were given much more latitude in the use of evidence than they would have otherwise received.

A second illustration of the absence of central judicial supervision comes from the English colonies in North America, where there was no circuit court system and where men without legal training served as judges. The danger inherent in such an arrangement became evident in

---

[47] On Anderson see Michael MacDonald, *Witchcraft and Hysteria in Elizabethan London* (London, 1990), pp. xvi–xix. On the prosecutions at Exeter and the failure of Sir Thomas Raymond to instruct the jury regarding the use of confessions as evidence see Roger North, *The Lives of the Rt. Hon. Francis North; the Hon. Sir Dudley North; and the Hon. and Rev. Dr. John North*, ed. A. Jessop, 3 vols. (London, 1890), pp. 9, 167–8; *A True and Impartial Relation of the Informations against Three Witches* (London, 1682).

[48] For the negative effect of Sir John Holt on prosecutions see Wallace Notestein, *A History of Witchcraft in England* (Washington, DC, 1912), pp. 320–1. For the action of the judge in the trial of the women accused of causing the possession of Edward Fairfax's children in 1622 see Edward Fairfax, *Daemonologia: A Discourse on Witchcraft*, ed. W. Grainge (1882), pp. 126–7.

[49] Keith Thomas, *Religion and the Decline of Magic* (London, 1971), p. 458.

Massachusetts in 1692, when 156 persons, most of them from Salem Village and Andover, were charged with witchcraft, a relatively large witch-hunt that led to 19 executions. The judges who presided over these trials failed to enforce the fairly strict standards of judicial proof that had been applied both in English witchcraft trials and in those held in New England prior to the Salem episode.[50] They also tolerated the use of both physical and psychological pressures in order to obtain confessions, thereby violating one of the most important procedural safeguards in Anglo-American criminal law.[51] It is interesting to note that these legally untrained men all came from the general vicinity where the accusations originated and were affected, therefore, by the highly charged emotional atmosphere that developed during the early stages of the hunt. Thus the Salem judges had more in common with the elders and lairds who served as local commissioners of justiciary in Scotland than with the central judges who went on circuit in England.

A final illustration of the role of central authorities in English witch-craft prosecutions comes from the one court in which the state could proceed by information, the central court of Star Chamber. In that conciliar court we find the government using its special judicial powers not to prosecute witches but to take action against their accusers. Indeed, the first trial in England in which the state actively prosecuted the accusers of witches for fraud was the Star Chamber case of Anne and Brian Gunter in 1606–7, an action initiated by the attorney general, Sir Edward Coke. The action followed the acquittal of two women at the Berkshire assizes in 1605 for having allegedly caused the demonic affliction of Anne, a teenage girl.[52]

Crossing the channel to France, we find ourselves in a very different political environment, as both contemporaries like Sir John Fortescue and subsequent historians have never failed to point out. Here it seems we might expect to find the strongest support for the 'state thesis', if we may call it that. In France the prosecution of witches has been associated

---

[50] On the problem of proof in New England see Richard Weisman, *Witchcraft, Magic and Religion in 17th-Century Massachusetts* (Amherst, MA, 1984), chs. 7–10. The main decision of the judges was to accept spectral evidence. The judges also disregarded the two-witness rule, which was part of New England criminal procedure.

[51] Richard Godbeer, *The Devil's Dominion* (Cambridge, 1992), pp. 206–10.

[52] The interrogatories and depositions are available in PRO, STAC 8/4/10, a volume of more than 200 folios. There are additional depositions in the Ellesmere Papers at the Huntington Library, Ellesmere MS 5955/2. L'Estrange Ewen gives a summary of the case in *Witchcraft in the Star Chamber* (London, 1938), pp. 28–36.

not only with 'centralising absolutism' and an attack on particularism but with the efforts of the state to discipline the population. Robert Muchembled has seen witch hunting as part of a larger attack on popular culture that was conducted by agents of state and church and was inspired by both the Counter-Reformation and a programme of royal absolutism. Now if we consider the 'state' to comprise all 'natural rulers' from the king down through the hierarchy of provincial and local officials to parish priests and fathers within families, as Muchembled does, and if we consider absolutism to have entailed an assertion of power by all these authorities, then it is hard to deny that witchcraft prosecutions, which usually involved the exercise of power by elites over their inferiors, were the result of the rise of the absolutist state.[53] The difficulty arises only when we attribute the inspiration of these witchcraft prosecutions to those royal officials who stood at the top of this hierarchy and when we see these trials as part of a policy of centralisation. It is true that most of those prosecutions took place in the peripheral regions of the kingdom, outside 'royal' France, but it is difficult to see this as part of an effort to destroy particularism. Indeed, the main reason why prosecutions flourished in these outlying regions was the failure of the government to supervise the judicial process. Local elites in these areas, to be sure, did everything they could to use state power to their advantage, just as they did in Scotland, but they did not prosecute witches as part of some centrally managed or centrally inspired campaign.[54]

Further evidence for the negative role of the French absolutist state in witchcraft prosecutions comes from the work of Alfred Soman on the decriminalisation of witchcraft in those areas which came under the jurisdiction of the *parlement* of Paris. According to Soman, the source of the *parlement*'s policy of obligatory judicial review of all witchcraft convictions, which was proposed in 1588, enacted in 1604 and reenacted in 1624, was a local panic in the Champagne-Ardennes region in 1587–8. In this episode, which was not unlike the Scottish panic of 1591–7, local officials were swimming suspected witches, using the courts to settle personal disputes, and executing suspects in summary fashion, some- times by lynching. The process of establishing control over these local panics was a delicate one, but it eventually succeeded. Part of this

---

[53] Muchembled, *Popular Culture*, passim.
[54] In *Les derniers Bûchers: un village de Flandre et ses sorcières sous Louis XIV* (Paris, 1981), Muchembled modifies his previous emphasis on external forces by revealing the importance of local initiatives and the autonomy of the village authorities.

process, it should be noted, was the effort of the *parlement* to restrict the administration of torture to itself, just as the Scottish privy council had tried to do.[55]

The important consideration for our purposes, however, is the fact that the process of state-building, the process of controlling the periphery, indeed the process of establishing anything more than the most tenuous links between the centre and the periphery, had nothing to do with the encouragement of prosecutions and everything to do with its restraint. The effect of judicial centralisation in France was that the higher courts could monitor the actions of local judges, as they did frequently between 1580 and 1650, and even bring criminal charges against those who used abusive procedures in trying witches.[56] It has been argued that one of the reasons for the high incidence of witchcraft prosecutions in the outlying regions of France was precisely the fact that they did *not* fit into the centralised judicial system of the absolute state and therefore did not have an automatic review or appeals process.[57]

When we turn our attention to Germany, we find ourselves in a somewhat different political world. Here we have difficulty identifying the central state authorities. Should they be the officials of the large and amorphous empire or those of the 350 smaller political units that it comprised? If we decide upon the former, the main argument of this chapter finds strong, albeit negative, support. Even though the famous imperial law code of 1532, the Carolina, included a provision for prosecuting witches, imperial authorities did not actively pursue witches or encourage subordinate officials to do so. Even if they had, their task would have been difficult since imperial power was exceptionally weak. That of course is the reason why the smaller political units within the empire were able to prosecute witches with such freedom. However much the emperor might have wished to emulate the national states of Europe in restraining witchcraft prosecutions, he had virtually no jurisdictional weapons with which to act. He had no intendants, no viceroys, no circuit judges. He had a central imperial court, the *Reichskammergericht*, but no method of making appeals to it mandatory. In fact the only provision that imperial authorities could make for local

---

[55] Soman, 'Decriminalizing witchcraft', p. 6.

[56] Briggs, *Communities of Belief*, pp. 45–6.

[57] Ibid., pp. 13–14. Briggs argues that witches were worse off in these outlying regions because 'the local community found it easier to use the legal system for its own purposes, and it is to those communities that we should look for the driving force behind the persecution'.

witchcraft trials was the requirement that law professors from nearby universities provide instruction in a crime about which those local authorities knew little. This provision, of course, had a devastating effect on witchcraft prosecutions, since it was these very jurists who provided local magistrates with demonological theories as well as a certain amount of procedural training.[58]

As we turn from Germany to Spain, the terms of the argument change once again, since many witchcraft cases were heard before the tribunals of the inquisition, which was of course an ecclesiastical institution. It was, however, also a royal institution, under the control of the king, and therefore can legitimately be considered as part of the state apparatus. Indeed, the inquisition has been referred to as 'an instrument of royal policy, an agent of centralisation', and a defence against the 'centrifugal forces' in Spanish politics.[59] The extent to which the inquisition served to restrain the process of witch hunting, mainly by controlling the various tribunals through the central supreme council in Madrid, helps to illustrate how little witch hunting can be considered the result of centralisation or, more generally, the process of state-building.[60] Further support for this thesis comes from the evidence we have of intense witch hunting in the local municipalities, such as in the towns of Catalonia in 1618, which were sometimes able to evade strict control from the centre.[61]

Witch hunting in Italy, where most historians contend that the development of the modern state began, had much in common with the prosecutions that took place in Spain. In Italy, as in Spain, most witchcraft prosecutions came under the control of the inquisition, and as in Spain the judicial record is one of almost astonishing restraint. The main point to be made here is that it was in the courts of the Roman inquisition that inquisitorial procedure was perfected, and where the interest of the state in prosecutions was most boldly asserted. Yet that highly developed procedure, as John Tedeschi has shown, worked

---

[58] On this practice see Gerhard Schormann, *Hexenprozesse in Nordwestdeutschland* (Hildesheim, 1977), pp. 158–9.

[59] Bartolomé Bennassar, ed., *L'Inquisition espagnole (XVe–XIXe siècle)* (Paris, 1979), pp. 50–1.

[60] E. W. Monter, *Frontiers of Heresy* (Cambridge, 1990), p. 69, for the tightening of controls over the local inquisitors, who in the earlier period were 'virtually a law unto themselves'.

[61] Ibid., p. 274. See also Antoni Pladevall i Font, *Persecutió de bruixes a les comarques de Vic a principio del segle XVII* (Barcelona, 1974).

constantly in favour of the accused witch, certainly as much as the highly touted common law procedure that prevailed in England.[62]

The final country in this survey, Denmark, is especially relevant to our concerns, since that kingdom, like Scotland, had a monarch who developed a personal commitment to witch hunting. Christian IV (1588–1648), duly alarmed by a witch hunt that took the lives of eleven women in Køge in 1612, apparently was instrumental in the promulgation of the famous ordinance of 1617, which defined the crime of witchcraft for the first time and reserved the penalty of burning only to those who had made pacts with the devil. Since prosecutions increased dramatically after 1617, it is tempting to see them as the result of actions taken at the centre, especially since accompanying legislation against adultery and fornication suggests a broader policy of state-sponsored discipline.[63] Once again, however, appearances are deceptive. Whatever the role of King Christian in these trials – and it has not been established that there was any at all – his government can certainly not be assigned responsibility for the hunt that occurred. Quite to the contrary, the impulse to witch-hunting came from below, from the district courts, whereas the role of the central government was to ensure the adherence to established procedures, and to guarantee that all convictions from the lower courts be appealed to the county courts and, if necessary, to the supreme court. It is instructive to note that just under 90 per cent of the cases heard at the district level, where trials were held by juries that knew the accused, resulted in convictions, whereas the proportion at the royal county courts was approximately 50 per cent.[64] These percentages, it should be recalled, come remarkably close to those in Scotland, and in both cases the local courts proceeded by jury trial, whereas in the higher courts inquisitorial procedure prevailed.

Some of the conclusions that emerge from this study of witch hunting may not be all that startling. It has long been recognised that local courts pursued witches more aggressively than central courts; that many witch-craft convictions were reversed on appeal; that scepticism appeared first in the central courts. What is not often recognised, however, is the role that state-builders played in this whole process. However much they may

---

[62] John Tedeschi, 'Inquisitorial law and the witch', in *Early Modern European Witchcraft*, pp. 83–118.

[63] J. C. V. Johansen, 'Denmark: the sociology of accusations', in *Early Modern European Witchcraft*, pp. 345–6. Soman, 'Decriminalizing witchcraft', p. 17, sees Denmark and the Netherlands as the exceptions to the European pattern.

[64] Johansen, 'Denmark', pp. 349–50.

have wished for a more homogeneous population, however much they may have desired to discipline the lower classes and help the church wipe out superstition, they also were firm advocates of what has come to be called the rule of law, and that often meant adherence to strict legal procedure. These two goals, of social control and judicial restraint, came in conflict with each other, especially in cases of witchcraft, and the state found itself regulating over-zealous local authorities who exceeded the bounds of royal justice. If we wish to speak about reason of state and absolutism in connection with witch hunting, we should look less at the celebrated introduction of state-sponsored prosecutions and the application of judicial torture, and much more at the central regulation of local justice.

Page 116 blank

Part 2

Witchcraft and religion

5. *The devil's encounter with America*

FERNANDO CERVANTES

When future historians look back on witchcraft historiography as it has developed in recent decades it is likely that they will place it in the context of a reaction against the parochial tendencies of nineteenth-century positivism. This will look in vain for such misdescriptions of cultures and ages as can be detected in writers like Frazer and Tylor, or Lecky and Dickson White. They will find almost no attempts to analyse human society in terms of an opposition between reason and irrationality. And if they place the two historiographies in a comparative context they will no doubt find late-twentieth century scholarship, unlike that of the nineteenth century, conspicuous for its lack of self-confidence.

Some might place this apparent timidity in the context of a growing realisation that any distinction between 'reason' and 'superstition', however unavoidable it may seem, is riddled with difficulties, and they will thus value the shift from strictly intellectual explanations of witchcraft to the more helpful attempts to explain the phenomenon as the outcome of specific social strains and conflicts.

There can be no question that this shift has been a welcome development; but it cannot be denied that it has also led to a neglect of the more intellectual aspects of the problem. To suggest that there is now a need to redress this imbalance is not to advocate a return to the concepts of the late Victorian age but, as Alasdair MacIntyre has put it, to prevent 'the perception of those concepts as culture-bound' from leading 'to a blindness to the importance of ascriptions of rationality and irrationality in the human sciences'.[1]

One area in witchcraft studies where this danger is particularly clear is the one concerning the concept of the devil. Central as he was to the

---

[1] Alasdair MacIntyre, 'Rationality and the explanation of action', in *Against the Self-Images of the Age*, 2nd edn (London, 1983), p. 244.

whole phenomenon of witch prosecutions, the devil is nevertheless commonly portrayed in very stereotypical terms. Seen as God's grand cosmic antagonist, his historical development is often presented as the result of the efforts of generations of medieval theologians to develop an elaborate demonology which then filtered down to ordinary people in a cruder form.[2] Yet the picture cannot be so simple: the development of medieval demonology was by no means a progressive or a cumulative process; there existed different, often actually incompatible, theological traditions in the middle ages, some of which could not logically have led to the demonological developments that came to characterise the sixteenth and seventeenth centuries. If this is so, it seems important to identify those medieval theological traditions that prepared the background to the witch-hunts as well as the circumstances that allowed them to carry the day in the early modern period.

In this chapter I propose to focus on the role of the devil in the process of conversion in sixteenth-century Mexico. I see this process as especially relevant for my purpose not only because some of the best missionary minds of the time were active participants in it, but also because its concurrence with the threshold of early modern demonology allows an analysis of at least two conflicting theological traditions at work.

I

The discovery and colonisation of America has been the subject of endless controversy. From the earliest days, the theme of the primeval innocence and nobility of the American Indians ran parallel to the no less arresting insistence on their bestiality and the demonic character of their cultures and religions. Where Columbus and Vespucci pointed to the abundance and fertility of the New World and humanists like Peter Martyr contrasted the simplicity of the natives with the 'barbarism' of their European invaders, others, like Dr Chanca, had no qualms about writing of their 'bestiality . . . which seems to me greater than that of any beast in the world', or about the unlikelihood – in the words of Francisco

---

[2] See, for instance, Keith Thomas, *Religion and the Decline of Magic* (Harmondsworth, 1978 edn), pp. 559–60; and, more typically, Carlo Ginzburg, *I Benandanti: Stregoneria e culti agrari tra Cinquecento e Seicento* (Turin, 1966), English transl., *The Night Battles. Witchcraft and Agrarian Cults in the Sixteenth and Seventeenth Centuries* (London, 1983), passim.

de Aguilar – of the existence of 'another kingdom in the world where the devil was honoured with such reverence'.[3]

Implicit in these conflicting claims was the irksome issue of legitimation. The Castilian crown's principal claim to dominion in America rested on the bulls of donation made by Pope Alexander VI in 1493. These bulls were grounded on the papal assumption of 'plenitude of power', meaning temporal authority over both Christians and pagans, an assumption that has no basis in natural law and about which the lawyers and the theologians were known to be uneasy. Once the Caesaro–papal claims of the bulls were questioned, therefore, the Castilian crown was deprived of any rights and was left only with the duty to evangelise.[4]

It is in this insecure climate that the figure of the devil made its debut in America. If evangelisation was the only means to legitimise the European invasion, it followed that the more the natives were perceived to be under the power of Satan, the more urgent the European presence became. It is no accident that the bulk of the sermons, both lay and ecclesiastic, that were preached to the natives in these early years sought to provide syntheses of Christian doctrine centred on the themes of liberation from sin and from the power of the devil, where the Spanish appeared as bearers of the Gospel's message, sent 'to give Light to those in Darkness, those who dwell in the shadow of Death'.[5]

It would, of course, be presumptuous to reduce the figure of the devil to a mere instrument of political expediency and to ignore the genuine belief of most contemporaries in the reality of diabolism. But there is the opposite danger of giving the subject too much importance too early, and to place the devil of the discoverers in the context of the developments that would subsequently lead to European witch hunts.

The figure of the devil we are concerned with here should be set in the context of a pervasive optimism. As Inga Clendinnen has written, the early discoverers

---

[3] *Select Documents illustrating the Four Voyages of Columbus*, ed., Cecil Jane (London, 1930), I, p. 71; Francisco de Aguilar, *Relación breve de la conquista de Nueva España*, ed., F. Gómez de Orozco (Mexico City, 1954), p. 163. On humanist writers see J. H. Elliott, *The Old World and the New* (Cambridge, 1970), pp. 1–27.

[4] Anthony Pagden, *Spanish Imperialism and the Political Imagination* (New Haven and London, 1990), p. 14.

[5] Joaquín Antonio Peñalosa, *El Diablo en México* (Mexico City, 1970), p. 15. See especially the accounts of Bernal Díaz del Castillo (*Historia verdadera de la conquista de Nueva España*) and Hernán Cortés (*Cartas de Relación*). The Gospel passage is from Luke 1: 79.

were not vexed by Indian perfidy, nor deeply perturbed by grotesque idols, nor even by the possibility, suggested by some strange sculpted figures, that these people lacked a proper abhorrence of sodomy. For in those places they also found gold; and with gold, much more than a mere means to personal material advancement, they could transform the world . . . [6]

The famous assertion of Bernal Díaz that the Spaniards had gone to the New World 'to serve God and the King, and also to get rich' has, in the words of John Elliott, a 'disarming frankness'[7] that is difficult for us to appreciate. It is part of a wider vision where the world, although still the battleground of the conflict of good and evil, of the armies of God with his angels and his saints against Satan and his armies of demons, had nonetheless been redeemed. If the battle was extended in history, on the plane of eternity it had been won inexorably by the death and resurrection of Christ. No matter how formidable he might appear, the devil had no chance against the inevitable advance of the Christian church.

Such optimism was well illustrated in the conquest of Mexico, and particularly in Hernán Cortés' attitude towards the religious practices of the natives. In his second letter to the emperor, Charles V, Cortés gives a surprisingly level-headed account of the religious practices of the Mexicans, recounting how he made it clear to Moctezuma and his companions that their man-made idols were not worthy of the worship due to the one true God. 'And everyone', he wrote

especially the said Moctezuma, replied that . . . owing to the very long time that had passed since the arrival of their ancestors to these lands, it was perfectly possible that they could be mistaken in their beliefs . . . and that I, as a recent arrival, should know better the things that they should hold and believe.[8]

The significance of this passage lies in Cortés' firm conviction that the Indians were normal human beings, whose level of civilisation was 'almost the same as the Spanish',[9] and whose 'errors', far from being the result of direct demonic intervention, were more due to human weakness and thus susceptible to instruction and correction. Accordingly, whenever Cortés ordered the destruction of Indian 'idols' he invariably

---

[6] Inga Clendinnen, *Ambivalent Conquests. Maya and Spaniard in Yucatán (1517–1570)* (Cambridge, 1987), pp. 13–14.

[7] J. H. Elliott, *Imperial Spain* (Harmondsworth, 1970), p. 65.

[8] Hernán Cortés, *Cartas de Relación*, 10th edn (Mexico City, 1978), p. 65.

[9] Cortés, *Cartas*, p. 66.

replaced them with crosses and images of the Virgin Mary, often entrusting the very same Indians that had been responsible for the care and propitiation of the defeated idols with the care of the new Christian images.[10] Such initiatives reflect Cortés' hope that as soon as the Christian message was preached to the Indians they would readily accept the errors of their ways and set their house in order. Implicit in this was Cortés' belief in the intrinsic goodness of human nature, a belief that seemed to echo Aquinas' dictum that grace does not destroy nature but perfects it.

On a different level, Cortés' attitude reveals symptoms of a peculiar millenarianism that would soon come to inspire the Franciscan missions. In the 1520s the conversion of the Indians of central Mexico seemed imbued with an enthusiasm immersed in ritual euphoria. The way in which thousands of Indians flocked to hear the Christian message and submitted readily to baptism served to confirm the missionaries' belief that the millennium and the ultimate defeat of the devil were close at hand. It was in this spirit that most chronicles and early Franciscan plays were written, relating countless instances where the Indian leaders recognised the Spaniards as the 'children of the Sun' and acknowledged that they had been under Satan's rule. Through vivid representations of the battle between St Michael and Lucifer the Indians were persuaded that the demons were the erstwhile leaders of their doomed way of life, and many plays ended with the humiliation and defeat of the devil to mark the beginning of the millenial reign of true charity.[11]

Yet this optimism never went unchallenged. The Dominicans, for example, were often critical of the Franciscan approach to baptisms *en masse*, insisting on the need for careful instruction in the basic principles of the faith before the administration of baptism and the other sacraments. Nor was it too long before their observations began to ring true, for despite the destruction and confiscation of idols it was soon discovered that clandestine native practices had anything but disappeared. Idolatry was deemed so widespread that in the early 1530s the

[10] Bernal Díaz del Castillo, *Historia verdadera de la conquista de la Nueva España* (various edns), passim. The practice was repeatedly opposed by the Mercedarian chaplain, Bartolomé de Olmedo who favoured a more thorough instruction in the Christian faith.

[11] M. Ekdal Ravicz, *Early Colonial Religious Drama in Mexico. From Tzompantli to Golgotha* (Washington, DC, 1970), p. 73; Richard C. Textler, 'We think, they act: clerical readings of missionary theater in sixteenth-century New Spain', in Steven L. Kaplan, ed., *Understanding Popular Culture. Europe from the Middle Ages to the Nineteenth Century* (Berlin, 1984), pp. 192, 203–5.

Franciscan archbishop of Mexico, Fray Juan de Zumárraga, in sharp contrast with the policies of his coreligionists, saw fit to implement the first inquisitorial practices against idolatrous and superstitious Indians.

Few moments in history are filled with more bitter irony. The thought of a Franciscan friar who was also a humanist, conversant with the writings of Erasmus and author of a treatise which spelled out Christian doctrine in simple language, acting out the role of inquisitor general, engaged in a ruthless and frantic persecution of unfaithful Indian apostates which culminated in the burning at the stake of a charismatic Indian leader, would have seemed like a very bad kind of nightmare to the early missionaries.[12] And yet it is difficult to imagine an alternative course of action open to the archbishop. After all, the Indians were no longer innocent pagans awaiting Christian enlightenment, but proper Christians, baptised and allegedly instructed, and therefore subject to the same disciplinary treatment that was used in Europe against the sins of idolatry, heresy and apostasy. All these crimes were clearly widespread and thriving among the Indians. Idols were constantly being hidden in caves. Human sacrifice, although less frequent, lingered on, and it was very common to find young men with their legs cut open or with wounds in their ears and tongues inflicted with the purpose of providing human blood for the idols.[13] More alarming were a number of similarities that could be detected between Christian practices and native rites. Fasting, for instance, was an indispensable prelude to the sacrifices which, as a rule, ended in a communal banquet, often accompanied by the ingestion of hallucinogenic mushrooms, *teunanacatl* in Nahuatl. As Toribio de Motolinía explained to the Count of Benavente, this term, translated literally into Spanish, meant 'the flesh of god', 'or of the devil whom they adore'.[14]

How was it possible for the Christian sacraments to find such striking parallels in the idolatrous rites of remote pagans? At best the phenomenon could be explained as the result of a mysterious initiative on the part of God to prepare the Indians for the reception of the Gospel. This indeed

---

[12] Archivo General de la Nación, Mexico City, Ramo Inquisición (hereafter AGN Inq.), tomo 2, exp. 10 (hereafter 2.10); printed as *Proceso inquisitorial del Cacique de Texcoco*, publicationes del AGN, vol. 1 (Mexico City, 1910). A good summary is Richard E. Greenleaf, *Zumárraga and the Mexican Inquisition 1536–1543* (Washington, DC, 1961), pp. 68–74.

[13] AGN Inq. 37.1; 40.7; 30.9; 40.8.

[14] Fray Toribio de Motolinía, *Historia de los Indios de la Nueva España* (Mexico City, 1973), p. 20. AGN, Inq. 38(I).7. The ambivalent use of the words 'god' and 'devil' is not fortuitous: it corresponds to the ambivalent nature of Mesoamerican deities.

has been Motolinía's hope when confronted with some infant bathing ceremonies which seemed to him to resemble baptism.[15] But such hopes were not easy to hold in face of the more frequent orgiastic ceremonies that were encountered and which seemed to the friars to represent a form of pseudo-sacramentalism imbued with Satanic inversion.

The crumbling optimism of the second decade of Franciscan evangelisation was a reflection of the growing conviction among the friars that Satanic intervention was at the heart of Indian cultures. It had become clear to them that the deities of the Indians were not merely false idols but, in the words of Fray Bernardino de Sahagún, 'lying and deceitful devils'. 'And', he continued in the introduction to one of the sections of his monumental ethnographic compilation,

> if it be thought that these things are so forgotten and lost, and that faith in one God is so well planted and firmly rooted among these natives that there is no need to speak about them . . . I am also certain that the Devil neither sleeps nor has forgotten the cult that these Indian natives offered him in the past, and that he is awaiting a suitable conjuncture to return to his lost lordship.[16]

Such anxieties reached a dramatic climax in 1562, when the discovery of widespread idolatry at Mani, the centre of the missionary enterprise in Yucatán, led to the most extreme and ruthless interrogations and tortures in the history of conversion in Mexico. An official inquiry established that 158 Indians had died during or as a direct result of the interrogations. At least thirteen committed suicide rather than face the inquisitors. Eighteen disappeared; many were crippled for life, their shoulder muscles irreparably torn, their hands paralysed 'like hooks'. Although Fray Diego de Landa, the Franciscan provincial responsible for the campaign, was summoned to Spain to answer charges, it is symptomatic of the new preoccupation with diabolism that, in the event, he was exonerated and indeed subsequently appointed bishop of Yucatán. There was, after all, no question as to his honesty and zeal. 'Being idolaters', he had explained, 'it was not possible to proceed strictly juridically against them . . . because . . . in the meantime they would all become idolaters and go to hell'.[17]

---

[15] Ibid., p. 85.
[16] Bernardino de Sahagún, *Historia general de las cosas de Nueva España*, 6th edn (Mexico City, 1985), pp. 704–5.
[17] Inga Clendinnen, *Ambivalent Conquests*, pp. 76–7. See also her 'Disciplining the Indians: Franciscan ideology and missionary violence in sixteenth-century Yucatán', *Past and Present*, 94 (1982), 27–48.

Attempts to account for this dramatic change of attitude on the part of the missionaries have led historians into what Robin Briggs has called 'the problems of multiple explanation'. It could be said that 'the violence of the missionaries sprang in large measure from the shock of betrayal'.[18] Equally, it could be argued that the effects of the Reformation in Europe had tended to deprive the New World of some of the best elements of the Spanish missionary orders, now more concerned with the Protestant heretics than with those 'sad priests of the devil' with their 'obscene and bloody devotions and lacerations' as Diego de Landa would write.[19] Or again, one could say that as the colonisation of the new territories became the increasing concern of the state, evangelisation tended to become more a matter of acquiescence based on faith, authority and tradition than a matter of assent based on reason and argument.[20] As I have indicated, it will not be my intention to add a further explanation to the list, but rather to attempt to shed some light on such explanations by concentrating on the concept of the devil, a theme central to them all. My contention, in other words, is that a better appreciation of the philosophical intricacies of the idea of, and the belief in, the devil, can provide valuable clues for the understanding not just of the missionary change of attitude that we have highlighted, but of the early modern European obsession with diabolism as a whole.

II

A central and essential feature of the devil in Christian thought is his complete subordination to the will of God. From the earliest days Christian theologians repeatedly emphasised this point. Hermas and Polycarp taught that the devil had no power over the human soul; Justin Martyr, that the devil was a creature of God, with an essentially good nature which he had merely deformed through his own free will;[21] and Irenaeus and Tertullian, that the devil's powers over men were limited, since he could not force them to sin against their will. The view that evil

---

[18] D. A. Brading, 'Images and prophets: Indian religion and the Spanish Conquest', in Arij Ouweneel and Simon Miller, eds., *The Indian Community of Colonial Mexico* (Amsterdam, 1990), p. 185.

[19] Clendinnen, *Ambivalent Conquests*, pp. 50–1, 119–20.

[20] See, for example, Sabine MacCormack, '"The heart has its reasons": predicaments of missionary Christianity in early colonial Peru', *Hispanic American Historical Review*, 65: 3 (Aug. 1985), 443–5.

[21] J. B. Russell, *Satan. The Early Christian Tradition* (Ithaca and London, 1981), pp. 42–50, 60–72.

was not an independent principle was to be reinforced by Clement and Origen, who were among the first to assert that evil does not exist in itself[22] and whose teachings would in turn prepare the ground for St Augustine's classic definition which denied evil's ontological existence.[23]

If evil had no substance, no actual existence, no intrinsic reality – if nothing was by nature evil – then a principle of evil – an evil being independent from God – was an absurdity. The persuasive power of this philosophical principle in medieval Christian thought is difficult to overestimate. It can be seen at work even those areas furthest removed from philosophy. The vivid and frightening devil which characterised monastic spirituality, for instance, was effectively toned down in popular literature. Thus the stories of Gregory of Tours in sixth-century Gaul follow the guidelines of Evagrius Ponticus and John Cassian in aiming to be amusing and light and in invariably leading to happy endings in which the saints triumphed over their demonic adversaries, often in a humorous way.[24] Even the more strictly theological or juridical expressions of the Christian struggle against Satan, such as the exorcisms of the possessed, were set in a context of unshakeable confidence. As Peter Brown has explained, exorcism was held to be the one irrefutable sign of *praesentia* – the physical presence of the holy. It was 'the one demonstration of the power of God that carried unanswerable authority'.[25]

It would seem that this conviction about the impotence of Satan against God and his church was badly shaken in the late medieval period. The reasons for this are complex and well beyond my scope, but some significant developments can be stressed. Firstly, there is the transposition of monastic spirituality from the cloister into the secular world that the Gregorian reformers and their successors encouraged from the late eleventh century onwards. As Edward Peters has suggested, given that the secular world lacked the liturgical defences of the monastery, the motives and ideals that had led to the development of the monastic devil associated with sermons, *exempla* and hagiographies took on a very different character in the untrained minds of the secular clergy and lay

---

[22] Ibid., pp. 80–148.
[23] St Augustine, *City of God*, xi.22, xii.3.
[24] J. B. Russell, *Lucifer. The Devil in the Middle Ages* (Ithaca and London, 1984), pp. 154–7.
[25] Peter Brown, *The Cult of the Saints. Its Rise and Function in Latin Christianity* (London, 1981), pp. 106–7.

people.[26] As a result, quite independently of the rise in manifestations of dissent at this time – notably the Cathar movement – which indeed helped to sharpen the sense of the world's vulnerability to demonic influence, a feeling of helplessness against demonic instigations began to be felt in more personal and direct ways. Already in the writings of the Cistercian mystic and historian Cesarius of Heisterbach (c. 1180–1240) it is clear that demons had become no mere external enemies doomed to be defeated by the bearers of a militant faith, but that they had penetrated into every corner of life and into the souls of individual Christians. Much more than the causes of droughts or epidemics, demons had come to be regarded, outside as well as inside the cloister, as the instigators of interior desires that individuals could not acknowledge as belonging to themselves.[27]

All this forms part of that mood of spiritual introspection that gathered momentum towards the end of the medieval period and which was marked by an emphasis on domestic piety and an urge to achieve a closer identification of individual religious experiences with the sufferings of Christ. But the trend is also linked to a change of emphasis in late medieval perceptions of sin and penance. As John Bossy has explained, the traditional moral system taught throughout the medieval period was based on the seven 'deadly' or 'capital' sins, which could be viewed as a negative exposition of Jesus' twofold commandment to love God and one's neighbour. The system had the advantage of fitting into a whole string of septenary classifications and of providing a set of categories under which people could identify passions of hostility as un-Christian. Yet it had the disadvantage of making little of obligations to God and, more worrying still, of having no scriptural authority. This is one of the preoccupations behind the efforts of the scholastic theologians of the thirteenth century to build their treatment of Christian ethics around the Decalogue, and as the new system came to replace the old one, new perceptions of morality came to the fore whose effects, in Bossy's words, 'may fairly be described as revolutionary'.

One of these effects was a notable enhancement of the status of the devil. By treating idolatry as the primary offence that a Christian could commit, the Decalogue led to a change from the traditional role of the devil as the anti-type of Christ – the 'Fiend' who taught men to hate

[26] Edward Peters, *The Magician, the Witch and the Law* (Sussex, 1978), pp. 92–3.
[27] Norman Cohn, *Europe's Inner Demons. An Enquiry inspired by the Great Witch Hunt* (London, 1975), p. 73.

rather than to love – to his new role as the anti-type of God the Father and thus the source and object of idolatry and false worship. By analogy, whereas traditionally witchcraft had been seen as the offence of causing malicious harm to others – it is interesting, for instance, to note that in Chaucer's exposition it had been dealt with, rather loosely, under wrath – in the new context it became a clear offence against the First Commandment. So too, just as the phenomenon of Carnival could in the old context be explained as an inverted image of the traditional machinery of penance derived from a moral system based on the Seven Sins, in the new context, the phenomenon of the witch could be explained as an inverted image of a moral system founded on the Ten Commandments, particularly the first. It is thus no accident, according to Bossy, that in proportion as the Decalogue became established as the accepted system of Christian ethics, witchcraft and diabolism became increasingly persuasive.[28]

A problem with Bossy's argument is that it can easily be made to backfire. If we consider the case of Thomism, for example, it is well known that Aquinas maintained not only that the Decalogue was a compendium of the natural law, but also that the natural law was valid independently of the Decalogue. Aquinas' treatment of the Decalogue was thus an affirmation of the intrinsic goodness of nature independently of the effects of grace. And if nature was good, even regardless of whether God had willed it so or no, it is difficult to see how the devil could have any major influence upon it. Acceptance of the Decalogue, therefore, could also go hand in hand with a decline of diabolism. Certainly, the Aristotelian naturalism espoused by Aquinas would, in different contexts produce a marked *penchant* for scepticism with regard to devils, as is clear from the opinions of Ulrich Müller, Agostino Nifo and Pietro Pomponazzi.[29]

It is of course true that this scepticism never spread to strictly Thomist circles. The *Malleus Maleficarum*, for instance, a work that is clearly in the Thomist tradition, is widely regarded as central to early modern demonology. Yet it is revealing to notice the marked differences between

---

[28] John Bossy, *Christianity in the West 1400–1700* (Oxford, 1985), pp. 35–8, 138–9; Bossy, 'Moral arithmetic: seven sins into Ten Commandments', in Edmund Leites, ed., *Conscience and Casuistry in Early Modern Europe* (Cambridge, 1988), pp. 215–30.

[29] On this see H. R. Trevor-Roper, 'The European witch-craze of the sixteenth and seventeenth centuries', in *Religion, the Reformation and Social Change*, 3rd edn (London, 1984), pp. 130–1; and H. C. Lea, *Materials towards a History of Witchcraft* (Philadelphia, 1939), pp. 384, 377, 435, 366.

the assumptions that inspired the authors of the *Malleus* and those that came to characterise subsequent demonological works. The central argument of the *Malleus* is that the problem about witches was malefice, particularly malefice in relation to the sexual act and marriage, and consequently, that witchcraft was a conspiracy against nature, charity and the human race. By contrast, the bulk of sixteenth- and seventeenth-century demonologists would argue that the problem about witches was idolatry and devil worship, and consequently, that witchcraft was a conspiracy against God and his church, a conclusion that would have been difficult to reach in a context where the Thomist concordance between nature and grace was accepted.

Such a context clearly did not exist in the early modern period. The old assumption that Thomism was more or less universally accepted by intellectuals until the fourteenth century marked 'the end of the journey',[30] is now seen not merely as an exaggeration but as a fundamental misconception of the period. As Heiko Oberman insists, one only needs to remember Robert Kilwardby, Durandus de St Porciano, Robert Holcot and William Crathorn to realise that such compliance with Thomism was not even a feature of the Dominican order.[31] Indeed, the circumstances for the development of Thomism in the fourteenth century were particularly inauspicious, for the defenders of Aquinas had to cope with the legacy of the Parisian condemnation of Averroism in the 1270s and with the consequent urgent need to clear their master of the charge of Averroist tendencies. Since most of the charges addressed metaphysical issues, the consequence of the defence was the transmission of an over-metaphysical Aquinas which did not pay adequate attention to him as an interpreter of Scripture and Patristic theology. In this way there developed the caricature of an Aristotelian, anti-Augustinian and semi-Pelagian Aquinas which was offensive to mainstream theology and which explains why Thomism failed to appeal to philosophers and theologians well into the fifteenth century.[32]

As Oberman explains, the main effect of the concern with Averroism was the widespread Franciscan reaction against a 'metaphysically fool-proof causal system which embraces the whole chain of being, including

---

[30] This is the general assumption of research inspired by the work of pioneers like Etienne Gilson and Martin Grabmann.

[31] Heiko A. Oberman, 'The reorientation of the fourteenth century', in A. Maieru and A. Paravicini Bagliani, eds., *Studi sul XIV secolo in memoria di Anneliese Maier* (Rome, 1981), p. 515.

[32] Ibid., pp. 517–18.

God as first and final cause'. Although the chain of being itself was not called into question, the resulting association of God and necessity was.[33] Scholastics thus tended to reject Aquinas' moral system, seeing it as a threat to the freedom and omnipotence of God, or as an attempt to bind God's moral decisions within a normative system which could be conceived as separate or distinct from God. The Franciscan alternative, as represented by Duns Scotus and William of Ockham, invoked faith in God as person and free agent, rather than as 'first cause' or 'unmoved mover'. Their insistence that God was not tied to creation by causation but, rather, related to it by volition, seemed to make all metaphysical arguments based on necessary causal links lose their relevance in theological thought. To cite Oberman again, whereas in Aquinas' metaphysical ontology 'the natural and supernatural realms are organically joined by the being of God' in whom human beings participate by reason and faith, the Franciscan alternative 'retraces nature and supernature . . . to the *Person* of God, and points to God's will as . . . the "ceiling" of theology'. Little room was left here for the possibility of a natural knowledge of God or for the demonstrability of a natural religion. God's eternal decree of self-commitment had 'established the limits of theology which to surpass is to trespass, yielding sheer speculation'.[34]

This Franciscan school of thought dominated medieval intellectual history from Duns Scotus to the Great Schism and beyond. Indeed, it did not lose much of its impetus until the Erasmians and the reformers began to evoke a new longing for a comprehensive system of thought, which in part inspired the Catholic neo-Thomist revival of the sixteenth century. But even after the Council of Trent's catechism confirmed Aquinas' view of the Decalogue as a compendium of natural law, the increasingly fragmented and eclectic theological debates characteristic of the time proved fundamentally inimical to the Thomist conception of inquiry as a long-term, cooperative, pursuit of systematic understanding.[35] The most authoritative philosopher of the period, the Jesuit Francisco Suárez, for instance, formulated a philosophy that tended to an eclectic synthesis of the thought of Aquinas, Scotus and Ockham that was irreconcilable with the Thomist theory of matter and form (hylomorphism). Where Aquinas

---

[33] Ibid., pp. 518–19.
[34] Ibid., p. 519. See also Heiko A. Oberman, 'via antiqua and Via moderna: late medieval prolegomena to early Reformation thought', *Journal of the History of Ideas* (1987), 23–40.
[35] On this point see Alasdair MacIntyre, *Three Rival Versions of Moral Enquiry* (London, 1990), p. 150.

had applied the principles of Aristotelian physics to the nature of man, teaching that matter was the principle of human individuation and that the soul was the form of the body, Suárez insisted on a transition from apprehensions of essence to judgements of particular existence that necessarily implied a separation of matter and spirit.[36]

The effects that this nominalist persistence in post-Tridentine thought would have on subsequent demonological investigations would be difficult to exaggerate. For the position was irreconcilable with Aquinas' theory of the human intelligence, a theory that in turn was the keystone of the Thomist formulation of the concordance between nature and grace. Against the Platonists Aquinas had argued that man was not primarily a spiritual being confined in the 'prison' of the body, but a part of nature. Likewise, human intelligence was not that of a pure spirit; it was 'consubstantial' with matter, subject to the conditions of space and time, and only capable of knowing – i.e. constructing an intelligible order – through the data of sensible experience systematised by reason.[37] As Christopher Dawson put it, the intellectualism of Aquinas 'recognised the autonomous rights of the human reason and its scientific activity against the absolutism of a purely theological ideal of knowledge, and the rights of human nature and natural morality against the exclusive domination of the ascetic ideal'.[38]

As we have seen, the Franciscan nominalist school, by concentrating their attacks on the early metaphysical writings of Aquinas rather than on his mature synthesis in the *Summa Theologiae*, failed to see the significance of this balance, and it is in this anti-Thomist tendency, and in the way in which it coincided with a trend in favour of a moral system based more on the Decalogue than on the seven sins, that the foundations of early modern demonology are to be sought. It is no accident that it was precisely in the context of the twofold acceptance of nominalism as a philosophical system and of the Decalogue as a moral system that Jean Gerson influenced the famous conclusion of the University of Paris in 1398. Henceforth all strictly maleficient witchcraft, as well as all seemingly beneficient counter-witchcraft, would be regarded as

---

[36] Francisco Suárez, *Disputationes Metaphysicae*, V, 6, 15–17, and see F. C. Copleston, *A History of Philosophy. Volume III: Ockham to Suárez* (New York, 1953), pp. 360–1.

[37] St Thomas Aquinas, *Summa Contra Gentiles*, ii, 76. See also F. C. Copleston, *Aquinas* (Harmondsworth, 1955), pp. 156–98. A clear, brief account of the wider implications of the thesis is Christopher Dawson, 'The scientific development of medieval culture', in Dawson, *Medieval Essays* (London and New York, 1953), pp. 148–52.

[38] Dawson, 'Scientific Development'.

idolatrous and as necessarily involving apostasy and submission to the devil. Malefice ceased to be the centre of the problem and gave way to idolatry and devil worship as the main objects of concern.

All this, of course, emphatically does not mean that the witch hunts of the sixteenth and seventeenth centuries are to be blamed on the voluntarism encouraged by the Franciscan nominalists. In fact, as Stuart Clark has explained, the 'interiorisation' of the crime of witchcraft encouraged by the nominalists often played against witch prosecutions. By focusing on sin – especially on the sin of idolatry – rather than on sorcery and malefice, misfortune came to be seen in a more Jobian light and the devil came to be perceived increasingly in the context of the mystery of redemption: a completely subservient being used by God for the spiritual improvement of the pious.[39] Nevertheless, this incipient scepticism about the reality of witchcraft was nowhere accompanied by a decline of diabolism itself. Indeed, the implications of diabolism in relation to the individual soul became much more immediate and compelling. The nominalist tendency to separate nature and grace made the realm of 'the supernatural' much less accessible to reason, thereby enhancing the attributes of both the divine and the demonic in relation to the individual. If it is true that in the long run this tendency contributed to the decline of witch prosecution, it is no less clear that it also became a central element in the seventeenth-century proliferation of cases of diabolical obsession and possession on both sides of the confessional front.

III

When we turn our attention to the New World the influence of Franciscan nominalism becomes especially significant. It is revealing, for instance, that the first work written in Mexico dealing strictly with diabolism, Fray Andrés de Olmos' *Tratado de Hechicerías y Sortilegios*, was inspired almost entirely by the influential demonological treatise by the Basque Franciscan Fray Martín de Castañega,[40] a work in which

---

[39] Stuart Clark, 'Protestant demonology: sin, superstition and society (c. 1520–c. 1630)', in B. Ankarloo and G. Henningsen, eds., *Early Modern Witchcraft* (Oxford, 1990), pp. 45–81. Although Clark focuses on Protestant demonology, very much the same argument could be applied to the Catholic case.

[40] Fray Martín de Castañega, *Tratado muy sotil y bien fundado de las supersticiones y hechicerías y varios conjuros y abusiones y otras cosas tocantes al caso y de la posibilidad e remedio dellas* (Logroño, 1529).

idolatry and devil worship are the central objects of concern. Written in Nahuatl, the aim of Olmos' treatise in paraphrasing Castañega's work was to convince missionaries and Indians alike that diabolism was not primarily maleficent but idolatrous. Lapsed Indians should no longer be seen as gullible simpletons who had been deluded by the devil nor even as malicious sorcerers who used demonic power to harm their fellow beings. Much more serious than this, idolatrous Indians were active devil-worshippers, members of a counter-church set up by a devil anxious to be honoured like God. With this purpose Satan had set up his own church as a mimetic inversion of the Catholic Church. It had its 'excraments' to counter the Church's sacraments; it had its ministers, who were mostly women, as opposed to the predominance of male ministers in the church; and it had its human sacrifices which sought to imitate the supreme sacrifice of Christ in the Eucharist.[41]

How pervasive the rejection of Aristotelian naturalism and of the Thomist concordance between nature and grace became during this period can be seen not only in the complete disregard by contemporaries of works of a more strictly Thomist inspiration (notably Vitoria's *De magia*, which deals much more with malefice than with idolatry), but also in the way in which it seemed to carry the day even among those thinkers who considered themselves to be in the mainstream of Thomist orthodoxy. This is especially clear in the thought of perhaps the most intelligent and systematic thinker to write about the cultures of the American Indians in the sixteenth century: the Spanish Jesuit José de Acosta (1540–1600).

In the work of Acosta, the rejection of the Thomist concordance between nature and grace, albeit not made explicit, seems to be all-important. Indeed, the contrast between his treatment of what he regarded as natural and his analysis of what he thought to belong to the 'supernatural' sphere in the cultures of America is so striking that, at first sight, it is hard to believe that they are the constructs of the same mind.

As far as the 'natural' sphere was concerned, Acosta's account of the native cultures of the New World was one of the most objective and original to have hitherto appeared. In easy, fluent style, the reader was provided with a concise and lucid exposition of the nature, origins and organisation of Indian cultures which clarified complex questions with confident and critical acumen. Where previous writers had been content

---

[41] Georges Baudot, *Utopía e Historia en México. Los primeros cronistas de la civilización mexicana (1520–1569)* (Madrid, 1983), p. 243.

to revert to tradition or to ancient wisdom. Acosta insisted that empirical knowledge and experience should always take precedence over the doctrines of ancient philosophers in any examination of the causes and effects of natural phenomena. Accordingly, native cultures had to be understood on their own terms, since comparisons with other races would only lead to absurd and inappropriate analogies. 'So long as they do not contradict the law of Christ and his Holy Church', he wrote, the Indians

> should be governed according to their own laws, the ignorance of which has led to many errors . . . For, when the judges and rulers are ignorant of the ways in which their subjects are to be judged and ruled, they not only inflict grief and injustice upon them, but they also . . . encourage them to abhor us as men who in all things, be they good or bad, have always opposed them.[42]

This seemed a long cry from Zumárraga and Olmos and Sahagún. Indeed, Acosta's insistence on the urgent need to assess Indian cultures on their own terms and his pursuit of causality and generality where his predecessors had been content with the mere observation and description of phenomena, in some ways resembled the purpose and method of modern science. It is no doubt this quality that gained Acosta the respect of William Robertson in the eighteenth century, when the Scotsman pronounced the *Historia* to be 'one of the most accurate and best informed writings concerning the West Indies', an opinion that found a recent echo when Anthony Pagden concluded that Acosta's work had made 'some kind of comparative ethnology, and ultimately some measure of historical relativism, inescapable'.[43]

The fact that the devil had little or no room in this scheme was reflected in Acosta's frequent impatience with the opinions of 'ignorant friars' who imagined the whole of the Indian past as a diabolical hallucination.[44] Rather than blaming the devil, Acosta was at pains to stress the natural goodness of Indian cultures. 'If anyone – he wrote – is amazed at the rites and customs of the Indians . . . and detests them as inhuman and diabolical . . . let him remember that among the Greeks and

---

[42] Ibid., p. 281. See also Acosta, *De Procuranda Indorum Salute* (Cologne, 1596), pp. 483, 517

[43] Anthony Pagden, *The Fall of Natural Man. The American Indian and the Origins of Comparative Ethnology* (Cambridge, 1982), p. 200. Robertson is quoted in David Brading, *The First America. The Spanish Monarchy, Creole Patriots and the Liberal State* (Cambridge, 1991), p. 184.

[44] Acosta, *Historia*, pp. 188–9.

the Romans one finds the same kind of crimes and often even worse ones.' So too, he reminded his readers that according to Bede, the Irish and the English, 'in their heathen days', has been no more enlightened than the Indians.[45] In their refusal to abandon their ancient rites and customs the Indians were not necessarily playing into the hands of the devil. Their behaviour, in fact, was no different from that of the bulk of the Castilian peasantry who merely needed instruction to 'submit to the truth as a thief surprised in his crime'.[46]

In all this, Acosta seemed poles apart from the demonology of his time. Even when dealing with the irksome question of conversion, Acosta's insistence on the need to preserve those pagan rites and ceremonies that did not conflict with Christianity[47] seemed to echo St Gregory the Great's advice to St Augustine of Canterbury, and was in perfect tune with the current Jesuit missionary practice which produced its most illustrative representatives in China and India with Matteo Ricci and Roberto de Nobili. But Acosta was only willing to deploy such analytical acumen when dealing with natural phenomena or with cultural expressions that could be explained from a strictly natural standpoint. As soon as he entered the field of religion proper Acosta seemed to join the voluntarist camp and all his insistence on empirical knowledge and analysis was brought to a complete standstill. To enter the sphere of the supernatural was to enter the sphere of theological certainty, where the divine law was the one and only standard of truth and where the divine will was alone sovereign. Thus, when faced with the curious similarities that existed between Christian and pagan religious practices, Acosta was as baffled as his predecessors. Yet, unlike Motolinía, he could find no room for providentialist hopes. Despite his conviction that in the wider structure of the divine plan good would always triumph over evil, when faced with Indian religions Acosta could not bring himself to anticipate God's plan. To his mind, the evident similarities between Christian and pagan religious ceremonies necessarily pointed to a super-natural origin in the latter, and since it would be absurd to think of God as attempting to imitate himself, the only alternative source to account for such similarities had to be a diabolical one.

It is true that Acosta, in Thomist fashion, would have accepted that

---

[45]   Ibid., pp. 216, 228.
[46]   Acosta, *De Procuranda*, p. 150; the quotation, from Acosta, *Confesionario para los curas de Indios* (Lima, 1588), is from Pagden, *Fall of Natural Man*, p. 161.
[47]   Acosta, *De Procuranda*, p. 483.

man was capable of grasping religious truth by the mere encouragement of his own innate and natural desire for truth. But this desire seemed in itself insufficient to produce religious expressions that so closely resembled Christian religious practices, especially in milieux where Christianity had been hitherto unknown. Conversely, it was a common-place in contemporary theological thought that Satan, the *Simia Dei*, was forever seeking to imitate his creator, so that, as Pedro Ciruelo had put it, 'the more saintly and devout the things he made men do, the greater was the sin against God'.[48] From this it followed that the more highly structured was the social order of pagan peoples, and the more refined and complex was their civility and religious organisation, the more idolatrous and perverted were the results.[49]

It was in his analysis of Indian religions, therefore, that the nominalist separation of nature and grace was taken by Acosta, with impeccable logic, to its most extreme and dramatic conclusions. Defined in the book of Wisdom as the 'beginning cause and end of every evil', idolatry had always been regarded as the worst of all sins: the means through which the Prince of Lies, moved by pride and envy, had blinded men to the true shape of God's design for nature.[50] Now, by denying paganism any natural means towards a supernatural end – unless, of course, both the means and the end could be classed as diabolical – Acosta effectively equated paganism with idolatry. Anything faintly religious in pagan cultures was necessarily the result of Satan's incorrigible 'mimetic desire'.[51] It was precisely this mimetic desire that was at the root of the existence of counter-religious practices among the Indians of America; for the devil was constantly taking advantage of any opportunity that would allow him to imitate the divine cult. In America he had his own priests who offered sacrifices and administered sacraments in his honour. He had many followers who led lives of 'recollection and sham sanctity'. He had 'a thousand types of false prophets' through whom he sought to 'usurp the glory of God and feign light with darkness'. Indeed, there was 'hardly anything that had been instituted by Jesus Christ . . . which, in some way or other, the devil had not sophisticated and incorporated

---

[48] Pedro Ciruelo, *Tratado en el qual se repruevan todas las supersticiones y hechicerías* (Barcelona, 1628), p. 183.

[49] Acosta, *De Procuranda*, p. 474.

[50] Wisdom, xiv.27; St Thomas Aquinas, *Summa Theologiae*, IIa–IIae, a.94a. 4 resp.; Acosta, *De Procuranda*, p. 486; Acosta, *Historia*, pp. 217–18.

[51] I have borrowed this term from René Girard. See especially *Le Bouc Emissaire* (Paris, 1982).

into their [the Indians] heathendom'. In his attempt to imitate Catholic ritual Satan had distinguished between 'minor, major and supreme priests, and a type of acolyte', and had founded 'monasteries' where chastity was rigorously observed, 'not because of any love of cleanliness . . . but because of his desire to deprive God, in any way that he can, of the glory of being served with integrity and cleanliness'. It was in the same spirit that Satan had encouraged 'penances and ascetic disciplines' in his honour, and sacrifices where he not only competed with the divine law, but actually tried to overstep it, for God had stopped Abraham's sacrifice of Isaac, whereas Satan encouraged human sacrifices on a massive scale. His frantic mimetic desire had even culminated in a desperate attempt to imitate the mystery of the Trinity.[52]

Such Satanic 'envy and urge to compete' became even more explicit in the devil's attempts to imitate the Christian sacraments. For he had instituted sham imitations of baptism, marriage, confession and sacerdotal unction. More histrionically, the Eucharist had been copied and mocked by the Mexicans in their rituals involving communal banquets which, in the May celebrations of the god Huitzilopochtli, reached the level of an elaborate parody of the feast of Corpus Christi when, after a long procession, the celebrations culminated in the communal ingestion of a small idol made of maize pastry and honey. 'Who could fail to be astonished', Acosta exclaimed, 'that the devil should take so much care to have himself adored and received in the same way that Jesus Christ . . . commanded and taught [to be received]!'[53]

Since, however, such similarities were a clear proof of the demonic nature of Indian religions, Acosta chose to overlook the chastity of the 'monasteries' and the asceticism of the 'penitential' practices and to stress that pagan religious ceremonies were invariably mixed with all types of 'abominations' that inverted and perverted the natural order. The unctions of priests, for instance, were carried out with a substance amassed with every last sort of 'poisonous vermin', such as spiders, scorpions, snakes and centipedes, which, when burnt and mixed with the hallucinogen *ololhiuqui*, had the power of turning the newly ordained priests into witches who saw the devil, spoke to him and visited him by night in 'dark and sinister mountains and caves'. Similarly, the parody of the Eucharist host was made from a mixture of human blood and

[52] Acosta, *Historia*, pp. 235, 238, 240, 242, 246, 248, 249, 268.
[53] Ibid., pp. 266, 259–65, 255–9.

amaranth seeds; the walls of the 'oratories' were always stained with blood and the long hair of the priests had been hardened by the clotted blood of sacrificial victims. Satanic pollution and ritual filth invaded every corner of Indian religion. A manifest inversion of the Christian ideals of sacramental purity and ritual cleanliness, their ritualism culminated in the comparably offensive practice of human sacrifice which, in an unthinkably perverted fashion, was often accompanied by cannibalism. This was not merely an 'unnatural crime' like sodomy and onanism; it was the ultimate expression of idolatry: its self-consuming nature associated it with Satanic desire itself.[54]

In his account of Indian religions, Acosta made the Indians guilty of all the idolatrous aberrations listed in the book of Wisdom: 'With their child murdering initiations, their secret mysteries, their orgies with outlandish ceremonies, they no longer retain any purity in their lives . . . Everywhere a welter of blood and murder, theft and fraud, corruption, treachery, riots, perjury, disturbance . . . pollution of souls, sins against nature.'[55]

IV

The contrast between Acosta's analysis of indigenous cultures and his assessment of native religions could not be more marked, and it becomes even more striking when we compare his method with the way in which his Dominican predecessor, Fray Bartolomé de Las Casas (1484–1566), had dealt with the same problem a few decades earlier. For Las Casas' background and intellectual concerns were very similar to Acosta's. His thought, like Acosta's, had been moulded by the theological tradition of the School of Salamanca and, consequently, like Acosta, he had grounded his anthropology upon the premise that all human minds were the same in essence, that all men were innately susceptible to moral training, and that any analysis of cultural differences needed to be based on an historical explanation. Like Acosta, too, he had insisted on the primacy of empirical knowledge as the basis of any fruitful analysis of the American reality.[56] Apart from their clear differences in style, structure and length (Las Casas' writings being as voluminous as they are convoluted), their arguments and their appreciation of Indian cultures

---

[54] Ibid., pp. 262–5, 248; Pagden, *Fall of Natural Man*, p. 176.
[55] Wisdom, xiv.22–30.
[56] Pagden, *Fall of Natural Man*, p. 146.

were surprisingly similar. The one essential difference between them was that, unlike Acosta. Las Casas did not appear to have been influenced by the voluntarist separation of nature and grace. This left him with the freedom to approach the supernatural manifestations of Indian cultures from an essentially naturalistic standpoint.

It is for this reason that we find no sharp contrast between the natural and the supernatural in the writings of Las Casas. Although he distinguished clearly between the two spheres, he thought it a mistake to separate them. Following Aquinas he concluded that the supernatural, albeit beyond human reason and understanding, was nonetheless as rational as the natural and that, consequently, any human desire for the supernatural was rooted in nature.[57] Although he would have agreed with St Augustine, as Aquinas himself had done, that the original initiative always came from God, he was adamant that this did not do away with the essential goodness rooted in human nature itself. The desire for God was a universal and perfectly natural phenomenon which responded to an essential human need and which sought expression in the worship of God – *latria*. By analogy, *idolatria* was not a demonic invention, but an equally natural – albeit disordered – phenomenon, responding to a natural desire for good and emerging from an error of reason caused by the ignorance and weakness of a fallen nature. Although a degeneration of the original *latria*, idolatry tended to be the rule, the 'natural' state among the higher civilisations, whenever grace was absent. It could not, therefore, have a diabolical origin. No matter how disordered it might appear, or how much it might be used by the devil to perpetuate his perversities, the basic desire behind idolatry was essentially good: a proof, indeed, that the Indians were eager for evangelisation.[58]

This did not mean of course that the devil was not as important for Las Casas as he was for Acosta. Indeed, the reality of Satanic intervention in human affairs was just as present in the writings of the Dominican as in those of the Jesuit, and it was often presented in an even more vivid and pervasive way. In the writings of Las Casas the devil was deemed to be constantly transporting men through the air and tempting witches to obtain unbaptised infants for their cannibalistic rites; he would also turn men into beasts; he would perform false miracles and he would

[57] Fray Bartolomé de Las Casas, *Apologética Historia Sumaria*, ed., Edmundo O'Gorman, 2 vols. (Mexico City, 1967), I, p. 539.
[58] For a different view see Carmen Bernand and Serge Gruzinski, *De l'Idolâtrie. Une archéologie des sciences réligieuses* (Paris, 1988), pp. 45–74.

constantly appear in human and animal forms.[59] Yet, all these demonic actions were set by Las Casas unquestionably in the context of malefice,[60] and his demonology was more in tune with the Thomist tradition that had inspired the authors of the *Malleus Maleficarum*, than with the nominalist tradition at the root of the demonology that became prevalent in the early modern period.

Consequently, Las Casas' agreement with Aquinas on the question of the relation between nature and grace, which, as we have seen, allowed him to give a naturalistic explanation to the problem of idolatry, invested the devil with a justifying rather than a condemnatory role as far as Indian religious expressions were concerned. Where Acosta had initiated his discussion with a furious denunciation of Satan as the author and fount of idolatry, Las Casas began by invoking Aristotle's criteria for a true city, only moving to a discussion of religion once he had demonstrated the essential goodness of its natural foundations. If the devil was indeed the culprit of all native vices and crimes, he could easily be brought to heel once 'doctrine and grace' were made to work on the essentially good religious expressions of the Indians.[61] In all this, Las Casas emerges as one of the last upholders of Thomist naturalism. His views on Indian religions were destined to become the last, desperate cry of this short-lived tradition. They had, ironically, much more in common with the optimism about human nature that we detected in the writings of his rivals, Cortés and Motolinía, than with the sombre pessimism that in his own lifetime he would witness permeating Christian thought.

V

It is clear that Acosta's ambivalent analysis of Amerindian culture is a direct result of the voluntarist streak in his demonology. If this factor is not taken into account, his work inevitably appears riddled with what David Brading has called 'a latent contradiction which he fails to resolve in any satisfactory manner' and which might be explained as the result of 'his subordination of humanitarian and religious interests to political expediency'.[62] In the light of my argument, however, Acosta's position is perfectly coherent. Despite the clear political slant that can be detected

---

[59] Bartolomé de las Casas, *Apologética Historia*, ed., Juan Perez de Tudela Bueso, 2 vols. *Biblioteca de Autores Españoles* (Madrid, 1958), cv, pp. 299–345.

[60] Ibid., esp. pp. 308–9.

[61] Las Casas, *Apologética Historia*, ed., E. O'Gorman, I, p. 183; II, pp. 177, 178, 215.

[62] Brading, *The First America*, pp. 193–4.

in his triumphalist celebrations of the Spanish conquest as the fulfilment of a providential design, Acosta's work is undeniably the most able and persuasive exposition of an attitude to the Indian past that would become dominant until the first half of the eighteenth century.

Any attempt to explain what made this voluntarist tendency so compelling from the sixteenth to the eighteenth centuries inevitably sends us back to the impact of the Reformation on both sides of the confessional front. We have seen how the anti-Averroist tendencies of the fourteenth century played against an organic development of Thomism by encouraging an over-metaphysical and semi-Pelagian view of Aquinas' thought. By the fifteenth century, however, it was becoming clear that Thomism presented formidable alternatives to the nominalist school. It is in fact to the fifteenth and sixteenth centuries that some of the greatest names in neo-Thomist scholasticism belong. With a few exceptions like the Italian Thomas de Vio, better known as Cajetan (1468–1534), the Thomistic revival was dominated by Spanish Dominicans like Francisco de Vitoria (1480–1546), Domingo de Soto (1494–1560), Melchor Cano (1509–60) and Domingo Ibáñez (1528–1604). The chief centre of this revival was the school of Salamanca which, as we have seen, had been tremendously influential in the intellectual formation of both Las Casas and Acosta.

Thus the explanation for the differences that we detected in the thought of these two thinkers should take chronology carefully into account. On the one hand, Las Casas was essentially a pre-Tridentine thinker and a Dominican, and his thought faithfully reflected the strict Thomism whose best representative was the Dominican Francisco de Vitoria. On the other, Acosta was essentially a Tridentine thinker and a Jesuit, and his thought was inspired by the not-so-strict Thomism of the Jesuit school represented especially by Francisco Suárez.

It might be thought ironic that Tridentine theology should have become less strictly Thomist than the theology advocated by the pre-Reformation Dominican school. But it is becoming increasingly clear that the idea of a Thomist preponderance in Tridentine Catholicism is likely to be as flawed as the 'myth of the Thomist phalanx' – as Oberman has called it[63] – in the fourteenth century. For despite the existence of some first-rate Thomist commentators in the seventeenth century, notably John of St Thomas (1589–1644), 'neo-Thomism' came unquestionably under the influence of Suárez. The latter, as we have

---

[63] Oberman, 'Reorientation . . . ', pp. 516–18.

seen, attempted an eclectic synthesis of the thought of Aquinas, Ockham and Scotus which proved irreconcilable with Aquinas' views on the human intelligence and on the concordance between nature and grace.

It is likely that in this, Suárez – as, indeed, Tridentine theology as a whole – was swayed by the apologetic need to prove that all Catholic thinkers were fundamentally in agreement.[64] But a further and perhaps more fundamental factor in this trend was the immense weight the thought of St Augustine had acquired in the late middle ages. From about 1330 the African saint began to be regarded no longer as one of the four church fathers but as *the* authoritative and definitive interpreter of the Scriptures. The subsequent merging of this exaggerated Augustinianism with Franciscan nominalism led to a recurring insistence on the separation of the natural and the supernatural, of divine and human values, which became characteristic of both Protestant and Catholic Christianity in the early modern period.

This tendency, sometimes referred to as 'ultrasupernaturalism' or 'hyper-Augustinianism'[65] can be detected in the most representative thinkers of the time from the Jesuit-trained philosopher René Descartes to the Oratorian theologian Nicolas Malebranche. By the end of the seventeenth century it was so widespread that Pierre Bayle had no qualms about classing it as characteristic of Christianity *tout court*, and his criticism is a clear illustration of how extreme the claims of both God and the devil had become. The division of the natural and the super-natural, Bayle claimed, had at best reduced religiously based morality to a servile observance of capricious norms instituted by divine decree; at worst it led men into positive wickedness by the imitation of God's arbitrary exercise of power. In this way, Bayle not only highlighted the logic behind the accusations of devil-worship often levelled against Calvinists and Jansenists; he also helped to place the proliferation of cases of diabolical possession and obsession, and the general obsession with diabolism, into a recognisable intellectual context.[66]

It is likely, therefore, that the final demise of diabolism in Western thought on both sides of the Atlantic had much less to do with the rise of

---

[64] A point made by Pietro Redondi, *Galileo: Heretic* (Princeton, 1987), pp. 222–3.

[65] The term 'Ultrasupernaturalism' was coined by R. A. Knox in *Enthusiasm* (Oxford, 1950); 'Hyper-Augustinianism' is used by Charles Taylor, *Sources of the Self* (Cambridge, 1989).

[66] On this see D. P. Walker, *The Decline of Hell* (London, 1964), pp. 53–7, 202–13.

This chapter has been adapted from the first chapter of the author's *The Devil in the New World*, Yale University Press (New Haven and London, 1994).

scepticism than is commonly assumed. A more convincing explanation would need to take into account the increasing realisation among Christian thinkers from about the time of the publication of Leibniz's *Theodicy* that the only way to preserve a viable defence of God's omnipotence that left any room for a credible demonology was a return to some kind of concordance between nature and grace. It was the persistence of the voluntarist opposition to this attempt that eventually opened the doors to modern scepticism and to the secularist assault on the reality of the supernatural.

6. 'Saints or sorcerers': Quakerism, demonology and the decline of witchcraft in seventeenth-century England

PETER ELMER

'Strange creatures, not like other men and women' is how one Welsh Quaker described the contemporary response to his coreligionists. Mary Penington, an early Quaker convert, agreed: 'to every class we were a by-word: they would wag the head at us, accounting us fools, mad, and bewitched [and] as such they stoned, abused and imprisoned us'.[1] The rich literature of Quaker sufferings attests to the almost universal fear and hatred which first greeted their appearance on the stage of inter-regnum England. It is also an invaluable source for one particular accusation that was levelled at the Quakers with inordinate frequency, that of using diabolical witchcraft to promote the new heresy and subvert the established order. Historians of Quakerism have often noted this trend. More recently, Barry Reay has attempted to place such accusations within the wider framework of the perceived threat posed by the sect to social, religious and political order in mid-seventeenth-century Britain.[2] Somewhat surprisingly however, historians of witchcraft have been slower to fasten on to the potential significance and meaning of this large body of evidence.[3] In what follows, I hope to rectify this omission and

---

[1] R. Davies, *An Account of the Convincement, Exercises, Services and Travels of . . . Richard Davies* (London, 1710), p. 79; M. Penington, *Some Account of Circumstances in the Life of Mary Penington* (London, 1821), p. 41. Davies also reported how, following his conversion to Quakerism in 1657, he found it difficult to convince his mother that he 'was her Child, and that I was not . . . Bewitched, or Transformed into some other Likeness, which was reported of Quakers then, and that they bewitched People to their Religion'; Davies, *An Account*, p. 36.

[2] B. Reay, *The Quakers and the English Revolution* (London, 1985), pp. 68–71. For earlier Quaker historians on this subject, see, for example, A. M. Gummere, *Witchcraft and Quakerism* (London, 1908); W. C. Braithwaite, *The Beginnings of Quakerism* (London, 1923), pp. 53, 67, 102, 107, 181, 220, 487; R. M. Jones, *The Quakers in the American Colonies* (London, 1923), pp. 28–31, 275.

[3] It is briefly noted in K. V. Thomas, *Religion and the Decline of Magic* (London, 1978), pp. 580–1, and more recently in the American context in C. F. Karlsen, *The Devil in the*

to suggest possible ways in which the evidence of Quaker witchcraft might be used to shed important light on the history of educated belief in demonology in the second half of the seventeenth century. In particular, I wish to show its potential relevance to what Keith Thomas, in his pioneering work on witchcraft, has termed 'the most baffling aspect of this difficult subject', namely the roots of educated scepticism.[4]

Of all the practices of the early Quakers which aroused suspicions of diabolism, none was considered more dubious than the manner in which it was said that they made new converts. Opponents regularly claimed that Quaker preachers attracted proselytes by the use of a wide variety of enchanted objects including bottles, ribbons, strings and potions. How else might the godly explain the apparent ease with which men and women, some of high standing in their communities, were persuaded to join the Quaker movement? Margaret Fell, for example, the wife of a northern judge and MP, recounted how at her convincement, 'it raised such a Bitterness, & envy amongst ye preists & professors, that . . . they all concluded it was of ye Devill, and yt it was sorcery and witchcraft, & yt they gave us bottles to drink & tyed strings about our armes'.[5] Stories such as these proliferated in the pages of the yellow press of the 1650s, but as Fell hinted, the chief source of such allegations was not 'vulgar' opinion, but the men of learning, magistrates and the established clergy.[6] To cite just two examples of the latter, Richard Baxter repeated similar claims, both in published works and private correspondence, whilst his celebrated Presbyterian colleague Samuel Eaton recounted the tale of a Nottingham man who was seduced by the sorcery and witchcraft of the Quakers into attending their meetings. In the latter case, the individual eventually recanted, but not before he fell sick and languished in trances, only recovering from the Quakers' spells when removed from their

---

Shape of a Woman: Witchcraft in Colonial New England (New York and London, 1987), pp. 122–5; and R. Godbeer, *The Devil's Dominion: Magic and Religion in Early New England* (Cambridge, 1992), pp. 193–9.

[4] Thomas, *Religion and the Decline of Magic*, p. 681.

[5] Friends House Library (hereafter FHL), Spence MSS, vol. 3, fo. 135.

[6] For 'sensationalist' accounts of this kind in the popular press, see, for example, Anon., *The Quakers Fiery Beacon: or, the Shaking Ranters Ghost* (London, 1655), p. 8; *The Weekly Post* (London, 1655), no. 283 (31 July–7 Aug. 1655), pp. 1906–7; T. Underhill, *Hell Broke Loose* (London, 1660), pp. 36–7, 46–8. According to Samuel Pepys, such stories were still circulating in the coffee houses of Restoration London; see *The Diary of Samuel Pepys*, eds., R. Latham and W. Matthews, 11 vols. (London, 1970–83), IV, p. 438.

company.[7] Women and young men were particularly perceived to be prone to such diabolism. In Massachusetts, for example, in 1662, a young Quaker Mary Tilton was allegedly exiled from the Bay Colony for 'having like a sorceress gone from door to door to lure and seduce people, yea even young girls, to join the Quakers'.[8]

Not surprisingly, however, the vast majority of such claims were reserved for the Quaker leadership, and George Fox in particular. Described by Roger Williams as 'this bewitched and bewitching soul', Fox was credited with using all manner of unholy devices in order to ensnare potential converts. Among the tricks of his trade, Fox was said to have bewitched one female follower with the gift of a magic bracelet, to have used enchanted ribbons and bottles, and to have employed a familiar spirit. One northern minister, Francis Higginson, claimed that Fox, 'hath been and is vehemently suspected to be a sorcerer', citing as evidence his peculiar ability to out-stare and 'fascinate' onlookers.[9] Fox himself recorded in his *Journal* numerous instances of similar accusations, and seems to have regarded them as an essential element of his charismatic style of leadership. What others termed witchcraft, Fox clearly perceived as semi-miraculous acts of divine providence, as for example in 1652 when the local ministers and magistrates of Furness 'raised a report . . . yt neither water could drowne mee: nor coulde they draw blood of mee: and yt surely I was a witch'.[10]

If the methods used to convert followers were not in themselves sufficient evidence of Quaker diabolism, their habits and actions offered further confirmation, since they were widely considered to imitate the behaviour normally attributed to witches and sorcerers. The action of

---

[7] R. Baxter, *The Certainty of the World of Spirits* (London, 1691), p. 175; Dr Williams' Library, London, Baxter Treatises, vol. 3, fo. 309ʳ; S. Eaton, *The Quakers Confuted, being an Answer unto Nineteen Queries . . . sent to the Elders of the Church of Duckenfield in Cheshire* (London, 1654), sigs. A4ᵛ–Bʳ.

[8] S. S. Booth, *The Witches of Early America* (New York, 1975), p. 106.

[9] R. W[illiams], *George Fox Digg'd out of his Burrowes* (Boston, 1676), appendix, p. 116 (for further suggestions of Quaker witchcraft in this work, see pp. 2, 9, 22, 26–30, 49, 101, 181); [F. Higginson], *A Brief Relation of the Irreligion of the Northern Quakers* (London, 1653), pp. 18–19. Similar tales of Fox's witchcraft were repeated and endlessly recycled; see, for example, R. Farmer, *Sathan Inthron'd in his Chair of Pestilence* (London, 1657), pp. 38–9; [W. Fiennes], *Folly and Madnesse made Manifest* (Oxford, 1659), pp. 4–5, 66; [C. Leslie], *A Parallel between the Faith and Doctrine of the Present Quakers, and that of the Chief Hereticks in All Ages of the Church* (1700), sig. Bʳ.

[10] *The Journal of George Fox*, ed., N. Penney, 2 vols. (Cambridge, 1911), I, pp. 2–3, 38, 104–5, 169, 411n; *The Journal of George Fox: A Revised Edition*, ed., J. L. Nickalls (Cambridge, 1952), pp. 42–4, 179.

quaking itself, and the fits, trances and feats of fasting which characterised the activities of many early Quakers were all listed by their
enemies as certain evidence of diabolical infatuation. Higginson, for
example, cited William Perkins' *Discourse on the Damned Art of
Witchcraft* (1608) to prove that the Quakers' fits were truly from the
devil, not God, whilst the prominent New England minister John Norton
drew on classical and patristic sources to prove much the same point.[11]
Even more telling in the long run perhaps were the lurid contemporary
accounts of Quaker apostates who, having rejected the sect, accused their
erstwhile colleagues of practising all manner of diabolical tricks,
including possession. The most celebrated, or rather infamous, instance
was that of the Kendal ex-Quaker, John Gilpin, whose strange antics and
subsequent possession whilst under the care of the Quakers was widely
publicised throughout the second half of the seventeenth century.[12] No
doubt inspired by incidents such as these, puritan ministers were
constantly on the look-out for similar cases of feigned trances and
diabolical possessions. No less an expert on the subject than Richard
Baxter asserted that 'when the Quakers first rose here, their Societies
began like Witches, with Quaking and Vomiting, and Infecting others,
with breathing on them, and tying Ribbons on their Hands'. Written in
1691, such were the fruits of a life-time's study and observation, though
it is interesting to note that Baxter's views on this subject had remained
constant for over forty years. Thus, in a letter to a friend written in 1654,
Baxter opined that Quaker trances and feats of fasting 'com[e] not fr[om]
any ordinary Natural power', but were cited as evidence of a diabolical
conspiracy, orchestrated ultimately by the Papists, aimed at destroying
all order and godly religion in England. As if to underline the point, five
years later Baxter confidently asserted in print that William Perry, the
infamous 'Boy of Bilson', whose feigned possession was a *cause célèbre*
in the 1620s, was now resident in Bristol as a Quaker.[13]

Though from the Quaker point of view, prodigious acts of fasting,
fits and the like were readily taken as evidence of saintliness, it is not

---

[11] [Higginson], *A Brief Relation*, p. 18; J. Norton, *The Heart of N England Rent at the
Blasphemies of the Present Generation* (Cambridge, MA, 1659), pp. 5–6.

[12] J. Gilpin, *The Quakers Shaken: or, a Fire-brand Snatch'd out of the Fire* (Newcastle,
1653).

[13] Baxter, *The Certainty of the World of Spirits*, p. 175; Dr Williams' Library, Baxter
Treatises, vol. 3, fo. 302^r and *passim*; R. Baxter, *A Key for Catholics* (London, 1659),
p. 187; see also W. M. Lamont, *Richard Baxter and the Millennium* (London, 1979) for
a useful discussion of Baxter's religious world view.

difficult to see how the Quakers' opponents might place a different construction upon them. As a method of making converts, it was fraught with potential problems, but then so too were the more conventional approaches employed by Quaker prophets and evangelists. Their enemies, for example, routinely claimed that their books and pamphlets were bewitched, and that those who read and digested their message often became distracted and possessed. Thus Mary White of Suffolk was said to have suffered terrible fits and 'become distracted or possessed with an evil spirit' after reading Quaker literature in 1655. Her subsequent death occasioned yet another anti-Quaker diatribe in which the diabolical vices of the Friends were painstakingly recounted.[14] In a similar case in late-seventeenth-century New England, Cotton Mather cited as evidence of the Quakers' diabolism the case of a possessed maid who could only read Quaker books 'as if . . . the Witches or evil Spirits liked the Quakers books better, or that they were more favourable to them'. And at Evesham in Worcestershire in 1656, a local magistrate, Thomas Milnard, accused the Quakers of having bewitched the mayor with their writings and bibles which he subsequently refused to buy on the grounds that it was 'Witchery stuff'.[15]

Further evidence to support the learned perception of the Quaker as a form of surrogate witch was afforded by the thoroughly unconventional behaviour of some of the early adherents. The attempt, for example, by Susan Pierson to raise a fellow Quaker from the dead at Worcester in the 1650s evoked dubious comparisons with the deeds of necromancers. Equally, the tendency of early Friends to pronounce terrible curses upon their oppressors may have back-fired, particularly when their judgements were vindicated in the outcome. Roger Williams was probably not alone when he reasoned that ''tis true some of their Predictions have and may come to pass', adding ominously 'as do many also of Conjurers and Witches, for the Devil knows the Complexion of persons and things, and what is like to pass'.[16] Another sinister feature of early Quakerism

---

[14] Anon. *Quakers are Inchanters, and Dangerous Seducers. Appearing in their Inchantment of one Mary White at Wickham-skeyth in Suffolk, 1655* (London, 1655).

[15] J. Whiting, *Truth and Innocency Defended . . . in Answer to Cotton Mather . . . his Late Church History of New England* (London, 1702), pp. 50–1; [H. Smith and T. Woodrove], *The Cruelty of the Magistrates of Evesham* (London, 1655), p. 3.

[16] Baxter, *The Certainty of the World of Spirits*, p. 175; F. Duke, *An Answer to some of the Principal Quakers* (London, 1660), p. 38 (see also pp. 35, 59 and 68 where explicit accusations of witchcraft are made against the Quakers); Williams, *George Fox Digg'd out of his Burrowes*, p. 181. Dorcas Erbury also claimed to have been resurrected from the dead by James Nayler; see Reay, *The Quakers and the English Revolution*, p. 55.

noted by its enemies was the tendency of the Quakers to meet in lonely, isolated places, frequently at night, thus raising the spectre of nocturnal gatherings with that 'grand Quaker' the Devil. Though descriptions of sabbats are very rare in English witchcraft, we have what looks suspiciously like a Quaker sabbat, replete with feasting, in the notorious case of the alleged bewitchment of the Cambridgeshire Quaker-apostate Mary Philipps (or Margaret Prior by another account) which reached the local assizes in the summer of 1659. Though this particular case was rapidly dismissed for want of reliable evidence, stories of the Quakers' strange nocturnal habits and meetings continued to circulate. Thus the Scottish Presbyterian and celebrated witch-finder Alexander Peden claimed to have attended a Quaker meeting in Ireland at which the devil appeared in the shape of a raven. Similar suspicions were aroused by the nightly activities of the Young Quakeress, Jane Holmes, in the north Yorkshire village of Malton in the 1650s. For some, the mere fact that the Quakers first appeared in the north, the acknowledged home of witches and papists, was enough to taint them with the stigma of diabolism.[17]

A common theme running through many of these accounts, and one which clearly added to the growing image of the Quaker as witch, was the prominence of animals, or familiar spirits, the latter a quintessentially English feature of witchcraft beliefs. In the Cambridge case cited above, Philipps (or Prior) accused the Quakers of transforming her into a mare and riding her to the feast, or sabbat, where there was apparently much talk of 'doctrine'. At the Cheshire Quarter Sessions in 1656, John Forshoe reported as suspicious a conversation with the Quaker William Mosse in which the latter claimed that he was converted to Quakerism following a diabolical ride on a large black horse.[18] And one of the proofs adduced in the case of Mary White (see above, p. 149) was that in her fits, it was reported 'something in her body did run up and down, and

---

[17] Anon., *Strange and Terrible Newes from Cambridge being a True Relation of the Quakers Bewitching of Mary Philips* (London, 1659); *The Life and Prophecies of Mr Alexander Peden*, ed., P. Walker (Falkirk, 1781), pp. 46–7 (for Peden's extraordinary ability to detect witches, see pp. 38, 39–40, 49–50); R. Farmer, *The Great Mysteries of Godlinesse and Ungodlinesse* (London, 1655), p. 77; C. Wade, *Quakery Slain Irrecoverably* (London, 1657), p. 8.

[18] [J. Blackley et al.], *A Lying Wonder Discovered, and the Strange and Terrible Newes from Cambridge Proved False* (London, 1659), pp. 3–4; *Quarter Sessions Records . . . for the County Palatine of Chester, 1559–1760*, eds., J. H. E. Bennett and J. C. Dewhurst (Record Society of Lancashire and Cheshire, xciv, 1940), p. 164. George Fox was accused of both employing a familiar spirit as well as riding a suspiciously large black horse; see Duke, *An Answer*, p. 35; *Journal of George Fox*, ed., Penney, I, p. 38.

somtime she roared like a Bull; somtime barked like a Dog, and some-
time blared like a Calf'. Overtones of lycanthropy are everywhere
apparent in the reports of Quaker meetings, descriptions of bestial
behaviour a commonplace. Some accused the Quakers of howling and
shrieking like 'Night owls . . . infernal spirits . . . dogs and wolves', whilst
in another widely reported case, a Wrexham ex-Quaker, William
Spencer, invoked the image of the devil as the lord of the flies when he
reported hearing strange buzzing noises emanating from the vicinity of
his Quaker hosts as they slept.[19]

The annals of the early Quaker movement provide ample evidence of
the 'demonisation' of the sect, and the practical measures which were
taken against them by those in authority to combat this new threat to the
ordered, godly commonwealth. In the most extreme cases, Quakers were
formally accused of the crime of witchcraft, imprisoned and prosecuted
for the offence, as at Cambridge in 1659 (see above, p. 150). In the
same year, two Devon Quakers, Sarah and Elizabeth Tripe, were
examined by the mayor of Dartmouth, having been formally accused of
witchcraft by one Richard Laing at the instigation of the local minister
John Flavell.[20] Far more dramatic however were the revelations in
1659–60 concerning a mass gathering of Quaker and Baptist witches at
Sherborne in Dorset which would appear to have led to the institution of
formal charges against a number of local sectaries. According to one
hostile account, 'three men and two Women formerly Quakers' had
confessed to a whole series of crimes, including the murder by witchcraft
of the late minister of Sherborne and a campaign of harrassment against
his successor. The two women, moreover, were said to have admitted
that 'the divel hath oft times had Actuall copulation with them in sundry

---

[19] Anon., *Quakers are Inchanters*, pp. 6, 7; Wade, *Quakery Slain Irrecoverably*, p. 56;
S. Clarke, *A Mirrour or Looking-Glasse both for Saints and Sinners . . . The Second
Edition Much Enlarged* (London, 1654), pp. 461–2. The story of Spencer is
immediately preceded by a section headed 'Examples of Gods judgements upon
Witches, Conjurers, Inchanters and Astrologers' (ibid., pp. 453–8).

[20] Devon Record Office, Exeter, 'Minute Book of the Meeting for Sufferings held
at Exeter, 1682–4', 874D/S10, 18 Jan. 1683, 8th minute; FHL, 'Great Book of
Sufferings', I, p. 354; J. Whiting, *Persecution Expos'd, in Some Memoirs Relating to
the Sufferings of John Whiting, and Many Others of the People Called Quakers*
(London, 1715), p. 191. A year earlier, one Thomas Harvey was imprisoned at Exeter
on suspicion of witchcraft where he was visited by two Devon Quakers, William
Hingston and Anthony Tucker. Harvey was probably a Quaker since he had travelled
with the two Devon men to Bristol without a pass; see Devon Record Office, Exeter,
'Minute Book of the Sessions of the Peace', C1/64, fo. 429. I should very much like to
thank Mr John Slate for his generous help in alerting me to the existence of these cases.

shapes, but most commonly in the shape of Mr Lyford and Mr Bamfield, the ministers of Sherburne, whom he and they most hated and endeavoured to destroy'. Once again, responsibility for these accusations seems to have originated with the local incumbent, Francis Bampfield, a man of unstable temperament who was finally ejected from the living in 1662.[21] Formal accusations of this kind were, however, relatively rare. Much more common were informal accusations and innuendo which, as Barry Reay has stressed, were largely the product of the ruling elites. Typical in this respect were the actions of the Evesham minister, George Hopkins, a close friend and colleague of Richard Baxter, who in August 1655 preached on the subject of the Quakers' diabolism and witchcraft and then proceeded to lead the whole congregation in a full-scale attack upon a local Quaker meeting.[22]

Two other types of action which were especially reminiscent of English witch hunting, and can be found extensively in the records of Quaker persecution, were pricking and swimming. Pricking, or the practice of searching for insensitive spots on the witch's body as proof of guilt, was widely employed in a ritualistic fashion against the Quakers. Quaker apologists routinely complained that female members of the sect were singled out for this treatment. John Crook, for example, claimed in 1664 that an arresting officer pricked the arms of several Quaker women 'till they were black', an experience confirmed by the personal testimony of Barbara Blaugdone who reported being assaulted by a man who 'run some sharp Knife or Instrument . . . into the side of my Belly'.[23] Moreover, male members of the sect were not immune from this barbarism. At both Oxford and Cambridge, scholars seem to have

---

[21] [T. Smith], *A Gagg for the Quakers* (London, 1659), unpaginated appendix entitled 'A Memorable Advertisement from Dorsetshire'; A. Wood, *Athenae Oxonienses*, ed., P. Bliss, 4 vols. (London, 1813–20), IV, cols. 126–7; Reay, *The Quakers and the English Revolution*, p. 68.

[22] H. Smith, *A Collection of the Several Writings and Faithful Testimonies of . . . Humphrey Smith* (London, 1683), 'The Sufferings, Tryals & Purgings of the Saints at Evesham', sigs. A2ʳ–ᵛ. Hopkins had in fact worked closely with Baxter in the case of a bewitched Evesham girl whose dispossession had led to the execution of a local witch; see British Library (hereafter BL) Egerton MS 2570, fo. 88ᵛ.

[23] J. C[rook], *A True Information to the Nation, from the People Called Quakers* (London, 1664), p. 11; B. Blaugdone, *An Account of the Travels, Sufferings & Persecutions of Barbara Blaugdone* (London, 1691), p. 10. Blaugdone herself had fallen under suspicion of witchcraft on a number of occasions. Whilst *en route* to Ireland, she was nearly thrown overboard by some of the crew who suspected her of raising a storm. On arrival, she was shunned by her erstwhile friends, some of whom claimed that she was a witch and treated her accordingly; see ibid., pp. 21, 27–8.

regularly abused Quakers in this manner, and James Parnell complained of the jailor's wife at Colchester that she 'swore she would have my blood several times . . . and that she would mark my face . . . calling me Witch and Rogue'.[24] However, by far the most dramatic instance of this particular practice comes from Restoration Reading where between 1664 and 1676 local Friends were regularly subjected to an appalling campaign of violent persecution by the magistrate, Sir William Armourer. During this period, Armourer seems to have become obsessed with the idea of Quaker bewitchment, frequently interrupting their meetings in order to search female members for signs of enchanted 'black strings and ribbons'. His favourite technique on such occasions was to pull out a 'sharp Instrument somewhat like a pack needle' with which, the Quakers claimed, he 'mischiefously prickt severall women untill he drew bloud'.[25] The whole episode is highly reminiscent of the treatment inflicted upon the prophetess Anna Trapnell in Cornwall in the early 1650s, though Trapnell was spared the attentions of Truro's "witch-tryer-woman' and 'her great pin' through what she claimed was an act of divine intervention.[26]

Swimming witches – a common English practice – is also echoed in the punishments suffered by many early Quakers. We have already seen how George Fox's crossing of the notorious stretch of tidal water between Furness and Lancaster gave rise to the rumour of his witch-like inability to drown (see above, p. 147). In addition, Quakers were often assaulted and ducked, as for example at Mitcham in Surrey in 1659 when a group of Friends was attacked, and individuals beaten and thrown into ditches and ponds, so that 'when they had soe donne then they said freindes looket like witches'. Punishment by water ordeal was also

---

24 [J. Haward et al.], *Here Followeth a True Relation of Some of the Sufferings Inflicted upon the . . . Quakers by . . . the Schollars and Proctors of the University of Oxford* (London?, 1654), p. 4; E. Sammon et al., *A Discovery of the Education of the Schollars of Cambridge* (London, 1659), p. 4; Anon., *The Lambs Defence Against Lyes. And a True Testimony Given Concerning the Suffering and Death of James Parnell* (London, 1656), p. 10. For further examples, see J. Besse, *A Collection of the Sufferings of the People Called Quakers*, 2 vols. (London, 1753), I, p. 711; F. Gawler, *A Record of Some Persecutions Inflicted upon Some Servants of the Lord in South-Wales* (London, 1659), p. 27; [E. Hookes], *For the King and Both Houses of Parliament* (London, 1675), p. 14.

25 Besse, *A Collection of the Sufferings*, I, pp. 15, 24, 25, 29, 32; Anon., *Persecution Appearing with Its Open Face, in William Armorer* (London, 1667), pp. 5, 18, 42, 57, 70, 71; BL, Dept. of MSS, Microfilm M863/7, fos. 81–5; Anon., *The Continued Cry of the Oppressed for Justice* (London?, 1676), pt. 1, p. 12.

26 A. Trapnell, *Anna Trapnell's Report and Plea. Or, a Narrative of Her Journey from London into Cornwal* (London, 1654), pp. 21–2, 24. For Trapnell, see below p. 167.

inflicted upon the first two female Quakers to visit Oxford, Elizabeth Heavens and Elizabeth Fletcher. According to one account:

the students, hating reproof, fell to abusing the innocent women, and drove them by Force, to the Pump in John's College, where they pump'd Water upon their Necks, and into their Mouths, till they were almost dead: After which they tied them Arm to Arm, and inhumanly dragged them up and down the College, and through a Pool of Water.[27]

The encouragement of these practices was almost certainly designed to forge a common core of opposition to the Quakers, one which joined popular suspicion and hostility with that of the learned, governing elites. One measure of its success may be found in the treatment of imprisoned Quakers who, if rarely prosecuted for witchcraft *per se*, were jailed in large numbers for all manner of other religious and civil offences. John Aynsloe, a Cambridgeshire Quaker, thus reported that his coreligionists were regularly 'shut up in Dungeons and Holes, where they keep their Felons, and Witches, and Murderers'. Similarly, Margaret Parker of Aynho was imprisoned at Northampton in 1659 for non-payment of tithes, but she nonetheless found herself 'closely confined among Murderers, Thieves, Whores, and some called Witches, in a close nasty Place, where her friends were not admitted'.[28] Jailors and their wives seem to have been particularly credulous on the subject of Quaker diabolism, and responded accordingly. George Fox, for example, claimed that the jailor at Launceston in Cornwall tried to employ a conjurer to murder him. In the same year, the same man accused the Quaker prophetess, Anne Blackling, of being a witch, though in this particular instance he may have been consciously echoing the views of the local magistrate who, prior to sentence, accused her of being a 'whore' and a 'witch' and told her 'she and that generation . . . were not fit to live'.[29]

[27] Besse, *A Collection of the Sufferings*, I, pp. 562, 689 (cf. II, p. 228); *The Journal of George Fox*, ed., Penney, I, p. 340; see also Sammon et al., *A Discovery*, p. 4; *Victoria County History of Nottinghamshire*, ed., W. Page, 2 vols. (London, 1910), II, p. 74.

[28] Besse, *A Collection of the Sufferings*, I, pp. 91, 530.

[29] *The Journal of George Fox*, ed., Penney, I, p. 330; [E. Pyott, W. Salt et al.], *The West Answering to the North* (London, 1657), pp. 49, 59, 62, 117. Rumours of Martha Simmonds' witchcraft, and her bewitchment of James Nayler, were circulating freely in Bristol following the Quaker's arrest for blasphemy in 1656. Most of these seem to have stemmed from the depositions of fellow prisoners; see Farmer, *Sathan Inthron'd*, pp. 7–8, 10–12, 20, 22, 23, 24, 38–9. Another Quaker, John Roberts, was accused by the jailor of Gloucester of bewitching one of his staff. Interestingly, Roberts seems to have possessed some skill in locating the lost goods of neighbours, an attribute unusual in a Quaker, but one that nonetheless undoubtedly exacerbated fears of his

There can be little doubt that the inability of the authorities to punish Quakerism with the full severity of the laws reserved for witches and other felons was seen by many as a grave omission. Indeed, Barry Reay has gone so far as to suggest that a Quaker Salem was only narrowly avoided in England in the 1650s because of the divisions within the Cromwellian ruling elite. The key turning point in this respect, and one which sheds much valuable light upon the subject, was the debate which took place in parliament in December 1656 in the wake of the Nayler affair.[30] Reaction to the special committee formed to deal with the case, and to suggest a suitable punishment for the blasphemer, was evenly divided, but the genuine strength of feeling aroused by the affair is beyond dispute. Hardliners such as Major-General William Boteler, who argued vociferously for the death penalty, did so, significantly, within the context of a wider debate which included reference to the existence of legal punishments reserved for witches:

> The magistrate is to be a terror unto evil works. If we punish murder and witchcraft, and let greater offences go, as heresie and blasphemy, which is under the same enumeration; for my part I could never reconcile myself nor others to leave out the latter and punish the former.[31]

Others, however, pleaded for clemency, one on the grounds that Nayler himself was the hapless victim of bewitchment, that of Martha Simmonds whose reputation for 'witchery' was given widespread

---

'supernatural' powers; see D. Roberts, *Some Memoirs of the Life of John Roberts* (London, 1859), pp. 26, 56–62; D. Rollison, *The Local Origins of Modern Society: Gloucestershire 1500–1800* (London, 1992), pp. 187–96.

[30] For the best study of elite attitudes to the early Quakers, see Reay, *The Quakers and the English Revolution*, pp. 49–61 where the Nayler case is fully discussed. Some indication of the seriousness with which those in authority greeted the Quaker menace can be gleaned from T. L. Underwood's comment that 'of approximately ninety-eight adverse authors of the Commonwealth period listed in Joseph Smith's *Bibliotheca Anti-Quakeriana*, nearly 40 per cent are included in the *Dictionary of National Biography*'; *The Miscellaneous Works of John Bunyan*, ed., R. Sharrock, 11 vols. (Oxford, 1980–5), I, p. xxi.

[31] *Diary of Thomas Burton*, ed., J. T. Rutt, 2 vols. (London, 1828), I, p. 25. Boteler's commitment to the punishment of witches is well attested. In the 1640s, as chair of the bench, Boteler on three occasions admonished the Grand Jury of Bedfordshire on the legal requirement to punish the felony of witchcraft; see R. Lee, *Law and Local Society in the Time of Charles I: Bedfordshire and the Civil War* (Bedfordshire Historical Record Society, lxv, 1986), pp. 85, 95, 102. I cannot concur with Lee's conclusion that reference to the statute against witchcraft on three out of four occasions represents an attitude of apathy to the subject on the part of Boteler; ibid., pp. 66–7.

publicity by the Bristol preacher, Ralph Farmer.[32] In the event, Nayler narrowly escaped execution, thus providing an apparent victory for Cromwellian moderation. In practice, however, the hand of conservatives like Boteler was strengthened, and much new legislation, designed to destroy the nascent Quaker movement, was placed on the statute book. Widespread persecution of Quakerism followed, both according to the new laws as well as by the ingenious application of existing legislation, but without the creation of Quaker martyrs in the form of surrogate witches. For some, in retrospect, this would remain a missed opportunity, and there may have been many more like the Irish Presbyterian, Lt-Col. Cunningham who in the early years of the Restoration continued to assert that it ought to be 'lawful to put the Quakers to Death as false Prophets and Witches'.[33]

The persecution of Quakers as what I have termed 'surrogate witches' was of course only part of a much wider campaign of vilification levelled at members of the sect in its early years. Hostility to the Quakers, much of it promoted and encouraged by those in authority, probably peaked around 1659–60, and has prompted one historian of the sect to speculate that it was partially responsible for the Restoration of 1660.[34] With the change of regime, however, the persecution continued unabated, and Quaker records amply testify to the general fear and suspicion generated by Quaker activities in the post-Restoration period. Throughout this time, new allegations of Quaker witchcraft continued to surface in print to take their place alongside more established tales of Quaker diabolism. As late as the 1690s, there still seemed to be an audience for such

---

[32] *Diary of Thomas Burton*, ed. Rutt, I, pp. 153, 155; for Simmonds, see above p. 154 n. 29 and P. Mack, *Visionary Women: Ecstatic Prophecy in Seventeenth-Century England* (Berkeley, 1992), pp. 197–208.

[33] Besse, *A Collection of the Sufferings*, II, pp. 472–3. Some indication of what might have taken place in England, if the more conservative puritan element had gained mastery of the Commonwealth is suggested by the intensity of the campaign against Quakers in New England from 1656 onwards. From their first arrival, the Quakers were rapidly perceived as part of a diabolical conspiracy to undermine the godly establishment of the colony, and accusations of witchcraft were widespread; see especially Karlsen, *The Devil in the Shape of a Woman*, pp. 122–5. For attempts to link the Salem trials in 1692 to popular antipathy for local Quakers, see C. L. Heyrman, 'Specters of Subversion, Societies of Friends: Dissent and the Devil in Provincial Essex County, Massachusetts', in D. M. Hall, J. M. Murrin and T. W. Tate, eds., *Saints and Revolutionaries: Essays on Early American History* (London, 1984), pp. 38–74 (esp. pp. 47–54); Godbeer, *The Devil's Dominion*, pp. 193–9.

[34] Reay, *The Quakers and the English Revolution*, p. 81 (see esp. pp. 81–100).

senastionalist journalism.[35] The negative effect of this publicity upon the reception accorded to Quakerism in late-seventeenth-century England is beyond doubt. What remains largely unexamined, however, is the extent to which the stigma of Quaker diabolism had an impact upon contemporary perceptions of traditional belief in witches and witchcraft.

In confronting this issue, one is immediately struck by a coincidence – namely, that the 'construction' of the Quaker-witch stereotype took place at roughly the same moment in English history when, according to most historians of English witchcraft, belief in traditional learned demonology was in decline.[36] At first sight, this might appear paradoxical, but it is possible, I believe, to show that the two processes may in fact be linked, part of a complex and barely perceptible shift in the intellectual outlook of the learned. However, in order to explore this vital realignment of educated belief, it is first essential to grasp the extent to which Quaker actions and doctrines offended against conventional assumptions and appeared to threaten the whole edifice of life and belief in mid-seventeenth-century England. In the eyes of the governing elites, Quakerism represented not merely a challenge to the religious status quo, but a threat to some of the most cherished assumptions of their society and the world view upon which they rested. In the words of one Cromwellian MP, its 'principles and practises are diametrically opposite both to magistracy and ministry . . . [and] will level the foundation of government into a bog of confusion'.[37]

---

[35] See, for example [C. Leslie], *The Snake in the Grass: or Satan Transformed into an Angel of Light . . . the Second Edition* (London, 1697), pp. 300–9 where an incident which occurred in 1674 was used by the author to prove the existence of witchcraft among Cumberland Friends. As late as 1701, George Whitehead still felt that it was necessary to discredit the notorious fabrication of the discovery of a nest of Quaker witches at Sherborne in 1659; see G. Whitehead, *Truth Prevalent: and the Quakers Discharged from the Norfolk-Rectors Furious Charge* (London, 1701), p. 125. The original incident is described above, pp. 151–2.

[36] Among contemporary figures, John Aubrey, Sir William Temple and the radical minister, John Everard, all attest to the significance of the civil war period as a turning-point in this respect; see M. Hunter, *John Aubrey and the Realm of Learning* (New York, 1975), p. 220; W. Temple, *Miscellanea. The Second Part. In Four Essays* (London, 1690), pt. iv ('On poetry'), pp. 6–7, 43; J. Everard, *Some Gospel-Treasures Opened* (London, 1653), p. 148. Dr Stuart Clark quite rightly reminds me however that this is a claim which has never been fully authenticated by hard evidence, and that it is possible that much of the Anglican establishment before 1640 may have been more than a little sceptical of witchcraft. I intend to confront this, and many other related issues, in my forthcoming book on English witchcraft, of which this essay represents one small part.

[37] Reay, *The Quakers and the English Revolution*, p. 57.

Concerns of this nature permeate the literature of the interregnum and Restoration, and were particularly uppermost in the minds of those who attempted to draw the link between Quakerism and witchcraft. Thus the Quakers' object, according to the title-page of one Quaker demonology, was to 'subvert all Civil Government both in Church and State', whilst others pointedly referred to their stubborn refusal to bow or perform hat service as yet further evidence of their wizardry.[38] Indeed, the Quaker contempt for all forms of authority was axiomatic, rooted as it was in their obdurate adherence to the 'light within' as the sole guide to all matters, human and divine. That these impulses were construed by their opponents as demonic rather than divine was equally axiomatic given the fruits of such wayward thinking. For example, the minister Ellis Bradshawe, in a work dedicated to Oliver Cromwell, bewailed the blasphemous outpourings of the Quakers, and their assault upon godly ministers, by recounting the manner in which Satan first established contact with apostate witches:

> And is it not always so with Satan in his trading with Witches, that before he granteth them a familiar spirit to be their servant, hee ever ingageth them under a degree of blasphemie . . . And then hee knoweth that he hath them sure as quite from under the protection of God, and so ingageth them in covenant . . . with himselfe . . . as I might instance in many examples that I have read in Histories concerning divers Witches.[39]

Moreover, it was not only the outward authority of church and state that was threatened by these 'Quaker-witches'. One of the most frequent complaints levelled against the early Quakers was that their teachings

---

[38] [R. Blome], *The Fanatick History: or an Exact Relation and Account of the Old Anabaptists, and the New Quakers* (London, 1660); H. Howet, *Quaking Principles Dashed in Pieces by the Standing and Unshaken Truth* (London, 1655), p. 14 (where the Quakers' refusal to honour men is compared to the irreverent actions of wizards); Anon., *The Continued Cry*, p. 107 (case of William Moxham, accused of being 'bewitched' for refusing to bare his head in the Bishop's Court at Salisbury, 1676); cf. remark of a Leicestershire minister that the Quakers will 'allow of now Lawes of God, nor Scriptures; but the Revelations and Edicts of their own bewitched fancies'; J. Timson, *The Quakers Apostasie from the Perfect Rule of the Scriptures Discovered* (London, 1656), p. 33.

[39] E. Bradshawe, *The Quakers Quaking Principles Examined and Refuted* (London, 1656), pp. 31–2. Much the same point was made by the Norfolk Presbyterian Jonathan Clapham in yet another work dedicated to Cromwell; see J. Clapham, *A Full Discovery and Confutation of the Wicked and Damnable Doctrines of the Quakers* (London, 1656), p. 38. Clapham went on to raise the spectre of the diabolical sabbat which he compared to Quaker gatherings, p. 43.

fostered familial divisions and disorder, thus undermining one of the central tenets of early modern political thought, patriarchalism. Stories of bewitched sons, daughters and wives turning Quaker are legion, and though some were certainly published for polemical purposes only, not all took this form.[40] Quaker testimonies themselves testify to the generation of deep familial division and conflict. Thus when Josiah Langdale turned Quaker in 1693 at the age of twenty, he began to 'thou and thee' his mother who, in turn, 'said I was bewitched, and that she would never own me to be her Son more'.[41]

The rebelliousness of the Quakers – their profound antipathy for traditional forms of order and social convention – became a commonplace of late-seventeenth-century English thought. 'Rebels against Christ' was how one of their opponents styled them, 'children of disobedience', according to another, in whom 'the Devil reigns and rules'. There can be little doubt that such epithets only accentuated the likelihood that the Quakers' crimes would be conflated with those of witches since the refusal of the latter to bow to authority, and their subversion of normal social relations, was equally platitudinous. From the perspective of the godly, puritan and non-puritan, what was under attack here was the whole metaphysic of order upon which early modern English society was built. The Quaker vision of society was nothing less than a Satanic inversion of the godly commonwealth, a point graphically made by Richard Baxter in 1654 when he confided to a friend that the Quakers:

> worke no miracles but are as men posest by evill spirits . . . these pr[e]scrib[e] ye laws of hell, destroying relations, & endevouring to blot out ye light & law of nature . . . even parents so disowne their owne children, husbands their wives & all nations their govern[o]rs & would dissolve all societies, so yt ye very image of ye de[vill] is visible in their doctrine.[42]

Just as historians have tended to dismiss the reality of witchcraft for early modern Europeans on the grounds of its apparent illogicality, so too

---

[40] See for example the case cited in Anon., *An Answer to a Scandalous Paper . . . Dated from Dorchester in New-England, August 17. 1655, subscribed, Edward Breck* (London, 1656), sigs. A4ᵛ–Bʳ.

[41] FHL, 'Some Account of the Birth, Education, & Religious Exercises and Visitations of God, to . . . Josiah Langdale' (1723), MS Box 10 (10), p. 15; cf. [D. Lupton], *The Quacking Mountebanck or the Jesuite Turn'd Quaker* (London, 1655), p. 19.

[42] S. Scandrett, *An Antidote Against Quakerisme* (London, 1671), p. 81; Anon., *The Devil Turned Quaker* (London, 1656), sig. A3ᵛ (cf. sig. A5ʳ); Dr Williams' Library, Baxter Treatises, vol. 3, fol. 309ʳ.

historians of Quakerism are in danger of discrediting contemporary perceptions of the reality of the Quaker threat by intimating that it too, like witchcraft, was the product of an irrational hysteria. Yet to do so would be to perpetrate a gross distortion of the motives of those who wrote such diatribes against the Quakers. When, for example, seventeenth-century Englishmen of various Protestant leanings made the link between Quakerism, witchcraft and Catholicism, and suggested that the Quaker panic was part of a Jesuit-inspired plot designed to subvert the 'true faith' in England, it made perfect sense for them to do so. Catholicism and witchcraft had long gone hand in hand in the mental outlook of Protestant Englishmen, so much so that by the 1650s countless authorities could be cited to support the equation of witches with papists.[43] The civil war itself, and the religious and political turmoil which it engendered, were all commonly ascribed to the machinations of the papacy which continued into the 1650s with the attempt to undermine the godly commonwealth of the Republic. The appearance of the Quakers at this time was therefore seen as a logical development in the on-going process of Catholic subversion which was of course masterminded by those two arch-apostates, the Pope and the devil. In no time at all, men of learning, preachers and governors were making explicit references to the Catholic sources of Quaker diabolism, and focusing particular attention upon the role of the Jesuits in spreading such 'doctrines of devils'.

That these were genuine expressions of fear and moral outrage is beyond question. William Prynne, for example, cited dozens of references to learned demonologists and contemporary authorities (including Weyer, del Rio, Petrus Thyraeus and Georgius Pictorius) in

---

[43] For just a few examples among many of works equating the witchcraft of the Quakers with the subtle plots of Jesuits and Catholics, see G. Bishop et al., *The Cry of Blood* (London, 1656), sig. C^r, p. 14 [a Quaker account of this process]; C. Gilbert, *The Libertine School'd or a Vindication of the Magistrates Power in Religious Matters* (London, 1657), sig. C^v, pp. 13, 18; Baxter, *A Key for Catholics*, pp. 184–9; W. Prynne, *The Quakers Unmasked, and Clearly Detected to be the Spawn of Romish Frogs, Jesuits And Franciscan Fryers . . . The Second Edition Enlarged* (London, 1664), pp. 8–13, 21–4. A Quaker from Woodbridge in Suffolk was apparently beaten by a priest who called him 'rogue, witch, devil, papist'; see Besse, *A Collection of the Sufferings*, I, p. 666. For Catholicism and witchcraft, see for example P. Lake, 'Anti-Popery: the structure of a prejudice', in R. Cust and A. Hughes, eds., *Conflict in Early Stuart England: Studies in Religion and Politics 1603–1642* (London and New York, 1989), pp. 75, 93, 100n. Popular identification of the Quakers with the activities of Roman Catholics is discussed in S. A. Kent, 'The papist charges against the interregnum Quakers', *Journal of Religious History*, 2 (1982–3), 180–90.

order to substantiate the claim that the Quakers' possessions, strange prophesyings and eccentric behaviour were part of a diabolical conspiracy, masterminded by the Jesuits, to turn the English away from 'our Reformed Church and Religion'.[44] Others repeated the charge – albeit in less fulsome style – in pamphlet after pamphlet.[45] Elite anxiety of this kind probably reached fever pitch in the wake of the Nayler affair, if we can trust the evidence of Thomas Burton's parliamentary diary. On 5 January 1657, Burton recorded that MPs in the Grand Committee for Religion, prompted by discussion of a magical book by one Robert Turner, 'fell into a long debate how the papists laboured to delude us and intricate us, by obtruding doctrines of all sizes in their books dispersed abroad'. The entry ends with the telling shorthand note: 'Quakers, and magic, and all devils, &c'.[46]

When men like Prynne and Baxter described the threat of Quakerism within the wider context of a diabolically inspired Catholic plot, they unwittingly evoked deeply engrained habits of thought which were widely shared by their fellow countrymen. At the heart of their antipathy toward the sect, as well as other religious and political malcontents, lay an overwhelming belief in the sanctity of social, religious and political conformity, and a corresponding distaste for what Prynne termed the 'Anti-magistratical as well as Anti-ministeriall' tendencies of radical sectarianism.[47] Such concerns, however, were not limited to those in authority in the 1650s. Belief in what one might term the 'unitary state' wherein authority and order was vested in a single individual or body (one ruler, one church, etc.) continued to dominate the thinking of the vast majority of the political nation throughout the middle decades of the seventeenth century, despite (or perhaps in part because of) the

---

[44] Prynne, *The Quakers Unmasked*, pp. 8–10, 11–12, 21–2, 24.

[45] See, for example, the opinion of the minister Richard Standfast who asserted that it was undoubtedly the case that the Quakers, acting as the Jesuits' emissaries, had used the 'black arts' of sorcery and witchcraft; R. Standfast, *A Caveat Against Seducers* (London, 1660), pp. 24–5.

[46] *Diary of Thomas Burton*, ed., Rutt, I, pp. 80, 305–7, 331.

[47] Prynne, *The Quakers Unmasked*, p. 8; cf. Anon., *The Quakers Fiery Beacon*, p. 8, where the passage from Prynne is cited *verbatim* from the first edition of 1655. Such plagiarism provides an excellent example of the way in which 'serious' works of anti-Quaker sentiment were recycled for popular consumption in the 'tabloid' press of the 1650s. The publisher of *The Quakers Fiery Beacon* and many similar compilations was George Horton who had earlier played a key role in the 'creation' of the Ranter scare; see J. C. Davis, *Fear, Myth and History: The Ranters and the Historians* (Cambridge, 1986), p. 108.

radical aspirations of a minority. As a result, faith in a divinely ordained, ordered polity, reflective of the wider harmony exhibited by the Creation, remained a commonplace of political thought in this period, notwithstanding the fact that different factions or groups might differ in the stress which they placed on specific aspects of this harmonic world view.[48] A by-product of this dominant metaphysic was the hermeneutic principle that the best way to understand the world of God, man and nature was through an exploration of its antithesis, the disorderly world of Satan, devils and Hell.[49] In plain terms, this meant subscription to the language of binary oppositions and the logic of argument *a contrariis*, which as Stuart Clark has shown informed all manner of Renaissance thinking, but was particularly appropriate when invoked within the context of early modern demonology.[50]

Educated belief in witchcraft and the detailed theories of the demonologists was thus part of a much broader intellectual spectrum – a whole universe of moral meanings – which was firmly rooted in the early modern preoccupation with order, authority and uniformity. In England, prior to the civil war, support for the godly commonwealth was thus

[48] It is not my purpose here to resurrect that monolith of early modern political thought, the great chain of being, which some historians have too readily accepted as the sole source of political authority in England before 1640. On the other hand, I am inclined to the view that for the majority of the political nation before 1640, subscription to a divinely ordained civil polity, in which unity, uniformity and hierarchy were the chief defining characteristics, was largely automatic (regardless of specific differences of opinion as to what precise form this polity might take). This is a complex issue to which I intend to return at a later date. For two studies which stress the flexibility of conventional harmonist thinking, see R. Eccleshall, *Order and Reason in Politics: Theories of Absolute and Limited Monarchy in Early Modern England* (Oxford, 1978) and J. Daly, 'Cosmic harmony and political thinking in early Stuart England', *Transactions of the American Philosophical Society*, 69 (1979), 3–40. More recently, interest in this controversial subject has been revived by Kevin Sharpe who, like Eccleshall and Daly, infers that the civil war acted as an essential solvent of consensual harmonism; see K. Sharpe, 'A Commonwealth of meanings: languages, analogues, ideas and politics', in Sharpe, *Politics and Ideas in Early Stuart England* (London and New York, 1989), pp. 1–71.

[49] Such thinking has recently been invoked in order to shed light on two vital areas of seventeenth-century life in England, anti-popery and puritanism. See P. Lake, 'Anti-Popery', p. 73 and P. Collinson, *The Birthpangs of Protestant England: Religious and Cultural Change in the Sixteenth and Seventeenth Centuries* (London, 1988), pp. 146–8.

[50] S. Clark, 'Inversion, misrule and the meaning of witchcraft', *Past and Present*, 87 (1980), 118. I should like to thank Dr Clark, not only for numerous illuminating discussions on this subject, but also for permission to read the drafts of various chapters of his forthcoming *Witchcraft in Early Modern Thought* (Oxford), in which these and many related issues are discussed.

reinforced by the recognition of its opposite, demonic disorder, which for true patriots took the form of devil-worshipping witches, aided and abetted by Catholic fifth columnists. The wide appeal of such ideas was undoubtedly conducive to the promotion of unity in the body politic, and arguably acted as a deterrent to rebellion and the expression of dissent.[51] The collapse of religious and political consensus after 1640 however challenged the whole edifice upon which Protestant unity under the Stuarts was based, and as England fragmented into parties, factions and sects, so too did these groups attempt to appropriate for themselves the sole custodianship of traditional moral, religious and political authority. One aspect of this process was the attempt by all sides to lay claim to the authorising language of demonic inversion and witchcraft. During the civil war itself, both sides sought to depict the conflict as a struggle of cosmic proportions, an apocalyptic encounter between the forces of good and evil, order and disorder, God and the devil. Thereafter, the inability of successive governments to resolve the deep divisions exposed by civil war ensured that the politicisation of witchcraft would continue to grow apace with each new political crisis (the Restoration; Exclusion Crisis; the 'rage of party'). Seen against this background, the demonisation of the Quakers was just one example (though a particularly well documented one) of a long process which had its roots in the disintegration of consensus in the 1640s, and which was itself prefigured to some extent by the gradual polarisation of the political nation in the reign of Charles I.[52]

There is insufficient space here to document these developments in full, but some examples taken from the post-civil war period should help to illustrate the general point, namely that from 1640 onward no one was immune from the charge of diabolism since there was no longer a single standard of good and evil, or right and wrong, by which to judge the

---

[51] The Jacobean preacher, Samuel Garey's view that 'Popery is a witchcraft of religion' would appear to have attracted near universal assent. The celebrated Elizabethan jurist William Lambarde consistently linked the activities of witches with those of Jesuits and papists in his charges to the Kent Grand Jury, on one occasion referring to the Pope as 'that witch of the world'; see S. Garey, *Great Brittans Little Calendar: Or, Triple Diarie* (London, 1618), appendix ('A Short Disswasive from Popery'), sig. I2ʳ; *William Lambarde and Local Government: His Ephemeris and Twenty-Nine Charges to Juries and Commissions*, ed., C. Read (Ithaca, 1962), pp. 101, 110–11, 115. It would be easy to multiply examples of this kind for the late sixteenth and seventeenth century.

[52] For examples of such polarisation, accompanied by the language of demonic inversion, before 1640, see: *CSPD, 1628–9*, p. 43; J. Forster, *Sir John Eliot: A Biography, 1592–1632*, 2 vols. (London, 1872), II, pp. 13, 111–12; J. Rushworth, *Historical Collections*, 8 vols. (London, 1721–2), I, pp. 362, 391, 618.

actions of men. During the civil war itself, both sides habitually resorted to the language of witchcraft, most obviously as a form of crude propaganda, but equally as a valuable authorising agent in the struggle to establish the righteousness of one's particular cause. On the parliamentary side, for example, the supporters of godly reform were bombarded with sermon after sermon in which it was alleged that closet papists, posing as royal counsellors, had 'bewitched the Court and Country' and threatened to destroy the godly commonwealth. Biblical sources were ransacked in order to show that the king, in the guise of Saul or Pharaoh, had been deluded by the 'sorcery' of evil advisers in the shape of latter-day witches of Endor and Egyptian magicians.[53] The cure, as in the case of the bewitched, lay in an act of dispossession, which for most Puritans implied the thorough-going reform of the liturgy, administration and teachings of the Anglican church. The correlation between public and private exorcism (itself suggested by the therapeutic performance of regular *fast* sermons) is also evident in the career of the Puritan minister, Lewis Hughes, who as a young man in 1602 had played a leading role in the celebrated dispossession of Mary Glover.[54] Now, forty years on, Hughes campaigned for the reform of the Laudian Prayer Book on the grounds that some of its prescribed ceremonies (e.g. churching) were directly comparable to those practised by devil-worshipping witches.[55]

Not surprisingly, supporters of the king and the established church took a rather different view of events, though they too invoked demonological precedents in order to explain the recalcitrance of the rebels. The Bible in particular provided valuable comfort for royalists in the shape of 1 Samuel, 15, 23: 'For Rebellion is as the sin of witchcraft'.

---

[53] For just a sample of the fast sermons preached before parliament which made such inferences and connections, see T. Wilson, *Jerichoes Downfall* (London, 1643), pp. 31, 33–4; T. Hill, *The Militant Church, Triumphant over the Dragon and his Angels* (London, 1643), p. 20; E. Staunton, *Rupes Israelis: The Rock of Israel* (London, 1644), pp. 10–11; J. Caryl, *Joy Out-Joyed: Or Joy in Overcoming Evil Spirits and Evil Men* (London, 1646), pp. 5–6; H. Wilkinson, *Miranda, Stupenda. Or, the Wonderful and Astonishing Mercies which the Lord hath Wrought for England* (London, 1646), pp. 1–3; P. Sterry, *The Commings Forth of Christ in the Power of the Death* (London, 1650), pp. 7, 40, 41.

[54] L. Hughes, *Certain Grievances, or, the Popish Errors and Ungodlinesse of the Service Book* (London, 1642), pp. 17–20; *Witchcraft and Hysteria in Elizabethan London: Edward Jorden and the Mary Glover Case*, ed., M. MacDonald (London and New York, 1991), pp. xxii–xxiii. Fasting and prayer were of course the traditional puritan remedies for bewitchment.

[55] Hughes, *Certain Grievances*, pp. 14–16.

The learned image of the witch as an archetypal rebel afforded a distinctly political resonance to this text which was fully utilised by the defenders of the religious and political status quo. On at least two occasions during the civil war, loyalist clergymen preached before the Oxford parliament on 1 Samuel, 15, 23. The distinguished jurist and royalist Sir Robert Heath felt impelled to compose a private, manuscript meditation on the subject in order to demonstrate the point that when we understand 'the true nature of witchcraft, then in that as in a glass shall we the better see the true p[or]trature of Rebellion, which we are soe naturally inclined unto'.[56]

Following the end of the first civil war in 1646, references to the 'witchcraft' of the victors continued, and were, more often than not, couched in terms of the general collapse of established order and religious unity in the country. 'Are there not now as many minds as men?' lamented one disgruntled royalist in 1647. In calling the citizens of London to arms, he implored them to 'arise, and bee noe longer deluded and infatuated with the false prophitts of these tymes . . . which seek the ruine of your soules and bodyes by lulling you asleep in that which is worse then witchcraft'.[57] Fabian Philipps echoed these sentiments in 1649 when he cited as one of the reasons for parliament's victory in the war 'the fiery Zeale of a Seditious Clergie to preach the people into a Rebellion, and the People head-long lie runing into the Witchcraft of it'. In the post-mortem which followed defeat, Philipps reckoned that 'seven years mistaken, preaching and pratling' had brought nothing but confusion, and he concluded by comparing the recent blood-letting in England (most notably the execution of the king) with the 'witchcraft and cousenage . . . of Medea when shee set Pelias daughters to let out his blood that young might come in the place of it'.[58]

---

56 N. Bernard, *ΕΣΟΠΤΡΟΝ ΤΗΣ ΑΝΤΙΜΑΧΙΑΣ, or a Looking-Glasse for Rebellion* [16 June 1644] (Oxford, 1644); B. Holyday, *Against Disloyalty, Fower Sermons Preach'd in the Times of the Late Troubles* ['Of rebellion', 19 May 1644] (Oxford, 1661); BL, Egerton MS 2982, 'A Meditation uppon thes wordes Rebellion is as the Sinn of Witchcraft, 1 Samuel 15. 23', fo. 81ʳ. For Heath's life and career, see P. E. Kopperman, *Sir Robert Heath, 1575–1649: The Window of an Age* (Woodbridge, 1989).

57 *Historical Manuscripts Commission. Calendar of the Manuscripts of . . . the Marquess of Salisbury . . . Part XXII*, ed., D. Owen (London, 1971), pp. 398–9; the anonymous author pointedly reminded his audience that 'there is but one truth and one way to that *Summum Bonum*, the true Protestant religion', ibid., p. 398.

58 [F. Philipps], *King Charles the First, No Man of Blood; But a Martyr for his People* (London, 1649), pp. 21, 66. This work was republished in expanded form in 1660 as *Veritas Inconcussa* (London, 1660), the relevant references appearing on pp. 75, 235–6.

On all sides of the political and religious divide, the language of witchcraft was thus invoked as a natural and rational response to the unprecedented divisions and disorder ushered in by civil war. Newspapers, pamphlets and private journals abound in examples of this kind.[59] Just as the *maleficium* of the village witch was cited to explain unforeseen accidents within the context of parochial life, so in the 1640s was the language of popular demonology utilised in national politics to account for sudden desertions or unexpected rebuffs. Thus, when Sir Edward Dering appeared to effect a dramatic *volte-face* in 1642 by promoting a petition in Kent in favour of episcopacy and the old Prayer Book, John Pym roundly condemned such actions in the Commons as those more suited to a witch.[60] Most dramatic of all, however, was the vehemently demonic language used by the Presbyterian Denzil Holles in February 1649 in order to explain the treachery of Cromwell and his associates in their dealings with the king. In his *Memoirs*, Holles berated Cromwell and his 'Fellow-Witches' for plotting the destruction of the kingdom in their meetings or 'Sabbaths' with the result that 'England is become, by the actings of these men, that Monster, whose shape is perverted, the head standing where the feet, and the feet where the head, should be . . . '.[61]

The references to inversion, disorder and universal chaos in the body politic invoked by Holles are typically those of conventional demonology and underline the extent to which mid-seventeenth-century Englishmen were liable to perceive the disintegration of political and religious order in demonic terms. These were not mere rhetorical flourishes or crude propaganda designed simply to comfort and reassure an anxious audience. On the contrary, in an age in which metaphors, like analogues, were widely held to convey universal truths, citations such as these reflected a genuine desire to come to terms with the unprecedented upheavals of the age. And what is more, they would continue to be

---

[59] Royalist newspapers in particular were quick to detect the demonological significance of their opponents' actions; see, for example, *Mercurius Aulicus*, 25 June 1643, p. 331; 17 Aug. 1643, p. 447; 27 Sept. 1643, p. 543; 1 Apr. 1644, p. 917; 27 Apr. 1644, p. 962; 14 Oct. 1644, p. 1204; 10 Aug. 1645, pp. 1697–8; *Mercurius Academicus*, 9 Feb. 1646, pp. 81–2; *Mercurius Anti-Britannicus*, 4 Aug. 1645, pp. 5–6; Anon., *A Wonder a Mercury Without a Lye in's Mouth* (London, 1648), pp. 1–2.

[60] J. Forster, *Lives of Eminent British Statesmen: John Pym and John Hampden* (London, 1837), p. 272.

[61] 'Memoirs of Denzil, Lord Holles . . . from the Year 1641 to 1648', in F. Maseres, ed., *Select Tracts Relating to the Civil Wars in England*, 2 vols. (London, 1815), I, pp. 189–90, 256, 307.

invoked for the rest of the century, particularly at moments of acute religious and political crisis. During the 1650s, for example, the Quakers were only one of a number of sects who were stigmatised with the taint of demonolatry. The Baptists had long shared a similar fate, their denial of infant baptism readily conflated with the witch's spiritual rejection of christian baptism.[62] Similarly, as Professor Davis has shown, the 'fabrication' of a Ranter conspiracy in the early 1650s owed much to the propensity of a new ruling class to envisage Ranter opposition within the framework of demonic inversion.[63] Other examples from the 1650s include the accusations of witchcraft which surfaced at the trial of the pseudo-messiah William Franklin and his 'spouse' Mary Gadbury in January 1650, and the allegations levelled at the radical minister, John Pordage in the mid-1650s, part of a concerted effort by the local Puritan authorities to dispossess him of the rich living of Bradfield.[64] One of the best documented examples of this process of demonisation is to be found in the autobiography of the fifth monarchist and prophetess, Anna Trapnell, where she describes her treatment at the hands of the authorities in Truro in 1653. Here, she recalled how she was harried by 'Englands Rulers and Clergie' who adjudged her to be 'under the administration of evil angels, and a witch'. One of her persecutors, the St Ives minister, Leonard Welstead, even refused to take direct action against Trapnell until 'the Rulers came, for then they say, the witches can have no power over them'. Thus, she concluded, 'one depends upon another, Ruler upon Clergie, and Clergie upon Rulers'. Finally, she was

---

[62] The Presbyterian Thomas Hall, for example, regarded Baptism as 'little better then Witchcraft: for Witches, before they can make a league with the Devil, must renounce their Infant-Baptism'; T. Hall, *The Font Guarded with XX Arguments* (London, 1652), sig. A2ᵛ. Much the same point was made by Hall's puritan colleagues Nathaniel Stephens and John Eachard; see N. Stephens, *A Precept for the Baptisme of Infants out of the New Testament* (London, 1651), pp. 38, 61; J. Eachard, *The Axe, Against Sin and Error; and the Truth Conquering* (London, 1646), pp. 16–17, 27. It was widely rumoured that Colonel Thomas Robinson, a notorious persecutor of nonconformists in Cornwall, was killed by a witch, 'either a Presbyterian or "Baptize"', see *CSPD, 1671*, p. 105; *Journal of George Fox*, ed. Penney, II, pp. 30–1.

[63] Davis, *Fear, Myth and History*, pp. 120–1.

[64] H. Ellis, *Pseudochristus: or, a True and Faithful Relation of the Grand Impostures . . . Lately Spread Abroad . . . by William Franklin and Mary Gadbury and their Companions* (London, 1650), pp. 9, 43, 55–6; C. Fowler, *Daemonium Meridianum. Satan at Noon* (London, 1655), pp. 18, 55, 80, 87, 135, 148, 149. In the same tract, the Presbyterian Fowler referred to the Quakers as 'not Men but Monsters', p. 162. Pordage himself claimed that Fowler's Reading colleague, Simon Ford, had preached a sermon on the subject of Pordage's alleged diabolism 'and so excited Magistrates to persecute me', p. 87.

brought to court where it was generally believed that she would prove herself to be a witch since 'it used to be so among witches, they could not speak before the Magistrates'. In the circumstances, she signally failed to ratify this test with the result, according to Trapnell, that the 'rude multitude said, "Sure this woman is no witch, for she speaks many good words, which the witches could not" '.[65]

Equally significant perhaps in the long term was the response of the radical sectaries to such charges of witchcraft. Once again, the example of the Quakers is illuminating. Much to the dismay of their enemies, many of whom prayed for a return to religious and doctrinal unity, the new breed of Quaker 'witches' responded to their critics by invoking the age-old principle of *lex talionis*. Thus it was the latter who were routinely subjected to the charge that it was they, and not the Quakers, who practised sorcery and witchcraft in order to delude the people. Yet the Quaker definition of witchcraft, like that of many of their fellow sectaries, was very different from that favoured by their more orthodox opponents.[66] Based largely on biblical precedents, the Quakers characteristically envisaged witchcraft not as a physical manifestation of the power of evil, but rather as a form of spiritual apostasy. Biblical archetypes included Simon Magus[67], Elymas the Sorcerer[68] and pharaoh's magicians, Jannes and Jambres.[69] No credence however was paid to the conjectures of learned demonologists and theologians.[70]

---

[65] Trapnell, *Anna Trapnel's Report and Plea*, sig. A3ʳ, pp. 21, 25, 28. Trapnell's commentary on this episode suggests further ways in which accusations of witchcraft aimed against sectaries might help inadvertently to spread popular scepticism.

[66] Interestingly, Quaker citations of witchcraft bear a close affinity with those repeatedly invoked by the sceptic and radical nonconformist John Webster in the 1650s; see P. Elmer, *The Library of Dr John Webster: The Making of a Seventeenth-Century Radical*, *Medical History*, supplement no. 6 (1986), pp. 2–3, 12–13.

[67] A. Stodard et al., *Something Written in Answer to a Lying, Scandalous Book* (London, 1955), p. 2; G. Fox, *A Declaration of the Ground of Error & Errors* (London, 1657), p. 23; G. F[ox], *Old Simon the Sorcerer who hath Bewitched the Whole City of Christendom* (London, 1663); W. Bingley, *A Lamentation over England* (London, 1683), p. 24.

[68] Fox, *A Declaration*, pp. 22–3; Besse, *A Collection of the Sufferings*, I, pp. 101–2; J. Audland, *The School-Master Disciplin'd* (London, 1655), p. 2.

[69] Fox, *A Declaration*, p. 34; R. Farnsworth, *Gods Covenanting with his People* (London, 1653), p. 2; J. Parnell, *A Collection of the Several Writings* (London, 1675), pp. 66, 159, 167, 203, 257.

[70] Despite the constant resort to the language of witchcraft, I have found no references in the Quaker archives to traditional demonological sources. Quaker scepticism of the powers normally ascribed to witches is evident, however, in a number of tracts; see, for example [Blackley et al.], *A Lying Wonder Discovered*, pp. 3–4 and passim; G. Fox, *A Testimony for all the Masters of Ships and Seamen to Read Over* (London, 1677),

From the 1650s onwards, the personnel and institutions of the established church were subjected to an orchestrated campaign of vilification, much of it clothed in the language of this distinct Quaker demonology. 'A spiritual Witch and a Magician' was how James Parnell described the Huntingdonshire minister, Thomas Drayton. Similar descriptions can be found scattered throughout the writings of the early Quakers.[71] No aspect of the established church was immune from such invective. The universities in particular were singled out for their role in plying the trade of 'divination' (that is, teaching the clergy to 'divine' for money) and teaching the 'magick arts' of pharaoh's magicians. Moreover, excessive reliance on books and human learning to the detriment of the 'spirit within' often led the Quakers to accuse orthodox ministers of practising a form of necromancy, that is, raising the living spirit of God from the dead letter of the Bible.[72] 'Who are the sorcerers who deceive all Nations but their national Teachers?' was a familiar refrain of Quaker pamphleteers. Such ideas seem to have percolated down to the grassroots of the movement. In 1677, for example, Joanna Mare, a Yorkshire Quaker, was presented at the archdeacon's visitation for disparaging the Book of Common Prayer and 'calling itt witchcraft'. Likewise, Nicholas Gibbens, a Dorset priest, was accused by the Quaker Anthony Mellidge of behaving 'like a sorcerer, making signs with his fingers in a scoffing manner' as he interrupted a meeting of Friends at Corfe in 1657.[73]

pp. 16–18; *Adventures by Sea of Edward Coxere*, ed. E. H. W. Meyerstein (Oxford, 1945), pp. 27, 30, 31. Even the Quaker disapproval of popular magic and astrology was largely couched in terms of the spiritual apostasy involved, rather than its overt diabolism; see, for example, R. F[arnsworth], *Witchcraft Cast Out from the Religious Seed and Israel of God* (London, 1655); E. Burrough, *A Trumpet of the Lord Sounded out of Sion* (London, 1656), pp. 5–6.

[71] Parnell, *A Collection*, pp. 311–12, 393, 393–4. The Quakers frequently claimed that it was part of their mission to cleanse the land 'of all false teachers and seducers . . . and witches, who beguile the people, and inchanters, and diviners, and Sorcerers, and hirelings'; Anon., *A Paper Sent Forth into the World from Them that are Scornfully Called Quakers* (London, 1654), p. 8; cf. [I. Penington et al.], *Some Principles of the Elect People of God . . . Quakers* (London, 1671), p. 15.

[72] For criticism of the universities in these terms, see T. Lawson, *Dagon's Fall Before the Ark* (London, 1679), pp. 2–3; Parnell, *A Collection*, pp. 66, 207, 311–12, 460; R. Hubberthorne, *A True Testimony of the Zeal of Oxford-Professors and University-Men* (London, 1654), p. 9; E. B[illing], *A Word of Reproof* (London, 1659), pp. 19–20, 35–6. For the 'necromancy' of the clergy, see G. Fox et al., *Sauls Errand to Damascus* (London, 1654), p. 7; [R. Farnsworth], *The Priests Ignorance* (London, 1655), pp. 4–5.

[73] W. Tomlinson, *A Word of Reproof to the Priests or Ministers* (London, 1656), p. 7; *The Diary of Abraham de la Pryme*, ed. C. Jackson (Surtees Society, liv, 1869), p. 293; A. Mellidge, *A True Relation . . . of Anthony Mellidge* (?, 1656), p. 5.

In this interchange of invective and innuendo, the language of witch-craft habitually invoked by the Quakers was perhaps not so radically different from that levelled against them by their adversaries. True, the Quaker conception of witchcraft as primarily a spiritual crime, based largely on scriptural precedents, did preclude reference to the spurious claims of learned demonologists. But, in other respects, the various participants in this on-going debate shared much the same conceptual framework in which the merits of unity and the fear of discord were paramount. The early Quakers were not therefore averse from reminding their persecutors of the religious chaos which they had spawned and the concomitant diversity of opinion which one of their number described as the 'womb of Witchcraft'. There was no safe middle ground here, only the option of light or dark: 'your Rebellion is the crime of Witchcraft, who cannot cease to do evill, for you have bound your selves in the Covenant with hell'.[74] The dualism which pervaded so much of the discourse of mid-seventeenth-century England, and featured so prominently in orthodox Puritanism, was thus also a part of the mental outlook of the early Quakers. That such thinking helped to sustain belief in witchcraft (however defined) is equally apparent. What we now need to consider are the consequences for the latter in a world that after 1640 was becoming slowly accustomed to the notion of difference and diversity (pluralism in the broadest sense of the word) and which precluded the simple classification of social realities along the lines suggested by such dualism.[75]

Most historians are agreed that some time between 1640 and 1700, elite belief in the reality of diabolical witchcraft underwent radical revision

---

[74] Burrough, *A Trumpet of the Lord*, pp. 11–13, 20; cf. the view of one of their opponents that the logic of Quakerism forced members of the sect to believe, *ipso facto*, that all their enemies were to be excommunicated for 'Dogs, Devils . . . Whores, Antichrist, Witches, Sorcerers'; M. Byne, *The Scornfull Quakers Answeres* (London, 1656), pp. 78–9, 100. We should perhaps remember that just as the early Quakers were not wedded to the notion of pacifism, nor were they initially outspoken advocates of a general religious toleration.

[75] At precisely what point English society can be fairly described as 'pluralistic' is of course a matter of some debate. What does seem beyond reasonable doubt, however, is that from 1640 onward, and with each successive political crisis, the political and religious divisions unleashed by the civil war, more and more Englishmen were forced (albeit reluctantly) to acknowledge the existence of difference as a permanent feature of the English ideological landscape. For a recent analysis of the seemingly insoluble divisions in English society after 1660, see T. Harris, *Politics under the Later Stuarts: Party Conflict in a Divided Society, 1660–1715* (London, 1993).

and gradual extinction. Traditionally, historians anxious to explain this phenomenon have focused on the emergence of a sceptical tradition, dating from the sixteenth century and the works of Johann Weyer and Reginald Scot, which reached its apogee a century later when it coalesced with the growing rationalism of the new empirical science.[76] Today, however, this explanation looks increasingly untenable. Two main objections have been proposed. Firstly, there is precious little evidence to support the view that those who were active in promoting the values of the new science were equally forthright in their rejection of traditional witchcraft beliefs.[77] And secondly, as Keith Thomas himself confessed, the arguments of the sceptics of the late seventeenth century differed little in tone or substance from those first articulated by Weyer and Scot a century earlier.[78] The search for a mono-causal explanation for the decline of educated belief in witchcraft has thus proved highly elusive. It has surely not been helped by the tendency of all such accounts to intimate that the whole edifice of Renaissance demonology was somehow suffused with a fallacious rationale which was ultimately bound to crack under the weight of its own internal contradictions.[79] Contemptuous of the intellectual rigour and inner coherence of such beliefs, modern commentators have thus tended to imply that it was only a matter of time before the 'enlightened' few were able to persuade their more 'credulous' compatriots of the blinding error of their ways. Yet as recent studies have shown, analyses of this kind have radically distorted the role of such ideas in the wider realm of early modern discourse. Far

---

[76] See, for example, Thomas, *Religion and the Decline of Magic*, pp. 689–92; R. Holmes, *Witchcraft in British History* (London, 1974), p. 156. Related to this idea is the belief that the continuing faith in 'occult' science and medicine helped to perpetuate 'superstitions' such as witchcraft; see, for example, G. Tourney, 'The physician and witchcraft in Restoration England', *Medical History*, 16 (1972), 153–4.

[77] See, for example, C. Webster, *From Paracelsus to Newton* (Cambridge, 1982), pp. 99–100.

[78] Thomas, *Religion and the Decline of Magic*, p. 684. Much the same point is made by Hugh Trevor-Roper in his 'The European witch-craze of the sixteenth and seventeenth centuries', in Trevor-Roper, *Religion, the Reformation, and Social Change* (London, 1967), p. 169.

[79] Clark, 'Inversion, misrule and the meaning of witchcraft', pp. 98–9. But, as Dr Clark suggests in his forthcoming study, this is not to deny the point that the doctrines of the demonologists did contain within them the seed of their own destruction since they rested on a logic of contrariety that was inherently liable to self-deconstruct. That this should occur in a world in which there was no longer an absolute fixed point from which to measure right and wrong, good and evil, would seem to complement the main thrust of my argument here, namely that the decline of educated belief in witchcraft took place against a background of emerging cultural, religious and political pluralism.

from representing outmoded and irrational systems of belief which were marginal to the interests of the men of this age, we are now being told that the sophisticated texts of the demonologists were central to the intellectual concerns of the era, so much so that 'it becomes difficult to explain, not how men accepted the rationality of the arguments, but how, occasionally, sceptics doubted it'.[80]

A subsidiary, but related, problem has been the tendency to view early modern opinion on this subject as polarised into two distinctive camps: sceptics and believers. This simplistic division is, however, virtually impossible to document. Individuals displayed a bewildering variety of views on the subject which seem to have been shaped more by circumstances than the dictates of ideological consistency. King James I and Richard Baxter provide just two examples.[81] Moreover, contemporaries were quite capable of subverting, or deconstructing, 'sceptical' authorities for their own ends. Amongst other examples, William Prynne's citation of Weyer in order to substantiate the witchcraft of the Quakers should alert us to the dangers of attaching too much significance to the published works of celebrated sceptics.[82]

Rather than seek explanations in 'great texts', or attach excessive importance to the explanatory status of a sceptical tradition, I would like to suggest an alternative line of inquiry which takes as its starting point the relocation of the language of demonology within the wider context of

---

[80] Ibid., p. 127.

[81] S. Clark, 'King James's *Daemonologie*: witchcraft and kingship', in S. Anglo, ed., *The Damned Art: Essays in the Literature of Witchcraft* (London, 1977), pp. 161–3. I am particularly impressed by the knowledge that James' so-called conversion to scepticism took place after his succession to the English throne when, as Clark points out, 'it was the Jesuits who became the principal objects of his lively apprehensions' and whom he now regarded 'with a horror previously reserved for witches'; ibid., p. 164. Baxter, on the other hand, was scrupulous in the application of rational 'empirical' methods to suspected cases of bewitchment and possession. On numerous occasions, he seems to have diagnosed the 'suffocation of the mother' and prescribed medical help, yet he remained throughout his life a fervent believer in the reality of witchcraft and demonic activity; see Baxter, *A Key for Catholics*, pp. 184–9; cf. the similar approach adopted by the Anglican minister and healer Richard Napier: M. MacDonald, *Mystical Bedlam: Madness, Anxiety and Healing in Seventeenth-Century England* (Cambridge, 1981), pp. 211–12.

[82] Prynne, *The Quakers Unmasked*, pp. 8–9, 22. Likewise, the Presbyterian Samuel Jeake the elder saw no inconsistency in citing Reginald Scot as a witness against 'popish miracles' in a letter in which he also assented to the reality of diabolical possession and dispossession; see East Sussex Record Office, Lewes, Frewen MS 4223, 'Some Contranimadversions & Counter Consideracōns to ye Animadversions & Consideracōns of . . . Mr T[homas] M[orris] in his last Epistle' [28 Dec. 1667], fos. 197ᵛ, 198ʳ.

early modern thought in England. Integral to this approach is a greater sensitivity to the linguistic conventions of the age, and the manner in which these were exposed to revision in the light of the events of the 1640s and succeeding decades. Though historians have been slow to chart these important developments, contemporaries seem to have been fully aware of what today we might term an on-going process of linguistic deconstruction. The shock of civil war, and the attempt to come to terms with the legacy of division unleashed by the conflict, forced men to confront the inadequacies of inherited languages and traditional modes of discourse. As the newspaper *Mercurius Aulicus* reported in 1644, the word 'rebel' was 'a good old statutible word, though scarce high enough for these rare moderne Rebels, *who have as much out-done Language as Men'*.[83]

The acts of men which 'out-do language' are not easily reduced to the terms of conventional usage. In mid-seventeenth century England, learned men, regardless of their particular religious or political affiliation, were confronted with precisely this problem: how to signify the collapse of traditional forms of life in a world in which there were no longer any universal 'signifiers'. Some, like Thomas Hobbes, immediately perceived the need to create an alternative 'language' of civil society which owed nothing to divine or cosmic models, and everything to the artifice of man. Consequently, in his *Leviathan* (1651), common metaphors and analogues take on new meanings, amongst them witchcraft, which now came to represent little more than a substitute phrase, literally a metaphor, for the act of disobedience.[84]

---

[83] *Mercurius Aulicus*, 11 Feb. 1645, pp. 1378–9 (my emphasis). According to Thomas Sprat, official historian of the Royal Society, the 1640s were 'a time, wherein all Languages use, if ever, to increase by extraordinary degrees; for in such busie and active times, there arise more new thoughts of men, which must be signifi'd, and varied by new expressions'; T. Sprat, *The History of the Royal Society of London* (London, 1667), p. 42. Other examples of this process of linguistic change are noted in C. Hill, 'The word "revolution" in seventeenth-century England', in R. Ollard and P. Tudor-Craig, eds., *For Veronica Wedgwood These Studies in Seventeenth-Century History* (London, 1986), pp. 134–51; and R. Ashcraft, *Revolutionary Politics and Locke's Two Treatises of Government* (Princeton, 1986), p. 69.

[84] T. Hobbes, *Leviathan*, ed., R. Tuck (Cambridge, 1991), pp. 18, 300, 303–4, 422–4. Hobbes' friend and staunch royalist, William Cavendish, seems to have shared his views on witchcraft, as well as those on the state; see M. Cavendish, duchess of Newcastle, *The Life of . . . William Cavendishe, Duke, Marquess, and Earl of Newcastle* (London, 1667), pp. 144–5; T. P. Slaughter, *Ideology and Politics on the Eve of the Restoration: Newcastle's Advice to Charles II* (Philadelphia, 1984). The latter contains the transcript of a letter in which Newcastle advises the future king to forego reliance on outmoded 'harmonist' notions of government, and to rely instead upon

The vast majority of Hobbes' learned contemporaries, however, were either unable or unwilling to make such a leap in the dark. They chose instead to seek intellectual solace in a traditional world view which stressed the principle of a god-given, universal order and provided familiar linguistic conventions with which to make sense of the unfolding events of the 1640s and 1650s. As a result, as I have tried to show, all forms of opposition, recalcitrance, rebellion or apostasy were now susceptible to demonological explication.

Two conclusions may be drawn. Firstly, the politicisation of demonology (or alternatively the demonisation of politics) ensured that witchcraft was much less likely to act as a normative system of discourse which fostered unity and concord in the body politic. On the contrary, it, like language itself, had become the prey of faction and party, an instrument more likely to encourage continuing division and schism than religious and political harmony.[85] The best illustration of this point is to be found in the evidence from witchcraft trials in this period, many of which on closer inspection reveal a large degree of partiality and factionalism. The Hopkins trials in East Anglia in the mid-1640s, the Faversham witches (1645) and the Bodenham case at Salisbury (1653) all testify to the use of witchcraft trials as a means to identify and punish

Machiavellian deceit and the Hobbesian threat of force in the government of the realm; ibid., pp. 34–5, 69. The implication here is that the civil war destroyed the faith of some royalists in traditional consensual politics, and with it belief in ideas such as witchcraft which had once seemed a natural part of that pre-civil war world view. If so, then such a process might also account for the scepticism of a man like Sir Robert Filmer whose *An Advertisement to the Jury-Men of England* (London, 1653) represented a radical *volte-face* from views held in the 1640s; for an illuminating discussion of Filmer's changing views on this subject, see I. Bostridge, 'Debates about witchcraft in England 1650–1736', Oxford D.Phil thesis, 1990, pp. 27–55.

[85] Nowhere is this more apparent than in the struggle for the single most important source of authority, the Bible. After 1660, Restoration divines frequently lamented the way in which non-conformists had attempted to appropriate specific scriptural texts for partisan ends. The most frequently cited in loyalist circles was Judges 5, 23 ('Curse ye Meroz') which at least one Restoration cleric attempted to reappropriate on the grounds that it was 'the most loyal Text in all the Bible', notwithstanding the fact that 'with this Text . . . was the Kings Army rooted [sic], our Blessed King Martyr'd and Murther'd, and the Kingdom Ruined'; E. Hickeringill, *Curse Ye Meroz. Or the Fatal Doom. In a Sermon Preached in Guild-hall-Chappel, London* [9 May 1680] (London, 1680), pp. 1–3. On a broader scale, the whole language of pre-civil war harmonism, incorporating an appeal to patriarchal authority and divine right monarchy became a trade-mark of loyal support for the restored regime after 1660. One facet of such loyalism was the repeated recitation of 1 Samuel 15, 23; see below p. 178, n. 94 for examples.

religious and political dissidents.[86] During the early years of the Restoration, witchcraft and claims of bewitchment were also used as a vehicle for the expression of nonconformist dissent, most notably in Suffolk where leading Puritans took an active part in the promotion of such cases which were clearly designed as some form of veiled protest against the new regime.[87] In such instances, it is difficult to escape the conclusion that expressions of scepticism or credulity were far more likely to be conditioned by religious and political considerations than they were by the actual 'facts' of the case. By the 1680s, events such as these would appear to have led to the growth of a culture of scepticism in Anglican and Tory circles, despite the constant resort of apologists for the restored regime to demonological precedents in order to stigmatise their opponents.[88]

---

[86] Kent Archives Office, Maidstone, Fa/JQe 14; Anon., *The Examination, Confession, Triall and Execution of Joan Williford, Joan Cariden, and Joan Hott . . . at Faversham in Kent* (London, 1645); Bostridge, 'Debates about witchcraft', p. 26; E. Bower, *Doctor Lamb Revived* (London, 1653). I am currently undertaking a major reappraisal of the Hopkins' trials, though already it is clear from initial research that much of the impetus for witch-hunting came from local puritan elites intent on eradicating all manner of dissident behaviour as part of a much wider campaign of 'moral cleansing' in the puritan stronghold of East Anglia.

[87] The best illustration of this process can be found in the witchcraft-induced fits of the Dunwich nonconformist preacher, Thomas Spatchet which lasted from 1660 to 1667. The most remarkable feature of the physical torments suffered by the body of Spatchet was the manner in which they so closely paralleled events in the wider *body politic* at this time. They began for example in March 1660, just one month before the Restoration, and reached a climax in mid-1662 at which time Spatchet became completely incapacitated from engagement in prayer and worship (i.e. at the time of the St Bartholomew's Day ejection). For a brief period at the end of 1662, coinciding with the issue of Charles II's first Declaration of Indulgence, he experienced a 'partial . . . freedom from his fits'. They soon returned, however, and by 1665 he became totally immobilised ('his feet would be as if they were nailed to the ground'), an allusion no doubt to the passage and implementation of the Five Mile Act. The fits finally ceased, albeit gradually, in 1667, ostensibly because of the death of the witch whom Spatchet held responsible for his miserable condition. But a more likely explanation was the change of religious climate in this year following the fall of Clarendon when once again comprehension was on the royal political agenda, and discussions were reopened nationwide with the non-conformist leadership; see S. Petto, *A Faithful Narrative of the Wonderful and Extraordinary Fits which Mr Tho Spatchet . . . was under by Witchcraft* (London, 1693), pp. 6, 8, 21, 27 and passim; A. G. Matthews, *Calamy Revised* (Oxford, 1934), p. 454; *The Correspondence of Henry Oldenburg*, 11 vols. (Madison, Milwaukee and London, 1966–75), V, pp. 14–15.

[88] In the Spatchet case cited above, for example, one gentleman is said to have remarked 'that if she Bewitched none but Spatchet and Manning [a fellow congregationalist preacher, Samuel Manning], and *such as they are*, she should never be Hanged by him'. Significantly perhaps no action was taken against the witch; Petto, *A Faithful Narrative*, p. 19. For a particularly good example of Tory scepticism, see *The Lives*

Secondly, and perhaps less easily demonstrated, I should like to suggest that the politicisation of the crime of witchcraft was accompanied by a radical reorientation on the part of England's ruling class as to the chief source of dissent in the body politic. During the 1640s and 1650s, the puritan authorities clearly saw the greatest threat to orderly government emanating from *de facto* toleration and unbridled liberty, a consequence of the fact that in the words of one of their number 'famous England' had now become 'an Amsterdam of mixtures [and] an Island of Monsters'. One consequence of this was the severity of punishment afforded to the Quakers, whose ubiquity, prominence, beliefs and behaviour made them ideal candidates for the role of surrogate witch. Though hard to prove, there is some evidence to suggest that the Quakers were beginning to take the place of the witch in the minds of some of the men who ruled England in the 1650s. The diary of the puritan minister, Ralph Josselin, for example, testifies to the genuine sense of fear and panic induced by the arrival of the Quakers in rural Essex in the mid-1650s. At the same time, in one of the few recorded instances of witchcraft in the diary, Josselin displayed remarkable scepticism in the case of a 'poore wretch' who had been accused of bewitching the child of a local dignitary.[89] In neighbouring Suffolk, the Presbyterian Edward Willan, who had played a prominent role in detecting witches during the Hopkins' episode in 1645, was particularly active in persecuting local Quakers, even perhaps

---

of the Right Hon Francis North . . . by the Hon Roger North. Together with the Autobiography of the Author, ed. A. Jessopp, 3 vols. (London, 1890), I, pp. 166–9; III, pp. 130–2. In one of the cases cited by North, the Exeter witches of 1682, there is a clear suggestion that the trial was being used by some to foment political unrest in the wake of the Exclusion Crisis; see *CSPD, 1682*, p. 347.

[89] T. Hodges, *The Growth and Spreading of Haeresie* (London, 1647), p. 46; *The Diary of Ralph Josselin, 1616–1683*, ed. A. MacFarlane (London, 1976), pp. 366, 379; A. MacFarlane, *The Family Life of Ralph Josselin* (Cambridge, 1970), pp. 26–7. For the size and rapid spread of the Quakers, see Reay, *The Quakers and the English Revolution*, pp. 11, 26–31 where it is suggested that by 1660 they may have formed 1 per cent of the total population of England, of which nearly half were women. Moreover, the rural nature of the sect meant that 'not one county escaped the effects of Quaker proselytizing'; ibid., p. 11. According to a survey conducted in 1680, nearly 11,000 Quakers had been imprisoned since the Restoration. In the event, the authorities did not need to resort to witchcraft legislation in order to entrap Quaker suspects. There already existed extensive laws with which to punish them, and Quaker offences, 'unlike many alleged cases of witchcraft . . . actually took place' (or rather, one might say that the former were more easily proven than the latter). In addition, unlike the majority of witches, the Quakers frequently admitted their guilt; see ibid., pp. 43, 44, 64, 106, 140n, 143n and W. C. Braithwaite, *The Second Period of Quakerism* (London, 1919), p. 98 and passim.

to the extent of fomenting accusations of witchcraft against the sect in 1655.[90]

Obviously, prioritisation of this kind did not in itself preclude continuing belief in the existence of conventional witchcraft. For many, the two went hand in hand, part of the same species of dissent and diabolical subversion. Others, however, clearly saw the witchcraft of the Quakers as of a different order from that normally ascribed to old, poor and obscure women. As one opponent of the Quakers put it in an admonitory letter of 1655, 'the Devil hath a finer way of witchcraft now, then ever he had since the world began'.[91] In her pioneering account of Scottish witchcraft, Christina Larner pointed to the significance of labelling theory as a tool to help explain why Scottish witches did not always fulfil the ideal of the stereotypical witch (old, poor, female). In the event, she cited the sociologist's emphasis upon 'process' whereby any form of deviance was conceived 'not as a static entity but rather as a continuously shaped and reshaped outcome of dynamic processes of social interaction'.[92] Precisely the same forces seem to have been at work in the refashioning of the English witch after 1640. The cultural construction of the Quaker 'witch' should thus be seen as part of a wider process of intellectual realignment during which time the Quakers' actions and beliefs were readily integrated into the learned, pre-civil war model of the deviant witch. Within a few years of their appearance, the diabolism of the Quakers became firmly established in the minds of a large number of the ruling elite. 'That grand Quaker' the devil now worked a new kind of magic more suited to the millennial atmosphere of the times. Or, as one critic of the Quakers observed, Satan now 'seldom appears with his Horns and cloven feet, [for] his game is better played when he comes like an Angel of Light'.[93]

---

[90] C. L'Estrange Ewen, *Witchcraft and Demonianism* (London, 1933), pp. 282, 299; Besse, *A Collection of the Sufferings*, I, pp. 665–6. Willan's conflation of witchcraft with radical sectarianism is evident in the Hopkins' trials where he testified that one of the accused was 'an anabaptist and runner after new sects'; L'Estrange Ewen, *Witchcraft and Demonianism*, p. 282.

[91] Anon., *An Answer to a Scandalous Paper*, sigs. A4ᵛ, Bʳ.

[92] E. M. Schur, *Labelling Deviant Behaviour* (New York, 1971), cited in C. Larner, *Enemies of God: The Witch-Hunt in Scotland* (London, 1981), p. 98.

[93] Anon., *Work for a Cooper* (London, 1679), p. 2. For the Devil as 'that grand Quaker', and variations on this theme, see Anon., *The Devil Turned Quaker* (London, 1656); I. Bourne, *A Defence of the Scriptures* (London, 1656), p. 49; T. L[edger], *Anti-Quakisme* (1653), p. 2. The Fifth Monarchist, John Spittlehouse, described the Quakers as 'the Devils last game he hath to play'; see B. S. Capp, *The Fifth Monarchy Men: A Study in Seventeenth-Century English Millenarianism* (London, 1972), p. 183.

After 1660, the Quakers continued to suffer at the hands of the Restoration authorities, though now the object of magisterial attention was extended to all those religious and political dissidents who had cooperated or sympathised with the government of the interregnum. Now, the threat of the rebel, in the broadest sense of the term, as the arch-enemy of Restoration society, became paramount, and the eradication of this threat became *the* major preoccupation of the ruling class, a point readily confirmed by the briefest perusal of the sermon literature of this period. Between 1660 and 1688, the Anglican clergy repeatedly inveighed against the danger posed to the divinely ordained government of the restored Stuarts by rebels, nonconformists and assorted mal-contents. More often than not, they did so by recourse to the exemplary language of learned demonology.[94] The message, often delivered at assize time, was not lost on the Restoration magistracy who, for much of this period, proceeded against 'fanatics' and rebels with undue ferocity. At the same time, prosecutions for witchcraft dwindled to virtual extinction. As a threat to the peace of the ordered commonwealth, it would appear that witchcraft had become relegated in the hierarchy of concerns which most impinged upon the minds of England's ruling elite.[95]

[94] It is impossible to cite in full here the vast source material on this subject. For just a very small sample covering the years from the Restoration to the accession of James II, see J. Douch, *Englands Jubilee* (London, 1660), sig. A3ᵛ; W. Creed, *Judah's Return to their Allegiance* (London, 1660), pp. 29–30; J. Riland, *Elias the Second His Coming to Restore All Things* ['Moses the peace-maker', separately paginated], p. 41; G. Hascard, *Gladius Justitiae* (London, 1668), pp. 3–4; T. Bruce, *Monarchy Maintained* (London, 1682), pp. 19–20; J. Knight, *The Samaritan Rebels Perjured by a Covenant of Association* (London, 1682), pp. 19, 22–3, 28–9; J. Allen, *Of Perjury* (London, 1682), p. 22; W. Gostwyke, *A Sermon Preached at . . . Cambridge* (Cambridge, 1685), pp. 5–7; T. Heyricke, *The Character of a Rebel* (London, 1685), pp. 6–7, 13, 20. I am currently preparing a study of the politicisation of witchcraft in Restoration England which will utilise this and much other, hitherto disregarded, material.

[95] Anthony Fletcher, for example, has noted that after the Restoration, 'the focus of magisterial anxiety shifted from social disorder to political insecurity'; A. Fletcher, *Reform in the Provinces: The Government of Stuart England* (New Haven and London, 1986), pp. 333, 352. Occasionally this shift of emphasis is discernible in the actions and statements of prominent Restoration figures. Thus Sir John Keeling, a notorious persecutor of nonconformists (especially Quakers), expressed profound scepticism of the guilty verdict in the case of the Bury St Edmunds' witches in 1664. It seems highly probable that his views on this occasion were shaped to a large extent by the fact that the driving force behind the prosecution of the two witches was Samuel Pacey, a prominent merchant and nonconformist. Conversely, the presiding judge, Sir Matthew Hale, was renowned as an advocate of religious comprehension; see *A Tryal of Witches,*

In conclusion, I would support the view of Christina Larner that educated belief in witchcraft was not argued out of existence, but rather that 'it simply ceased to have political vitality'.[96] Once witchcraft became the property of parties, sects and factions, it ceased to function as a universal arbiter of divine truth or justice. In addition, with no agreed reference point from which to judge, with absolute certainty, the actions and beliefs of men, argument *a contrariis*, a fundamental assumption of traditional demonological discourse, was increasingly controversial and partisan. Accordingly, it became ever more difficult to answer the kind of question put to the Quaker James Nayler in 1656: 'whether the power that worketh in you and in the rest of your quaking fraternity, be divine or diabolical? . . . and hereby let us know whether you be Saints or Sorcerers?' More importantly, perhaps, it became increasingly unlikely with the passage of time that such questions might arise in the first place.[97]

at the Assizes held at Bury St Edmunds (London, 1682), appended to Matthew Hale, *A Short Treatise Touching Sheriffs Accompts* (London, 1683). For Keeling's persecution of nonconformists and Quakers, see Public Record Office, Assi 2/1, fo. 99; *Historical Manuscripts Commission. Fourteenth Report, Appendix. Part IV. The Manuscripts of Lord Kenyon* (London, 1894), p. 86; E. Stockdale, 'Sir John Kelyng, Chief Justice of the King's Bench 1665–1671', in *Miscellanea* (Bedfordshire Historical Record Society, lix, 1980), pp. 43–53.

96 Larner, *Enemies of God*, p. 176.

97 J. Deacon, *A Publick Discovery of the Secret Deceit . . . where may easily be discerned Satan Transformed into . . . an Angel of Light, in that Sect . . . called Quakers* (London, 1656), pp. 58–9. Rather than adopt a linear view of this process of decline, Jonathan Barry has suggested to me the advantage of a cyclical pattern whereby with each successive political crisis, the number of witchcraft sceptics grew. If so, then the work of Ian Bostridge which largely complements my own in terms of its basic emphasis upon patterns of linguistic change, would suggest that this process of decline continued well into the eighteenth century; see Bostridge, 'Debates about witchcraft', esp. chs. 4 and 5. I should like to thank Jonathan Barry for this point, as well as many other perceptive comments on the first draft of this paper.

Part 3

The making of a witch

7. The descendants of Circe: witches and Renaissance fictions

GARETH ROBERTS

This chapter begins with a magician's epilogue:

> Now my charms are all o'erthrown,
> And what strength I have's mine own,
> Which is most faint.

The words are Keith Thomas' at the beginning of the last chapter of *Religion and the Decline of Magic*.[1] The appropriation involved in the text's conceit of Keith Thomas as Prospero is wittily apt: at the end of their magical works, both Thomas and Prospero contemplate the decline of magic (the title of Thomas' last chapter), both ask for release from their labours, perhaps both anticipate the cooperation and applause of their audiences with 'the help of your good hands'.[2] There are further consequences to this historian of magic speaking the words of a Renaissance magician from a play. For Thomas' appropriation causes his text to play at this moment between Renaissance history and Renaissance fictions, so that we glimpse not only Keith Thomas as Prospero, but also Prospero as Keith Thomas. As a result of Thomas' appropriation, we can catch sight in *The Tempest*, particularly in Prospero's famous renunciation of magic,[3] as well as in this epilogue, of Prospero contemplating the prospect of magic's decline in the seventeenth century, and perhaps even the decline in that century of princely theurgy as it was exercised in what Orgel has called the 'illusion of power' of the Jacobean and Caroline court masque.[4]

---

[1] K. Thomas, *Religion and the Decline of Magic: Studies in Popular Beliefs in Sixteenth and Seventeenth Century England* (London, 1971), p. 641.

[2] Shakespeare, *The Tempest*, ed., Stephen Orgel (Oxford and New York, 1987), V.i.328.

[3] *The Tempest*, ed., Orgel, V.i.33ff.

[4] Stephen Orgel, *The Illusion of Power: Political Theater in the English Renaissance* (Berkeley, Los Angeles and London, 1975).

To extend this play between history and fiction in Thomas' epigraph a little further: it is extraordinarily difficult to get at any 'history' of events in *The Tempest* in a version not mediated to us by Prospero's authority, retelling or memory.[5] In Prospero, especially in his difficult relationship with Caliban (according to Prospero the son of an incubus), and in Prospero's account of Caliban's mother the witch Sycorax, we may see the Renaissance scholars who wrote the treatises, made the fine demonological distinctions and tried the cases. We may see too the humanist historians of witchcraft who recorded, repeated, rewrote, discussed and transmitted accounts of the nature and activities of witches from Circe and Medea onwards (Prospero quotes the latter at length in a catalogue of his magical powers).[6] In the difficulty of access to an alternative history to Prospero's we have expressed the problems of the modern historian who wants to address the problem of the 'reality' of witchcraft, or who desires to recuperate popular belief, intent on excavating whatever there may be under or behind the written treatises, the trial accounts and the confessions. These inquiries in search of an authentic history are heard in the titles of articles such as Horsley's 'Who were the witches?' and Midelfort's (rather plaintive) 'Were there really witches?'[7] In Prospero's construction of the foul and uneducated witch Sycorax (old, ugly, dark, sexually contaminated), the binary opposite to his humanistically educated daughter, the Renaissance princess Miranda (young, beautiful, white, virgin), we have both a stereotype of the witch familiar from many Renaissance treatises,[8] and also an issue confronting

---

[5] Cf. Orgel's introduction to his edition of *The Tempest*, especially pp. 5–28.

[6] *The Tempest*, ed., Orgel, V.i.33–50.

[7] Richard A. Horsley, 'Who were the witches? The social roles of the accused in European witch trials', *Journal of Interdisciplinary History*, 9 (1979), 689–715; H. C. Erik Midelfort, 'Were there really witches?', in *Transition and Revolution: Problems and Issues of European Renaissance and Reformation History*, ed., Robert M. Kingdon (Minneapolis, MN, 1974), pp. 189–233.

[8] The most famous is Reginald Scot's: 'One sort of such as are said to bee witches, are women which be commonly old, lame, beare-eied, pale, fowle, and full of wrinkles; poore, sullen . . . ', *Discoverie of Witchcraft* (1584), ed., Brinsley Nicholson (London, 1886), I, iii, 5. See also Elizabeth Sawyer's self-description: 'poor, deformed and ignorant, / And like a bow buckled and bent together', *The Witch of Edmonton*, II.i.3–4 in *Three Jacobean Witchcraft Plays*, ed., Peter Corbin and Douglas Sedge (Manchester, 1986). The 'historical' Elizabeth Sawyer was 'most pale & ghoast-like without any bloud at all . . . Her body was crooked and deformed, even bending together' in a source for this play, Henry Goodcole's pamphlet *The Wonderfull Discoverie of Elizabeth Saywer* (1621), sig. A4ᵛ. See also Malcolm Gaskill's chapter in this volume pp. 257–87.

feminist historians of witchcraft, that of male authors and authorities writing the predominantly female witch figure.

The opening of this chapter is partly a tribute to the eager use Renaissance literary studies has made of Thomas' book, and also an implicit acknowledgement of Thomas' own use of 'literary' sources in writing about witchcraft: a quotation from Chaucer's 'Canon Yeoman's Tale' follows on the next page after the lines from *The Tempest* and Thomas Heywood's play *The wise woman of Hogsdon* provides one of the epigraphs to chapter 8 of *Religion and the Decline of Magic*. This chapter's opening also invokes the dual categories of Renaissance 'history' and 'fiction' in the particular case of writing on witchcraft only to imply the uncertainty of their distinction from each other. There are many senses in which any writing about witchcraft must be a species of fiction. If we follow Stuart Clark's lead and talk of 'the language of early modern witchcraft beliefs'[9] then one could say that in terms of Saussure's theory of the linguistic sign we can deal with the signifier and signified of witchcraft's language, but much research admits to severe problems about witchcraft's referent. In strictly technical ways learned opinion in the Renaissance made a similar point about the fictions of magic and witchcraft: the witch in fact had no power of her own to harm, magic produced no real effects, the devil and magic could not produce true miracles, and any apparent wonders the devil and his human agents managed between them were only certain sorts of illusions produced by demonic sleights of hand. In numerous ways demonologists had been declaring since Augustine that magic and witchcraft were not 'real' things and worked through a series of lies, illusions and fictions,[10] a tradition which may have contributed to the frequent use

---

[9] Stuart Clarke, 'Inversion, misrule and the meaning of witchcraft', *Past and Present*, 87 (1980), 98–127.

[10] Augustine's seminal discussion of the possibility of the magical transformations of men into animals in *De civitate dei*, XVIII, xviii opens, 'But perhaps readers of this are waiting to hear what I have to say about this great trickery of demons [*ista tanta ludificatione daemonum*]'. On the illusion of the apparent transformation of men into animals Augustine was followed by Aquinas: it is brought about in an imaginary appearance [*phantasticam apparitionem*] rather than in fact, *De malo*, cited H. C. Lea, *Materials Toward a History of Witchcraft*, arranged and ed., Arthur C. Howland, 3 vols. (New York, 1957), I, p. 93. On Augustine and magic see Claude Jenkins, 'Saint Augustine and magic', in E. Ashworth Underwood, ed., *Science, Medicine and History: Essays on the Evolution of Scientific Thought and Medical Practice Written in Honour of Charles Singer*, 2 vols. (Oxford, 1953), I, pp. 131–40 and Lynn Thorndike, *A History of Magic and Experimental Science*, 8 vols. (New York, 1923–58), I, pp. 504–22.

in the Renaissance of the magician as a metaphor for the poet and dramatist.

The not-quite new historicist approach this chapter is adopting was signalled by its not-quite new historicist opening: ideally it should have started with a sixteenth-century traveller's anecdote about America. Although one may have reservations about new historicism, especially about its use of gobbets of texts as synecdoches for 'history', witchcraft and its representation seems an ideal subject for its critical practice, and indeed one of Stephen Greenblatt's best essays is about exorcism.[11] Greenblatt's 'cultural poetics' is liminally situated, like the study of witchcraft: between disciplines, between fact and fiction, between history and literature, between different sorts of texts. It is new historicism's declaration of the mutual 'permeability' of what used to be called history and literature that makes it attractive as a critical practice with which to approach witchcraft. Greenblatt rejects an older dichotomy between history and literary texts:

> that finds history to lie outside the texts . . . For history is not simply discovered in the precincts surrounding the literary text or the performance or the image; it is found in the artworks themselves as enabling condition, shaping force, forger of meaning . . . And the work of art is not the passive surface on which this historical experience leaves its stamp but one of the creative agents in the fashioning and re-fashioning of this experience.[12]

Similarly, Montrose finds the same active relation between the text and culture in one of Shakespeare's plays. *A Midsummer Night's Dream* is not 'merely an inert "product" of Elizabethan culture. The play is rather a new *production* of Elizabethan culture'.[13]

Magical practitioners in plays, fictions and treatises (and also outside them, although this relation is more problematical and controversial), are largely textual creations from a whole range of texts from classical antiquity onwards which have a genealogy of reproducing, transmitting and informing each other. Treatises on witchcraft sometimes reflect on their own use of the authority of 'poets', that is writers of fiction, as evidence for witchcraft. They admit that poets do not always tell the

---

[11] S. Greenblatt, 'Shakespeare and the exorcists', in *Shakespearean Negotiations: The Circulation of Social Energy in Renaissance England* (Oxford, 1988), pp. 94–128.

[12] *Representing the English Renaissance*, ed., Stephen Greenblatt (Berkeley, Los Angeles and London, 1988), p. viii.

[13] Louis Montrose, '"Shaping fantasies": figurations of gender and power in Elizabethan culture', in *Representing the English Renaissance*, ed., Greenblatt, p. 32.

truth, but often claim that the ancient poets offer reliable testimony on the subject of witchcraft. The 1575 English translation of Lambert Daneau's treatise *De veneficis* cites Homer's Circe as an example of a witch and says of classical writers, 'although they bee Poetes, yet in this point faigned they or devised nothing beside the truth, but such thinges as they sawe were knowne, and frequented in their time'.[14] In 1616 Alexander Roberts cites Circe as one of the devil's troop and makes the same point about ancient poets' veracity at greater length:

> But because the reports of these may seeme to carry small credit, for that they come from Poets, who are stained with the note of licentious faining, and so put off as vaine fictions; yet seeing they deliver nothing herein but that which was well knowne and usuall in those times wherein they lived, they are not slightly, and upon an imagined conceit, to be rejected: for they affirme no more then is manifest in the records of most approved Histories, whose essence is and must be truth.[15]

There are many more instances, but perhaps the most unexpected is in William Perkins, given Perkins' almost exclusive use of Scriptural authority, suggested by the full title of his treatise on witchcraft, *A discourse of the damned art of witchcraft, so farre forth as it is revealed in the Scriptures, and manifest by true experience.* Arguing that witches in his day are the same as in the past, Perkins says that records show that about 100 years after the building of the Temple of Solomon and just after the Trojan war 'there were the same Witches that are now, as the *Circes* and *Syrenes*'.[16]

In their considerations of antique 'feigning' poets as authorities, Daneau, Roberts and Perkins cite the figure of the classical demi-goddess and enchantress Circe as evidence of witchcraft. Now Circe is ubiquitous in Renaissance culture, in its emblems, poems, masques and entertainments: she has been described as 'one of the best-known symbolical figures of the Renaissance',[17] and 'the moralized myth most typical of the Renaissance'.[18] 'Who knows not Circe / The daughter of the Sun?' as

---

[14] Lambert Daneau, *A Dialogue of Witches* (1575), sig. C6v.

[15] Alexander Roberts, *A Treatise of Witchcraft* (1916), p. 9.

[16] William Perkins, *A Discourse of the Damned Art of Witchcraft* (Cambridge, 1608), p. 197.

[17] Rosemund Tuve, "Image, form and theme in "A Mask"' in *Images and Themes in Five Poems by Milton* (Cambridge, MA, 1962), p. 130.

[18] Douglas Bush, *Pagan Myth and Christian Tradition in English Poetry* (Philadelphia, 1968), p. 13. On Circe generally see now Judith Yarnall, *Transformations of Circe: The History of an Enchantress* (Urbana and Chicago, 1994) and for some references to

the Attendant Spirit in *Comus* asks.[19] She is the subject of two paintings
by the Italian Dosso Dossi,[20] of an engraving attributed to Dürer,[21] of
emblems of Alciati (*Cavendum a meretricibus*: 'one should beware
of whores' warns Alciati), and of Geoffrey Whitney.[22] For Dante, Luther
and Roger Ascham she is a figure with which to admonish their
countrymen: Ascham fears the transformation of a young Englishman
going to Italy, 'Some *Circes* shall make him, of a plaine English man, a
right *Italian.*'[23] Montaigne's thoughts turn to her as he contemplates
'custome'.[24] Circe is the central device and the rebellious protagonist in
the French *ballet de court* performed before Henri III and Catherine
de' Medici, the *Ballet comique de la reine* of 1581,[25] and she is the hinge
of Milton's invention for his masque *Comus* performed before the
Bridgewater family in September 1634. Milton's constant rewritings of
Circe are a synecdoche for her pervasive presence in Renaissance culture

Circe in classical antiquity and later Robert Brown Jnr, *The Myth of Kirke* (London, 1883), and Momolina Marconi, 'Da Circe a Morgana', *Rendiconti del R. istituto Lombardo di Scienze e Lettere: Classe lettere*, 74 (Turin, 1940–1), pp. 533–73. For fuller documentation of Circe's presence in Renaissance culture see Merritt Y. Hughes, 'Spenser's Acrasia and the Circe of the Renaissance', *Journal of the History of Ideas*, 4 (1943), 381–99; Leonora Leet Brodwin, 'Milton and the Renaissance Circe', *Milton Studies*, 6 (1974), 21–83; Gareth Roberts, 'Circe', in *The Spenser Encyclopaedia*, ed., A. C. Hamilton et al. (Toronto, Buffalo and London, 1990), pp. 165–7.

[19] Milton, *Comus* in *The Poems of John Milton*, ed., John Carey and Alastair Fowler (London and New York, 1968), pp. 50–1. All quotations from Milton's poems are from this edition.

[20] 'Circe', Galleria Borghese, Rome; 'Circe and her lovers', National Gallery of Art, Washington. See also Felton Gibbons, *Dosso and Battista Dossi: Court Painters at Ferrara* (Princeton, NJ, 1968), esp. pp. 198–200, 215–16. Gibbons rehearses the arguments that the Galleria Borghese painting may depict an Ariostan enchantress, Melissa or the Circean Alcina, rather than Circe herself. I am grateful to Machteld Lowensteyn for drawing my attention to the painting by Jacob Cornelisz van Oostsanen (c. 1470–1533) of 'Saul at the Witch of Endor' in the Rijksmuseum, Amsterdam, which is influenced by Dossi. It is reproduced in Max J. Friedländer, *Early Netherlandish Painting*, transl. Heinz Norden, 14 vols. in 16 (Leyden, 1967–76), XII, plate 139.

[21] Hartmannus Schedel, *Registrum huius operis libri cronicarum cum figuris et ymaginibus ab inicio mundi* ['The Nuremberg chronicle'] (Nuremberg, 1493), f. 41.

[22] Andrea Alciati, *Emblemata cum commentariis* (Padua, 1621), Emblem 76, p. 336; Geoffrey Whitney, *A Choice of Emblemes, and Other Devises* (Leiden, 1586), p. 82.

[23] Roger Ascham, *The Scholemaster* in *English Works*, ed., W. A. Wright (Cambridge, 1904), p. 225.

[24] 'Of experience', *Montaigne's Essays*, trans. John Florio, 3 vols. (London and Toronto, 1928), vol. iii, III, xiii, 340.

[25] On this see Francis Yates, *The French Academies of the Sixteenth Century*, Studies of the Warburg Institute, XV (1947), pp. 236–74.

and a testimony to one Renaissance male poet's obsession with Homer's 'beautiful-haired Circe, a formidable goddess with human speech'.[26] In Milton's first Latin elegy, written at the age of 18, the attractions of London and its girls are 'the infamous halls of faithless Circe'[27] abandoned in favour of a hasty retreat to Cambridge. At the opposite pole of Milton's literary career in time and genre, in austere tragedy as opposed to light elegy, we find Samson berating the beguiling Dalila as Circe with her cup of magical potions:

> I know thy trains
> Though dearly to my cost, thy gins, and toils;
> Thy fair enchanted cup, . . . [28]

And at the turning point in human history, just before the fall, Eve in *Paradise Lost* is unconcerned by a rustling in Eden's bushes and a serpent's wanton wreaths. Why should she concern herself?

> . . . every beast, more duteous at her call,
> Than at Circean call the herd disguised.[29]

As Milton's writings suggest, Circe occupies sites in Renaissance literature where pleasure and virtue are not reconcilable with Jonsonian amicableness. There is a long history of critical debate over Circean conflicts of pleasure with virtue in two moments in English Renaissance texts with a direct genealogy: in Spenser, *Faerie Queene* II xii in Acrasia's Bower of Bliss, and in Milton's *Comus*, where a Lady of impeccably Spenserian literary descent (her unlikely pedigree is surely Guyon, the Knight of Temperance, out of Amoret) confronts the male Circean enchanter Comus. The relation of pleasure to virtue is a deep Renaissance concern, not least in the problematic pleasures of fiction itself. These relations are dramatised in *The Faerie Queene* II xii and in *Comus*, and whatever positions are adopted in the critical debate over these texts, the issues hinge on the symbolical figures of a Circean Acrasia and a Circean Comus, so that Circe may serve as a figure of internal and external critical problems about these two moments in Spenser and Milton.

But Circe is more than Tuve's 'symbolical figure', for from very early times she also figures as a witch in writings about witchcraft. For St

---

[26] *'Kirke euplokamos, deine theos audeessa'*, *Odyssey*, X.136.
[27] *'malefidae infamia Circes / Atria'*, 'Elegia prima', 87–8.
[28] *Samson Agonistes*, 932–4.   [29] *Paradise Lost*, IX. 521–2,

Augustine she was 'that notorious witch Circe',[30] for the authors of the Dominican manual *Malleus maleficarum* 'a certain witch named Circe'.[31] The sixteenth-century Dutch sceptic and doctor Johann Weyer remembers her Homeric beauty, 'Circe, that most beautiful witch'.[32] whereas the English physician and demonologist, John Cotta, referred more rudely in 1616 to Medea and Circe as 'those old famous Hags'.[33] To think of Circe as a witch was fairly commonplace and not confined to demonologists. Fynes Moryson's *Itinerary* (printed 1617) records him on the way to Naples and notes the mountain named Circello 'of the famous Witch *Circe*'.[34]

Circe, on the strength of the directions about raising the shades of the dead she gives Odysseus in *Odyssey*, X, occasionally appears in witch-craft treatises as evidence for necromancy: John Cotta notes not only the raising of Saul by the witch of Endor, but also the practices of Medea and Circe.[35] But more generally Circe was already being cited in the seventh century as evidence for the reality and continuance of witchcraft itself. While for Boethius it was the *sensus moralis* of Circe which was paramount,[36] she appeared as an historical example in the sections 'De magis' and 'De transformatis' of Isidore of Seville's *Etymologies*[37] and in Rabanus Maurus.[38]

As we have seen in cases like those of Lambert Daneau and Alexander Roberts, writers of Renaissance witchcraft treatises admit that poets do not always tell the truth, but claim that the ancient poets do offer reliable testimony on witchcraft. And more particularly, because of her

---

[30] '*illa maga famosissima Circe*', *De civitate Dei*, XVIII, xvii.
[31] '*quadam Maga dicta Circe*', Jakob Sprenger and Heinrich Kramer, *Malleus maleficarum* in *Malleorum quorundam maleficarum* (Frankfurt, 1582), tom 1, pars 1; pars 1, quaestio 10, p. 145.
[32] '*Circe maga formosissima*', Johann Weyer, *De praestigiis daemonum* (Basle, 1566), II, xviii, 208.
[33] John Cotta, *The Triall of Witch-craft* (1616), p. 40.
[34] Fynes Moryson, *An Itinerary Containing his Ten Yeeres Travell* (1617), II, ii, 105.
[35] Cotta, *Triall*, p. 37.
[36] *De consolatione philosophiae*, IV, iii. Boethius also remarks on her beauty, '*Pulchra . . . dea*'.
[37] *Isidori Hispalensis episcopi etymologiarum sive originum libri XX*, ed., W. M. Lindsay, 2 vols. (Oxford, 1911), VIII, ix, 5 and XI, iv.
[38] Rabanus Maurus, 'De magis artibus' in *De consanguineorum nuptiis et de magorum praestigiis* (Migne, *Patrologia latina*, vol. CX), column 1097. See also Richard Kieckhefer, *Magic in the Middle Ages* (Cambridge, 1989), p. 29 and Valerie Flint, *The Rise of Magic in Early Medieval Europe* (Oxford, 1991), pp. 51–8. On Isidore's discussions of magic and Rabanus' extensive borrowings from them see Thorndike, *A History of Magic and Experimental Science*, I, pp. 623–33.

celebrated transformation of Ulysses' companions ('By her spells Circe changed the comrades of Ulysses')[39] Circe occurs in discussions of transformation. She regularly appears, especially in continental demon-ologists, in discussions of whether witches can transform themselves or others into animals. Clearly, the frequency of this discursive set-piece and the habitual inclusion of Circe in it is attributable to a passage in St Augustine's *De civitate dei*, XVIII and the persistence of the debate may be the consequence of the absence of a clearly final decision by Augustine.

The issue of transformation crops up almost incidentally in *De civitate* XVIII xiv when Augustine notes the emergence in human history of certain 'theological poets' [*qui etiam theologi dicerentur*], i.e. poets like Homer and Hesiod, who may have written some true things among their frivolous lies. The story of the transformation of the companions of Diomedes into birds, reported by both Virgil and Ovid,[40] reminds Augustine of Circe's transformation of the companions of Ulysses. Augustine seems eventually to deny to humans and demons the ability to transform: 'And so I should not believe on any account, that the body, let alone the soul, can really be converted into the limbs and features of animals by the craft or power of demons.'[41] This pronouncement is cited with approval by sceptics such as Weyer and Reginald Scot.[42] But the English translation here captures an awkward and ambiguous inflexion in Augustine's tone, 'And so I should not believe . . . [*Non . . . ulla ratione crediderim . . .*]' which is heard elsewhere in his discussion" 'If I were to say that we should refuse to believe these reports . . . [*Si enim dixerimus ea non esse credenda . . .*]'. His statement about the story in Apuleius, *The golden ass* is 'this may be a fact or a fiction' and Augustine, having proposed that demons may through illusions make it *seem* that men are transformed, is still uneasily equivocating when Circe appears again, this time in a line from Virgil, *Eclogues* VIII:

> For that reason it seems to me that this thing, generally talked about and reported in literature – that people are wont to be changed into wolves by Arcadian gods (or rather demons) and that 'by songs

---

[39] Virgil, *Eclogues*, VIII. 70.

[40] Virgil, *Aeneid*, XI. 271–7; Ovid, *Metamorphoses*, XIV. 495–511.

[41] Augustine, *De civitate dei*, XVIII, xviii.

[42] Scot, *Discoverie*, V, i, 73. Scot's quotation of Augustine here is not verbatim and his marginal reference to *De civitate dei*, VIII (rather than XVIII), xviii incorrect; Weyer, *De praestigiis*, III, xx.

Circe transformed the comrades of Ulysses' – could have come about, if indeed it did come about, by these means I have stated.[43]

A marginal in a Renaissance edition of *De civitate dei* senses Augustine's difficulties in the ingenious explanation he gives of how demons may *appear* to transform, when it comments that the means Augustine proposes seem difficult to understand to the less learned.[44] And Augustine's apparent reluctance to pronounce unreservedly is implicitly registered by two sixteenth-century writers on witchcraft with diametrically opposite views. Jean Bodin, for whom the story of Circe is not a fable, takes Augustine to mean that transformation *is* possible. All those who have written on lycanthropy, both ancient and modern, are in agreement that lycanthropy is possible: the human figure changes but the spirit and reason remain the same, as (Bodin triumphantly concludes) Homer says. He then quotes two lines of Greek from the Circe episode in the *Odyssey*: 'And they had the heads, voice, bristles and shape of swine, but their minds remained unchanged just as before.'[45] Earlier, at the end of the fifteenth century, the authors of the *Malleus maleficarum*, citing the discussion in Augustine, had argued that Circe transformed Ulysses' companions only in appearance.[46] At the other pole to Bodin, Reginald Scot, anxious to retain Augustine's authority, finds that Augustine has rather too much time for foolish fables such as justifying the story of Circe. Scot trusts that this sort of passage has been foisted into the saint's work by a papist.[47]

Circe, then, often figures as evidence of witchcraft, and her reputed power to transform obviously exercised demonological discussions. Homer's story of Circean transformation is the archetype, with later analogues which it was surely instrumental in forming and which are themselves then incorporated in and transmitted by witchcraft discourse, constituting, taken together, a Circean configuration of narrative and motifs whose features I now propose to identify. Augustine's discussion

---

[43] '*Proinde quod homines dicuntur mandatumque est litteris ab diis vel potius daemonibus Arcadibus in lupos solere converti, et quod 'Carminibus Circe socios mutavit Ulixi', secundum istum modum mihi videtur fieri potuisse quem dixi, si tamen factum est*', XVIII, xviii.

[44] Augustine, *De civitate dei cum commento* (Freiburg, 1494), sig. K3.

[45] '*oi de suon men echon kephalas phonen te trichas te / kai demas, autar nous en empedos, os to paros per*', *Odyssey*, X. 239–40; Jean Bodin, *De la démonomanie et des sorciers* (Paris, 1580), II, vi, ff. 101^v–102. Bodin quotes these lines in a slightly corrupt form.

[46] *Malleus*, pars II, quaestio 1, cap 8, 298–301.

[47] *Discoverie*, V, iii, 76.

in *De civitate dei* XVIII xvii–xviii cites Circe at the beginning of xvii and then in xviii mentions analogical narratives of transformation. Augustine heard in Italy of landladies steeped in magic who transformed men into beasts of burden [*iumenta*] by giving them something in cheese: he mentions Apuleius' account of his transformation into an ass ('which he reported – or made up'),[48] and the transformation of the father of Praestantius into a pack-horse. Collocations of these small narratives are found together in numerous later discussions.[49]

One story of transformation often given in later discussions is that of a young man transformed into an ass by a Cyprian witch. Scot gives it in the *Discoverie*, V, iii, noting that Bodin gives an epitome of it and the *Malleus*[50] a fuller version. The authors of *Malleus* claimed to have learned this [*percepimus*] from the Knights of St John at Rhodes. Bodin commenting on the *Malleus* version says that an identical one [*du tout semblable*] is to be found in William Archbishop of Tyre. If Bodin was right,[51] then the authors may have been disingenuous about their source, and in any event this particular analogue of the Circe story would go back to at least the twelfth century. Scot's version is a faithful and lively translation of the *Malleus*, omitting a passage of demonological theory and adding a few ribald asides quite deliberately at the expense of the marvellous in a narrative he wants to appear ludicrous. A merchant ship arrived at Cyprus and among those who went ashore in search of supplies was 'a certaine English man, being a sturdie yoong fellowe'.[52] He found a woman who offered him eggs which he ate. Returning to his ship he was beaten back by sailors crying 'What a murren lacks the asse? Whither the divell will this ass?' He had no alternative but to return to the witch's house where, in the form of an ass, he served her three years carrying her burdens. One day, hearing the church bell ringing at the elevation of the host, he fell on his knees. The witch came to beat him but

---

[48] '*aut indicavit aut finxit*', XVIII, xviii.

[49] Scot, *Discoverie*, V, i–vi; Weyer, *De praestigiis*, II, xxvii, 240–3 and III, xx, 446–53; Bodin, *Démonomanie*, II, vi; Cotta, *Triall*, VI, 33–6.

[50] *Malleus*, pars 2, quaestio 2, cap 4, 423–7.

[51] Bodin, *Démonomanie*, II, vi, f. 100. I have not been able to discover this in *Guillaume de Tyr. Cronique*, ed., R. B. C. Huygens, *Corpus Christianorum. Continuatio mediaevalis*, vols. lxiii and lxiii^a (Turnholti, 1986).

[52] *Discoverie*, V, iii, 75. The protagonist of this story is English, young and sturdy only in Scot. *Malleus* testifies to his youth and sturdiness [*iuvenis quidam . . . robustus*, pars II, q2, cap 4, 424], Bodin to his nationality [*un jeune soldat Anglois*, II, vi, f. 100]. This is a small but telling example of the way that Circean narratives rewrite each other in the transmission of this witchcraft story.

her sorcery was discovered. He was returned to his own shape and the witch was burned. Here clearly discernible features mark the story as a Circean 'fantasia'. These features, since they can be observed clustered in a comparatively developed narrative, may then be perceived in other analogues, particularly Augustine's Italian landladies in *De civitate* XVIII, xviii. A full structural analysis of Homer's archetype in relation to its later and developing versions would be rewarding, but mention will be made only of some characteristic features. The stories begin with arrival by sea in a strange land: in Scot the man is a 'stranger and far from his countrie' [*Malleus*, '*alienum a patria*']. As in the *Odyssey*, food is the agent of transformation. Men are transformed by a woman into very particular sorts of domestic animals. Although Homer's Circe has changed men into wolves and lions, it is for transformations of men into swine she is chiefly remembered. Transformation into beasts of burden, especially asses, mark the later analogues and the transformed beasts are to be kept in servitude. These features may be suggested as constituting a Circean narrative configuration.

The figure of Circe, then, and also a Circean configuration may be traced in demonological discussions of witches and particularly of their power, or that of devils, to transform: Circe is the archetype in demonological discussions of transformation. In these discussions, by and large and with the exception of Bodin, the theorists were more sceptical, although in a highly technical way, than popular opinion. As has been seen, most discussions allow transformation only in appearance or through demonic deception. Popular opinion seems to have accepted that witches could really transform at least themselves into animals. Gifford's uneducated Samuel suspects a hare 'which my conscience giveth me is a witch', while the learned and orthodox Daniel reports stories from Germany about witches deluded by devils into believing they are werewolves.[53]

I want now to turn from demonological discussions to what are more patent Renaissance fictions and argue first, as a sort of literary analogy to my tracing Circe in demonological discussions, for the pervasive and transforming presence of Circe in Shakespeare's *The Comedy of Errors*.

---

[53] George Gifford, *A Dialogue Concerning Witches and Witchcraftes* (Oxford, 1931), sigs. A4ᵛ, K2ᵛ–K3. In the Lancashire witch trials of 1634 the ten-year-old Edmund Robinson claimed to have encountered witches in the shape of greyhounds and to have seen a witch transform a boy into a horse, BL Harley MS 6854, ff. 22ᵛ–23ᵛ.

Two of the twins in *The comedy of errors*, Syracusan Antipholus and his servant Dromio, arrive as strangers in Shakespeare's Ephesus in I ii and Antipholus expresses a traveller's fear about the town's ominous reputation. In Shakespeare's long-acknowledged main source, the *Menaechmi* of Plautus, the slave Messenio's fears are that 'in Epidamnum there are the greatest pleasure-lovers and drinkers, while an enormous number of swindlers and tricksters also live in the town. And as for the prostitutes, it's said that there's nowhere in the world where they're more alluring'.[54] William Warner's translation of the Plautus play, printed 1595, which Shakespeare might or might not have seen in manuscript before writing *Errors*, is more robust, more exaggerated and much freer: 'this Towne *Epidamnum*, is a place of outragious expences, exceeding in all ryot and lasciviousnesse: and (I heare) as full of Ribaulds, Parasites, Drunkards, Catchpoles, Cony-catchers, and Sycophants, as it can hold: then for Curtizans, why here's the currantest stamp of them in the world'.[55] Shakespeare shifted the location of his play about twins and mistaken identity from Epidamnum to a more magical town: Ephesus is the home of the goddess Diana, possession, exorcisms and magic books in Acts XIX. But nothing in Plautus, Warner or Acts XIX prepares us for Syracusan Antipholus' very specific fears of deception of the eyes, and terrifying magical transformations of mind and body:

> They say this town is full of cozenage,
> As nimble jugglers that deceive the eye,
> Dark-working sorcerers that change the mind,
> Soul-killing witches that deform the body,
> Disguised cheaters, prating mountebanks, . . . [56]

In these lines, particularly in the fear of transformed minds and bodies, the first symptoms of Circe's pervasive presence can be felt in the play.

Two elements of a Circean configuration may be isolated in *The Comedy of Errors*: transformation and the ambiguities of Circe's perilous attraction. In an article on Circe in Milton, Leonora Leet Brodwin's

---

[54] Plautus, *Menaechmi* in *Works* (5 vols., Loeb edn), II, lines 258–62.
[55] Geoffrey Bullough, *Narrative and Dramatic Sources of Shakespeare*, 8 vols. (London and New York, 1957–75), I, p. 17.
[56] Shakespeare, *The Comedy of Errors*, ed., R. A. Foakes (The Arden Shakespeare, London, 1962), I.ii.97–101. All references to *The Comedy of Errors* are to this edition.

reading of the significance of Homer's narrative identifies three 'temptations' offered by Circe: bestial enslavement, degradation of masculinity and carefree happiness.[57] All three terms of Brodwin's analysis articulate the simultaneous attraction and threat offered to men by Circe's magical female sexuality: the first two involve a female subversion of male authority, the last a perilous offer of irresponsible pleasure. In Homer's story, in its successive analogues and influences, developments, exegeses and uses, is exhibited a configuration of attitudes, anxieties and fears about the magical transformation of men by women.

So, from Act II onwards in *The Comedy of Errors*, both the servant Dromios talk of themselves as transformed into asses, of being abused, loaded down and beaten. In later developments, Circe's literary descendants such as Ariosto's Alcina, Tasso's Armida and Spenser's Acrasia did not confine themselves to pigs but transformed men into various animals: an ass is prominent among other animals in the emblems of Whitney and in some editions of Alciati (e.g. Paris 1583).[58] So too in later analogues to the Circe story, themselves shaped by Homer's narrative like those mentioned above, men are changed into asses.[59] It seems to me likely that Shakespeare read Scot's story of the sturdy young Englishman transformed into an ass by the Cyprian witch and that it influenced *The Comedy of Errors*. He had certainly read Scot by the time he wrote *A Midsummer Night's Dream* and *1 Henry IV*.[60] I do not simply want to make a point about Shakespeare's sources here, although I do think that Scot's *Discoverie* book V influenced *Errors*, but I want to suggest how in the Dromios' fears of transformation, subjugation and beating, Circe's presence is detectable in the play, and also to see *Errors* as part of the transmission of the changing configuration of elements which constitute Circe: to suggest, as Lévi-Strauss does with Oedipus, that the Circe myth is the sum of all its constituent versions.[61]

---

[57] Brodwin, 'Milton and the Renaissance Circe', 23–6.

[58] Alciati reproduced in Hughes, 'Spenser's Acrasia and the Circe of the Renaissance', facing 386.

[59] Scot, *Discoverie*, V, iii–v.

[60] See *A Midsummer Night's Dream*, ed., Harold F. Brooks (Arden Shakespeare, London, 1979), esp. pp. lviii–lx and 146–9; Bullough, *Narrative and Dramatic Sources of Shakespeare*, I, pp. 370–3, 394–7; and the note on the name of the devil 'Amamon' at *1 Henry IV*, ed., A. R. Humphreys (Arden Shakespeare, London, 1961), II.iv.332.

[61] Claude Lévi-Strauss, 'The structural study of myth', *Structural Anthropology*, 2 vols. (Harmondsworth, 1977), I, esp. pp. 216–19.

The perils and ambiguous attractiveness of the erotic and magical in Circe manifest themselves in what is usually acknowledged as *The Comedy of Errors'* greatest lyrical speech in III ii. In it Antipholus of Syracuse woos Luciana in terms which reveal that his urgent but anxious desire for her causes him (unconsciously) to figure her as Circean. Circe's traces might be characterised in one of Antipholus' phrases about Luciana later in this scene, 'enchanting presence and discourse'.[62] The speech must be quoted in its entirety,

> Sweet mistress, what your name is else I know not,
> Nor by what wonder you do hit of mine;   30
> Less in your knowledge and your grace you show not
> Than our earth's wonder, more than earth divine.
> Teach me, dear creature, how to think and speak;
> Lay open to my earthy gross conceit,
> Smother'd in errors, feeble, shallow, weak,   35
> The folded meaning of your words' deceit.
> Against my soul's pure truth, why labour you
> To make it wander in an unknown field?
> Are you a god? would you create me new?
> Transform me then, and to your power I'll yield.   40
> But if that I am I, then well I know
> Your weeping sister is no wife of mine,
> Nor to her bed no homage do I owe;
> Far more, far more to you do I decline;
> O, train me not, sweet mermaid, with thy note   45
> To drown me in thy sister's flood of tears;
> Sing, siren, for thyself, and I will dote;
> Spread o'er the silver waves thy golden hairs,
> And as a bed I'll take thee, and there lie,
> And in that glorious supposition think   50
> He gains by death that hath such means to die;
> Let love, being light, be drowned if she sink.[63]

This *admiratio* initially addresses Luciana as wonderful, more than human, preternaturally possessed with knowledge. The language of 37–8 bears traces of the enchantress who can transform 'love's pure truth' into an ass wandering in a field. Line 40 appeals for transformation and invites subjugation, and 39 in its identification of a new creation as

---

[62] *The Comedy of Errors*, III.ii.160.   [63] Ibid., III.ii.29–52.

an attribute of deity perhaps reveals the speech as informed by the theological point central to demonological discussions of transformation and agreed by the great consensus of theologians, as Vives points out in a comment on *De civitate dei* XVIII xviii,[64] and expressly made by Scot: only God can accomplish the new creation that substantial transformation would necessitate.[65] But almost immediately Luciana's nature declines from goddess to the siren and mermaid of lines 45ff. The sirens' dangerous beauty was a Renaissance commonplace and they are often the attendants of Circe in poetry and mythography;[66] line 49 sees Antipholus wishing to succumb to their beauty and song and leaving a safe Odyssean position tethered to the mast. The water imagery shifts into the last line of this speech, 'Let love, being light, be drowned if she sink.' Currently available explanations of this line seem to me inadequate. In it 'Love' rather than Antipholus is now floating and she is female. Surely she is being 'swum' as a witch. In these tests women were proved guilty as witches if they floated for, as demonologists like James I argued, the water, as agent of the baptism they had denied, refused them. Love in Antipholus' conceit, will paradoxically be proved innocent and worthy if it sinks heavily. It is being swum on the suspicion of being 'light' (i.e. wanton) and if it does prove 'light' (i.e. it floats) it will be witch-like and suspicious. The paradoxes of the conceit of a swimming-test for witchcraft bring to a culmination those paradoxes, ambiguities and anxieties about Luciana and the women of Ephesus subtly voiced in Antipholus' speech, and express the ambivalence characteristic of male reactions to a Circean presence.

Because of increasingly complex and distressing mistakings of identity, by the beginning of Act V the two male visitors to Ephesus are convinced that the city is full of spirits, goblins, devils and witches. The women of Ephesus are feared as supernatural agents, particularly in the threat they pose to transform, and all are termed with mounting anxiety and violence, siren, witch, sorceress and devil. Circe emerges explicitly as the figure for the play's fears of the women of Ephesus in what is surprisingly the play's only allusion to classical mythology. (*The taming of the shrew*, another very early Shakespearian comedy and written at about the same time, has at least eleven decorative classical

---

[64] *De civitate dei . . . commentariis per . . . Ioannem Lodovicum Vivem* (Basle, 1555), column 1050.

[65] Scot cites the *Canon episcopi*'s assertion of God's sole power as creator to transform, *Discoverie*, V, iii, 77.

[66] William Perkins also thinks of them together. See above p. 187.

similes.)[67] Duke Solinus reviewing the confusions at the end of the play, as a prelude to their disentanglement and rational explanation which begins some sixty lines later says, 'I think you all have drunk of Circe's cup' (V.i.271). As the play moves towards its comedic resolution, a male authority provides an attempt at rationality in the common tropological reading of Circe as the loss of reason, which offers an alternative to the escalating fears of a Circean configuration which supernaturally threatened the transformation of men.

Circe's beauty holds out the promise of pleasure, a pleasure Homer's Odysseus successfully negotiates on *his* terms. But Hermes warns him that to have sex with Circe on *her* terms would unman him, 'when she has you stripped naked she may make you worthless and unmanned'.[68] The danger of succumbing to Circe's pleasures rather than mastering them, dangers of unmanning and of subjugation, are clearly articulated in Horace's reading of Homer's Circe in *Epistles* I.ii: if Ulysses had drunk of Circe's cup 'enslaved by a whorish mistress, he would have become shamed and witless' [*sub domina meretrice fuisset turpis et excors*].[69] That Circe offers pleasure is expressly stated in the motto to Whitney's Circe emblem *Homines voluptatibus transformantur* ('men are transformed by pleasures') and is a Renaissance commonplace. Equally clear in Alciati's motto is the stigmatisation both of these pleasures and the female figure who offers them, *Cavendum meretricibus* ('beware of whores'). Commentaries in Renaissance editions of Horace on *Epistles* I ii make clear the threat of female subversion Circe posed to male virtue, control and rationality: Circe was in fact a stunningly beautiful woman [*mulier fuit speciossima*] who estranged the minds of men through excessive love, and the Stoics called avarice, greed and lust 'whorish mistresses' and those who serve them slaves.[70] The commentator Lambinus quotes Dion Chrysostom on Circe signifying pleasure, which fights not with weapons but with luxury, pleasures, feasts, allurements, softness and sex; and entices, deceives, unmans, liquifies [*liquefacit*] and

---

[67] *The Taming of the Shrew*, ed., Brian Morris (Arden Shakespeare, Routledge: London and New York, 1981), p. 61, citing Mincoff.

[68] '*me s'apogumnothenta kakon kai anenora thee*', *Odyssey*, X. 301.

[69] Horace, *Epistles*, I. ii. 25. My colleague, Matthew Leigh, tells me that Horace is here using the language of *servitium amoris*, the slavery of love to a typically self-willed and dominant woman, which can be found in the love elegies of Propertius, Tibullus and Ovid.

[70] *Q Horatius Flaccus cum commentariis et enarrationibus commentatoris veteris* (Lugduni Batavorum, 1597), 520.

enervates men. Circe was a shameless and lascivious woman who enticed men from proper business and duty to a life of pleasure.[71]

Two of Spenser's beautiful Circean witches, Duessa and Acrasia, both offer pleasure and sex, and cause unmanning. In *Faerie Queene* I, dalliance with Duessa enfeebles Fradubio and the Redcrosse knight: the sprinkling of Duessa's cup on Timias, significantly on his 'weaker parts', temporarily disables him in the fight with her.[72] In *Faerie Queene* II xii, the emasculating effects of the pleasures of Acrasia and her Bower of Bliss are seen in the arrested manhood (and perhaps infantilisation) of the adolescent Verdant who sleeps in Acrasia's lap, his knightly weapons idly hung on a tree.[73] A more explicit manifestation of Circean unmanning is Genius, the epicene porter to Acrasia's Bower of Bliss, who holds a Circean bowl and staff: an effeminated man with his loose garments flowing about his heels.[74]

A Circean offer of perilous pleasures is one of the ways in which witchcraft and magic were seen by the treatise writers. The devil seduced witches, witches seduced men, witchcraft itself was a seduction to and of mankind. The twelfth-century mystic and exegete Hugh of St Victor had severely segregated *magica* from *philosophia*, personified her and described her dangerous seductions: 'the mistress of iniquity and malice, lying about the truth, and truly harming souls, she seduces [*seducit*] from divine religion, suggests as pleasant [*suadet*] the worship of demons'.[75] George Gifford often uses the verb: the devil seduces multitudes by means of witches, witches are seduced by the devil to be his servants, Satan seduces men into error, is given power to seduce because of men's wickedness, and witches seduce men to run after devils.[76] The sceptical Reginald Scot registers the fact that continental demonologists would have witches executed 'for seducing the people. But God knoweth they have small store of Rhetorike or art to seduce.'[77] In the opinion of a Scottish bishop, the worst crime of the three witches burned at St Andrews in 1542 was that they strove with their incantations and witchcraft to steal away and ruin [*subtrahere et subvertere*] many of the

---

[71] *Dionysii Lambini . . . in Q Horatium Flaccum* (Frankfurt, 1596), commentary on Satires and Epistles, 252–3.

[72] Spenser, *The Faerie Queene*, I. viii. 14.7.

[73] Ibid., II. xii. 79–80.

[74] Ibid., II. xii. 46–9.

[75] *Eruditiones didascalicae libri septem* in Migne, *Patrologia latina*, 176 (Paris, 1754), column 810.

[76] *Dialogue*, sigs. A2, B3, B4, D4, Hᵛ.

[77] Scot, *Discoverie*, III, xix, 56.

Christian faithful of both sexes.[78] Later in sixteenth-century Scotland, the North Berwickshire witches had allowed themselves 'to be allured and inticed by the Divell' and had then seduced by their sorcery a number of other people, and Dr Fian had followed the 'allurements and entisements of sathan'.[79] Even the honourable and learned can be seduced to sorcery.[80] The devil offered various illicit but ultimately destructive pleasures to the witch: success, revenge, sexual gratification according to some continental theorists, sometimes just an easier life for the poor, sometimes just a promise of food.[81] Recourse to witchcraft of various sorts, including comparatively harmless or merely superstitious kinds, was seen as a seductive alternative to a hard Christian quest in life. Erasmus interprets Circe's cup as pleasure and equates it with witchcraft in the *Enchiridion*: 'the cuppe of Cyrces teche [*sic*, the Latin is "*docent . . . pocula*"], that men with voluptuousnes, as with wytchecrafte [*veneficiis*] fall out of their mynde'.[82] Arthur Golding's Epistle to Leicester prefatory to his translation of Ovid's *Metamorphoses* (1567) makes the same equation between witchcraft and pleasure: 'What else are Circes witchcrafts and enchauntments than the vyle / And filthy pleasures of the flesh which doo our sences defyle?'

A metaphoric extension of the idea that witchcraft is seductive, pleasurable and unmanning is the use of this nexus of ideas for purposes of Protestant propaganda in sixteenth- and seventeenth-century England. Like Spenser's Duessa, the Roman church was often seen as explicitly Circean. The English translation of Bullinger's sermons on the Apocalypse call her 'that great witche *Circes*' and William Fulke saw the Roman Church as a '*Babylonicall Circe*'.[83] The Roman Church was

---

[78] See Christina Larner (*née* Ross), 'Scottish demonology in the sixteenth and seventeenth centuries and its theological background' (Ph.D. thesis, University of Edinburgh, 1962), 49–52.

[79] *Newes from Scotland* (?1592), sigs. A4–A4ᵛ, D.

[80] Danaeus, *Dialogue*, sig. E3.

[81] See Thomas, *Religion and the Decline of Magic*, pp. 519–26; on poverty as a temptation see Danaeus, *Dialogue*, sig. E2ᵛ; revenge and greed, poverty, riches, desire for revenge, and the satisfaction of cruel minds, James VI and I, *Daemonologie* (Edinburgh, 1597), II, iii; desire for revenge, *The Wonderful Discoverie of the Witchcrafts of Margaret and Phillip Flower* (1619), sigs. B2ᵛ–B3; poverty and revenge, Thomas Potts, *The Wonderfull Discoverie of Witches in the Countie of Lancaster* (1613), sig. O3.

[82] Erasmus, *Enchiridion militis Christiani: An English Version*, ed., Anne M. O'Donnell, *EETS*, original series 282 (Oxford, 1981), p. 109; *Opera omnia* (Leiden, 1703–6), vol. v, column 29C.

[83] See Gareth Roberts, 'Three notes on uses of Circe by Spenser, Marlowe and Milton', *Notes & Queries* (October, 1978), 433–5.

seductive, glamorous, magical, bestially transforming, poisonous, enfeebling, effeminating.[84] Here, as Spenser's Duessa, Bullinger and Fulke show, part of the Circean configuration included an analogue from the Apocalypse, the great Whore of Babylon of Revelation XVII, with her magical and enfeebling cup. In the late sixteenth century one of the Roman church's most visible and demonised adherents, Mary Queen of Scots, was often referred to as a witch and a seductive Circe: she appears as Circe in three poems in 1586.[85]

The Faerie Queene's final Circe is in the Mutabilitie Cantos and is Mutabilitie herself. Her lineaments are less obviously Circean than those of Duessa or Acrasia. Like Circe she is extremely beautiful, has the golden wand Renaissance mythographers attribute to Circe, magically interferes with the moon (as does Virgil's Circe in *Eclogues* VIII), and encounters her old opponent Mercury. Her constant epithet 'Titanesse', which is Spenser's coinage, echoes Ovid's favourite use in the *Metamorphoses* of Circe's patronymic, *Titania*. (Contact with the fairy queen with Circe's patronymic turns Shakespeare's Bottom into an ass.) In her ambition to take Circe's power of change to cosmic proportions in Spenser's poem and to disorder the created universe, Mutabilitie embodies the last Circean characteristic I want to make clear: female rebellion. This threat (and the associated danger of female tyranny)[86] was observable in the struggle for sexual dominance between Odysseus and Circe implied in Homer and in Horace. Adriana in *The Comedy of Errors* exhibits the characteristics of the impatient and rebellious wife, especially in II.i. She is later reproved by the abbess for shrewishness, and her sister Luciana delivers her a homily on men as 'masters to their females' in II.i. Commentators on the play have noted the influence of Ephesians 5 and 6, which contain Paul's most famous exhortations to domestic and social ordering, 'Wives, submit your selves unto your owne husbands, as unto the Lord: . . . '[87] The discourses of witchcraft too used the homologies of male dominance. The Biblical verse 'For rebellion is as the sin of witchcraft' (1 Samuel 15.23) was often quoted

---

[84] See D. Douglas Waters, 'Errour's den and Archimago's hermitage: symbolic lust and symbolic witchcraft', *English Literary History*, 33 (1966), reproduced in *Critical Essays on Spenser from ELH* (Baltimore and London, 1970), pp. 158–77.

[85] Kerby Neill, 'Spenser's Acrasia and Mary Queen of Scots', *PMLA*, 60 (1945), 682–8.

[86] See Brodwin, 'Milton and the Renaissance Circe' 54ff.

[87] Bishops' Bible, Ephesians 5.22. See especially *The Comedy of Errors*, ed. T. S. Dorsch (Cambridge, 1988), pp. 10–11, 113–14, and also T. W. Baldwin, 'Three homilies in *The Comedy of Errors*' in *Essays on Shakespeare and Elizabethan Drama in Honour of Hardin Craig*, ed., Richard Hosley (London, 1963), pp. 137–47.

in all sorts of writing, not only those on witchcraft. In the writings of the learned on witchcraft, witches were rebels and traitors. The authors of the *Malleus* thought witches should be treated in law as are those in cases of lese-majesty for 'they strike against [*pulsant*] the Divine Majesty'.[88] Indeed, many argued that this defection and treachery was the reason why they should be executed rather than for *maleficium*. William Perkins thought witches should be punished with death like traitors for the witch is 'the most notorious traytor and rebell that can be".[89] Circean seduction was a form of rebellion. One of her dangers is the usurpation and consequently the subjugation of the male by the female. Perhaps one should remember that the primary meaning of 'seduce' is political rather than sexual: 'to persuade (a vassal, servant, soldier etc.) to desert his allegiance or service'. Circean transformation, rebellion, threats to male ordering, dominance and rationality may be seen as part of what Stuart Clark reads as the language of inversion and misrule in the discourse of witchcraft. Indeed Clark mentions Circe as part of his discussion of the motif of 'overturning'.[90]

There is a dense collocation of all these Circean dangers in the first couple of pages of Samuel Harsnet's exposé of fraudulent Catholic exorcisms in England in the 1580s, *A declaration of egregious popish impostures, to with-draw the harts of her Majesties subjects from their allegeance* (1603). At the opening of the address to the 'seduced' Catholics of England, political and erotic senses of the word are interrelated as Harsnet warns the 'seduced and disunited Brethren' against two great witches, lying wonders and counterfeit zeal. On the next page the seductive witchcraft of the Roman church is named explicitly as Circean,[91] as Harsnet appeals to Englishmen in a passage that plays on the anxieties about Circe I have been describing – seduction, rebellion, subversive enthralment of men by women, loss of male rationality:

> that men as you are, borne free of an understanding spirit, and
> ingenious disposition, should basely degenerate, as to captivate your
> wits, wils and spirits, to a forraine Idol Gull, composed of palpable

---

[88] *Malleus maleficarum*, pars 1, quaestio 1, 9.

[89] Perkins, *A Discourse of the Damned Art*, p. 248.

[90] 'Inversion, misrule and the meaning of witchcraft', esp. 114–15. For a reading of some sixteenth-century German visual representations of witches as a 'fear of female sexuality as an appropriation of male power and as an inversion of the proper order', see also Charles Zika, 'Fears of flying: representations of witchcraft and sexuality in early sixteenth-century Germany', *Australian Journal of Art*, 8 (1989–90), 19–47.

[91] Cf. above pp. 195–9, for the way in *The Comedy of Errors* that Circe is the name eventually given to figure the anxieties subliminally present earlier on in the text.

fiction and diabolicall fascination, whose enchaunted chalice of heathenish drugs, and Lamian superstition, hath the power of *Circes* and *Medaea*'s cup, to metamorphose men into asses, bayards [bay horses], and swine.

Part of the iconography of Circe which always attracted attention, commentary and exegesis was her magic cup, the very tool of her power to transform and weaken. In Homer it contains a rich and sweet mixture, 'a potion of cheese and barley meal and yellow honey with Pramnian wine; but in the food she mixed baleful drugs'.[92] In Ovid's imitation of this Homeric passage in the *Metamorphoses* the sense of deceptive intention in concealing the magical drugs is stronger. Ovid's Circe 'added juices to lie hidden under the sweetness' [*quique sub hac lateant furtim dulcedine, sucos / adicit*].[93] Both descriptions provided hints to mythographers (and certainly Spenser) about Circe as mixture, for Spenser the bad mixture which is intemperance, *akrasia*. In his reading of Circe in his witch Acrasia and her Bower Spenser saw in Circe's cup an inversion of a cherished humanist commonplace for the harmony of the delightful and the educative. The image of the sweetened and medicinal cup of delightful fiction has a history going back at least as far as Lucretius. In Castiglione's manual for Italian courtiers *The book of the courtier* it is a metaphor for how a courtier might delightfully instruct his prince in virtue, and Sir Philip Sidney in his *Apology for poetry* justifies the writing of fiction by comparing the delightful instruction of fiction to a doctor administering sweetened medicine, 'even as the child is often brought to take most wholesome things by hiding them in such other as have a pleasant taste'.[94]

Sidney defended poetry from the charge that it threatened to seduce men from obligations, the active life and duty. In this charge of pleasurable seduction from active duty poetry itself, like Acrasia, is Circean. In Sidney's *Apology for poetry* one of the charges against poetry figures its pleasurable seduction as Circe's Renaissance attendants, 'with a siren's sweetness drawing the mind to the serpent's tail of sinful fancy'.[95]

---

[92] *Odyssey*, X. 234–6.

[93] *Metamorphoses*, XIV, 275–6.

[94] Lucretius, *De rerum natura*, I, 936–50, IV, 11–25; Baldessare Castiglione, *The Book of the Courtier*, Sir Thomas Hoby (trans.) (London, 1975), p. 265; Sidney, *An Apology for Poetry*, ed., Geoffrey Shepherd (Manchester, 1973), p. 113. The extensive history of this commonplace can be traced through Shepherd's note in his edition of the *Apology*, p. 182.

[95] *Apology*, p. 123.

Sidney also defended fiction from the charge that it lies. The Renaissance poet-magician asks to be trusted to use sweetened and pleasurable deceptions, including the licence given him (and it is always 'him') of lying benevolently to us for our instruction. In his own eyes at least he could therefore claim to be the opposite to the devil, the father of lies, and to the witch, both of whom deceive to destroy us with their mingling of fact and fiction. But ironically, and Sidney was probably unaware of this, Augustine used precisely the same *topos* of the sweetened and concealing cup for the deceitful mixture by which evil spirits with their deceptive fictions [*fingunt*] lead Christians astray and poison them. The same image which for Castiglione expressed the justifiable and pleasurable deceptions used by the courtier to educate his prince and which for Sidney images the healthful depiction of fiction, is used by Augustine of the deceptive practice of using the name of Christ in magic. Augustine talks of

> those who lead astray [*seducunt*] by magical bindings [*ligaturas*], by spells, by the devices of the Enemy, and mix the Name of Christ in with their spells. Because they are now not able to lead Christians astray, in order to give them poison they add a little honey, so that which is bitter lies hidden by the sweet, and is drunk destroying them.[96]

Sidney at one point sharply distinguishes his truth-telling poet from a magician, but only at the risk of reminding us, as this chapter earlier noted in passing, that the magician was frequently in the Renaissance a figure for the poet or dramatist.[97] The moment occurs crucially in the context of one of Sidney's most important defences against the charge of lying against poetry, the fine point that the poet can never lie because he

---

[96] *In Joannis Evangelium tractatus CXXIV* in Migne, *Patrologia latina*, 35 (1845), column 1440. On Augustine's vocabulary for magic see Sister Mary Emily Keenan, 'The terminology of witchcraft in the works of Augustine', *Classical Philology*, 35 (1940), 294–7. There may be a variation on this motif of hiding magical poison with sweetened deception in a story from Byzantine hagiography in the *Acta sanctorum*. The magician Gourias, 'a misleader of the people' who feigned holiness and an eremitic life, attempted to destroy St Joannikios with a poisoned honey and milk mixture, Dorothy de F. Abrahamse, 'Magic and sorcery in the hagiography of the middle Byzantine period', *Byzantinische Forschungen*, 8 (1982), 3–17.

[97] On the poet-magician in Spenser see William Blackburn, 'Spenser's Merlin', *Renaissance and Reformation*, n.s. 4 (1980), 179–98 and William Blackburn, 'Merlin' in *The Spenser Encyclopaedia*, pp. 470–1; Gareth Roberts, 'Magic', in *The Spenser Encyclopaedia*, pp. 445–6; Alvin Kernan, *The Playwright as Magician: Shakespeare's Image of the Poet in the English Public Theatre* (New Haven, 1979), esp. pp. 146–59.

affirms nothing to be so, 'Now for the poet, he nothing affirms, and therefore never lieth. For, as I take it, to lie is to affirm that to be true which is false . . . But the poet (as I said before) never affirmeth. The poet never maketh any circles about your imagination, to conjure you to believe for true what he writes.'[98] This, like much of the *Apology*, is a brilliant rhetorical sleight of hand which serves Sidney's polemical purposes at this moment. In fact Sidney will himself 'conjure' his readers at the end of the *Apology*.[99] There is an unspoken admission here of the danger of slippage between benevolent and malevolent deceptions of magic.

In Isidore's section on transformations 'history' and 'fiction' mutually confirm each other on the reality of transformation. The transformation of the companions of Diomedes into birds is not fiction and lies but is confirmed by history.[100] In Spenser's Bower of Bliss, however, with Circean Acrasia as its final and central revelation, the relations of fiction, pleasure and truth are problematic. In his reading of the figure of the witch Circe Spenser saw her at her most radically subversive for male humanist poets like himself, for he saw her perilous and unlicensed power to destabilise the relation between fiction and truth.

---

[98] *Apology*, pp. 123–4.
[99] Ibid., p. 141.
[100] '*non fabuloso mendacio, sed historica adfirmatione confirmant*', *Etymologies*, XI, iv, 2.
    I am grateful to Jonathan Barry and Lawrence Normand for their close and painstaking reading of drafts of this chapter.

8. *Witchcraft and fantasy in early Modern Germany*

LYNDAL ROPER

In January 1669, Anna Ebeler found herself accused of murdering the woman for whom she had worked as a lying-in maid. The means was a bowl of soup. Instead of restoring the young mother's strength, the soup, made of malmsey and brandy in place of Rhine wine, had increased her fever. The mother became delirious but, as the watchers at her deathbed claimed, she was of sound mind when she blamed the lying-in maid for her death. As word spread, other women came forward stating that Ebeler had poisoned their young children too. The child of one had lost its baby flesh and its whole little body had become pitifully thin and dried out. Another's child had been unable to suckle from its mother, even though it was greedy for milk and able to suck vigorously from other women: shortly after, it died in agony. In a third house, an infant had died after its body had suddenly become covered in hot, poisonous pustules and blisters which broke open. The baby's 7-year-old brother suffered from aches and pains caused by sorcery and saw strange visions, his mother suffered from headaches and the whole household started to notice strange growths on their bodies. And a fourth woman found her infant covered with red splotches and blisters, her baby's skin drying out until it could be peeled off like a shirt. The child died most piteously, and its mother's menstruation ceased. All had employed Ebeler as their lying-in maid. Anna Ebeler was interrogated six times and confessed at the end of the second interrogation, when torture was threatened. She was executed and her body burnt on 23 March 1669 – a 'merciful' punishment practised in place of burning in the humane city of Augsburg. She was aged 67. Just two months had elapsed since she was first accused.[1]

---

[1] Stadtarchiv Augsburg (hereafter cited as StadtAA), Urgichtensammlung (hereafter cited as Urg.), 28 Jan. 1669, Anna Ebeler.

1 The case of Anna Ebeler, 1669, *Relation Oder Beschreibung so Anno 1669 . . . von einer Weibs/Person . . .* (Augsburg 1669).

Note: These images might be used and reused for different cases. Thus, some of the same scenes are to be found in *Warhaffte Historische Abbild: und kurtze Beschreibung, was sich unlangst in . . . Augspurg . . . zugetragen . . .* (Augsburg 1654); and *Wahraffte Beschreibung des Urthels . . .* (Augsburg 1666).

Anna Ebeler was one of eighteen witches executed in Augsburg. As many more were interrogated by the authorities but cleared of witchcraft; others faced religious courts and yet further cases never reached the courts. Augsburg saw no witchcraze. Unlike its south German neighbours, it executed no witch before 1625 and its cases tended to come singly, one or two every few years after 1650.[2] Witchcraft of an

---

[2] StadtAA, Stafbücher des Rats, 1563–1703. For the indispensable, pathbreaking study of witchcraft in Bavaria, see Wolfgang Behringer, *Hexenverfolgung in Bayern. Volksmagie, Glaubenseifer und Staatsräson in der Frühen Neuzeit* (Munich, 1987), pp. 431–69: there is one unclear case from 1563; one woman died under arrest in 1591 (p. 157), and another in 1699 (Strafbuch des Rats, 1654–99, 24 Sept. 1699, Elisabeth Memminger). See also Bernd Roeck, *Eine Stadt in Krieg und Frieden. Studien zur Geschichte der Reichsstadt Augsburg zwischen Kalenderstreit und Parität* (Schriftenreihe des Historischen Kommission bei der Bayerischen Akademie der Wissenschaften 37) (Göttingen, 1989), esp. I, pp. 113–16, 445–54; and II, pp. 539–52 on the witch trial of 1625; and on the cases of 1654, see Wolfgang Wüst, 'Inquisitionsprozess und Hexenverfolgung im Hochstift Augsburg im 17. und 18. Jahrhundert', *Zeitschrift für Bayerische Landesgeschichte*, 50 (1987), 109–26. On witch hunting in the neighbouring region, H. C. Erik Midelfort, *Witch Hunting in Southwestern Germany 1562–1684. The Social and Intellectual Foundations* (Stanford, CA, 1972).

2 A: Anna Ebeler is abducted from a dance by the devil and led to her house.

everyday, unremarkable kind, the themes of the cases can tell us a great deal about early modern psyches. For Ebeler's crimes were not unusual. It was typical, too, that of her accusers all except one should have been women, and that her victims were young infants aged up to about six weeks and women who had just given birth.

One dominant theme in witch trials in Augsburg is motherhood. Relations between mothers, those occupying maternal roles and children, formed the stuff of most, though not all, witchcraft accusations in the town.[3] To this extent, early feminist works which focused on birth and midwives in their explanations of witchcraft were making an important observation.[4] But though the trials were concerned with the question of

---

[3] Three of those executed were lying-in maids, and a fourth was a failed midwife. Four of those heavily suspected were lying-in maids and most were expelled from the town on other pretexts. Other cases were closely related. One executed witch killed her own child, another committed incest with her own son who later died, while a third had worked as a childminder. In seven further cases, themes were borrowed from the same paradigm: the executed witches had harmed children for whom they were in some sense responsible.

[4] Barbara Ehrenreich and Deirdre English, *Witches, Midwives and Nurses. A History of Women Healers* (New York and London, 1973). See also, for a survey of feminist views of witchcraft, Dagmar Unverhau, 'Frauenbewegung und historische Hexenverfolgung', in Andreas Blauert, ed., *Ketzer, Zauberer, Hexen. Die Anfänge der europäischen Hexenverfolgungen* (Frankfurt am Main, 1990). Recently it has been argued that witchcraft accusations were an attempt to destroy a female science of birth control: Gunnar Heinsohn and Otto Steiger, *Die Vernichtung der weisen Frauen. Beiträge zur Theorie und Geschichte von Bevölkerung und Kindheit* (Part A,

motherhood they were not, it seems to me, male attempts to destroy a female science of birth nor were they concerned with wresting control of reproduction from women. What is striking is that they were typically accusations brought by mothers, soon after giving birth, against women intimately concerned with the care of the child, most often the lying-in maid and not the midwife.

Many investigations of witchcraft proceed by trying to explain why women should be scapegoated as witches or what other conflicts may have been at the root of the case – conflicts involving issues with which we are more comfortable, such as struggles over charity, property or political power. However, I want to argue that the cases need to be understood in their own terms by means of the themes they develop. As historians, I think we may best interpret them as psychic documents which recount particular predicaments. Witchcraft cases seem to epitomise the bizarre and irrational, exemplifying the distance that separates us from the past. What interests me, however, is the extent to which early modern subjectivities are different or similar to ours. I shall argue that unless we attend to the imaginative themes of the interrogations themselves, we shall not understand witchcraft. This project has to investigate two sides of the story, the fears of those who accused, and the self-understanding of people who in the end, as I shall argue, came to see themselves as witches.

Our perplexity in dealing with witchcraft confessions derives in part from their epistemological status. In a profession used to assessing documents for their reliability, it is hard to know how to interpret documents which we do not believe to be factual. But witchcraft

Hexenverfolgung, Kinderwelten, Menschenproduktion, Bevölkerungswissenschaft) (Herbstein, 1985). However, the cases the authors cite are actually about hostility to children, not about birth control: see, for example, pp. 149–56. For a critique of the Heinsohn-Steiger thesis, see Robert Jütte, 'Die Persistenz des Verhütungswissens in der Volkskultur. Sozial- und medizinhistorische Ammerkungen zur These von der "Vernichtung der weisen Frauen"', *Medizinhistorisches Journal*, 24 (1989), 214–31. David Harley has argued that there is little evidence for the importance of midwives among those executed in England: 'Historians as demonologists: the myth of the midwife-witch', *Social History of Medicine*, 3: 1 (1900), 1–26; and for a similar argument, Peter Kriedte, 'Die Hexen und ihre Ankläger. Zu den lokalen Voraussetzungen der Hexenverfolgungen in der frühen Neuzeit – Ein Forschungsbericht', *Zeitschrift für historische Forschung*, 14 (1987), 47–71, 60. While it may be true that the absolute figure of midwives accused or executed was small, they are none the less a recognisable occupational group in the German evidence where only a few other work patterns may be discerned. Their significance might be better related to the involvement of mothers, lying-in maids and others connected with the care of mothers and infants.

confessions and accusations are not products of realism, and they cannot be analysed with the methods of historical realism. This is not to say that they are meaningless: on the contrary, they are vivid, organised products of the mind. Our problem is not that early modern people had a different ontology to our own, believing in a world populated by ghosts who walked at night, devils who might appear in the form of young journeymen, severed arms carrying needles or wandering souls inhabiting household dust. Rather, all phenomena in the early modern world, natural and fantastic, had a kind of hyper-reality which resided in their significance. Circumstantial details were ransacked for their meaning for the individual, and for what they might reveal about causation and destiny. Causation, which could involve divine or diabolic intervention in human affairs, was understood in terms both moral and religious. Consequently, we need to understand confessions and accusations as mental productions with an organisation that is in itself significant. This means analysing the themes of witchcraft not to tell us about the genealogy of magical beliefs – the approach taken by Carlo Ginzburg in his recent book[5] – but to tell us about the conflicts of the actors.

In the cases I have explored, witchcraft accusations centrally involved deep antagonisms between women, enmities so intense that neighbours could testify against a woman they had known for years in full knowledge that they were sending her 'to a blood bath' as one accused woman cried to her neighbours as they left the house for the chancellery.[6] Their main motifs concern suckling, giving birth, food and feeding; the capacities of parturient women's bodies and the vulnerability of infants. This was surprising, at least to me: I had expected to find in witchcraft a culmination of the sexual antagonism which I have discussed in sixteenth- and seventeenth-century German culture. The idea of flight astride a broom or pitchfork, the notions of a pact with the devil sealed by intercourse, the sexual abandonment of the dance at the witches' sabbath, all seemed to suggest that witchcraft had to do with sexual guilt and attraction between men and women, and that its explanation might

[5] Carlo Ginzburg, *Ecstasies. Deciphering the Witches' Sabbath*, trans. Gregory Roberts (London, 1990) (first published in Italian 1989): interestingly, one of the effects of Ginzburg's brilliant analysis is that women's predominance as victims in the witchhunt tends to slip from the explanation.

[6] StadtAA, Urg., 15 July 1650, Ursula Neher, testimony Sabina Stoltz, 29 July 1650. Anna Ebeler screamed that her persecutors were sending her 'to the butcher's slab', 'to the raven stone': StadtAA, Urg., 28 Jan. 1669, Anna Ebeler, testimony of Catharina Mörz, and Anna Ebeler, 24 Jan. 1669.

lie in the moralism of the Reformation and Counter-Reformation years, when Catholics and Protestants sought to root out prostitution and adultery, shame women who became pregnant before marriage and impose a rigorous sexual code which cast the women as Eve, the temptress who was to blame for mankind's fall.[7]

Some of the cases I found certainly dealt with these themes, but the primary issue in what we might term a stereotypical case of witchcraft was maternity. The conflicts were not concerned with the social construction of gender but were related much more closely to the physical changes a woman's body undergoes when she bears children.[8] While these clearly have a social meaning and thus a history, the issues were so closely tied to the physical reality of the female sex and to sexual identity at the deepest level that they seemed to elude off-the-peg explanations in terms of female roles and gender conflict. The stuff of much of the accusations made by the mothers was not femininity or genital sexuality, but was pre-Oedipal in content, turning on the relationship to the breast and to the mother in the period before the infant has a sense of sexual identity.[9] The primary emotion of the witch-craft cases, envy, also originates in this early period of life.[10] Witchcraft accusations followed a pattern with a psychic logic: the accusations were made by women who experienced childbirth and their most common type of target was a post-menopausal, infertile woman who was caring

---

[7] See, on the sexual themes of images of witchcraft, Charles Zika, 'Fears of flying: representations of witchcraft and sexuality in early sixteenth-century Germany', *Australian Journal of Art*, 8 (1989–90), 19–48; and on the themes of witch fantasy and their historical elaboration, Richard van Dülmen, 'Imaginationen des Teuflischen. Nächtliche Zusammenkünfte, Hexentänze, Teufelssabbate', and Eva Labouvie, 'Hexenspuk und Hexenabwehr. Volksmagie und volkstümlicher Hexenglaube', both in Richard van Dülmen, ed., *Hexenwelten. Magie und Imagination vom 16.–20. Jahrhundert* (Frankfurt am Main, 1987); Robert Rowland, '"Fantasticall and devilishe persons": European witch-beliefs in comparative perspective', in Bengt Ankarloo and Gustav Henningsen, eds., *Early Modern European Witchcraft: Centres and Peripheries* (Oxford, 1990). On the project of sexual regulation, Lyndal Roper, *The Holy Household. Women and Morals in Reformation Augsburg* (Oxford, 1989) and *Oedipus and the Devil* (London, 1994); and R. Po-Chia Hsia, *Social Discipline in the Reformation, Central Europe 1550–1750* (London, 1989), pp. 122–73.

[8] See Estela V. Welldon, *Mother, Madonna, Whore. The Idealization and Denigration of Motherhood* (London, 1988), for an illuminating attempt to deal with the issues of female psychosexual identity.

[9] John Demos has also noticed the importance of pre-Oedipal themes in Salem witch-craft: *Entertaining Satan. Witchcraft and the Culture of Early New England* (Oxford, 1982), esp. pp. 116ff, 179ff.

[10] Melanie Klein, 'Envy and gratitude' (1957), in Klein, *Envy and Gratitude and Other Works 1946–1963* (London, 1975).

for the infant. Often, as in the case we have just explored, she was the lying-in maid.

Here it might be objected that witchcraft interrogations and confessions cannot be used to give us insight into early modern psychic life in this way. They are stereotyped products, it might be argued, not of those interrogated but of the minds of the interrogators. These men wanted to know about witches' sabbaths, sex with the devil and cannibalism and they forced this information out of the women using leading questions and even outright promptings, resorting to torture to gain the confession they needed to convict the woman. However, such an objection does not recognise the cultural attitude to pain nor its place in the dynamic of interrogation in early modern society. Witches were women who could not feel pain as normal women could. They were unable to weep and they did not sense the witch-pricker's needle.[11] A measure of physical pain, so the interrogators believed, was a process of the body which enabled the witch to free herself from the devil's clutches, weakening her defences against the admission of guilt. The amount of pain had to be finely judged by the executioner, a scientist of the body. Using his knowledge of the victim's frailty, and in consultation with the council, he calculated the precise grades required at each stage of the process (from exhibition of the equipment, stretching on the rack without attaching weights, through to attaching weights of increasing size) so that the witch's integral, diabolic personality might be stripped away by the application of pain to uncover the truth.[12] Like a kind of

---

[11] See, for example, StadtAA, Urg., 20 Dec. 1685, Euphrosina Endriss, 6 Mar. 1686, final observation that Endriss had often looked as though she were going to cry but not a single tear escaped from her; Urg., 28 Jan. 1669, Anna Ebeler: at the interrogation of 11 Mar. 1669, Ebeler noted that the devil had not allowed her to cry properly, but, as the scribe noted, she then began to cry heartily and to pray the Lord's Prayer, the Ave Maria, and deliver a 'beautiful' extempore confession. Urg., 11 Feb. 1666, Anna Schwayhofer, 15 Mar. 1666, interrogators noted that she apparently felt no pain from the thumbscrews, a fact which the executioner explained by saying this was a mild form of torture. The executioner pricked a suspicious looking mark on Anna Elisabeth Christeiner but it disappeared, strong proof, he thought, of the devil's work: Urg., Apr. 1701, fourth interrogation, 3 Aug. 1701.

[12] See Edward Peters, *Torture* (Oxford, 1985); on the executioner, often a key figure in the generation of a witch hunt, Helmut Schuhmann, *Der Scharfrichter, Seine Gestalt – Seine Funktion* (Allgäuer Heimatbücher 67) (Kempten, 1964); Ch. Hinckeldy, *Strafjustiz in alter Zeit* (Rothenburg, 1980); Werner Danckert, *Unehrliche Berufe. Die verfemten Leute* (Munich, 1963); Franz Irsigler and Arnold Lassotta, *Bettler und Gaukler, Dirnen und Henker, Aussenseiter in einer mittelalterlichen Stadt* (Cologne, 1984), pp. 228–82. The duration of torture might also be measured by the time it took to say particular prayers, a technique which tacitly invoked divine assistance against

medicine of salvation, it assisted her travail to return to the Christian community in contrition so that she might die in a state of grace. Torture was part of an understanding, shared by the witch and her persecutors, of the interrelation of body and soul: the skin of the outer person had to be flayed away to arrive at psychological truth. Those who did not crack under torture were set free despite the seriousness of the accusations against them, because they were said to have proven their innocence: they lacked a diabolic interiority of this kind.

Pain had a religious significance too. By experiencing the pain of flagellation, or participating in the procession of the Twelve Stations of the Cross, a ritual which reached its final form in the Counter-Reformation in Augsburg,[13] one could come closer to Christ by physical imitation of His sufferings. Maternity involved pain. Mary herself had borne Jesus in suffering, and the seven swords of grief piercing the suffering Madonna were a powerful Baroque image. Luisa Accati has written of the importance of the Madonna in agony to Baroque under-standings of both Marian piety and motherhood.[14] Soothsayers told of spells in which they appealed to 'the suffering of Mary as she lay on her martyr-bed of straw'.[15] The witch, the women whose capacity to feel pain was impaired, was thus an unmaternal woman, alienated from the realm of pain so manifestly experienced by the new mothers who accused her of sorcery. Devoid of maternal affection, the witch was incapable of feeling pity for her victims.

diabolic power: see, for example, StadtAA, Urg., 30 June 1650, Barbara Fischer, for the use of the Miserere and Lord's Prayer. In some Bavarian trials, torture becomes part of an almost physical struggle against the devil's power: see Michael Kunze, *Highroad to the Stake*, trans. William E. Yuill (Chicago, IL and London, 1987); and Wolfgang Behringer, 'Hexenverfolgung als Machtspiel', in R. Po-Chia Hsia and B. Scribner, eds., *History and Anthropology in Early Modern Europe. Papers from the Wolfenbüttel conference 1991*, forthcoming. Kathy Start has researched the role of executioners and dishonourable people in Augsburg in the early modern period, and she has a great deal to say about the executioner as an expert on the body and its capacity to withstand pain, knowledge which also made his skills as a healer greatly valued: Kathy Start, 'The boundaries of honor. "Dishonorable people" in Augsburg 1500–1800', Ph.D. diss., Yale University, 1993.

13 Louis Châtellier, *The Europe of the Devout. The Catholic Reformation and the Formation of a New Society* (Cambridge, 1990), p. 150.

14 Luisa Accati, 'The larceny of desire: the madonna in seventeenth-century Catholic Europe', in Jim Obelkevich, Lyndal Roper and Raphael Samuel, eds., *Disciplines of Faith. Studies in Religion, Politics and Patriarchy* (London, 1987).

15 StadtAA, Urg., 2 July 1590, Anna Stauder. I have developed the theme of parallels between spells and Counter-Reformation religiosity in 'Magic and the theology of the body: exorcism in sixteenth-century Augsburg', in Charles Zika, ed., *No Other Gods Except Me: Orthodoxy and Religious Practice in Europe 1200–1700* (Melbourne, 1991).

Moreover, the system of confession also rested on a measure of collusion between witch and questioner. The witch had to freely affirm her confession after it had been given, in the absence of torture. This was a requirement of the Imperial Law Code of Charles V of 1532, and it was certainly not honoured all over the empire.[16] But in a place like Augsburg which did not experience mass witch hunts, the credibility of the phenomenon of witchcraft rested on the ultimate truth-telling of the witch. Witches could and did modify their confession: so, for instance, Anna Ebeler, who had confessed to having sex with the devil a countless number of times, insisted at the last that she had only rarely had diabolic intercourse, a disclaimer incorporated in her final public condemnation. Witches were commonly supposed to have renounced God, Jesus, Mary and the saints, but Ebeler was able to maintain that she had never forsworn the Virgin, who had comforted her during diabolic assaults, and that she had never desecrated the Host as she had earlier confessed she had.[17] Another who firmly denied that she was a witch was not described as such in her denunciation, even though she was executed for having used witchcraft.[18]

This freedom was in some sense apparent rather than real: witches who confessed and then revoked their confession embarked on a long and hideous game of cat and mouse with their interrogators, as they were reinterrogated and tortured until their narrative was consistent. But interrogators knew when a confession was simply a result of torture or its fear, and they noted this. Crucial to their own understanding of their task was the belief that, by repetition and forcing the culprit to describe and redescribe the minutiae of the crime, checking with witnesses, the truth would eventually be uncovered. That truth took on a kind of talismanic quality, as the witch was forced to tell and retell it in up to ten sessions of questioning, making it consistent. Her statements were then read out in full to the assembled council before condemnation could be agreed; a summary of her crimes was recorded in the Council's Punishment Book and read out before her execution; and this material formed the basis for the broadsheets and pamphlets that were written about

---

[16] *Die peinliche Gerichtsordnung Kaiser Karls V. von 1532*, 4th edn, A. Kaufmann, ed. (Munich, 1975), arts no. 48–58, pp. 50–6.

[17] StadtAA, Urg., 28 Jan. 1669, Anna Ebeler, interrogations 28 Jan. to 23 Mar. 1669; Verruf, 32 Mar. 1669; and Strafbuch Des Rats, 23 March. 1669, pp. 312–14.

[18] She also denied intercourse with the devil. StadtAA, Urg., 20 Dec. 1685, Euphrosina Endriss, 4 Mar. 1686, and condemnation, 16 Mar. 1686; Strafbuch des Rats, 1654–99, pp. 57–8.

the case.[19] The reiteration fixed the details until there could be no doubt about the narrative. It was a truth which the witch herself freely acknowledged and for which she alone had provided the material. For despite the power of the stereotypes in the witch's confession, these do not explain the particular inflections individual witches gave to them, as they described how they went to a sabbath that was held just by the gallows outside Augsburg, or how the devil appeared to them in a long black coat, dressed for all the world like a merchant.[20]

There is a further collusive dynamic at work in interrogation, that between witch and torturer. Torture was carried out by the town hangman, who would eventually be responsible for the convicted witch's execution. Justice in the early modern period was not impersonal: the act of execution involved two individuals who, by the time of execution, were well acquainted with each other. Particularly in witch trials, torture and the long period of time it took for a conviction to be secured gave the executioner a unique knowledge of an individual's capacity to withstand pain, and of their physiological and spiritual reactions to touch. In a society where nakedness was rare, he knew her body better than anyone else. He washed and shaved the witch, searching all the surfaces of her body for the tell-tale diabolic marks – sometimes hidden 'in her shame', her genitals. He bound up her wounds after the torture. On the other hand, he was a dishonourable member of society, excluded from civic intercourse, and forced to intermarry among his own kind. His touch might pollute; yet his craft involved him in physically investigating a witch, a woman who if innocent was forbidden him. He advised on the mode of execution, assessing how much pain the witch might stand, a function he could potentially exploit to show mercy or practise cruelty.[21] In consequence, a bond of intense personal dependence on the part of the witch on her persecutor might be established. Euphrosina Endriss was greatly agitated when a visiting executioner from nearby Memmingen inspected

---

[19] The procedure is described in Staatsbibliothek München, Handschriftenabteilung, Cgm 2026, fos. 1v–5r. For pamphlets describing the cases, see, for example, *Warhaffter Sumarisch: aussführlicher Bericht vnd Erzehlung. Was die in des Heyligen Röm. ReichsStatt Augspurg etlich Wochen lang in verhafft gelegne zwo Hexen/benandtlich Barbara Frölin von Rieden/vnnd Anna Schäflerin von Etringen . . .* (Augsburg, 1654); *Relation Oder Beschreibung so Anno 1669 . . . von einer Weibs-Person . . .* (Augsburg, 1669).

[20] StadtAA, Urg., 28 Jan. 1669, Anna Ebeler, interrogation 6 Mar. 1669; Strafbuch des Rats, 1654–99, 7 Feb. 1673, Regina Schiller, pp. 390ff.

[21] In 1587 the 'evil custom' of allowing the hangman to carry out torture unsupervised had to be explicitly abolished in Augsburg: Behringer, *Hexenverfolgung in Bayern*, p. 158.

her. She pleaded that 'this man should not execute her, she would rather that Hartman should execute her, for she knew him already'.[22]

Once the torturer's application of pain had brought the witch to confess, she knew she faced execution, and knew her executioner. In the procedure of interrogation itself, carried out in the presence of council interrogators, scribes and executioner, there is an unmistakable sado-masochistic logic, as the witch, in response to pain, might reveal details of her crimes only to deny them subsequently; or as she proffered scattered scraps of information about diabolic sex only then to tantalise her questioners with contradiction or silence. In this sadistic game of showing and concealing, the witch forced her persecutors to apply and reapply pain, prising her body apart to find her secret. Once it was found, she might herself identify with the aggressor: so, at the conclusion of her final confession as a witch, when it was plain she faced death, Anna Ebeler fell at her persecutors' feet in tears, asking for a merciful execution. 'She begged my lords for forgiveness for what she had done wrong. She thanked them for granting her such a good imprisonment and treatment.'[23] Masochism, however, has its twin in sadism. Even in death, the resolution of the game, the witch herself was believed able to retaliate against her tormentor. One hangman found his hands suddenly crippled after he executed two witches in 1685, and his colleague had to execute the third. Just before Barbara Fischer was executed, so one chronicler noted, a powerful rainstorm struck as if everything must drown: this witch, the writer observed, had shown no signs of contrition.[24] At every stage, the trial progressed through a combustion

---

[22] StadtAA, Urg., 20 Dec. 1685, Euphrosina Endriss, report of Hans Adam Hartman, 5 Feb. 1686: Hans Adam Hartman, executioner of Donauwörth, was the son of the Augsburg executioner Mattheus Hartman who had been crippled in both hands (see text above).

[23] 'bitt in fine nochmalen feussfellig vnd mit Weinen vmb Ein gnedig urthel, vnd Meine herrn vmb verzeihung, wass sie vnrechts gethan. bedankt sich auch dass man ihr so ein gute gefangnuss vnd tractament zukommen lassen', StadtAA, Urg., 28 Jan. 1669, Anna Ebeler, testimony of 21 Mar. 1669. Anna Schwayhofer also concluded her final testimony by saying this was the confession by which she wanted to live and die, 'confessing also, that she was a heavy, yes, the greatest sinner, and therefore she would gladly die, only begging hereby for a merciful judgement': Urg., 11 Feb. 1666, Anna Schwayhofer, interrogation 31 Mar. 1666. On sadism and masochism see Joyce McDougall, *Plea for a Measure of Abnormality* (London, 1990, 1st edn, France, 1978); Sigmund Freud, 'Three essays on the theory of sexuality', in *On Sexuality* (Pelican Freud Library 7), trans. James Strachey, ed., Angela Richards (London, 1977); Freud, 'The economic problem of masochism (1924)', in *On Metapsychology* (Penguin Freud Library 11), trans. James Strachey, ed., Angela Richards (London, 1984).

[24] Staatsbibliothek München, Handschriftenabteilung, Cgm 2026, fols. 64v–65r, 61r.

of sadism, retaliation and masochism, in which each actor might in fantasy veer from persecutor to victim to tormentor.

How can the historian make use of material generated in such circumstances? In spite of the geographical specificity and precision of detail we noted earlier in the confession material, witchcraft confessions certainly do possess a stereotypical aspect. There are elements, like the diabolic pact, the sabbath, the power the devil gave them to do harm, which appear in most confessions. But the basic psychic images of any society are usually the stuff of cliché. It is their commonness which makes these images seem banal, yet enables them to give form to inchoate, shared terrors and common predicaments. It is undoubtedly true that the pressures of interrogation and pain caused accused witches to shape their accounts of their own emotions and present a narrative of their psychic worlds in a particular way – the language of witchcraft forced them to present the devil as their seducer and the ultimate cause of their fall. But narratives in which people try to make sense of their psychic conflicts usually involve borrowing from a language which is not at first the individual's own. We might say that coming to understand oneself can involve learning to recognise one's feelings in the terms of a theory, psychoanalytic or diabolic, which one might not originally have applied to oneself, and it can also entail a kind of violence.

What was the substance of the witches' crime? The grief and terror of the witnesses concentrated on the bodies of those who were the victims of witchcraft. Their bodies bore the signs of their martyrdom. As one mother put it, her dead child was covered in sores so that he looked like a devotional image of a martyr.[25] Strange signs were seen: nipples appeared all over the body of one infant, erupting into pussy sores. The legs of another were misshapen and bent.[26] Repeatedly, witnesses stress the physical character of the victim's agony, incomprehensible suffering which cannot be alleviated by the onlookers or by the mother, and which excites hatred, revenge and guilt feelings in part because of the sufferer's innocence. In emotionally laden language, the witnesses describe the 'piteous' way the child died, and their own failure to get the child to thrive. It is in this collective world of gossip and advice that the rumours of witchcraft first began, in the grief and guilt of the mother at the loss of

---

[25] StadtAA, Urg., 11 Feb. 1666, Anna Schwayhofer, testimony of Margaretha Höcht, 19 Feb. 1666.

[26] StadtAA, Urg., 15 July 1650, Ursula Neher, testimony of Susanna Custodis, 11 July 1650.

the tiny baby, and as the women around them sought to identify the cause of the inexplicable, unbearable suffering. Such gossip could be deadly. It was her employer's tongue, her 'wicked gob' as Barbara Fischer put it, using the term applied to animals' mouths, which caused one lying-in maid to retaliate against her maligner by poisoning her.[27]

The themes of the inquiry are not only pitiful but frightening. These terrors circle around nourishment and oral satisfaction, evoking powerful pre-Oedipal feelings. The breast, milk and nourishment were its key images. The food the witch gave the mother was sprinkled with white or black diabolic powders or the soups she was fed were poisonous, and these of course influenced the milk the infant received in a very immediate way. Attacks on the mother's food were thus attacks on her infant as well. When the witch killed, she often used poison, perverting the female capacity to nourish and heal. So one grandmother was interrogated three times and tortured because her young grandson suspected witchcraft when he felt queasy after drinking an aniseed water tonic she had given him.[28] The witch could be a kind of evil mother who harmed instead of nourishing her charge. The flow of nourishment could be disrupted so that the child dried out and died. In one case, the witch was accused of literally reversing the flow of the maternal fluids, herself sucking the infant dry and feeding on it. Its mother described how 'its little breasts had been sucked out so that milk had been pressed out from the child's little teats contrary to nature, . . . and from this time on the child had lost weight so that it looked as if hardly a pound of flesh remained on it'.[29]

Another baby was found to be covered with a myriad of tiny teats as if it had become a mere drinking vessel for the thirsty witch; yet another baby's teats produced 'a little drop of white watery liquid'.[30] The signs that sorcery was afoot were clearly written on the infant's body. Its skin dried out for lack of fluid, or else erupted in sores as if evil fluids within its body were forcing their way out. Its entire little body might become 'red and blue, all mixed up, and rigid and hard, like a plank of

---

[27] 'nur vmb Jhres bösen Maules Willen', StadtAA, Urg., 14 June 1650, Barbara Fischer.

[28] StadtAA, Urg., 13 May 1654, Anna Zoller.

[29] StadtAA, Urg., 15 July 1650, Ursula Neher, testimony of Sabina Stoltz, 11 July 1650. See also Urg., 25 Jan. 1695, Barbara Melder, testimony of Judith Wolf, 23 Feb. 1695 who saw Melder, the suspected witch, suck her baby's breast.

[30] StadtAA, Urg., 15 July 1650, Ursula Neher, testimony of Anna Erhardt, 29 July 1650: at the time, she interpreted this naturalistically and only considered sorcery when Stoltz and Vetter accused Neher.

wood'.[31] The infant might be unable to drink from its own mother, yet when given to another woman, be 'so hearty in sucking that it made her weep'.[32] (These themes could also emerge in cases which did not correspond to the classic accusation against a maid: so Regina Schiller denied that she had had sex with the devil. He had tried to seduce her but instead 'had come to her breasts, and had tried to give her a little powder so that she could harm people, especially children'.[33] Here, too, a woman was thinking of herself as a witch who was the possessor of a poisonous breast, harming children, again working the images of pre-Oedipal nourishing rather than exploring fantasies of sex with the devil.) In all these cases, the infant's feeding had been disrupted so that no satisfactory nourishing could take place and the relation between mother and child was destroyed. Feeding had been reversed and the infant's young rosy flesh was wasting away while the old witch thrived.

These beliefs rested on a whole economy of bodily fluids. A postmenopausal woman, the old witch was in a sense a dry woman who, instead of feeding others well, diverted nourishment to her own selfish ends. Older widows were believed to have the power to ruin young men sexually, and youths were warned against marrying such women because they were sexually ravenous, and would suck out their seed, weakening them with their insatiable hunger for seminal fluid and contaminating them with their own impurities.[34] The old witch's fluids did not flow outwards. Often her magic was directed against fertility, making women barren.[35] As was well known, witches could not weep, and old widows

---

[31] 'am ganzen leiblen ganz roht vnd blaw durcheinander, auch ganz stärr vnd hart, wie ein holz', StadtAA, Urg., 11 Feb. 1666, Anna Schwayhofer, testimony of Hans Adam Sperl, 19 Feb. 1666.

[32] 'da habe das kind so herzhafft angefallen vnd von Ihr getrunken dass sie Köfppin sich geJammert vnd dorüber Weinen müssen', StadtAA, Urg., 28 Jan. 1669, Anna Ebeler, testimony of Anna Maria Kopf, 13 Feb. 1669.

[33] 'Er ihr zu den Prüssten khomben, vnd ein pulverlin geben wollen, damit den Leüthen, vnd sonderlich Khinder zuschaden', StadtAA, Strafbuch des Rats, 1654–99, 7 Feb. 1673, p. 390, Regina Schiller.

[34] See Fredericus Petrus Gayer, *Viereckichtes Eheschätzlein. Da ist: Die vier Gradus der Eheleute*, Erfurt, Johann Beck 1602, esp. fos. C iii r ff. on widows' lust, D vii v ff. and E ii v where the writer warns that young men who marry old widows are likely to pine and die in their youth before their elderly wives do, because these old widows have concentrated impurities in them (presumably owing to the cessation of menstruation) and even have impure, poisonous breath.

[35] See, for example, Emmanuel Le Roy Ladurie, *Jasmin's Witch. An Investigation into Witchcraft and Magic in South-west France During the Seventeenth Century*, trans. Brian Pearce (London, 1987), pp. 25, 43, 59–60: in rural communities in particular, the hostility to fecundity also involves destruction of the earth's fertility.

3 B: Ebeler's night ride with the evil one; C: Ebeler at the witches' dance; D: The Witches' assembly and the diabolic feast.

could neither menstruate nor suckle children. Instead, so the science of demonology explained, she was nourishing the devil. The warts for which the executioner searched her naked body were the diabolic teats on which the devil sucked. Witches were also believed to communicate without confessing, and to secrete the Host in their mouths, taking it home to trample upon and dishonour. In doing so they were not only misusing holy food but maltreating a child, the infant Jesus whose saving death provided the Bread of salvation, squashing him and making him suffer pain. This motif is clearly taken from the older myth of Jewish ritual murder, the belief that Jews were stealing the Host and torturing it to make it bleed, and that they stole Christian children so that they could use their blood in secret rituals.[36] Yet even this hoary fantasy was incorporated into the fabric of daily life: Anna Schwayhofer confessed to this crime in the apocalyptic year 1666, and described how, housewife to the fingertips, she had afterwards swept the crumbs of the desecrated Host off the floor of her lodgings with a broom.[37]

Witches were women who did not feed others except to harm them. Failed exchanges of food typified a witch's interactions with her neighbours. So one woman, suspected of being a witch, offered two sisters

---

[36] See R. Po-Chia Hsia, *The Myth of Ritual Murder. Jews and Magic in Reformation Germany* (New Haven, CO and London, 1988).
[37] StadtAA, Urg., 11 Feb. 1666, Anna Schwayhofer, interrogation 19 Mar. 1666.

who lived in her house a dish of Bavarian carrots. Yet this was a two-edged peace offering. The woman insisted the sisters eat the food, and sat with them until it was all consumed. One of the two was pregnant, and the dish made her ill.[38] The witch said the food would strengthen the child within her, yet this wish for the child's health actually meant its opposite. Like the fairies of fairytale who are not invited to the baptism, the old woman's evil 'wishes' for the infant's future blighted its life. And this could happen in a trice, even without the witch's intention: Maria Gogel explained how 'if a person ate plain milk, peas, meat or cheese, and chanced upon a child and merely said "Oh, what a beautiful child" immediately it is bewitched'.[39]

Witches' other means of harming was by *trucken*, pressing down on the infant or its mother. The verb may also refer to the effort of pushing down in labour. In witchcraft it is used in at least three different contexts: to describe the way the devil forces one woman to do evil, the smothering of an infant, and a mysterious kind of oppression felt by the woman who has just given birth. Georg Schmetzer's wife complained of feeling that something was coming to her at night, lying on her and pressing her so that she suffered from pain down one side. She suspected the lying-in maid of coming to her bed in the evening and lying on top of her – a fear strengthened by the maid's unorthodox suggested remedy for her backache that she should undress and lie on top of her in a kind of all over massage.[40] Anna Maria Cramer believed a witch was coming to her at night and lying on her, pressing down on her pregnant body.[41] Another woman heard a mysterious voice crying *druckdich, Madelin, druckdich* (be pressed down, Maggie, be pressed down) and she felt something trying to bite her neck. Her lying-in maid Euphrosina Endriss was finally brought to confess that she had 'pressed' the baby she carried about with her, squashing its skull so that it died.[42] The themes here do not appear to be directly sexual. Rather, what is described is a kind of heavy, deadly

---

[38] StadtAA, Urg., 11 Feb. 1666, Anna Schwayhofer, testimony of Anna Corona Cramer, 19 Feb. 1666; 25 Feb. 1666, Anna Maria Cramer; testimony Anna Maria Cramer and Anna Corona Cramer, 13 Mar. 1666; and interrogations.

[39] StadtAA, Urg., 15 July 1650, Ursula Neher, testimony of Maria Gogel, 29 July 1650.

[40] StadtAA, Urg., 20 Dec. 1685, Euphrosina Endriss, testimony of Georg Schmetzer, 24 Dec. 1685.

[41] StadtAA, Urg., 11 Feb. 1666, Anna Schwayhofer, testimony of Anna Corona Cramer, 19 Feb. 1666; 25 Feb. 1666, Anna Maria Cramer; testimony of Anna Maria Cramer and Anna Corona Cramer, 13 Mar. 1666.

[42] StadtAA, Urg., 20 Dec. 1685, Euphrosina Endriss, testimony of Magdelena Hornung, 24 Dec. 1685.

4 E: Ebeler's interrogation and confession of witchcraft; F: Ebeler perverts two innocent children, a boy and a girl.

embrace, again typified by an ambiguous mixture of love and hatred which might kill the infant with a kind of excess of maternality. The mother's feelings have more to do with extreme depression, immobility and passivity. In all these cases, the mother seems to suffer from a kind of lassitude, unable to move or act to protect herself and her child beyond screaming for help – she cannot fight back, and the oppressive sensation of smothering symbolises her inaction and the diffusive nature of the threat to herself and her child, causing harm not from within her own body but in a kind of anonymous pressure from without. As with the disturbances of nourishment, the violence is indirect, its source unclear and retaliation impossible.

Why should it have been motherhood which engendered these murderous antagonisms between women? Mothers in the early modern period spent the first few weeks of their child's life 'lying in', recuperating from the birth. These six or so weeks were set apart from normal life as the woman retreated into the lying-in room, resting in the bed from which the husband would be banished. There she was the centre of the house, and there, lying in bed, she would entertain her female friends who had supported her during the birth, holding a women-only birth party with wine and delicacies to celebrate her delivery. If she could afford it, she would employ a lying-in maid, whose job it was to care for both mother and child. During this period when her life was predominantly lived in the world of women, she could not leave the house and some believed her to be under the power of the devil.[43] Evil influences might make their presence felt; ghosts might appear. At the end of this time she would go to church for the ceremony of purification or churching, which marked her return to marital cohabitation and public life, and the lying-in maid would be dismissed. Today the attendant psychic conflicts of this period of the mother's life might be described as relating to the loss of the pregnant state and the ending of the unity of mother and child. Together with the incessant demands on time and energy that the new infant makes, these might be related to maternal depression and to a mixture of feelings towards the infant which may extend to anger, envy or even to wishing harm to the child.

What seems to emerge from these cases, however, is a different set of historically formed psychic mechanisms for dealing with this predicament. The time of separation of mother and child was clearly marked in ritual terms.[44] The mother's re-entry into society as a single being, uncontaminated by what can – if she bears a male child – seem to be the bisexuality of pregnancy, was celebrated in churching, a ritual which remained an important ceremony despite the Reformation's attempt to curtail it. These few weeks were also full of danger for mother and child. According to English figures, a woman had a 6 to 7 per cent chance of dying in childbed, and while this figure may seem low, it was an ever-present terror, doubtless added to by the stories passed around by her women visitors.[45] In the first few weeks of life the child was at its most delicate, as feeding had to be established, either with the mother, a wet-nurse, or else by hand. Interestingly, it was during this period or else immediately after the lying-in maid's departure that the child began to ail. But instead of seeking the source of her ills in post-natal depression, within herself, as we would, the mother's anxieties about the child's fate

---

[43] On churching, see Susan C. Karant-Nunn, 'A women's rite: Churching and the Lutheran Reformation', Hsia and Scribner, eds., *History and Anthropology*, forthcoming. See also, for example, *Andreas Osiander d. A. Gesamtausgabe*, eds., Gerhard Müller and Gottfried Seebass (Gütersloh, 1975–), V, Brandenburg-Nuremberg church ordinance 1533, p. 128: women who have just borne children should be instructed by the pastor and preacher that they are not under the power of the devil, as had previously been believed: 'das sie nicht in gewalt des teueffels sein, wie mans bisshere nicht on sundern nachteyl der gewissen darfür gehalten und groeblich daran geyrret hat'.

[44] For an excellent account of these rituals in England, see Adrian Wilson, 'The ceremony of childbirth and its interpretation', in Valeries Fildes, ed., *Women as Mothers in Pre-Industrial England* (London and New York, 1990).

[45] Patricia Crawford, 'The construction and experience of maternity in seventeenth-century England', in Fildes, ed., *Women as Mothers*.

and her own ability to nourish it were directed outwards, so that harm to either mother or baby was believed to have been caused by another. Here we might make use of what Melanie Klein says about splitting, which allows intolerable feelings of hostility and malice to be projected on to another, so that the mother recognises only benevolence in herself, projecting the evil feelings about herself on to the 'other' mother.[46] The lying-in maid was thus destined for the role of the evil mother, because she could be seen to use her feminine power to give oral gratification to do the reverse – to suck the infant dry, poison the mother and her milk and, in the most extreme form of witch fantasies, to kill, dismember and eat the child at the witches' sabbath. At a time when the new mother's experience of giving birth and caring for an infant might raise memories of her own infancy, recalling the terrifying dependence on the maternal figure for whom she may have experienced unadmitted, intolerable feelings of hatred as well as love, there was another person playing the maternal role to hand. We might say that during the new mother's period of feeling complete inertia, 'pressed down upon', she finally gained the strength to retaliate, resolving her state by accusing the witch of harming her child. In this sense, so far from being a simple expression of misogyny, early modern society can be said to have taken the fears of the mother seriously, supporting her search for the culprit instead of describing her as suffering from post-natal depression or attributing a kind of madness to her – women today may attempt to use the defence of post-partum psychosis to argue that they were not legally responsible for crimes committed during the first few weeks after giving birth.

The lying-in maid was almost over-determined as the culprit, should witchcraft be suspected. Old, no longer capable of bearing a child herself and widowed, she was a woman who housed alone and was a transitory member of the households of others. No longer at the heart of a bustling household of her own, she was a hired member of the family for whom she worked, privy to the most intimate physical secrets of the bodies of those she tended. An interloper, she was never accorded a real place of her own – one even had to share a cramped bed with a servant which was so narrow that she fell out of it in the night.[47] The lying-in maid

---

[46] See, for example, Melanie Klein, 'Envy and gratitude' (1957), 'Some theoretical conclusions regarding the emotional life of the infant' (1952), 'On identification' (1955), in *Envy and Gratitude and Other Works*.

[47] StadtAA, Urg., 28 Jan. 1669, Anna Ebeler, testimony of Anna Maria Schmuckher, 1 Feb. 1669.

undermined the settled hierarchies of a household at a time when the new baby's arrival overturned the workshop's rhythm. For the six to eight weeks after the mother had given birth, she alone carried out the duties of a mother, dandling, washing and swaddling the baby, and caring for its mother, giving her nourishing soups. Just as she had no place in the house she might call her own, so also her work life left her humiliatingly dependent on others: on the midwife, who trained her, recommended her and from whom she might hear of her next job; on her employer, the mother, who might choose not to re-employ her and who could blacken or enhance her reputation by gossiping with other mothers about her. She lacked the midwife's qualifications and official status as an employee of the council, nor did she have the luxury of the midwife's official retainer to tide her over slack periods. Often, it was her very insecurity which was turned against her. One woman who went down on her knees to plead with her accusers only made them the more convinced that something was amiss; frightened people were likely to be caught in the devil's snares.[48]

But she was also invested with awesome power. She had her particular recipes for strengthening soups, she had her methods for bringing up young infants, she 'alone cared for the child, and it was in no one's hand but hers' as one lying-in maid accused of witchcraft put it.[49] She was strong at a time when the new mother was ill and weakened, and she was fulfilling her tasks. The new mother, sleeping alone in the marital bed, was not 'mistress of the household' in sexual terms: old, infertile and unhusbanded as the lying-in maid was, she represented a double threat to the mother, standing both for the mother's own future and sometimes representing a sexual threat as well. If the husband were 'up to no good', the lying-in maid, who in many cases had borne illegitimate children, might be suspected.[50]

The lying-in maid dealt with the waste products of the body, she had access to the afterbirth and to cauls and she had the care of the infant's body.[51] One lying-in maid was accused of purloining the afterbirth,

---

[48] StadtAA, Urg., 28 Jan. 1669, Anna Ebeler, testimony of Benedict Widenmann, 24 Jan. 1669.

[49] StadtAA, Urg., 20 Dec. 1685, Euphrosina Endriss, pre-trial testimony of Endriss, 4 Dec. 1685.

[50] For example, Ursula Neher, StadtAA, Urg., 15 July 1650; Barbara Fischer, Strafbuch des Rats, 1615–32, p. 397, 13 May 1623; tried as a witch in 1650.

[51] On the different ways men and women used sorcery and bodily products, see Ruth Martin, *Witchcraft and the Inquisition in Venice, 1550–1650* (Oxford, 1898); Ingrid Ahrendt-Schulte, 'Schadenzauber und Konflikte. Sozialgeschichte von Frauen im

burning it at night under her bed in a bid to harm mother and child, and it was only with great difficulty that she managed to persuade the judges that she had merely been attempting to clean a pewter bowl.[52] Another was foolish enough to accuse the midwife of hiding a baby's caul. Taking the 'little net' to the father in the hope of gaining a handsome tip for her trouble, she not only antagonised the midwife but led people to suspect that she had her own nefarious purposes for the caul.[53] Through the waste products of the body, things invested with their owner's power – hair, nails, afterbirth – the sorcerer could control the individual to whom they had belonged. These substances could be used to direct the emotions, causing the bewitched person to fall in love, and they could be used to harm. In this cosmology, emotions were highly sensitive to manipulation of the body. Emotions, like physical pains, could be the result of external events and could readily be ascribed to other people, their source sought outside rather than in the self.

As any mother knew, to antagonise a lying-in maid was to court disaster. 'I gave her good words until she left the house', so one young mother said.[54] Many of the witnesses mention the time when the lying-in maid was 'out of the house', a phrase which captures the element of menace the maid was thought to represent. Only then might an accusation be safely made, because then the maid could not revenge herself by bewitching the child. (One seer refused to help an ailing child until the maid had gone: then she succeeded in restoring its rosy flesh, but it began to waste away again when the maid returned shortly after to collect money she was owed.)[55] So fraught was the moment of the maid's departure that her formal relinquishing of responsibility could also become a test of whether the child had thrived. One woman repeated the ambiguous rhyme she had spoken on parting from the child:

> My dear little treasure, now you are well recovered
> Look master and mistress
> Now I depart from the child

Spiegel der Hexenprozesse des 16. Jahrhunderts in der Grafschaft Lippe', in Heide Wunder and Christina Vanja, eds., *Wandel der Geschlechterbeziehungen zu Beginn der Neuzeit* (Frankfurt am Main, 1991); Roper, 'Magic and the theology of the body'.

[52] StadtAA, Urg., 15 July 1650, Ursula Neher, and testimony Hans and Jacobina Vetter, 11 July 1650.
[53] StadtAA, Urg., 28 Jan. 1669, Anna Ebeler.
[54] 'immerdar guete worth gegeben, biss Sie aus dem haus kommen', StadtAA, Urg., 29 Jan. 1669, Anna Ebeler, testimony of Eleonora Schmidt, 1 Feb. 1669.
[55] StadtAA, Urg., 15 July 1650, Ursula Neher, testimony of Sabina Stoltz, 29 July 1650.

Whatever may happen to him now
I will not be held to blame.[56]

Such a jingle, with its careful divestment of responsibility, has a menacing tone. It is a double-edged wish. An attempt to free the speaker of blame, it carries the implied threat that something *will* happen to the infant, and it prophylactically points the finger at someone else, by implication the mother, who now assumes the maternal role alone. Indeed, harm often came to the child after the lying-in maid had departed. 'It was the first night . . . that the lying-in maid was out of the house', one mother remembered, that strange things began to happen; it was just after the maid had left, another mother noted, when her child had suddenly sickened.[57] Something of the uncertain nature of the relationship between mother and lying-in maid is caught in the way one maid kept referring to the presents she had received, listing them and naming their giver, in a fruitless attempt to determine the relationship as one of goodwill – yet even the mothers she thought had valued her care were now willing to testify against her conduct.[58] Her behaviour was always indeterminate, its meaning open to a subsequent hostile reinterpretation.

Above all, it was the lying-in maid's maternal role which placed her in the role of suspect. Sometimes this might lead to straightforward conflicts over upbringing – Euphrosina Endriss was blamed for mollycoddling a child, giving it too many warm cushions.[59] Midwives and mothers suspected maids of bathing the child in water that was too hot, or of swaddling its limbs too tightly so that it might become deformed.[60] Injuries inflicted in the first few weeks of the infant's life might not manifest themselves for years: the failure of one child to speak, harm to one girl's reproductive organs, were all blamed on the lying-in maid.[61] 'Why must it always be the lying-in maid who is to blame?' asked one

---

[56] StadtAA, Urg., 20 Dec. 1685, Euphrosina Endriss, qu. 47, and testimony of Georg Schmetzer, 4 Dec. 1685: 'mein Schäzle du bist wohl auf, sehet Herr und Frau, iezo gehe ich Von dem Kind, es geschehe ihm was da wolle, so will ich entschuldiget sine'. The next day, the child began to sicken.

[57] StadtAA, Urg., 28 Jan. 1669, Anna Ebeler, testimony of Juditha Schorr, 13 Feb. 1669; Euphrosina Hayd, 1 Feb. 1669.

[58] StadtAA, Urg., 29 Jan. 1669, Anna Ebeler, and interrogation, 19 Feb. 1669.

[59] StadtAA, Urg., 20 Dec. 1685, Euphrosina Endriss, qu. 50.

[60] StadtAA, Urg., 15 July 1650, Ursula Neher, testimony of Jacobina Vetter, 29 July 1650; testimony of Susanna Custodis, 11 July 1650.

[61] StadtAA, Urg., 15 July 1650, Ursula Neher; testimony of Adam Schuster, 11 July 1650; testimony of Anna Erhardt, 29 July 1650.

accused woman.[62] A woman who could not be trusted, a woman unable to bear children herself, she was tailor-made for the role of the ultimate evil mother. The very intensity of the bonds between her and the child, as the person who enjoyed a primary attachment to the baby in its first weeks of life, were also the reason to suspect her. As with all witchcraft, it was the powerful ambivalence of feeling which nourished witchery: witchcraft was to be feared not from those indifferent to you, but from those whose relationship was close and whose intimate knowledge of your secrets could be turned to harm. Consequently every good wish a suspected woman might make for the health and well-being of an infant was charged with its opposite. So one young mother feared the frequent visits the lying-in maid made to her infant's cradle, standing over it. She later discovered a knife underneath its crib.[63]

And the lying-in maid had a motive: envy. Envy was the motor of witchcraft as seventeenth-century people understood it. One of the seven deadly sins, it was a feeling which could have material force. It is also an emotion which, according to Melanie Klein, first develops in the early months of an infant's life and is deeply connected to feelings of love and hate. Envy involves wishing harm towards an object. In the logic of sorcery, where emotions might be externalised on to things outside the person and where feelings had active force, the emotion itself was the wellspring of injury. Circumstances conspired to make the lying-in maid appear a likely sufferer from envy and hatred. As seventeenth-century people saw it, she was poor and single; her employer had a workshop and was comfortably off. Infertile herself, she tended a mother who was surrounded by the love, attention and presents of other women, and who had a baby. By contrast her own children had been conceived illegitimately or had died in infancy. So Barbara Fischer had been raped by her stepfather twenty years before she found herself accused of witchcraft. The child of their relationship had died just a few days after birth. At the time, she had begged the council to let her marry, blaming her stepfather's refusal to let her wed for her own fall into sin with him. But the council had punished her by confining her inside the house for her shame, and, two decades later, she explained her fall into witchcraft as the consequence of not being allowed to marry and become a

---

[62] 'was die kellerin vmb solche sachen red vnd antwort geben', StadtAA, Urg., 28 Jan. 1669, Anna Ebeler, interrogation, 19 Feb. 1669, qu. 49.

[63] StadtAA, Urg., 11 Feb. 1666, Anna Schwayhofer, testimony of Euphrosina Sperl, 19 Feb. 1666, the knife was her husband's but it had been moved.

mother.[64] Interestingly, her diabolic lover appeared to her in the form of a journeyman dyer, the trade her stepfather had followed. Admission of the envy she felt for the mother she tended was, in her case as in many others, the first step in her interrogation towards a full confession.[65] The witch, too, fully believed that to feel envy for a woman was to wish to harm her, and in this emotional world, where things were invested with meaning, emotions could also act directly. Anna Schwayhofer explained she had summoned the devil when, conscious of her own sins, she despaired of God's mercy: she had taken communion without confession, and she felt 'great envy, resentment and enmity to various persons'.[66]

To this point I have been exploring the psychic world of those who made the accusation, arguing that it is best understood as invoking deep emotions from the early period of the mother's own infant life. She and those around her are able to crystallise their own ambivalence towards her infant by projecting intolerable feelings on to the lying-in maid. I am not arguing that this always happened: in the vast majority of cases, the childbed was concluded happily and the maid was dismissed with mutual goodwill. But I am claiming that the social organisation of mothering practices allowed this to happen, so that a certain kind of psychic dramatic script was available should things go wrong.

But the witch herself had an understanding of her own behaviour. Its main element concerned her own admission of envy. This was the breaking point which then catapulted her into a range of other confessions about the devil. These form a distinct layer of testimony,

---

[64] StadtAA, Strafbuch des Rats, 1615–23, 13 May 1623, p. 397; and notes of 19 Oct. 1624, 30 Aug. 1625, 22 Nov. 1625, 29 Jan. 1626; Urg., 10 May 1623, Barbara Fischer; Strafbuch des Rats, 1633–53, 23 July 1650, fo. 337r–v; Urg., 14 June 1650, Barbara Fischer.

[65] StadtAA, Urg., 14 June 1650, Barbara Fischer, see interrogation of 20 June 1650.

[66] 'gegen vnderschidlichen Personen grossen Neid, grollen vnd feindtschafft getragen', StadtAA, Urg., 11 Feb. 1666, Anna Schwayhofer, interrogation, 31 Mar. 1666; and see also Urg., 28 Jan. 1669, Anna Ebeler, throughout. On enmity and exclusion from community, see David W. Sabean, *Power in the Blood* (Cambridge, 1984), pp. 31–60; for a strict Lutheran interpretation of confession and enmity, *Andreas Osiander d. A Gesamtausgabe*, VII, p. 663, Kirchenordnung Pfalz-Neuburg 1543, no absolution to be granted if someone still bears enmity. On the role of envy and hatred in the bringing of witchcraft accusations see Heide Wunder, 'Hexenprozesse im Herzogtum Preussen während des 16. Jahrhunderts', in Christian Degn, Hartmut Lehman and Dagmar Unverhau, eds., *Hexenprozesse. Deutsche und skandinavische Beiträge*, Studien zur Volkskunde und Kulturgeschichte Schleswig-Holsteins 12 (Neumünster, 1983), esp. pp. 188–9; Robin Briggs, *Communities of Belief. Cultural and Social Tensions in Early Modern France* (Oxford, 1989), pp. 7–65, 83–105.

5 G: Ebeler is led to execution and branded with burning tongs.

elicited under torture and often given with a considerable degree of reluctance. In other contexts, however, where children were not the target of malice, the devil could be a dominant theme: so the young Regina Schiller baffled authorities all over southern Germany for over a decade with her bizarre physical contortions and extravagant confessions, telling the authorities about her lurid pacts with the devil and showing the written contract for so many years and so many days, the number indicated with little strokes of blood because she could not count so far.[67]

By contrast, the witches whose fates we have considered here were chary of admitting even to flying or attending the witches' sabbath, and when they did so they presented themselves as outsiders, women who hung at the edges of the wild assemblies, without finding friends among the fellow witches. One witch recalled that the others came from elsewhere, they wore masks and spoke with accents she could not understand, and they were well-dressed, not of her class. She did not dance, and at the feast, few people sat at her table.[68] This was certainly a means of cutting down their involvement and guilt and yet the strong sense of being outsiders which their words convey suggests that the fantasies mirrored their current experience of isolation, socially marginal and

[67] Staats- und Stadtbibliothek Augsburg, 2o Cod Aug. 288, Schilleriana; Strafbuch des Rats, 1654–99, 7 Feb. 1673, Regina Schiller, pp. 390ff.
[68] StadtAA, Urg., June 1625, Dorothea Braun, interrogation, 22 Aug. 1625.

shorn of friends who might succour them. Their relations with the devil were distant and unsatisfactory. Even when conviction was a certainty, these accused witches still tried to minimise the extent of their sexual involvement with the devil, Dorothea Braun insisting at the last that, contrary to her earlier confessions, she had never had sex with the devil and had always resisted him; Anna Ebeler saying that she had told the devil she was too old for such things; Anna Schwayhofer firmly denying that intercourse had ever taken place.[69] Indeed, Braun presents the devil as a kind of peremptory employer, a master whose whims she was condemned never to satisfy. She was too slow learning the craft, she explained, and so the devil beat her.[70] Their accounts usually give only the merest description of the devil – he came as a journeyman, or dressed in black, he was a disembodied arm – and they try to argue that their bodies remained intact. Diabolic invasion presents a taboo from which they wanted to shield themselves. But genital sexuality is seldom their own explanation of what they do, even though the sexual narrative would excuse their deed with the culpability of Eve. Instead, dirt and degradation feature. This is most evident in the names of their diabolic lovers, which had names such as Hendirt, Gooseshit and the like, names which combine animality with excrement.[71] Common to almost all is the acknowledgement of the feeling of hatred and the sense of being deserted by God, exiled from the community of fellow Christians. Yet their deeds are projected on to the devil: he whispers what they should do, he gives them the powder, he forces them to harm the children. In this way their hostile emotions (apart from the first feelings of hatred) could be projected on to the devil and dissociated from themselves, in a kind of splitting characteristic of witchcraft at every level.

But if I am right that witchcraft could involve conflicts between women that have to be understood in psychic terms, we still need to explain why such conflicts were open to expression through witchcraft at a particular historical moment. After all, even in the town we have been considering here, there were witchcraft cases which followed this pattern

---

[69] StadtAA, Urg., June 1625, Dorothea Braun, statement, 18 Sept. 1625; Urg., 28 Jan. 1669, Anna Ebeler, interrogation, 23 Feb. 1669; Urg., 11 Feb. 1666, Anna Schwayhofer, interrogation, 26 Mar. 1666; and Strafbuch des Rats, 1654–99, 15 Apr. 1666, pp. 235–6.

[70] StadtAA, Urg., June 1625, Dorothea Braun, interrogation, 22 Aug. 1625. An older witch also tried to teach her to fly on a cat, but the cat refused to carry her!

[71] 'Hennendreckele': StadtAA, Strafbuch des Rats, 1633–53, 23 July 1650, Barbara Fischer, fo. 337r–v; 'Gändsreckh', Strafbuch des Rats, 1654–99, 18 Apr. 1654, Anna Schäffler, pp. 4–7.

or drew on these motifs for only a little over a century, and they were concentrated in the years from 1650 to 1700. After 1700, we can notice a dramatic inversion of the pattern. Now, children rather than their mothers became the objects of suspicion. Between 1724 and 1730, thirty-one child witches were locked up,[72] while after the death of one suspected witch in custody in 1699, no older women were condemned.[73] This reversal suggests to me that the dynamics of much witch hunting have to be sought in the relationship between mother and child which, after a certain point, switched to the child rather than its mother. I suspect that witch hunting in the seventeenth century must in part be related to the idealisation of motherhood in Baroque society. This is not simply a matter of misogyny: after all, it was because the state took the fears and accusations of suffering mothers seriously that cases could be prosecuted. Germany in the later seventeenth century was a society recovering from the ravages of the Thirty Years War. In Augsburg, the population had halved: small wonder that people feared attacks on fertility.[74] Here the widow played a double role. On the one hand, attacks on old, post-menopausal women are a staple of misogynist tract from the late sixteenth century onwards. But on the other, the widow, I have been suggesting, was merely the mother's mirror image, a woman who could be the repository of all the fears about evil mothers. Maternal hostility and fears about evil mothers could not easily be expressed directly in a society where Mary was revered by both Catholics and Protestants, and

---

[72] Behringer, *Hexenverfolgung in Bayern*, p. 466; Stadt- und Staatsbibliothek Augsburg, 2o Cod Aug. 289, Acta puncto maleficii et tentationis diabolicae.

[73] Wolfgang Behringer has noted a general rise in cases of child witches from the last quarter of the seventeenth century onwards. See his 'Kinderhexenprozesse. Zur Rolle von Kindern in der Geschichte der Hexenverfolgungen', *Zeitschrift für historische Forschung*, 16 (1989), 31–47. StadtAA, Strafbuch des Rats, 1654–99, p. 722, Elisabeth Memminger: since she was considered to have been a witch, her corpse was publicly carted out and buried under the gallows. There were two further similar cases: Christina Haber, a lying-in maid, was interrogated and tortured, 12 Dec. 1699, but eventually let out on recall: Strafbuch des Rats, 1654–99, p. 725. Anna Maria Christeiner and her daughter were accused of abducting and harming children, Verbrecherbuch, 1700–1806, p. 31, 20 Aug. 1701; Urg., 3 Aug. 1701. They were severely tortured but eventually freed on recall. By contrast, a case of 1700 to 1703 concerns the plight of the daughter of Hans Georg Groninger, a suspected girl witch aged 14 in 1702, who ate lice and her own excrement: Stadt- und Staatsbibliothek Augsburg, 2o Cod Aug. 289, Acta puncto maleficii et tentationis diabolicae; StadtAA, Urg., 17 May 1702, Regina Groninger.

[74] Barbara Rajkay, 'Die Bevölkerungsentwicklung von 1500 bis 1648', in Günther Gottlieb et al., eds., *Geschichte der Stadt Augsburg* (Stuttgart, 1985); Roeck, *Eine Stadt in Krieg und Frieden*, II, pp. 775–85, 880–9.

where the image of the suffering Madonna was ubiquitous. Hence, too, the tendency in folktale to populate a story with evil stepmothers who alone can represent the bad mother, keeping pure the image of the good, dead mother.[75] Here it is no coincidence that this period also saw a dramatic increase in executions of the ultimate evil mother, the woman who commits infanticide: such women had to be executed. This rise occurred from the early seventeenth century onwards, even though the Imperial Law Code of 1532 had paved the way for such executions three generations before. Together with witchcraft, this accounted for the vast bulk of women executed in Augsburg in the seventeenth century.[76] The themes of much witchcraft, I would argue, are to be found not in a simple sexual antagonism between men and women, but in deeply conflicted feelings about motherhood. At this level, we can talk about misogyny: one trouble with modern psychoanalysis, I think, as with seventeenth-century witchcraft, is that in the end, a mother, or a figure in a maternal position, is made responsible for our psychic ills.

What I have been trying to do here is to explore the themes of early modern witchcraft not so much in order to explain that phenomenon, but in order to see, in the one area where we do have detailed documentation, whether early modern subjectivities were radically different from our own. That is, I have been asking whether and how there is a history of mind and emotion. It might be objected that I have used psychoanalytic categories in order to explore past mental phenomena, and to that extent, my argument is circular, but I think this conceptual difficulty is inherent in the productive use of ideas. One current problem is whether a body of theoretical work like psychoanalysis, designed in a particular historical period, can possibly do justice to the mental lives of people in quite a different time. It is certainly true that psychoanalytic theory can be used to reduce all symbolic worlds to the same meaning, so that everything

---

[75] Bernd Roeck argues that Marian devotion was a line of division between the two confessions, but his evidence from baptismal registers also shows that while Catholics favoured the name 'Maria' for girls, the most popular name choice among Protestants was 'Annamaria'. This name choice combined the names of both the mother of Jesus and her mother, suggesting the centrality of Marian ideals and motherhood to Protestant understandings of womanhood. Protestants also strongly favoured the names 'Maria' and 'Regina' (associated with the Queen of Heaven): Roeck, *Eine Stadt*, II, pp. 847, 862–5. See the rich paper of Maria Warner, 'The absent mother, or women against women in the Old Wives' Tale', inaugural lecture, Tinbergen Professor, Erasmus University, Rotterdam, 1991.

[76] StadtAA, Strafbücher des Rats. Between 1633 and 1699 nine women were punished for this offence, six of whom were executed while a further six women and two men were suspected of the crime.

6 H: Ebeler is executed and her body burnt to ashes.

speaks of phallologocentrism, or betrays the Oedipal complex. I do not think testimony should be read reductively in this way. In the material I was reading, basic psychic conflicts which did not accord with what I expected to find were emerging from witness statements. It seems to me that there are some primary areas of attachment and conflict – between those in maternal positions and children – which are pretty fundamental to human existence, but the form those conflicts may take and the attitude societies adopt to them may change.[77] This, it seems to me, is the territory of the historian. If historians declare the effects of primary emotions of this kind to be unknowable, they will be condemning us to

[77] For a different, path-breaking use of psychoanalysis to study witchcraft in New England, see Demos, *Entertaining Satan*. Demos notes the importance of maternal themes in witchcraft material (pp. 181, 198–206) but then goes on to argue that since mothers are almost universally responsible for the care of children, the prevalence of witchcraft is best explained by general child-rearing practices among early New Englanders which resulted in a weak ego structure and a tendency to engage in a good deal of projective behaviour. He uses psychoanalysis, linked with attention to child-rearing practices, to construct a general pathology of New England society; I am using it rather to elucidate particular conflicts between people and illuminate psychic functioning in a manner which does not derive psychic meaning reductively from child-rearing practices. On psychic creativity, see Joyce McDougall, *Plea for a Measure of Abnormality; Theatres of the Body: A Psychoanalytic Approach to Psychosomatic Illness* (London, 1989); and *Theatres of the Mind: Illusion and Truth on the Psychoanalytic Stage* (New York, 1985). A similar emphasis on projective identification is to be found in Evelyn Heinemann, *Hexen und Hexenangst. Eine psychoanalytische Studie über den Hexenwahn der frühen Neuzeit* (Frankfurt am Main, 1986).

use of a 'common-sense' model of psychological explanation which makes no sense at all because it leaves out of account the extent to which irrational, deep and unconscious feeling can determine human action – and it is hard to see how any history of witchcraft or even of religion can be satisfactory without exploring this dimension.

9. *The devil in East Anglia: the Matthew Hopkins trials reconsidered*

JIM SHARPE

The East Anglian witchcraft trials of 1645–7 constitute one of the most remarkable episodes in the history of the European witchcraze. Despite the survival of a large body of relevant source material,[1] there are sufficient gaps in the records to make it unlikely that the full story of what happened during this outbreak of witch hunting will ever be completely reconstructed. Let us remind ourselves, however, of the main outlines. Over the winter of 1644–5 Matthew Hopkins, an obscure petty gentleman living at Manningtree in north-east Essex, became worried about witches in his neighbourhood. His worries bore fruit in the

---

[1] There is an extensive body of material, both manuscript and printed, relating to the East Anglian trials of 1645–7. The most important manuscript sources are: indictments and gaol delivery roll relating to prosecution of witches at the Essex assizes, Summer 1645, PRO ASSI 35/86/1/7–13, 19, 32–3, 41–3, 46, 51–6, 58–64, 66–73, 78–80, 82–91, 98; a large body of what appear to be notes taken from depositions relating to the investigation of witchcraft in 1645 in Suffolk, written in a mid-seventeenth-century hand, British Library Additional MSS 27402 ff. 104–21; and sets of depositions relating to the examination of seventeen witches held in the Isle of Ely's gaol delivery records, Michaelmas 1647, Cambridge University Library, EDR E.12. Printed sources include: *A True and Exact Relation of the severall Informations, Examinations, and Confessions of the late Witches arraigned . . . and condemned at the late Sessions holden at Chelmsford before the Right Honorable Robert, Earle of Warwicke, and severall of his Majesties Justices of the Peace, the 29 of July, 1645* (London, 1645); *A True Relation of the Arraignment of eighteene Witches at St. Edmondsbury, 27th August 1645* (London, 1645); John Davenport, *The Witches of Huntingdon, their Examinations and Confessions* (London, 1646). Both of the main protagonists in the trials put their thoughts on their activities into print: Matthew Hopkins, *The Discovery of Witches* (London, 1647); John Stearne, *A Confirmation and Discovery of Witchcraft* (London, 1648). The 1645–7 trials have not been the subject of a full-scale scholarly study, although references to many of the relevant sources can be found in Richard Deacon, *Matthew Hopkins: Witch Finder General* (London, 1976), while Essex's contribution is discussed in Alan Macfarlane, 'The witch-finding movement of 1645 in Essex', in Macfarlane, *Witchcraft in Tudor and Stuart England: a Regional and Comparative Study* (London, 1970), ch. 9.

prosecution of thirty-six witches, of whom perhaps nineteen were executed, at the summer 1645 assizes in Essex. Accusations spread rapidly over the Suffolk border, and we know of 117 witches who were examined or tried in that county. A stray reference[2] suggests that another forty were tried at the Norfolk assizes, while it seems that a further six were tried (and five subsequently executed) at the Great Yarmouth borough sessions.[3] Further trials (we have no way of calculating their total, although they were probably not numerous) occurred in Cambridgeshire, Huntingdonshire, Bedfordshire and Northamptonshire during 1645–6, while a body of depositions in the records of the Isle of Ely assizes reveals that a further seventeen suspected witches were examined there in 1646–7. Altogether we have references to some 240 alleged witches who came before the authorities during this episode, over 200 of them between July and December 1645.

In terms of statistics, then, these trials represent a major witch panic, comparable with those experienced in a number of continental outbreaks. Indeed, there were few continental crazes which witnessed the prosecution (frequently followed by execution) of 200 witches over a six-month period. Yet these East Anglian trials have been regarded also as remarkable for a number of other reasons. With the presence of Matthew Hopkins, and his associate John Stearne, we have, unusually for England, if not 'professional' witch hunters, certainly two men who were interested in hunting witches, and who were to come to claim expertise in this activity.[4] Also, in the sleep deprivation and other forms of pressure used in the interrogation of suspects, there was something approximating to the torture and inquisitorial procedures so familiar in European trials. And lastly, many of those accused were suspected not merely of *maleficium*, doing harm through witchcraft, but also of keeping and consorting with evil spirits. What we can reconstruct of

---

[2] *Signs and Wonders from Heaven. With a true Relation of a Monster borne in Ratcliffe Highway* (London, 1645), p. 4.

[3] J. G. Nall, *Great Yarmouth and Lowestoft* (London, 1867), p. 92 n. 2. Wallace Notestein, *A History of Witchcraft in England from 1558 to 1718* (1911: reprinted New York, 1965), p. 181 n. 50, regards this total as more reliable than the figure of sixteen which has frequently been cited.

[4] It is this emphasis on Hopkins' role in 1645–7 which has allowed me to use the term 'the Matthew Hopkins trials' as a convenient shorthand to describe the East Anglian trials of those years. This is not to deny that Hopkins was frequently operating with the active cooperation of local people who evidently held suspicions of witchcraft against their neighbours. For some observations on this point see Macfarlane, *Witchcraft*, pp. 137–8.

pre-trial depositions demonstrates that many of those who were examined confessed to keeping familiars, allowing to suck their blood, making pacts with the devil and (less frequently) having sexual intercourse with him.

It is this last issue which creates the greatest problems. The Matthew Hopkins trials offer a challenge to the standard interpretation of English witchcraft. English witch beliefs, let us remind ourselves, according to this interpretation, were not meant to be much concerned with the devil or his works, and witches were rarely thought to make pacts with the devil, and almost never to have sexual intercourse with him. What witches were meant to do usually was to inflict harm on their neighbours or their goods. Suspicion that they had done so, as Macfarlane demonstrated more than twenty years ago, normally followed neighbourly tensions or arguments which made English witchcraft accusations explicable more readily in terms of twentieth-century social anthropology than early modern demonology. The confessions and indictments of 1645–7 sit uncomfortably with such views, and, understandably, historians of English witchcraft have tended firstly to stress the peculiarities of these trials, and secondly to attribute those peculiarities to the presence of Hopkins. In 1933 Ewen suggested that the demonic aspects of the Essex and Suffolk trials were connected with 'Master Hopkins' reading of some continental authority'.[5] Later researchers have reached much the same conclusion. Macfarlane, for example, likewise attributed the peculiarities of the 1645 Essex trials to 'the influence of continental ideas, perhaps mediated through Matthew Hopkins'.[6] We are tempted, therefore, to write off the Hopkins trials as an aberration, in which 'continental ideas' temporarily sullied the English witch's normal image as 'a curiously tame and homely creature':[7] it is no accident that Keith Thomas should describe the Hopkins prosecutions as 'highly untypical'.[8]

While not wishing to get too deeply into what a 'typical' English witchcraft prosecution was like, and while accepting that the context of

---

[5] C. L. Ewen, *Witchcraft and Demonianism: a Concise Account derived from sworn Depositions and Confessions obtained in the Courts of England and Wales* (London, 1933), p. 52.

[6] Macfarlane, *Witchcraft*, p. 139.

[7] Alan Macfarlane, *The Culture of Capitalism* (Oxford, 1987), p. 110.

[8] Keith Thomas, 'The relevance of social anthropology to the historical study of English witchcraft', in Mary Douglas, ed., *Witchcraft Confessions and Accusations* (London, 1970), p. 50.

1645–7 was exceptional, it nevertheless seems to me that the Matthew Hopkins trials are too important to be written off as an aberration. Records relating to them do, after all, provide evidence of the largest single sample we have of English witches, and it would be unhelpful to dismiss their apparently unusual features as untypical and probably generated by Matthew Hopkins' alleged familiarity with continental witch beliefs. What I intend to do in this chapter is to examine the records of these trials, and analyse the alleged witches, what they were meant to have done, and what were the beliefs about them. The outcome of this exercise, it is to be hoped, will be not only to reassess the significance of the Hopkins trials, but also to demonstrate that they suggest that we need to make some modifications to the current orthodoxy about witchcraft in early modern England.

Any discussion of the typicality of the Hopkins trials ought to begin with a consideration of who the witches tried were, and what they were supposed to have done. Firstly, it is obvious that the traditional stereotype of the witch did not break down. During the Hopkins period, of 184 witches whose sex can be determined, 161, or 87.5 per cent, were women. This is a slightly lower female participation rate than that found by Macfarlane in his study of Essex witchcraft,[9] but hardly sufficiently so to suggest a breakdown in gender stereotypes about malefic witchcraft.

Similarly, although detailed research on this point has still to be undertaken, most of those accused seem to have come from the poorer elements of village and small-town society.[10] There were exceptions, but the trials under consideration here do not seem to have brought about that erosion of the social stereotype of the witch that occurred, for example, in some of the larger German persecutions.[11] Intriguingly, however, there were a few exceptions. A contemporary newsletter mentioned 'a

---

[9] Macfarlane, *Witchcraft*, p. 160, notes that only 23 of the 291 persons accused of witchcraft at the Essex assizes in the period of his study were men, making 92 per cent of this sample female.

[10] Records from the unusually well documented Suffolk parish of Framlingham, for example, which was the home of possibly as many as sixteen suspected witches in 1645, demonstrate that suspects were drawn from the local poor, while their accusers and witnesses against them were usually persons of at least some substance: Suffolk Record Office, FC 101/E2/26 (Framlingham Churchwardens' Accounts, 1642–6); FC 101/G7/1–2 (Framlingham Overseers of the Poor Accounts, 1640, 1645).

[11] H. C. Erik Midelfort, *Witch-Hunting in Southwestern Germany, 1562–1684: The Social and Intellectual Foundations* (Stanford, CA, 1972), pp. 137, 150.

parson's wife' named Weight among the early Essex accused, although no further reference has been found to her.[12] John Stearne noted 'one Henry Carre of Ratlesden, in Suffolke, who I have heard was a scholler fit for Cambridge (if not a Cambridge scholler) and was well educated' who died in gaol before trial.[13] Mother Lakeland, burned at Ipswich in 1645 for killing her husband by witchcraft, clearly had good social connections and had been thought of as a godly and respectable woman.[14] Perhaps the best documented of these socially exceptional witches was John Lowes, vicar of Brandeston in Suffolk. Although the tradition that Lowes had popish leanings is probably unfounded, it is clear that he was, as a later note in the Brandeston parish register put it, 'a contentious man', who had been prosecuted for barratry, and who had already aroused his flock's suspicion that he was a witch. Lowes had been instituted to his living in 1596, and was an octogenarian when he was swum in the castle ditch at Framlingham, subsequently being subjected to sleep deprivation for several nights and being run around the room in which he was kept until he was breathless.[15]

Lowes was also unusual in the type of harm he was meant to have caused. Some of the witnesses against him testified that he had inflicted the normal damage attributed to witches: the death of a child after an altercation with its father, or the killing of numerous cattle. Yet one witness, Daniel Rayner, also claimed that Lowes had confessed to using a familiar to do all the harm he could between Great Yarmouth and Winterton, while Hopkins testified that Lowes had admitted using a familiar to sink a ship off Landguard Fort, near Harwich. There are few other indications that the witches in our sample were thought to have inflicted unusual harm. Anne West was alleged to have sunk Thomas Turner's hoy and drowned him. Walter Maye claimed that Ann Dewsburowe fell out with his maidservant, and twice sank a boat that was carrying her. A Suffolk woman confessed that the devil told her to blast corn, while Thomasine Reade, one of the Isle of Ely accused, sent

[12] Notestein, *History of Witchcraft*, p. 174, citing *A Diary or an Exact Journal* (24–31 July 1645).

[13] Stearne, *Confirmation and Discovery*, p. 25.

[14] *The Lawes against Witches and Coniuration. And some brief Notes and Observations for the Discovery of Witches . . . Also the Confession of Mother Lakeland, who was arraigned and condemned for a Witch at Ipswich in Suffolke* (London, 1645), pp. 7–8.

[15] Relevant details are given in Deacon, 'The extraordinary case of John Lowes', in *Matthew Hopkins*, ch. 9. A note on the case, apparently dating from the early eighteenth century but incorporating the memories of persons present in 1645, survives in the parish register for Brandeston: Suffolk Record Office, FC 105/D1/1.

an imp to 'destroy the corn that groweth in Hillbrow field'. In another Ely case, Henry Freeman claimed that after an altercation Peter Burbush caused his mill to fall down.[16]

For the most part, however, the harm inflicted was similar to that which had formed the basis for English witchcraft prosecutions over the previous eighty years, namely minor matters, like bewitching a cow so that it gave 'naughty milk of two of her teats and since hath dried upp',[17] and more serious accusations like causing the death or sickness of cattle and human beings. The source materials surviving for the Hopkins period permit us to reconstruct 110 narratives of witchcraft suspicions: these include 36 incidents where the targets of the witch's wrath were adult humans, 56 children, 53 cattle, and 9 inanimate objects, ranging, as we have seen, from a mill which was demolished to beer which refused to brew.[18] These figures can be compared with those for the Home Circuit of the assizes between 1610 and 1659, when of 192 indictments for witchcraft alleging harm to persons or property, 61 involved adults, 44 children, 29 animals, and 2 other forms of property.[19] Thus the East Anglian trials of 1645–7 seem to demonstrate an unusual emphasis on the killing of children and cattle. The youth of witches' human victims in the Hopkins trials becomes more marked when it is realised that a large number of those classified here as adults were servants, so often in the front line of altercations with suspected witches, many of whom must have been in or barely out of their teens. It may be that in these trials, as in the rather different contexts of Mora in Sweden or Salem in Massachusetts, the misfortunes of children and adolescents played a crucial role in fuelling a large-scale witch panic.

Many of the witches and witnesses, again along very familiar lines, testified how witchcraft fears followed an altercation, or 'falling out' as they most frequently put it. Many of these incidents involved those tensions following a refusal to give goods which so often precipitated a witchcraft accusation. Margaret Benet, a Suffolk witch, told how she sent her imp to afflict Goody Gunshaw 'and that because she refused to let her

---

[16] BL Add. MSS 27402, f. 114v; *A True and Exact Relation*, pp. 4–5; Cambridge University Library, EDR 12/19; BL Add. MSS 27402, f. 118; Cambridge UL, EDR 12/11, 12/2.

[17] BL Add. MSS 27402, f. 110.

[18] Ibid., f. 117v.

[19] These calculations are based on the details of Home Circuit assize indictments given in C. L. Ewen, *Witch Hunting and Witch Trials* (London, 1929), pp. 200–52, augmented by additional information on Essex cases given in Macfarlane, *Witchcraft*, pp. 265–70.

have half a pint of butter'. Mary Bush, obviously a very poor woman, simply sent her imp to anyone who refused her relief. A woman witness deposed how a child in her master's house was stricken and died the day after Mary Edwards came to her house and was given 'some milk but not so much as she desired, and she went away mumblinge'. In another case a servant told how mother Palmer came to her master's house and asked for beer. Refused it, 'she went away thretning . . . she might want a cup of beere her selfe ear longe', from which moment no beer could be brewed successfully in that household. Susan Cocke of St Osyth in Essex sent her imps to torment the servant of John Turner after he refused to give her a sack of woodchips.[20]

A number of other bases for 'falling out' were recorded, although, as might be imagined, these were too varied to allow categorisation. Mary Sexton told how a dog came to her, and asked 'if she would revenge her self of the constables that had carried her to Ipswitch upon [a] misdemeanor'. Elizabeth Clarke, one of the first Essex witches to be examined, was thought to have killed the couple in whose favour her landlord, Richard Caley, had turned her out of her tenancy. Elizabeth Chandler, one of the Huntingdonshire accused, claimed she desired revenge on goodwife Darnell, 'having received some hard usage from the said goodwife Darnell, by causing her to be duckt'. Francis Moore told how 'one William Foster, some sixteen years since, would have hanged two of her children, for offering to take a piece of bread', and how she subsequently cursed him and caused his death. Two witches, one in Essex and one in the Isle of Ely, were thought to have used their powers against parish officers who tried to press their sons into the army.[21] The tensions underlying a witchcraft accusation in the Hopkins period could, therefore, be very varied: indeed, one witch, Elizabeth Weed of Catworth in Huntingdonshire, recalled sending an imp to kill a child, adding 'she wisht him to doe the same when she was angrie, but doth not well remember for what'.[22] In general, however, the impression in 1645–7, as was usually the case, was that members of the community with limited access to other forms of power were suspected of using witchcraft to revenge themselves on those who had offended them.

This being so, it is hardly surprising that another familiar theme to

---

[20] BL Add. MSS 27402, ff. 115, 114v, 116v, 117v; *A True and Exact Relation*, p. 29. Cf. the examples given in Stearne, *Confirmation and Discovery*, p. 36.

[21] BL Add. MSS 27402, f. 121v; *A True and Exact Relation*, pp. 21–2; *Witches of Huntingdon*, pp. 7, 8; *A True and Exact Relation*, p. 25; Cambridge UL, EDR 12/1.

[22] *Witches of Huntingdon*, p. 2.

surface in these trials is the frequency with which suspects had a long-established reputation for witchcraft. A witness deposed of a Suffolk witch that 'the parents of this woman and this woman have been formerly counted and commonly reputed for a witch'. John Abrahams claimed of Peter Burbush of Ely that 'he hath bin com[m]only reputed a witch & his mother before him'. In another Ely case, an alleged victim accused Joan Briggs of being a witch 'because they have had many fallens out & the s[ai]d Jone hath used many threatning speeches ag[ains]t this informant she having been a woman that hath a long tyme been suspected for a witch'. A fuller denunciation was made by one of the witnesses against Anne Morrice of Upwell: 'she hath bin a long tyme accompted a witche and her mother before her, and that shee is a com[m]on curser, and that by reporte of her neighbours much harme and damage hath befallen such as had difference with her'.Voicing such suspicions too vociferously could, of course, bring trouble down upon the accuser: Dorothy Ellis, another of the Isle of Ely accused, confessed to laming John Gotobed by witchcraft 'because he cald this ex[aminate] old witch & flung stones att this ex[aminate]'.[23]

On one level, then, the witchcraft detected in the East Anglian outbreak of 1645–7 was hardly atypical: most of those accused of witchcraft were women from the lower orders; many of them had a long-standing reputation for practising witchcraft. Their *maleficium*, overwhelmingly involving harm to children, adult humans and cattle, followed the pattern long familiar in England and most of the occasions when this harm was inflicted followed altercations, 'fallings out', between the witch and a neighbour in which those disputes over loans, alms or favours delineated by Macfarlane constituted a recurrent theme. Thus the alleged atypicality of the Hopkins trials lay not in these areas, but rather in the high profile which the devil enjoyed in the witches' account of their activities: John Stearne, indeed, after recounting a number of such cases, declared 'if I should goe to pen all of these sorts, then I should have no end, or at least too big a volume'.[24] Stearne's opinion is confirmed when we find that of our 110 witchcraft narratives, 63 involve accounts of the witch's meeting with the devil in one form or another (as we shall see, the varied nature of those forms raises a number of interesting issues). These cases obviously challenge the accepted interpretation of English

[23] BL Add. MSS 27402, f. 110; Cambridge UL, EDR 12/2, 12/10, 12/1, 12/15.
[24] Stearne, *Confirmation and Discovery*, p. 32.

witchcraft as non-diabolical, and obviously need some serious attention before we can dismiss them as untypical.

In fact, these accounts of dealings with the devil open up a rich seam of contemporary beliefs about him. Witches under examination confessed to meeting him for the first time in a number of different circumstances. Susan Marchant, a Suffolk witch, told how the devil first came to her when she was 'milking off a cow and singing off a psalme, and asked her why she singe psalmes as she was a damned creature', from which time she received familiars. The devil came to Priscilla Collet and tempted her to do away with herself or her children 'or else she sho'd always continue poore'; she did, in fact, subsequently try to kill one of her children, although it was rescued by another. Some first saw the devil, as demonologists warned their readers people would, when they were riven by despair or anger. The devil first came to Abigail Briggs a month after her husband died, and she told how he came 'to her shop and lay heavy upon her', and spoke to her 'in the voyce of her husband'. Similarly, the devil appeared to Mary Skipper shortly after her husband's death, and told her 'if she would make a covenant w[i]th him he wold pay her debts'. Mary Beckett recounted how the devil came to her 'and told her her sins weare so great that there was no heaven for her'. The devil first appeared to Ann Moats 'after she had beene cursinge of her husband and her childering'. Mary Wyard was offered material temptations when the devil told her that 'there weare soame witches had gold ringes on theyr fingers'.[25]

At the first meeting, or shortly after it, the devil began to try to convince the witch to enter into a covenant with him. He usually offered revenge or, as the case of Mary Wyard suggests, material wealth. Abigail Briggs, according to John Stearne's evidence, said the devil told her she would be revenged on her enemies, but [as was so often the case] 'she s[ai]d she found Satan a liar'. Elizabeth Richmond told how the devil 'came to her & imbraced her and asked her to love him & trust in him & would defend her & curse her enemies'. Elizabeth Hobard confessed that the devil came to her thirty years previously, that he took blood of her against her will, and 'at the same time she covenanted w[i]th him that he shold have her body and soule and wold avenge her of those that angered her', adding that 'he would furnish her w[i]th money but never p[er]formed it'. Similarly, the devil promised Ann Usher that if she denied Christ she would get richer, but he brought her nothing. Elizabeth

[25] BL Add. MSS 27402, ff. 110v, 111v, 114, 121, 117, 117v.

Currey, a widow of Riseley in Bedfordshire, confessed that the devil 'had the use of her body, and lay heavie upon her, and that through her wilfulnesse, and poverty, with desire of revenge, she denied God, and Christ, and sealed it with her blood'.[26]

The motif of the devil taking a few drops of blood to seal the covenant between him and the witch, and sometimes making a writing, runs through these narratives. Even more unexpectedly, as this last case suggests, there are fairly frequent references to sexual liaisons between the devil and the witch. In a practically unique case, Ellen Driver of Framlingham in Suffolk, aged 60, confessed that many years previously 'the devill appeared to her like a man & that she was married to him . . . and that he had lived with her 3 years and that she had 2 children by him in that time w[hi]ch weare changelinges . . . after she was married he had the use of her but was cold, and inioyned her before marriage to deny God and Christ'. Most of those who confessed to having intercourse with the devil found the experience an odd and not entirely pleasurable one. As we have seen, Elizabeth Currey felt the devil 'lay heavie upon her', while Ellen Driver felt him physically cold. These notions, strikingly similar to those attributed by continental writers to witches who had copulated with the devil, were echoed by other alleged witches. The devil came two or three times a week to widow Bush of Barton, 'but she said he was colder than a man, and heavier, and could not performe nature as a man'. The devil constantly had the use of Mary Skipper's body after she made a covenant with him, 'but she felt him always cold'. Other cases were less clear cut, and sometimes involved the devil in an animal shape. Alice Marsh, a Suffolk witch, claimed that the devil came to her in the shape of a rat, and desired her soul, 'but she wold not give it to him but she gave him hir body & after this he had the use of her body and so dep[ar]ted'. Margaret Bayle, also from Suffolk, told how 'when she was at work she felt a thing come upon her legs and so into her secret p[ar]tes and nipped her in that secret part where her markes weare found'. Ann Usher, probably a relative of Bayle's, simply 'felt 2 things like butterflies in her secret p[ar]tes'.[27]

These last cases introduce a major complication: the devil appeared in a variety of shapes. Frequently, of course, he was of human appearance:

---

[26] BL Add. MSS 27402, ff. 114, 108, 107, 117v; Stearne, *Confirmation and Discovery*, p. 31.

[27] BL Add. MSS 27402, f. 116v; Stearne, *Confirmation and Discovery*, pp. 28–9; BL Add. MSS 27402, ff. 121v, 108, 117.

'in the shadow of a man'; 'a handsome young gentleman with yellow hayre and black cloathes'; 'in the shape of a proper gentleman, with a laced band, having the whole proportion of a man'; 'in the likeness of a man called Daniel the Prophet'. Even with the devil in his human shape, however, there might be problems. Some of these East Anglian villagers knew that the devil was meant to have a cloven foot. Ellen Driver of Framlingham recounted that while she was in bed with the devil 'she felt his feet and they weare cloven'. Margaret Wyard, in the very act of making a covenant with the devil, 'observed he had a cloven foot'. Even more alarming was the experience of the Huntingdonshire witch Jane Wallis, who noticed the ugly feet of a man she met, 'and then she was very fearfull of him for that he would seem sometimes to be tall and sometimes lesse, and suddenly vanished away'. Others told how the devil might appear in animal form. As Joan Salter was going from the house of one of the witnesses giving evidence against her 'a black horse came to hir & crept betwixt her legges & carried hir over the green to hir own house, w[hi]ch this inform[an]t beleaveth to be the divell in the likeness of a horse'. The devil came to one of the Isle of Ely witches in 'the likness of a great mouse', to a Suffolk witch in the 'shape of a crabfish'. Mary Scrutton, another Suffolk witch, reported seeing the devil variously in the shape of a cat, a bear, or a man.[28]

With such confessions we plunge directly into the problem of the interplay between educated (or 'continental') ideas on the devil's role in witchcraft, and those of the populace. As we have seen, some of our East Anglian witches encountered the devil of the learned demonologists: appearing in the shape of a man (sometimes a handsome young gentle-man, but sometimes with a cloven foot); offering wealth or the power to revenge wrongs; making a covenant, often sealed with the witch's blood, in which the witch renounced God and Christ; a covenant which was often followed by sexual relations between the devil and the witch, relations which were often unsatisfactory ('he was colder than a man, and heavier, and could not perform nature as a man'). Such a pattern would have been recognisable to continental writers of witchcraft tracts like Bodin or Remy, or to English ones like William Perkins, and there is every likelihood that their pervasiveness in 1645–7 owed much to the

---

[28] BL Add. MSS 27402, f. 110v, 117v; *A True and Exact Relation*, pp. 1–2; Stearne, *Confirmation and Discovery*, p. 30; BL Add. MSS 27402, f. 116; *Witches of Huntingdon*, p. 12; Cambridge UL, EDR 12/20, 12/16; BL Add. MSS 27402, ff. 111, 116v.

investigative techniques of Hopkins, Stearne and their associates. But what are we to make of witches confessing to seeing the devil in the shape of a cat, a black horse, a crabfish, or a 'great mouse', and what are we to make of Ann Usher, experiencing not the cold and unsatisfactory embraces of a humanoid devil, but rather the sensation of '2 things like butterflies in her secret p[ar]tes'? Here we are encountering, surely, not the devil of the learned demonologists, but rather something very like the animal familiars that had long been a staple of English witch beliefs. As Macfarlane noted, if English witches wanted a link with the devil 'it was not through weekly or monthly meetings with him, but rather by keeping a small domestic pet, thought to be her "imp" or "familiar"'.[29] Whatever was untypical in the Hopkins trials, the familiar was not: indeed, the very first pamphlet generated by an English witchcraft trial, published in 1566, depicted a witch called Mother Waterhouse having a familiar, called Sathan, in the shape of a cat. This familiar performed acts of vengeance for her in return for drops of her blood.[30]

The familiar presents a key area in English witchcraft beliefs which is, sadly, as yet under-researched. At the very least, as the case of Mother Waterhouse suggests, the widespread belief in familiars takes us away from a model of witchcraft which is based on village *maleficium* into one where something very like a diabolical element is present. And if trial records of 1645–7 furnish us with considerable evidence about popular beliefs about the devil, even more do they provide insights into the folklore of familiars, or 'imps' as they were more often referred to in the documentation in question. Of the 110 narratives, 78 involve familiars. They came in numerous animal guises: mice, dogs, chickens, rabbits, turkey-cocks, a rat, a polecat. They were given names: indeed, Macfarlane's observation that 'even in witchcraft, the English obsession with pet-keeping emerged', may well suggest an interesting line of approach.[31] Many witches claimed that their familiars were passed on to them after the covenant was sealed, although others received them from their mother,[32] grandmother,[33] or friends.[34] Witches occasionally used their familiars in unison to create harm, or shared or borrowed them,

[29] Macfarlane, *Culture of Capitalism*, p. 109.
[30] *The Examination and Confession of certaine Wytches at Chensforde in the Countie of Essex before the Quenes Majesties Judges, the XXVI daye of July Anno 1566* (London, 1566), reprinted in Barbara Rosen, *Witchcraft* (London, 1969), pp. 72–82.
[31] Macfarlane, *Culture of Capitalism*, p. 109.
[32] BL Add. MSS 27402, f. 115v.
[33] Ibid., ff. 110, 121.   [34] Ibid., f. 115.

while Margery Sparham, a Suffolk witch, told how she sent two of her three imps 'after her husband beeinge a soldier to p[ro]tect him'.[35] Most female witches confessed that they allowed their familiars to suck blood from them through teats in their genitalia, and the Hopkins materials contain rich details about the resultant witches' marks. Indeed, one of the most graphic images furnished by the documentation comes from Margaret Wyard, who confessed that she had seven imps, but only five teats, so that 'when they come to suck they fight like pigs with a sow'.[36] One suspects that Wyard did not owe this particular image to continental notions foisted upon her by Matthew Hopkins.

So how should we regard the supposed untypicality of the Matthew Hopkins trials? Obviously, the context was untypical: the disruption, both administrative and psychological, of three years of war on local society provided a unique context for an English witchcraze. Moreover, the presence of Hopkins and Stearne as catalysts was a novel feature in English trials. But, at the risk of overstating my case, I would contend that in the actual content of the witch beliefs that surfaced in the course of the trials, there was much more which was familiar than unfamiliar. As we have seen, the alleged witches, and the harm which they were meant to have done, were firmly in the English mainstream. The wealth of information about, for example, familiars, is remarkable, but then we are looking at a remarkably rich body of documentation. The presence of the devil is unusually marked, but even here, as we have seen, English beliefs were still, to a large extent, conflating the devil of the learned demonologists and the neo-diabolical familiars of English witchcraft tradition, thus demonstrating that the issue is a more complex one than the straightforward imposition of learned beliefs on the populace. The Hopkins trials, perhaps, do not so much confront us with the unusual, but rather furnish us with unusually rich evidence of an ever-developing body of beliefs about witchcraft.

The exact relationship between popular beliefs and the demonological input of Hopkins, Stearne and other interested parties remains, and is likely to remain, problematic. Clearly there is enough uniformity (the sealing of the covenant with a few drops of blood, the devil's limitations as a lover) in the accounts given by confessing witches to suggest that what they said owed much to the leading questions of their interrogators. It is probable that a broad cultural vocabulary of diabolic beliefs was

---

[35] Ibid., f. 120v.   [36] Ibid., f. 117v.

being focused in the process of interrogation. Yet it is likewise clear that the populace did possess a repertoire of beliefs about the devil, and that what appeared in the witches' confessions was not simply 'imposed'. Similarly, the exact position on the continuum between popular and learned beliefs of the familiar so often alluded to in 1645–7 is uncertain. The existence of familiars (not least because of their obvious connection with that most certain proof that a person was a witch, the witch's mark) was obviously something which witch hunters had an interest in establishing. Even so, after eighty years of their presence in accounts of English witch trials, it seems likely that, by 1645, they had entered the popular consciousness as an element in witchcraft beliefs.[37]

Doubtless, however, this popular consciousness had been sharpened, not least in Puritan East Anglia, by the experience of listening to sermons in which the devil and his works figured prominently. The degree to which sermons were attended, how much attention to their content was given by those who did attend, and how much of that content was internalised and affected subsequent behaviour or subsequent patterns of belief, remains unclear. Even so, the statements of some of those participating in the Hopkins trials, whether as accused, accusers, witnesses or assistants to Hopkins and Stearne, demonstrates that at least some of the middling and lower sorts of Essex, Suffolk and the Isle of Ely had acquired a basic awareness of the threat offered to the godly commonwealth by the devil. Two more immediate factors were also at work. The point awaits further investigation, but it is probable that the parliamentarian propaganda of 1642–5, in both print and sermon, was tending to view the struggle against the royalists in increasingly apocalyptic terms, and was coming increasingly to employ the rhetorical device of describing royalists as agents of the devil.[38] And, more concretely, a number of clergy were actively involved in the search for witches. Three were active in the early Essex investigations,[39] while others were involved in Suffolk.[40] More remarkably, the Special Commission of Oyer and Terminer sent to try witches in that latter county in 1645 included two divines, Samuel Fairclough and Edmund

---

[37] Belief in familiars, indeed, predated the witchcraft statutes: Ewen, *Witchcraft and Demonianism*, p. 73, cites a Yorkshire case of 1510 as the first occasion when familiars (in this instance bees) sucked blood from their owner.

[38] I am grateful to Peter Lake for suggesting this point to me.

[39] Macfarlane, *Witchcraft*, p. 137.

[40] E.g. BL Add. MSS 27402, ff. 111, 115v.

Calamy, both of whom had local connections. It should be noted, however, that the exact impact of these two worthies on the rhythm and content of accusations remains elusive.[41]

Similarly, examination of the works published by Hopkins and Stearne makes it difficult to accept that they were responsible, in any simple way, for the promotion of 'continental' ideas. Hopkins' tract, apart from a reference to James VI's views on the validity of the swimming test[42] demonstrates little by way of any acquaintance with learned writings on witchcraft. Indeed, he explicitly denied that his skill in witch hunting was founded on 'profound learning, or from much reading of learned authors concerning that subject', attributing it rather to 'experience, which though it be meanly esteemed of; yet the surest and safest way to judge by'.[43] Stearne's rather longer publication presents more complexities. It is evident that he was familiar with the Warboys case of 1593, the Lancashire trials of 1612, and the bewitching of Francis Manners, earl of Rutland, in 1618–19,[44] while he also alludes to Thomas Cooper's *Mystery of Witchcraft* of 1617.[45] As G. L. Kittredge demonstrates in 1929, he also made heavy and unacknowledged use ('enormous plagiarism' is Kittredge's phrase) of Richard Bernard's *Guide to Grand Jury Men*, first published in 1627.[46] Bernard's marginal references suggest that he was familiar with the works of Bodin and Del Rio, but 'continental' notions do not figure prominently in his work, far more attention being devoted to the 1612 Lancashire trials and other English cases.[47] Thus even what we can reconstruct of the intellectual

---

[41] Notestein, *History of Witchcraft*, pp. 177–8. I am grateful to Keith Thomas for informing me of Fairclough's involvement in the Suffolk trials. It should be noted, however, that of the two sermons he preached before the Commission's sitting, one confirmed the existence of witchcraft, but the second stressed 'the hainousness of the sins of those, who would violently prosecute, or unduly endeavour to convict any person, except plain convincing evidence could be brought', which suggests a somewhat guarded attitude: Samuel Clark, *The Lives of Sundry Eminent Persons in this Later Age* (London, 1683), p. 172. In any case, Fairclough's sermons in Suffolk in late August cannot have affected earlier investigations in that county or Essex. Fairclough was, indeed, almost certainly the 'Master Fairecloth . . . an able orthodox divine' whom Stearne records as being invoked by a Haverhill witch apparently in hopes of clearing her name: *Confirmation and Discovery*, p. 54.

[42] Hopkins, *Discovery of Witches*, p. 6.   [43] Ibid., p. 1.

[44] Stearne, *Confirmation and Discovery*, p. 11.

[45] Ibid., p. 26.

[46] G. L. Kittredge, *Witchcraft in Old and New England* (1929: repr. New York, 1959), pp. 273, 564 n. 146.

[47] Richard Bernard, *A Guide to Grand Jury Men: Divided into Two Books* (London, 1627). The demonic pact and related matters are discussed in Book 2, chapters 3–7.

background of Hopkins' and Stearne's views on witchcraft reflects the mainstream of English Protestant writing rather than continental publications, while for Stearne, as for Hopkins, the actual experience of witch hunting seems to have been a greater influence in forming a view of what witches did than reading demonological tracts.

What this evidence from 1645–7 demonstrates (and what, I think, has impeded our proper appreciation of the Hopkins episode) is that the notion of a polarity between a 'learned', 'continental', and 'demon-ological' set of beliefs held by the elite and a popular concern with witchcraft which centred on *maleficium* is a gross oversimplification.[48] Obviously, at certain points in the Hopkins trials it is possible to see confessions coming through under pressure from Hopkins and Stearne giving details of the diabolical pact which may well reflect the accused's thoughts being moulded by continental notions. A much more common impression, however, is that of a jumble of popular and 'educated' beliefs which were mobilised into an agitated interaction by the conditions of a mass witch hunt. So we have not just the devil of the demonologists, but also a devil as imagined by the population at large. As Clive Holmes has pointed out, whatever input Hopkins may have had into confessions giving details about the devil, these confessions were not stereotyped.[49] There were, of course, some common themes: the devil's appearance at moments of stress, the taking of blood when the covenant was sealed, the unsatisfactory aspects of the devil as a lover. But close reading of the confessions reveals a host of variations and the insertion of elements which owed little to learned demonology. And there remains the problem which many witnesses and confessing witches had in distinguishing between the devil and the animal familiar. We therefore have the sense not of the imposition of ideas about the devil's role in witchcraft, but rather of a wide range of ideas being allowed to run free, and being allowed to enter the historical record, due to an unusual set of circumstances.

Even the presence of the devil in these East Anglian trials may not have been so novel a feature as has been thought. I would suggest that there is a serious gap in our knowledge here, and that the folklore of the devil in early modern England is a subject which needs to be more

---

[48] This point has been made by Clive Holmes, 'Popular culture? Witches, magistrates and divines in early modern England', in Steven L. Kaplan, ed., *Understanding Popular Culture: Europe from the Middle Ages to the Nineteenth Century* (Berlin, 1984), pp. 85–110.

[49] Ibid., p. 101.

thoroughly researched.[50] Even on a superficial level, however, one comes across constant indications that the devil featured fairly prominently in people's consciousness in the first half of the seventeenth century. The case-books of the astrological physician Richard Napier contained numerous references to clients who were convinced of the threat offered to them by the devil and his agents.[51] In 1608 Roger Houlte of Bury found himself the defendant in an ecclesiastical court defamation suit for saying of some women that 'they are all witches, they have given theire selves to the devill'.[52] In 1621, Helen Fairfax, the daughter of a Yorkshire gentleman, in the course of a fit imagined one of the women whom she thought to be bewitching her confessing to making a pact with the devil 'like to a man of this world whom she met on the moors'.[53] In 1638 Jane Moxie, a young woman from Lympstone in Devon, among other thoughts on witchcraft, allegedly held that witches met with the devil once a year on a hill on midsummer eve.[54] In 1641 a Chester man found himself in trouble for drinking healths to the devil.[55] Late medieval sources demonstrate that the devil was already a familiar figure, and that the notion of the demonic pact was well established.[56] Arguably the image of the devil, and of the satanic pact, was not such a novelty in 1645 as has been claimed: even the suggestions of the sabbat that appeared in some of the Essex trials of 1645 were, to say the least, no stronger than those found in the Lancashire witch scare of 1633.[57]

Mention of the Lancashire episode of 1633 moves us to a final

---

[50] Some indication of the value to historians of folkloristic approaches to witchcraft can be gleaned from K. M. Briggs, *Pale Hecate's Team: An Examination of the Beliefs on Witchcraft and Magic among Shakespeare's Contemporaries and his Immediate Successors* (London, 1962).

[51] Michael MacDonald, *Mystical Bedlam: Madness, Anxiety and Healing in Seventeenth-Century England* (Cambridge, 1981), p. 175.

[52] Cheshire Record Office, Consistory Court Papers, EDC5 (1608) 11.

[53] *Daemonologie: a Discourse on Witchcraft. As it was acted in the Family of Mr. Edward Fairfax, of Fuyston in the County of York, in the Year 1621; along with the only two Eclogues of the same Author known to be in Existence*, ed., William Grange (Harrogate, 1882), p. 86.

[54] Devon Record Office, Quarter Sessions Rolls, Box 41, Bapt. 1638, docs. 52, 56–7. I am grateful to Mary Wolffe for bringing this reference to my attention.

[55] Cheshire Record Office, EDC5 (1641) 9.

[56] See Kittredge, *Witchcraft in Old and New England*, pp. 239–43.

[57] See the materials collected in Ewen, *Witchcraft and Demonianism*, pp. 244–51. Although the notion of the sabbat (a meeting of thirty or forty witches, to which they were conveyed by their familiars, and at which the devil might be present) was stronger than in the Essex cases, and sexual intercourse between witches and the devil or their familiars in human form was mentioned, this incident also demonstrated a conflation of the devil and animal familiars.

contention: that the Hopkins trials might well benefit from being studied on a comparative basis with other major outbreaks of witch hunting. Comparisons with the large-scale German and Scottish trials might well help deepen our understanding of the variables involved. More value, however, might be found in looking at other serious outbreaks which occurred more or less unexpectedly in areas which, like England in 1645, had not been experiencing high levels of witchcraft prosecution: the Swedish trials of 1668–76; the Salem trials of 1692; and (to move geographically and chronologically nearer to 1645), the above-mentioned Lancashire incident of 1633, this last an elusive and ill-documented example of a potential large-scale outbreak which was nipped in the bud by a sceptical officialdom. In all these outbreaks, as in East Anglia in 1645, a large-scale witch hunt developed against a background of apparently low levels of tension over witchcraft, and in all of them the dynamics of the interaction between popular and official attitudes to witchcraft, and of new and old beliefs on the subject, were marked. The Hopkins trials, starting as they did in Essex, where witchcraft indictments had been low in the 1630s, remind us of the gap between the pervasiveness and richness of witch beliefs and what entered the historical record.

Part 4

Witchcraft and the social environment

10. Witchcraft in early modern Kent: stereotypes and the background to accusations

MALCOLM GASKILL

The study of witchcraft has been one of the best ploughed fields in the landscape of early modern social history. There is scarcely an aspect of the accusation and prosecution of witches which has not been confronted, hardly a legal archive which has not been ransacked by scholars eager to make their contribution to one of the darker chapters of Europe's past. Yet it is clear that the greater part of this research, even among English-speaking scholars, has concerned continental as distinct from English witchcraft, an imbalance attributable in the main to the towering achievements of Alan Macfarlane and Keith Thomas whose books were published in 1970 and 1971 respectively.[1] A quarter of a century later, theirs is still the dominant interpretation, but it is clear that the time is now ripe for a reappraisal of the English experience of witchcraft, especially when one considers the occasionally limited scope and overly theoretical structuring of their research.[2] Despite his chosen title, Macfarlane's survey remains essentially a study of Essex – a county sometimes mistaken for a country by social historians overawed by its bountiful records, and keen to see national resonance in the events and

---

[1] Keith Thomas, *Religion and the Decline of Magic. Studies in Popular Belief in Sixteenth- and Seventeenth-Century England* (London, 1971; 1973 edn); Alan Macfarlane, *Witchcraft in Tudor and Stuart England. A Regional and Comparative Study* (London, 1970). Although these should be seen as distinct works, Thomas and Macfarlane's relationship, as research supervisor and student respectively, fostered a harmony of interpretation.

[2] A comprehensive and updated study of witchcraft in early modern England by Dr J. A. Sharpe is, at the time of writing, in the final stages of production. See also Malcolm Gaskill, 'Witches and witchcraft accusations in England 1560–1690', in Gaskill, 'Attitudes to crime in early modern England with special reference to witchcraft, coining and murder', Ph.D. thesis, Cambridge University, 1994, ch. 2. Many of the themes of this essay are expanded there to include evidence drawn from all over England.

257

characteristics of the locality.[3] Furthermore, although Thomas' instincts and industry were formidable, he himself admits that his search of local archives was incomplete.[4] This chapter is based upon a primarily qualitative analysis of the prosecution of witches in the south-eastern county of Kent after 1560, and seeks to demonstrate how the anthropological framework constructed by Thomas and Macfarlane should perhaps be adjusted or applied more selectively. It is evident from the relatively unexplored Kentish material that all too often the stereotype commonly associated with English witches and their accusation fails to embrace fully the diverse, contingent and chaotic circumstances surrounding real accusations.[5]

I

First of all, let us examine the prevailing witch stereotype. Macfarlane and Thomas argued convincingly that witches in England were usually female, economically marginal, elderly and rarely had living husbands. Indeed, of the 102 women executed for witchcraft at the Home Circuit assizes between 1563 and 1682, only 32 are recorded as having had a husband alive at the time of their trials.[6] Witches were not necessarily the poorest members of the community, but in general were less well off than their accusers; they were, at least, sufficiently poor, on the one hand to warrant reliance on alms and, on the other, to be suspected of harbouring resentments against those who refused them. Accusations

---

[3] Martin Ingram has written that 'Studies of witchcraft and magic in England have given too much attention to apparently exceptional areas, especially the county of Essex, where for reasons which have not yet been fully explained the numbers of witchcraft prosecutions were unusually high', *Church Courts, Sex and Marriage in England, 1570–1640* (Cambridge, 1987), p. 96.

[4] Thomas, *Religion and the Decline of Magic*, p. 536n.

[5] The only serious study of witchcraft in Kent is Adrian Pollock, 'Regions of evil: a geography of witchcraft and social change in early modern England', Ph.D. thesis, University of Michigan, 1977. Although Dr Pollock sees a broader range of circumstances behind accusations than just conflict over alms, he upholds the broad picture of social tensions due to economic change, concluding that 'In almost all respects these characteristics are identical to Macfarlane's findings for Essex', 'Regions of evil', pp. 53–61, 164, 167–9, chs. 4–5; 'Social and economic characteristics of witchcraft accusations in sixteenth- and seventeenth-century Kent', *Archaeologia Cantiana*, 95 (1979), 37–48, quotation at 47.

[6] Thomas, *Religion and the Decline of Magic*, p. 671. This figure is taken from the abstracts of indictments printed in C. L'Estrange Ewen, *Witch Hunting and Witch Trials. The Indictments for Witchcraft from the Records of 1373 Assizes held for the Home Circuit A.D. 1559–1736* (London, 1929).

were not, we are told, made randomly, but instead were levelled at a woman with whom the victim had lately had some dealings and who probably lived nearby, particularly if she already had a reputation for witchcraft. When misfortune struck, such an individual might be identified as its cause if Providence seemed an improbable or unacceptable explanation.[7]

This functionalist model of accusation continues to influence the historical interpretation of long-term trends in English witchcraft prosecutions. It is argued that, from the later sixteenth century, declining neighbourliness and growing individualism in an expanding market economy meant that both the tendency to refuse alms and the suspicion of others within the community were increasing. The poor were disadvantaged as villagers rejected their dependants, and guilt at failing to fulfil neighbourly duties was then projected as fear of the revenge of those who had been denied charity. In a climate of religious Reformation and centralisation of criminal justice, traditional recourse to counter-magic was forbidden, and instead people were obliged to counter witchcraft in the courts. In this sense, therefore, witchcraft can be linked to a profound socio-cultural transition. However, since Macfarlane's work on witchcraft in Essex was first published, he has relocated the development of the individualism upon which his witchcraft thesis largely depends, to a period at least three centuries before the onset of witchcraft prosecutions in England.[8] This in itself represents a significant adjustment to the thesis. In any case, as evidence from Kent will hopefully demonstrate, the varied and complex realities of witch trials frequently stretch such a narrowly defined model accusation beyond its limits.[9]

Nevertheless, it is important for us to recognise that contemporaries often thought in terms of a stereotype when describing witches and their activities. Although it is true that physical appearance alone was

---

[7] Macfarlane, *Witchcraft*, pp. 30, 104–5, 110–12, 150–1, 168–76, 196–7 and *passim*; Thomas, *Religion and the Decline of Magic*, pp. 630, 652, 656–77 and *passim*.

[8] Alan Macfarlane, *The Origins of English Individualism: The Family, Property and Social Transition* (Oxford, 1978), pp. 1–2, 59–61 and *passim*.

[9] It should be noted here that most criticism of the Macfarlane/Thomas thesis to date has focused on Thomas' distinction between religion and magic; in other words, his view of early modern mentalities and beliefs. For summaries, see David D. Hall, 'Witchcraft and the limits of interpretation', *New England Quarterly*, 58 (1985), 254–61; Malcolm Gaskill, 'Witchcraft and power in early modern England: the case of Margaret Moore', in Jenny Kermode and Garthine Walker, eds., *Women, Crime and the Courts in Early Modern England* (London, 1994), pp. 125–7.

insufficient to accuse someone of witchcraft,[10] the caricature of the aged, ill-favoured and bad-tempered widow was prevalent in many portrayals of witches real and imagined. In a popular fable of 1655, a Kentish witch is described as an elderly woman with a dish-cloth around her head, and a staff in her hand, 'long nos'd, blear ey'd, crooked-neckt, wry-mouth'd, crump-shoulder'd, beetle-browed, thin-bellied, bow-legg'd, and splay-footed'. Such a description made the story instantly accessible to those who had an idea what a witch looked like, and, arguably, helped to form an image in the minds of those who did not. Sceptics noted the influence of this folkloric image on the sort of woman commonly to be seen arraigned in the courtroom. The late sixteenth-century Kentish gentleman, Reginald Scot, described a typical defendant in a witchcraft trial as an ordinary old woman, 'lame, bleare-eied, pale, fowle, and full of wrinkles', and similarly in 1646 a minister, John Gaule, criticised those who saw a witch in 'every old woman with a wrinkled face, a furr'd brow, a hairy lip, a gobber tooth, a squint eye, a squeaking voyce, or a scolding tongue'.[11]

Recently, it has been suggested that historians have been guilty of repeating assumptions and generalisations about witchcraft taken from the work of contemporary authorities whose knowledge was far from accurate or comprehensive. Most of Reginald Scot's examples are drawn from continental sources such as Bodin, as were Henry More's for his influential work, and the Puritan minister George Gifford provided a generalised view of witchcraft in Essex which Macfarlane quoted at length in order to back up generalisations of his own concerning the same county.[12] Furthermore, popular accounts of trials, often illustrated with

---

[10] Cf. Macfarlane, *Witchcraft*, p. 158; Robert Rowland, '"Fantasticall and devilishe persons": European witch-beliefs in comparative perspective', in Bengt Ankarloo and Gustav Henningsen, eds., *Early Modern European Witchcraft. Centres and Peripheries* (Oxford, 1990), pp. 169–70.

[11] L[aurence] P[rice], *The Witch of the Wood-lands* (London, 1655); Reginald Scot, *The Discoverie of Witchcraft* (London, 1584), p. 7; John Gaule, *Select Cases of Conscience Touching Witches and Witchcraft* (London, 1646), pp. 4–5. See also Thomas Fuller, *The Profane State* (London, 1647), p. 351; Thomas Ady, *A Candle in the Dark* (London, 1655), p. 42; Francis Peck, *Desiderata Curiosa* (London, 1779), II, p. 476, quoted in Macfarlane, *Witchcraft*, p. 87.

[12] Joyce Gibson, *Hanged for Witchcraft: Elizabeth Lowys and her Successors* (Canberra, 1988), pp. 5–6, 206; Henry More, *An Antidote Against Atheisme* (London, 1653); George Gifford, *A Discourse of the Subtill Practises of Devilles by Witches and Sorcerers* (London, 1587); Macfarlane, *Witchcraft*, pp. 110–12; Alan Macfarlane, 'A Tudor anthropologist: George Gifford's *Discourse* and *Dialogue*', in Sydney Anglo, ed., *The Damned Art. Essays in the Literature of Witchcraft* (London, 1977), pp. 140–55.

woodcuts of malevolent decrepit old women, exaggerated the familiar traits of age, gender, reputation and isolation and played down details considered incongruous with received lore about witchcraft. Although Macfarlane is perhaps too ready to accept the reliability of pamphlets as historical evidence, even he concedes that 'descriptions of actual trials lay no particular emphasis on the physical stereotype of the witch', and that the familiar image mirrored reality only in a partial or distorted manner.[13]

Comparisons between first-hand legal accounts and second-hand literary versions of the same prosecution often produce discrepancies between the social characteristics of those actually tried and their sensational, popular and, therefore, saleable image. The pamphlet account of the Maidstone trials of 1652, for example, concentrates on the six Cranbrook widows whom it calls 'the most notorious', rather than the five married women and, most incongruous with the stereotype, the six *men* also arraigned at the same assizes. Indeed, only five of the eleven others are mentioned at all. But what the account lacked in comprehensive coverage it made up for in sensationalism, reporting that William Reynolds, Thomas Wilson and their wives confessed to bewitching £500 worth of cattle and nine children, including one 'whose pourtraiture in wax was found, where they had laid it, under the Threshold of a doore'. The author even suggested that the bodies of three children recently discovered at Chatham were their victims. These embellishments do not feature in the original trial documentation, and the two couples were convicted of second-degree witchcraft only.[14] It is apparent from court records that although villagers were influenced by the simple witchcraft imagery belonging to the oral tradition, and sustained by cheap print,

---

[13] Macfarlane, *Witchcraft*, pp. 81, 96, 158, 216. Some contemporaries were aware that pamphleteers gave a false image of witchcraft, see, for example, Henry Holland, *A Treatise Against Witchcraft* (Cambridge, 1590), sig. E3ᵛ; *A True Discourse. Declaring the damnable life and death of one Stubbe Peeter, a most wicked Sorcerer, who in the likenes of a Woolfe, committed many murders* (London, 1590), p. 1.

[14] H.F., *A Prodigious & Tragicall History of the Arraignment, Tryall, Confession, and Condemnation of six Witches at Maidstone, in Kent* (London, 1652), quotation at p. 6; P[ublic] R[ecord] O[ffice], ASSI 35/93/6/36–8, 41–9; 94/5. See also Ewen, *Witch Hunting and Witch Trials*, pp. 239–43 for abstracts of the original indictments. The account also failed to mention that, despite their 'notoriety', the case against three of the women was quashed by parliament; two of them were ultimately pardoned, but the executions had already taken place: PRO, ASSI 35/93/6/35; *Journals of the House of Commons*, VII, 1651–9, pp. 160, 173; C. L'Estrange Ewen, *Witchcraft and Demonianism* (London, 1933), p. 32. Sir Robert Filmer, a Kentish JP and spectator at the trials, believed the accused to be ordinary and innocent people: *An Advertisement to the Jury-Men of England, Touching Witches* (London, 1653), sig. A2 and *passim*.

they were clearly not restricted by it regarding whom they accused at law.[15] It is important to remember that neither the statute nor canon law specified who a witch should be, or how they should be known.[16] Therefore, as Bob Scribner has suggested, witch-stereotypes 'came to have a cultural life of their own among both the learned and the unlearned [who] could both believe in the broad stereotype of witchcraft, while being wholly sceptical of its particular application to their own circumstances'.[17]

The remainder of this chapter will examine what kinds of people were charged with witchcraft in sixteenth- and seventeenth-century Kent. As suggested above, the ordinary people who initiated prosecutions deployed a wider definition of a witch (and thus who might plausibly be considered to be one) than they have usually been credited with. Furthermore, given the obviously close relationship in Macfarlane and Thomas' interpretative scheme between the stereotype of the *witch* and the stereotype of the *accusation*, were a broader band of society to have been vulnerable to the charge of witchcraft, then a wider range of events and circumstances behind prosecutions might also be expected. Accordingly, one finds an array of different types of witchcraft accusation, notably – and significantly for the 'orthodox' model – between approximate social equals, and cutting across familiar patterns of gender relations.[18]

II

The idea was put forward over fifteen years ago that the high status of women in England relative to Europe meant that the intellectual frame-

---

[15] For other misleading or suspicious pamphlet accounts of witchcraft accusations, see Gaskill, 'Witches and witchcraft accusations', 46–7.

[16] On this point, see ibid., 39–41.

[17] Bob Scribner, 'Is a history of popular culture possible?', *History of European Ideas*, 10 (1989), 183–4. See also Wolfgang Behringer, *Hexenverfolgung in Bayern* (Munich, 1987), ch. 3.

[18] In all, over 200 accused witches have been traced for Kent 1560–1700 (half of which were church court cases, 1560–75). Kent witnessed a marked increase in assize prosecutions in the 1650s, accounting for 50 per cent of witches accused at the Home Circuit during the Interregnum (twenty-eight of fifty-six cases). The preponderance of ecclesiastical cases (particularly those involving *maleficium*) is highly unusual – witchcraft was the third most common offence tried at Canterbury 1559–60 – and may help to explain why the statute of 1563 was introduced: Arthur J. Willis, *Church Life in Kent being Church Court Records of the Canterbury Diocese, 1559–1565* (London, 1975), p. 73.

work supporting the concept of the female witch worked less efficiently than on the Continent. But the authors of this theory suggested not that this resulted in a larger proportion of male witches but in fewer witches altogether, and concluded that 'when accusations were made, it is hardly surprising that European stereotypes were invoked'. This interpretation was met with a reply from two historians who not only questioned why peculiarly English views about the status of women did not affect the choice of suspects, but also argued that detailed analysis of Scottish witchcraft trials revealed that 14 per cent of witches were men. In addition, only 20 per cent of all female witches whose marital status was known were widows, and overall it was suggested that evidence from Scotland 'seems to show a much greater variation amongst defendants than the stereotype would allow'.[19] More recently, interesting parallels have emerged from this side of the border. Joyce Gibson, for example, has argued of witches in Essex that 'far from being impotent with age or malicious beggars as they are often portrayed, they were people of significance in the community, and many were part of a large workforce of spinners in conflict with powerful vested interests'.[20]

Whilst this may be overstating the case a little, one of the first things that the Kent archives reveal is that by no means all of those arraigned as witches in late sixteenth- and seventeenth-century Kent were old, impecunious widows.[21] Of forty-nine women (for whom marital status is known) presented for both maleficent witchcraft and cunning magic in the Canterbury church courts between 1560 and 1575, thirty-three had husbands alive at the time of their accusation. In other words, for this particular jurisdiction and period, a female witch was twice as likely to

---

[19] Alan Anderson and Raymond Gordon, 'Witchcraft and the status of women – the case of England', *British Journal of Sociology*, 29 (1978), 181 and *passim*; J. K. Swales and Hugh V. McLachlan, 'Witchcraft and the status of women: a comment', *British Journal of Sociology*, 30 (1979), 356; Hugh V. McLachlan and J. K. Swales, 'Stereotypes and Scottish witchcraft', *Contemporary Review*, 234 (1979), 88–90, 93.

[20] Gibson, *Hanged for Witchcraft*, p. 199.

[21] Macfarlane gives the average age of an Essex witch as between 50 and 70, a calculation based on a mere fifteen women, nine of whom died from ill-treatment, and were therefore likely to have been the oldest and weakest. Moreover, the Essex data relating to gender and age seems to illustrate the stereotype unusually well when compared to continental averages: 92 per cent female defendants (against 76 per cent); and the highest percentage of witches aged over 50: 87 per cent (against 62 per cent). Although the Essex witches were usually poor, Macfarlane admits that 'No direct connexion can be drawn between poverty and accusations': Macfarlane, *Witchcraft*, pp. 150–1, 155, 161–2, quotation at p. 155; Gibson, *Hanged for Witchcraft*, pp. 205–6; Brian P. Levack, *The Witch-Hunt in Early Modern Europe* (London, 1987), pp. 124, 129.

be married as widowed. Corroborating evidence can be drawn from the secular courts of almost a century later. Between 1640 and 1660, when prosecutions in Kent were at their peak, only 30 per cent of all those accused at the county quarter sessions and assizes, for whom marital status is recorded, were widows, whereas spinsters and women specifically referred to as married comprised 48 per cent of the total. The remaining 22 per cent were men, a figure consistent with the proportion of male suspects in the period 1560–1640. Of the sample of church court defendants, 16 per cent were men.[22]

The background to witchcraft accusations was also frequently at variance with the Macfarlane/Thomas stereotype. In her study of crime in seventeenth-century Sussex, Cynthia Herrup describes a case in which a man accuses two other men and a woman of witchcraft in a normal neighbourly quarrel in which 'the accuser and accused were not exceptionally mismatched in terms of power'. Professor Herrup continues:

> In eastern Sussex the rare accusations of witchcraft stand out because of the prominence of male defendants and because of the economic and social parity of the accused and the accuser. The changes seem to express ongoing competition rather than guilt or anger born of spurned hospitality, and, as such, they seem of a kind with accusations of trespass, unlicensed alehouses, or trading without an apprenticeship.[23]

For northern England, J. A. Sharpe has argued that many prosecutions stemmed from tensions between women in competition for prominence

---

[22] The secular court statistics for 1640–60 are based on forty-eight accused witches of whom the status of only two was unspecified. Of the remaining forty-six, fourteen were named as widows, ten were men, and the rest were married and unmarried spinsters. In the period 1560–1640, six of twenty-six witches tried at the secular courts were men. In all, approximately 19 per cent of witches prosecuted in Kent at the church courts, quarter sessions and assizes between 1560 and 1660 were male. A tentative survey of Cambridgeshire and the Diocese of Ely produces a figure of 30 per cent, and continental countries range between 20 per cent and 50 per cent. Robin Briggs recently arrived at 28 per cent in a sample from Lorraine, and argues that 'over a large area of France witchcraft seems to have had no obvious link at all with gender': Levack, *Witch-Hunt*, p. 24; Carlo Ginzburg, *Ecstasies. Deciphering the Witches' Sabbath* (London, 1990), p. 311; H. C. Erik Midelfort, *Witch Hunting in Southwestern Germany 1562–1684. The Social and Intellectual Foundations* (Stanford, 1972), pp. 180–1; Robin Briggs, 'Women as victims? Witches, judges and the community', *French History*, 5 (1991), 441–2, quotation at 441.

[23] Cynthia B. Herrup, *The Common Peace. Participation and the Criminal Law in Seventeenth-Century England* (Cambridge, 1987), p. 33. For similar cases, see John Stearne, *A Confirmation and Discovery of Witchcraft* (London, 1648), pp. 34–5 (Northants.); H[istorical] M[anuscripts] C[ommission], *Salisbury MSS*, XIV (London, 1923), p. 70 (Gloucs.).

in the female realm, and evidence from the Continent certainly suggests that, far from being marginal figures, witches were more commonly active, even aggressive, personalities whose assertive behaviour led to conflicts of interest with their neighbours.[24] Arguments for the witch to be seen, not as a marginal figure, but as a competitors for power, space and resources, have been advanced for several countries, among them France, Germany, Sweden and New England.[25]

It is certainly true that many women accused of witchcraft in Kent were active and integrated in local society, rather than passive and isolated. In 1586 Joan Cason was brought before the mayor of Faversham, charged with invoking evil spirits to kill Thomas Cooke's three-year-old daughter after he had broken off her engagement to his servant.[26] Seven women and two men gave evidence, alleging that she had sworn revenge upon several of her neighbours who had then suffered misfortune. Katherine Kenwarde related how Cason had lamed her child, and had heard the witch recite the following spell:

> take the Gume of an Ivye Tree in the alleye & leye yt in the grownde & the name of the p[ar]tie uppon the Gume, that as the Gume consumyd as sholde the p[ar]tie consume in hys bodye.

Agnes Barton claimed that during a quarrel over a broken pot, Cason had told her that she would come to harm when she was least expecting it; four days later, a child which she was nursing 'was suddenlie taken sycke in the nyghte mooste straungely' and died soon after. But the most damning evidence against Cason related to her diabolic familiar, a rat, which she confessed 'came to her one nyght wyth long leane handes & a

---

[24] J. A. Sharpe, 'Witchcraft and women in seventeenth-century England: some northern evidence', *Continuity and Change*, 6 (1991), 179–99. See also Sharpe, 'Women, witchcraft and the legal process', in Kermode and Walker, eds., *Women, Crime and the Courts*, pp. 106–24. For an interpretation which places female accusers in a slightly more passive role, see Clive Holmes, 'Women: witnesses and witches', *Past and Present*, 140 (1993), 45–78, esp. 49, 54–6, 74–5.

[25] Jeanne Favret-Saada, *Deadly Words. Witchcraft in the Bocage* (Cambridge, 1990), pp. 32, 104, and *passim*; David Sabean, *Power in the Blood. Popular Culture and Village Discourse in Early Modern Germany* (Cambridge, 1984), pp. 56–8, 211; Lyndal Roper, 'Witchcraft and fantasy in early modern Germany', this volume, pp. 207–36; Bengt Ankarloo, 'Sweden; the mass burnings (1668–1676)', in Ankarloo and Henningsen, eds., *Early Modern European Witchcraft*, pp. 310–12; Carol F. Karlsen, *The Devil in the Shape of a Woman. Witchcraft in Colonial New England* (New York, 1987).

[26] The following case is drawn from *Holinshed's Chronicles of England, Scotland and Ireland*, 6 vols. (London, 1586), III, pp. 1560–1, and borough court depositions and sessions roll: K[ent] A[rchives] O[ffice], Fa/JQs 23 (bdl. 128); Fa/JQs 1 (bdl. 104).

leane face ryghte lyke her M[aste]r John Mason & dyd kysse her & the lyppes of yt was colde'. The animal made a blood-curdling noise and was apparently impossible to kill. In court, although she was acquitted on the charge of *maleficium*, a lawyer disputed over a legal technicality concerning the invocation of a spirit. His claim was upheld by the court, and, despite her vehement protestations of innocence, Joan Cason was condemned and executed.

The existence of detailed court depositions and a printed secondary account enable us to reconstruct some of the circumstances behind the trial, revealing that forces of social disparity between accuser and accused were not necessarily at work. John Waller, who related the story in *Holinshed's Chronicles*, describes the witnesses as 'all verie poore people', who soon regretted Cason's death – of which more later. We also learn not only that Thomas Cooke (whose wife was the principal witness) and Joan Cason's husband worked in the same trade (collar-making), but that Katharine Kenwarde was probably one of Cason's own kin. To cap it all, Cason may even have been slightly wealthier than those who prosecuted her, since she had recently inherited a sum of money from her master and lover, John Mason. The element of the denial of alms is entirely absent here, and the part which most closely resembles the typical chain of events described by Macfarlane and Thomas occurs when one of her accusers comes to the *witch's* house for fire and a quarrel ensues. The familiar paradigm was reversed in a dispute between neighbours of comparable social status, and most probably it was in this very similarity of social circumstance, and therefore of neighbourly competition, that this conflict has its source.

Sixty years later, such squabbles – and the serious consequences they could have – remained a part of Kentish provincial life. Indeed, in 1645 yet another witchcraft trial in Faversham attracted public attention. A cheap pamphlet records the trial before the mayor, Robert Greenstreet, of four witches, one of whom, Joan Cariden, alias Argoll or Argoe, confessed that ten years earlier in 1635, the devil first visited her 'in the shape of a blacke rugged Dog in the night time and crept into the bed [next] to her and spake to her in mumbling language'. The next night he returned and commanded her 'to deny God and to leane to him and that then he would revenge her of any one she owed ill will to'.[27] She agreed

---

[27] *The Examination, Confession, Triall and Execution of Joan Williford, Joan Cariden, Jane Hott, who were executed . . . at Faversham* (London, 1645).

to the devil's conditions, promised her soul to him, and he suckled her for the first time. She is portrayed precisely as a typical witch of the period: one of a group of deluded, poverty-stricken, old widows seeking company and sustenance from the devil.

The reality was probably somewhat different, especially regarding the reasons for Cariden's unpopularity in the community. An isolated document from 1635, which survives in the borough archives, tells of Joan Cariden's local unpopularity a decade prior to her trial for witchcraft, adding another dimension to her character which otherwise could only be assessed from the 1645 pamphlet. Although the earlier account alleged that Cariden 'doth wraile against her neighbours and saith they shall never prosper, Because she hath curst them', nowhere is witchcraft specifically mentioned.[28] As for her social standing, there are a number of clues. The 1645 account refers to Cariden ambiguously both as a widow and as William Argoe's wife, but from the 1635 report we learn also that she had a son and a daughter with whom she most probably dwelt. Overall, it is clear that she was a socially integrated, non-marginal, but – in some quarters at least – unpopular figure who sold food locally. Richard Hilton evidently held a grudge against her, for she cursed him and 'caled him puritent [i.e. Puritan] Roge for she said it was his doeings that her wheat was arested'. This last accusation is especially intriguing as it may suggest not only religious and cultural tension, but also intervention in the passage of food into the town, and may point to her unpopularity as a regrator of corn at a time of dearth. It is known, for example, that in Faversham in the early 1630s there was at least one grain riot where the kind of action allegedly taken by Hilton was common.[29] Certainly, the 1635 statement records that she was owed money, probably loans or debts for goods sold on credit. On seeking repayment from one man, Cariden claimed 'he took the tongs and hurld [them] at are [her?] and put her [out] of the house like a dog'. Also she protested that if Nathaniel Beesbedge had been mayor (as he was to be in 1637), he 'would wright her cause againe and help her to her mony of goodwife

---

[28] Public cursing by no means always led to accusations of witchcraft. Indeed, it was common to present the two offences separately against a suspect. See, for example, the case of Emme Merchante of Whitstable, who in 1572 was 'suspected to use sorcery and wytchcrafte and is a great cursor and blasphemer of the name of Allmighty god': Thomas, *Religion and the Decline of Magic*, pp. 610–11; C[athedral,] C[ity, and] D[iocesan] R[ecord] O[ffice, Canterbury], DCb/X.1.11, f. 103ᵛ.

[29] Buchanan Sharp, *In Contempt of All Authority. Rural Artisans and Riot in the West of England, 1586–1600* (Berkeley, 1980), p. 30.

Cose'. Joan Cariden was probably resented as a creditor and retailer, as much as reviled as an evil curser and sower of discord.[30]

This conflict should perhaps also be examined against a backdrop of popular discontent with the mayoralty, and possibly of factional conflict. It is known that attacks upon urban oligarchies in the early seventeenth century were common in Kent, particularly in Faversham in the decade after 1610, and Joan Cariden's verbal assault on Mayor Greenstreet and his jurats may well have been in that tradition. Clearly dissatisfied with the administration of justice, the troublesome woman threatened to petition the lord warden of the Cinque Ports and instructed her son to 'goe and arest goodman Chillenden', and her son also said that 'he could not have noe justice of Mr Maior'. By mid-September 1635 Faversham had a new mayor, but ten years later Robert Greenstreet once again took up office, and within twelve days, intriguingly, Cariden had been thrown into gaol. Soon afterwards she was tried and executed as a witch.[31]

In general, these two cases suggest the diversity and complexity of the social environment of witchcraft accusations, and specifically how integrated and even assertive the protagonist could be. Taking this a step further, it is easy to see how in certain cases witchcraft accusations might have played a part in power struggles between different camps within the community. Annabel Gregory, for example, has demonstrated that political faction provided the dynamic for a witchcraft trial in another Cinque Port, Rye, in the early seventeenth century.[32] This, and cases from around England, indicate that witchcraft accusations could polarise communities along pre-existing fault-lines, rather than binding them together in a collective censure of a scapegoat.[33] In this regard, however,

---

[30] KAO, Fa/JQe 14; Edward Jacob, *The History of the Town and Port of Faversham* (London, 1774), p. 124.

[31] Peter Clark, 'The migrant in Kentish towns 1580–1640', in Peter Clark and Paul Slack, eds., *Crisis and Order in English Towns 1500–1800. Essays in Urban History* (London, 1972), p. 151; KAO, Fa/JQe 14. Cariden was examined for the first time on 25 September. Greenstreet would have taken up office on 13 Sept., see Jacob, *History of . . . Faversham*, p. 69.

[32] Annabel Gregory, 'Witchcraft, politics and "good neighbourhood" in early seventeenth-century Rye', *Past and Present*, 133 (1991), 33–5, 37 and *passim*. For a dramatic parallel from New England, see Paul Boyer and Stephen Nissenbaum, *Salem Possessed. The Social Origins of Witchcraft* (Cambridge, MA, 1974), pp. 37–45, 51–8, 86–109, 147.

[33] As Dr Sharpe has suggested, 'against notions of "tyranny of local opinion" or of village communities being united against the witch might be set a number of cases where reactions to witchcraft reflected divisions rather than hegemony in local attitudes':

the Faversham cases are more suggestive than conclusive. It is true that events of 1635 show Cariden as having been more integrated in the community than the 1645 account, but if she had supporters then we can only guess at who they might have been – other traders, a possible anti-Puritan faction, Greenstreet's political opponents. And yet it remains important to accept that this theory is at least as plausible as one which automatically assigns to Cariden the role of outcast simply because she has been accused as a witch.

Other cases where the accused was not a marginal figure can be added to the above. When Dorothy Rawlins of St Dunstan's, Canterbury, appeared on a charge of *maleficium* in 1651, she was far from being an impoverished lonely figure; instead, she lived with her husband, a brewer, and sold food to local people. Mary Blyth, the wife of a rival brewer in the same parish, testified that having bought some 'seesing' (size?) from the accused, on the way home 'the pott gave a greate blowe & flew & broake and the seesing flew aboute her eares and upp unto the seeling'. She attested that Rawlins 'was a witch, if there were any in England', and other customers claimed that they had become sick after eating food bought from her. Although Rawlins was acquitted, the case shows how suspicions could develop even about a person who was well known in the community, married, and with whom her accusers had regular dealings of their own accord. Indeed, some accused witches were described as models of Christian conformity. In 1641 a gentleman, Henry Oxinden, stepped in to protect Goodwife Gilnot of Barham against the accusations of her neighbours, and spoke of a woman 'religiously disposed' and a dutiful mother who 'hath taken noe small care to have them instructed up in the feare of God'.[34]

Oxinden's intervention reinforces the impression that suspects were not necessarily universally reviled in Kent communities, and that individuals were often present who were prepared to defend them. Partly because of this, things did not always go as planned for the accuser. When John Northcliffe indicted Sibil Ferris of St Lawrence-in-Thanet

---

J. A. Sharpe, *Witchcraft in Seventeenth-Century Yorkshire: Accusations and Counter Measures*, Borthwick Papers, 81 (York, 1992), pp. 21–2. For other examples, see Cambridge University Library, EDR D/2/10, ff. 4ᵛ, 22, 37, 51ᵛ, 77ᵛ (Cambs., 1577); British Library, Add. MS 28223, f. 15 (Norfolk, 1600); PRO, ASSI 47/20/1/512–13; 45/11/1/90–3 (Yorks., 1651). See also Gaskill, 'Witches and witchcraft accusations', pp. 52–3.

[34] KAO, Q/SB 2/13; Q/SRc E4/111; *The Oxinden Letters, 1607–1642*, ed., Dorothy Gardiner (London, 1933), p. 222.

for *maleficium* in 1610, even though she already had a long reputation as a witch and had appeared before a church court in 1597, the magistrate, Thomas Harflete, took her side, and not only acquitted her but fined Northcliffe two shillings for scratching her face and assaulting her with a pitchfork.[35] Nor were witches always bereft of friends and family, and assistance was frequently forthcoming from less prominent figures than the likes of Oxinden or Harflete. For instance, many accused women were able to find neighbours to testify to their good name at church court hearings. In 1618 Mary Hunt of Sandwich had been spinning at a neighbour's house, when Elizabeth Clark publicly accused her of witchcraft. Offended, Hunt took her case to the Canterbury archdeacon's court, and the women who had witnessed the accusation turned up to testify to her character and bearing. Nor did Katherine Wilson and Wilman Worsiter of Ashford stand alone against the authorities when they were tried for witchcraft at Canterbury in 1651. Word reached Worsiter's husband who, working in another county at the time that his wife was accused, rushed home to raise the £40 bail for her with the assistance of Stephen Strong and John Richards, pledging that she would appear at the next sessions of the peace. Likewise, Widow Wilson was bailed by two local men – a husbandman and a labourer.[36]

Nor were such acts of communal generosity towards accused witches in Kent isolated occurrences. In 1653 alone, Anne Pottin was bailed by two local men; Richard Fosher of Brookland provided sureties for Widow Howell; and Mary Page of St Nicholas-in-Thanet was able to rely on her husband to do the same. Husbands sometimes went to even greater lengths to clear their wives' names. In 1561 a church court heard how Robert Brayne of Biddenden made diligent enquiries to discover why his 35-year-old bride was believed to be a witch, after their marriage had been objected to on these grounds, but had been unable to find any substance in the accusation. Similarly dutiful was Robert Staunton of Northfleet, whose petition resulted in a pardon for his wife in 1574, after she was convicted of bewitching a neighbour's livestock; some years later, when Ade Davie of Selling confessed to having sold her soul to the devil and bewitched her family, her husband stepped in to defend her

---

[35] KAO, QM/SI/9/9; Arthur Hussey, 'The visitations of the Archdeacon of Canterbury', *Arch. Cant.*, 27 (1905), 32; KAO, QM/SI 1610/14/12; QM/SB 989.

[36] CCDRO, DCb/PRC 39/34, ff. 52v–54v; KAO, Q/SB 2/12; Q/SRc E4/47, 50. Support could take many forms. After Katherine Fisher (see below) was charged with witchcraft in 1560, a Kenardington man was excommunicated for knowingly harbouring her: CCDRO, DCb/Y.2.24, f. 30v.

as 'a right honest bodie . . . of good parentage'. Less successful in his efforts, but equally loyal, was Thomas Sharpe of Minster, whose wife was sentenced to death in 1651 for bewitching a gelding and causing a languishing illness in a man. Sharpe petitioned magistrates for a re-trial and promised to provide evidence of his wife's good character giving assurance that he personally had 'alwaies demeaned himselfe as a Christian ought to doe'.[37]

It is evident, then, that although many witches conformed to the stereotype of the elderly woman reliant on alms, equally, many accused women in Kent emerge from the archives as altogether more potent characters, able to draw upon at least some support when they were accused. This fact alone makes a model of witchcraft, whereby an incongruous and unconforming individual was persecuted due to social and economic pressures, sometimes seem remote in its relevance. It may also help explain why so many witches, of whom no more is known than the bare details contained in an indictment, were actually acquitted – even in the sixteenth century. We need to remember that many women were significant actors in the parish, and rather than standing outside the structure of patriarchal authority – and therefore falling victim to its prejudices – were integrally involved in local networks of kinship, work and worship. As a consequence, many accused witches experienced varied currents of defence and attack emanating from both men and women in different spheres of daily life, but always inextricably bound up in very particular personal and local circumstances. Notwithstanding the argument that increasing female prominence might have put certain women at greater risk of being accused of witchcraft, a rise of prosecutions does not necessarily presuppose a crisis in gender relations. It does, however, suggest intense competition and conflict between competing households – households which comprised, naturally enough, both women and men.[38]

---

[37] KAO, Q/SRc E6/24, 38; E7/87–8; CCDRO, DCb/X.8.5, f. 87; *Calendar of the Patent Rolls, Elizabeth I, VI, 1572–1575* (London, 1973), p. 283; Scot, *Discoverie of Witchcraft*, pp. 55–7; KAO, Q/SRc E3/65–6; Q/SB 2/41. In 1606 Thomas Winter of Barham objected so strongly to a neighbour accusing his mother of witchcraft, that he took him to court to forestall future accusations: CCDRO, DCb/PRC 39/29, ff. 333ᵛ–377.

[38] As E. P. Thompson has remarked, many women occupied a central position in the market place, where they behaved not as passive adjuncts of husbands and masters, but as 'the initiators of community opinion, and the initiators of actions: *Customs in Common* (London, 1991), pp. 315–17, 322, quotation at p. 322. On crisis in gender relations, see: David Underdown, 'The taming of the scold: the enforcement of

III

However small their minority, it is important to consider the handful of men who were accused of witchcraft, maleficent and otherwise. Indeed, the husbands of accused witches were not always in a position to help their wives, as they themselves might be implicated in the charge. In 1560, for example, Robert and Katherine Fisher of Ruckinge were presented together at both the archdeaconry and consistory courts at Canterbury for using *ars magica* and incantations; and Nicholas Hardwyn of Kingsdown and his wife were accused of *maleficium*. Hardwyn, it was alleged, 'coulde saye mundayes prayer that one Seks soo cauled of the parryshe of Lynsted shoulde not lyve untyll satter daye in night'; and William Ames testified that after he fell out with Hardwyn's wife, she 'said unto me that she wolde be even w[i]t[h] me before the yeer came about And ymmediatelye I had a cowe that stode gryndinge w[i]t[h] her tethe and formynge at hyr mought as nev[er] hathe been seen hertofore as my neighbours can tell'. This indicates that both husband and wife might be seen by local people as equally active in the exercise of harmful magic, although we cannot be sure of the conflicts which lay behind suspicions that they were engaged in such practices.[39]

In the following year, however, we find a more telling case. Robert Brayne, who, as we saw above, had attempted to clear his bride's name, appeared before the ecclesiastical authorities jointly accused with his new wife of using witchcraft to kill livestock, ruin milk and beer, and cause sickness among their neighbours. Brayne was personally charged with killing James Sloman's best cow, and disabling his servant 'w[i]th a strange sycknes', after he and Sloman had fallen out whilst labouring together to repair the highway. Alice Brayne also came directly into conflict with neighbours, who were reported to be 'vexed by her p[e]rsuasion', but, as in her husband's case, this stemmed from participation in work and trade, not isolation from it. In one instance, which once again reminds us how the begging paradigm could be reversed, she declined to lend a horse to a neighbour, who then lost two bullocks; another man complained that

---

patriarchal authority in early modern England', in Anthony Fletcher and John Stevenson, eds., *Order and Disorder in Early Modern England* (Cambridge, 1985), pp. 116–36, esp. 119–22; Martin Ingram, '"Scolding women cucked or washed": a crisis in gender relations in early modern England?', in Kermode and Walker, eds., *Women, Crime and the Courts*, pp. 48–80, esp. p. 49.

[39] CCDRO, DCb/X.8.5, f. 23ᵛ; Y.2.24, f. 26; X.1.2, f. 1/50.

he solde her a busshell of graynes and becawse she might not have
helpe soo sonne as she called to lay them upon her backe the dryncke
that was made of the sayde graynes beganne to sethe abowte the tunne
an w[i]thin a whyle a man might have drawen yt to the toppe of the
howse at hys fingers ende

In this case, at least, the accusation makes more sense when one views
the accused parties less as unpopular individuals and more as members
of an unpopular household.[40] Other isolated cases strengthen this
impression. In 1573 Archbishop Parker's court heard how Stephen
Blusshe of Marden had encouraged a man to visit a witch who in this case
happened to be Blusshe's own wife; and, some months later, a few miles
away at Broomfield, William Evernden and his wife were both presented
as suspected witches. In the seventeenth century such charges were more
commonly heard in the secular courts, and with more serious penalties.
At the Maidstone summer assizes in 1603, for instance, George and Anne
Winchester confessed to having bewitched a woman to death; as already
mentioned, two married couples, William Reynolds, Thomas Wilson and
their wives, were indicted at the same court in 1652.[41]

But the role played by men in English witchcraft prosecutions could
extend beyond mere complicity in a female crime, and although the
overwhelming majority of English witches were women, 'there does not
seem to have been any obvious objection to the idea of male witches', as
Macfarlane himself observed.[42] Elizabethan divines were in agreement
on this point. The Puritan minister Henry Holland was less concerned
about 'poor doating old women (which are commonly called witches)'
than the 'wicked man or woman that worketh with the devill'; and
William Perkins argued that Moses' use of the feminine gender was
misleading, and that, in truth, the Hebrew patriarch 'exempteth not the
male'.[43] The same opinion was also current in the seventeenth century:

---

[40] CCDRO, DCb/X.1.3, ff. 156ᵛ–157Aᵛ.

[41] 'An unpublished record of Archbishop Parker's visitation in 1573', *Arch. Cant.*, 29
(1911), 306; CCDRO, X.1.12, ff. 52ᵛ, 132ᵛ; Ewen, *Witch Hunting and Witch Trials*,
pp. 195, 239–40.

[42] Macfarlane, *Witchcraft*, p. 160; Ronald C. Sawyer, '"Strangely handled in all her
lyms": witchcraft and healing in Jacobean England', *Journal of Social History*, 22
(1989), 465. Probably the first person to be charged under the 1604 statute was a man,
see HMC, *Salisbury MSS*, XVII (London, 1938), p. 36.

[43] Holland, *Treatise Against Witchcraft*, sigs. B3, E1; William Perkins, *A Discourse of the
Damned Art of Witchcraft* (Cambridge, 1608), p. 168. See also Gifford, *A Discourse of
the Subtill Practises of Devilles*, sig. B2. In general, see Stuart Clark, 'Protestant
demonology: sin, superstition and society (c. 1520–c. 1640)', in Ankarloo and
Henningsen, eds., *Early Modern European Witchcraft*, pp. 45–81.

in the 1640s, for example, learned men on either side of the witchcraft debate agreed that witchcraft was a sin like any other and as such, both sexes were vulnerable to its insinuations.[44]

These attitudes were made manifest in the Kent courts. In 1652, apart from Reynolds and Wilson, four other men were tried for maleficent witchcraft at Maidstone, a town where almost a century earlier the surgeon John Halle had railed against a different group of male suspects whom he described as 'divelishe wyches and sorcerers'. One of these earlier witches, William Winckfield, was whipped and excommunicated for necromancy by a church court and, so it was said, finally fled from the civil authorities at the introduction of the 1563 Witchcraft Act. In the early 1560s men from the parishes of Headcorn, Westwell, Otterden and Lyminge were all accused of witchcraft in the church courts, including one Kytterell, 'a sinister physicion', who had performed sorcery over a woman in labour. Visitations in the diocese of Canterbury in 1569 exposed a Westbere man as an experienced sorcerer, and one George Walcot was accused of 'the sin of witchcraft'. Similarly, in 1580 the privy council ordered that Richard Yeorke of Stoale be apprehended for 'sundry lewde and detestable practises aboute conjuracions'; a decade later, Thomas Fansome appeared before the high commission charged with practising amatory magic, principally, giving poor William Suttyll's wife 'a wrytinge or a charme to make hyr husband to love hyr'.[45] It is true that many such accusations concerned sorcery, necromancy, invocation of spirits and magical healing rather than *maleficium*, but in the eyes of the church, the distinction was less important than in the secular courts. Many entries in the ecclesiastical records fail to specify the type of witchcraft being prosecuted, and so we cannot fully assess how many men were actually accused of *maleficium*. Yet we must accept that in early modern communities, however rarely, the male witch

---

[44] Gaule, *Select Cases of Conscience*, p. 52; Stearne, *Confirmation and Discovery*, p. 12. For expressions of the same opinion, see Thomas Cooper, *The Mystery of Witch-Craft* (London, 1617), pp. 180–1; Richard Bernard, *A Guide to Grand-Jury Men* (London, 1627; 1629 edn), p. 87; Alexander Roberts, *A Treatise of Witchcraft . . . With a True Narration of the Witchcrafts which Mary Smith, wife of Henry Smith Glover, did Practice* (London, 1616), pp. 4–5.

[45] John Halle, *An Historiall Expostulation: Against the Beastlye Abusers, Both of Chyrurgerie and Physyke, in Oure Tyme* (London, 1565), ed., T. J. Pettigrew (London, 1844), pp. 7, 15 and *passim*; CCDRO, DCb/X.8.5, ff. 90ᵛ–91; X.1.2, ff. 1/35ᵛ, 1/40ᵛ; X.8.5, ff. 53, 72; Y.2.24, f. 36ᵛ; X.1.6, f. 76; X.1.4, f. 91ᵛ; Hussey, 'Visitations of the Archdeacon of Canterbury'', 221; 'Peter de Sandwich', 'Some East Kent parish history', *Home Counties Magazine*, 5 (1903), 13; *Acts of the Privy Council*, n.s. XII, 1580–1581 (London, 1896), pp. 21–2; KAO, DRb/PRC 44/3, pp. 166–9.

– both helpful and harmful – was a physical as well as a theoretical reality.

Not all such men were poor and marginal figures. In 1562 an elderly woman, Joan Basden of St Paul's in Canterbury, swore before the consistory that Alderman John Twyne was a conjuror who exerted a strange coercive force over others. Twyne, she alleged, had threatened to kill her after they had argued about a debt owed to him, and had conjured up 'a black thing like a great rugged blak dogg w[hi]ch wold danse about the house, and hurle fyer'. Yet again, the roles of witch and accuser according to the Macfarlane/Thomas model would seem to have been reversed. Other accusations of witchcraft show how the socially impotent could attack figures of authority, in particular clergymen. Even after the Reformation, ministers were still seen by many as guardians of an intangible power, the potential of which might be viewed ambiguously as beneficial or malevolent. Witches accused in the church courts usually had been seeking to harness divine – as opposed to diabolical – power (remember Nicholas Hardwyn's maleficent prayer), and it may have sometimes seemed that a double standard was being observed. Moreover, it is likely that on occasion unspecified charges of witchcraft were a veil for disciplinary action against the use of traditional liturgy after the Elizabethan Settlement of 1559, and especially after the publication of the Thirty-Nine Articles of 1563. For these reasons, a clergyman might find himself under suspicion, especially if he was disliked for other reasons. In 1561 there were at least three instances of alleged clerical sorcery in Kent: the curate of Biddenden was accused of setting a bad example by burning some of his cattle in an attempt to reverse a witch's hex; a man presented for witchcraft claimed that he had learned some of his magical skills from the parish priest at Sutton; and Thomas Thompson, the vicar of Godmersham and Challock, was excommunicated for *veneficium* and incantation. To a clergyman, the consequences of such accusations might not have always been as serious as excommunication or, far worse, conviction for felony, but in many cases the damage done to his reputation in that community may well have been permanent.[46]

---

[46] CCDRO, DCb/Y.2.24, ff. 69ᵛ–70ᵛ; X.1.3, f. 156ᵛ; X.8.5, f. 72; Y.2.24, f. 54. This inversion of the stereotype can be seen in other counties, see, for example: Ewen, *Witch Hunting and Witch Trials*, p. 283; J. C. Jeaffreson, ed., *Middlesex County Records*, 4 vols. (Clerkenwell, 1886–92), I, p. 197; J. C. Cox, *Three Centuries of Derbyshire Annals*, 2 vols. (London, 1890), II, p. 90. For other cases of clerical witchcraft, see Gaskill, 'Witches and witchcraft accusations', pp. 57–9.

The accusation of men continued into the seventeenth century when, due to the growing ascendancy of the secular courts over their ecclesiastical equivalents, the penalties were more often potentially greater. The year 1617 saw the prosecution of three Kentish men under the 1604 Witchcraft Act, one of them a minister. In the village of Halden (now High Halden), Andrew Loader told justices how he witnessed the rector of the parish, William Lawse, give William Childes a conjuring book and then saw

> a Circle made with Chalke in the middle of the roome, w[hi]ch the said Chiles said that hee had made, & that it was in Compasse nine foote & a halfe, and hee told Mr Lawse that hee had gone as far as hee Could till hee had written Latine words in the Circle whereupon Mr Lawse wrot w[i]th Chalke within the said Circle three or fowre words in fowre sundry places

The rector's servant, Isaac Mungery, confirmed that the two men 'often wheare in secrett conference togethere in Mr Lawes his studdie and in other places in the house where Childs dide show Mr Lawes the seaven plannetts and divers other things'. Mungery also claimed to have seen spirits in his master's house.[47] Other cases seem equally remote from the stereotype. In the same year as Lawes was accused, the mayor and jurats of New Romney heard how when some local inhabitants voiced their suspicions about William Godfrey – a middle-aged property-owning farmer supporting a wife and children – to Thomas Bennett of Newchurch, Bennett 'did saye unto them that he thought in his Conscience that the said Godfrey was a witch'. Eight men and women came forward to give evidence against Godfrey for a variety of witch-crafts including causing lameness in lambs, leaving the devil in a house which he rented out, using familiars to attempt the abduction of a child and to kill a pig, and staining laundry with blood.[48]

The range of persons who might be implicated in witchcraft accusations extended to other family members, and it was widely held

---

[47] KAO, QM/SI 1618/2/7; QM/SB 1306–7, 1311, 1315. William Lawse obtained his MA from Cambridge in 1581, was inducted as rector of Halden in 1600 and died in 1626: J. Venn and J. A. Venn, *The Book of Matriculations and Degrees 1544–1659* (Cambridge, 1913), p. 414; *Extracts from Registers and Records: Relating to the Collation, Institution, Induction, and Composition of the Rectors of High Halden* (London, 1900), p. 11. A number of educated men were accused, see for example, Stearne, *Confirmation and Discovery*, pp. 23, 25, 32. In 1646 John Gaule asserted that many 'men of the most eminent wisdome and holinesse' had been slandered as witches: *Select Cases of Conscience*, p. 8.

[48] KAO, NR/JQp 1/30.

that witchcraft could be passed on either as a skill to family, friends and servants, or by heredity.[49] The offspring of a suspected witch were particularly at risk, and as one Jacobean minister observed, 'all who are convented upon these unlawfull actions [witchcraft] are not strucken in yeares; but some even in the flower of their youth be nuzzled up in the same, and convicted to be practizers thereof'.[50] At the bishop's court at Rochester in 1562, Alexander Goody of Tudeley told how he overheard Edmund Peyrson inform Mary Wodd that 'Fremans wedowe doythe say that thowe & thy childer bi witches', and that this was 'a Comyn Talke in Tudeley'. Again, at Canterbury in 1571, Laurence Walker and his wife accused Goodwife Champnes and her daughter of working together to bewitch their child. In 1617 when the farmer Godfrey was accused by various members of the Clarke, Barber and Ladds families, his children also fell under suspicion. William Clarke informed a magistrate that when he asked his young son to chase Godfrey's ducks from his land, the accused's daughter said 'they should repent it & that they would be quit w[i]th them for it'. Sickness among Clarke's livestock, followed by a visit to a cunning woman, convinced him that his next-door neighbours were guilty of maleficent witchcraft. Another neighbour also implicated Godfrey's adolescent son for having displayed, three years earlier, an uncanny prescience regarding some pies in his kitchen cupboard and had offered some unusual advice about a sack of flour, after which both commodities mysteriously spoiled.[51]

In this way, as suggested earlier, whole households might be ranged against one another, resulting in multiple accusations at variance with the stereotype. In 1631 John Younge's wife, Catherine, and another female relative, were tried at the summer assizes at Maidstone, where the former was sentenced to be hanged. In 1657 Stephen Allen of Goudhurst lost both wife and daughter to the hangman after they pleaded guilty to the invocation of evil spirits for maleficent purposes, and the girl even testified against her mother. Similarly, in 1566 at Wittersham, Fryswid Appes confessed that her sister was a witch, and a century later

[49] Norman Cohn, *Europe's Inner Demons. An Inquiry Inspired by the Great Witch-Hunt* (London, 1975), pp. 248–9. Spectators at the Maidstone trials of 1652 wanted the blood-line of the witches to be broken by fire: H.F., *Prodigious & Tragicall History of . . . six Witches at Maidstone*, p. 5. However, this connection was not – as Clive Holmes has suggested – exclusively matrilineal: 'Women, witnesses and witches', p. 51. See Perkins, *Discourse*, pp. 201–4; Bernard, *Guide to Grand-Jury Men*, pp. 206–7.

[50] Roberts, *A Treatise of Witchcraft*, p. 4.

[51] KAO, DRb/Jdl, f. 98; CCDRO, DCb/X.1.10, f. 6; KAO, NR/JQp 1/30/2, 10–12.

Katherine Huse brought her mother to the attention of the Kent magistrates for allegedly bewitching a neighbour's ring from her finger. Condemnation, as well as defence and support, therefore, could originate or be compounded from within the family, possibly serving as an outlet for domestic tensions for which no other legitimate means of expression existed.[52]

IV

So far the intention has not been to suggest that the character of witchcraft prosecutions in Kent was intrinsically different from other counties, still less that Macfarlane and Thomas were fundamentally mistaken in their conclusions. Rather one feels that the history of English witchcraft – in Essex at least – has emphasised the model accusation at the expense of cases which fit the theory less well. One can see clearly that the process of identifying a witch could deviate markedly from the familiar progression of begging, denial, guilt, misfortune and accusation; nor did it always rely on gender or social stereotypes. In short, it is simply impossible to encapsulate the experience and meaning of witchcraft within such a narrowly conceived framework. A final observation to be made from the Kent material concerns the use and abuse of witchcraft accusations as an expression of hostility and a means to resolve local disputes – in particular, the association and conflation of the offence with a range of grievances in the community.

In the first place, a specific accusation against one person might be deflected by that individual towards another. In 1591 a church court heard how at West Farleigh, Agnes Joyner and Alice Roydon diverted the rumour that they were witches towards Joan Preble and Mary Cleeve. It was alleged that while Joyner and her husband spread vicious gossip about the two scapegoats, Rydon 'Counterfeited herself to be bewitched by them. And the same Joyner & his wife mayntayned her in that abuse.' Again, in 1617, William Lawse tried unsuccessfully to turn the tables on his servant, Isaac Mungery. Suspecting his master of witchcraft, Mungery challenged him with certain questions 'w[hi]ch he touke soe ill thatt presently he scited me upon it to the comessaries Court to my greatt trubble and charges'. The servant, however, decided to make a civil action of the affair and went to a magistrate who released him from

---

[52] Levack, *Witch-Hunt*, p. 133; Ewen, *Witch Hunting and Witch Trials*, pp. 91–2, 216–17, 249; PRO, ASSI 35/98/5/35–6; CCDRO, DCb/Z.4.12, f. 29; KAO, Q/SB 8/19.

the clutches of the ecclesiastical authorities and summoned the clergyman Lawse instead.[53]

Formal presentment for witchcraft was often accompanied by
prosecution of the same person for other offences. In April 1652 John
Wills of Warehorne took Anne Pottin and John Young to court. Pottin
was charged with 'entertaininge of Inmates, for livinge incontinentlie
with men and being suspected to receive & keepe Fellons goodes'.[54] A
note at the bottom of the recognizance recording her bail, adds the
specific charge 'receivinge John Yonge who is a marryed man'. Young,
a local tailor, was accused of 'dissertinge his wife: for being suspected to
be lewd with other women [and] for other misdemeanures'. Both were to
be indicted for evading magistrates. The outcome of the trial does not
survive, but clearly John Wills was dissatisfied. In September, John
Young was apprehended and imprisoned in Canterbury Castle, and early
in 1653 both he and Pottin were presented by Wills for witchcraft. Of
Pottin's fate the record is silent, but Young, presuming he was able to pay
his gaol fees, was released when the bill against him was thrown out by
the grand jury. There is nothing to suggest why Young and Pottin might
have been thought to have been witches, but it would seem likely that
they were engaged in an extra-marital relationship which Wills objected
to. His grievance, therefore, was most likely Young's abuse of another
man's wife, and his dissolute life in general, as much as a vague and
unsubstantiated act of *maleficium*.[55]

Other witchcraft accusations in seventeenth-century Kent were
accompanied by objections to other forms of unneighbourly conduct,
such as drunkenness and other disorderly behaviour. Alice Robert of
Goudhurst, for instance, was presented at a Canterbury church court in
1560 not only for witchcraft but also because she had 'Raysed Stryffe
betwene Rycharde Rode and his wiffe'.[56] Others were said to have
committed immoral acts. In 1563, at the same hearing as she was accused

---

[53] KAO, DRb/Pa 21, ff. 6, 55; QM/SB 1315.

[54] For a parallel case, see *APC*, n.s. XII, p. 228.

[55] KAO, Q/SRc E5/60–1; Q/SMc 1; Q/SRc E6/38, 64, 83.

[56] CCDRO, DCb/X.1.2, f. 1/63ᵛ. See also: X.1.7, f. 35ᵛ; X.1.12, f. 28. Religious
nonconformity, such as failure to receive communion, also accompanied accusations.
One Kentish woman was presented as a witch in part because she wore a rosary; in 1562
churchwardens at Chartham reported an Irish priest not just for fortune-telling and
sorcery but for seeking to persuade people 'to contemne and despyse the religion that
nowe ys set forthe': CCDRO, DCb/X.1.4, ff. 19–20ᵛ; X.1.4, f. 20ᵛ. On the Continent
witchcraft was linked to offences as varied as vagrancy and rebellion: Levack, *Witch-
Hunt*, pp. 137–9.

of running a brothel, a Cranbrook woman was also questioned about witchcraft. In the same decade, the necromancer Winckfield was tried by the ecclesiastical authorities 'as an adulterer, and a woorker by divilshe and magicall artes'; he was also reputed to be a notorious bigamist, having three wives living at Canterbury. Other infractions of household discipline might also compound suspicions of witchcraft. At Aldington in 1569, suspicion that Margaret Dale was a witch became a formal accusation when her neighbours learned that she was no longer living with her husband; and another accused witch, Goodwife Martyn of Warehorne, was also allegedly separated in the 1560s. Disapprobation at the adultery and sexual promiscuity of Goodwife Swayne of St John's-in-Thanet, was accompanied by a charge of witchcraft in 1582 when she was denounced for saying, 'that she can make a drink which she saith if she give it to any young man that she liketh well of, he shall be in love with her'. Likewise, Thomas Fansome, the pedlar of love charms, was also presented for seeking to interfere with the natural course of sexual relations, as well as being a nuisance and 'A longe Fornicator' living incontinently from his wife.[57]

Fansome was also condemned as a cheat who had obtained money by unscrupulous means. Disliked for similar reasons, Joan Cason, the witch hanged at Faversham in 1586, confessed not only that John Mason 'had the use hir bodie verie dishonestlie whilest she was wife to hir husband', but crucially that she had failed to make the bequests stipulated by her lover in his will. Guilt over this omission caused Cason herself to believe that the deceased Mason had sent the rat which paid frequent visits to her house, in order 'that she shoolde see hys wyll fulfylled & . . . she dothe thincke that yt was Masons soule'. Cason denied any crime 'but hir lewd life and adulterous conversation' which would seem to have been the greatest objection of her neighbours. An adulteress in the locality was undesirable, but someone who fraudulently profited from the offence was intolerable. Ill-gotten gains were also the downfall of Christopher Harrison and Margaret Baron of Saltwood, tried at the Canterbury quarter sessions in 1653 as much for their attempts to defraud 'the goode and honest persons of this comon wealth of England of theire Goods

---

[57] CCDRO, DCb/X.1.4, f. 94ᵛ; Halle, *Historiall Expostulation*, pp. 11–13; 'Some East Kent parish history', *HCM*, 5 (1903), 15; CCDRO, DCb.X.1.7, f. 48v; Hussey, 'Visitations of the Archdeacon of Canterbury', 19; KAO, DRb/PRC 44/3, pp. 85–6. Sometimes witchcraft and whoredom were associated, particularly when accusations of either were used primarily as insults. See, for example: CCDRO, DCb/X.1.7, f. 79ᵛ; 'Some East Kent parish history', *HCM*, 7 (1905), 130.

chattels and moneys', as claiming the ability to 'tell and knowe the chances and fortunes of men to come hereafter'. Although it is not recorded if Harrison was found guilty of palmistry, he was certainly punished as a vagrant and placed in the house of correction.[58] Additional charges could also be of a more serious nature. In 1641 Manly Stansall of Gillingham was charged with another man 'For practising Inchantm[en]t & Witchcraft' upon Stansall's daughter. This charge was not, however, pursued at the next assizes, and instead Stansall was convicted of a *physical* assault on the girl, and was fined and bound over to keep the peace. This case also reinforces the earlier point about conflict within the family, especially since at least four writs were issued against Stansall's wife to answer related charges at this time. Accused witches might be charged with other destructive behaviour such as arson. In 1675, when Mary Brice of Rochester was indicted for killing a woman with a broom and setting fire to property, she was also charged with bewitching a man and a woman. In a similar case in 1658, Judith Sawkins of Aylesford was condemned not just for her alleged *maleficia*, but for burning a barn by natural means.[59] Clearly, the nonconformity of the witch could comprise more than initially meets the eye.

Contributory motives for witchcraft accusations could be even more deeply embedded in a community. As already mentioned, it was the personal grudges of a neighbour and a servant which caused the rector of Halden, William Lawse, to be called before the local magistrate on a charge of witchcraft in 1617. But Lawse had not lived entirely at peace with others in the community prior to the accusation. He had quarrelled with John Whetcombe at a slaughterhouse, for instance, and Whetcombe had called him 'a skurvye shitten fellowe' for which Lawse prosecuted him. He was also frequently at law in these years over tithe disputes and may well have acquired an image as a contentious person. It would appear that one of the origins of his unpopularity was that for the past decade he had lived in a cottage without the statutory 4 acres of land, and in an inconvenient place in the village 'To the great annoyance of all the Inhabitants there'. An attempt to present Lawse for this offence resulted in failure, and soon after some of his neighbours assembled a charge of

---

[58] *Holinshed's Chronicles*, III, pp. 1560–1; KAO, Fa/JQs 23 (bdl. 128); Q/SRc E7/84; Q/SMc 1.

[59] Elizabeth Melling (ed.), *Kentish Sources, VI. Crime and Punishment* (Maidstone, 1969), p. 95; KAO, Q/SMc 1 (1640–1); J. S. Cockburn, ed., *Calendar of Assize Records. Kent Indictments, Charles I* (London, 1995), pp. 394, 399, 411, 432, 482, 502. Ewen, *Witch-Hunting and Witch Trials*, pp. 250–1, 259.

witchcraft loosely based on an event which supposedly had occurred almost a decade earlier. Although Lawse was again acquitted it is probable that his local standing was further diminished by this incident.[60] Many prosecutions were generated by the sheer malice of personal feuds. Even if a case were thrown out of court, an accused witch would not only lose reputation, but might spend weeks or months in a noisome gaol awaiting trial – and even after acquittal if fees could not be paid. Given the appalling conditions, a protracted spell of imprisonment might even amount to a death sentence.[61] Yet, despite its importance for the history of crime, vexatious prosecution has been neglected because it is almost impossible to prove in all but a handful of cases.[62] On the whole, the safest conclusion is simply that false accusations *must* have knowingly been made because, in theory at least, vaguely defined legal provisions against witchcraft 'gave an unprecedented power to all members of the community to solve their conflicts and to take revenge for anything'.[63] Contemporaries believed that many accusations were false. Scot warned that some 'maintaine and crie out for the execution of witches, that particularlie beleeve never a whit of that which is imputed unto them'; even the witch-finder Stearne conceded as much.[64] Although Keith Thomas rightly points out that fraudulent cases 'must be recognized as essentially parasitic to the witch-beliefs, and in no way their cause', unless an individual case was directly proven to be fraudulent, it remained as serious and real as an accusation where the motive was sincere.[65]

---

[60] KAO, QM/SB 1306–7, 1311, 1315; QM/SB 1265; QM/SI 1618/2/7; CCDRO, DCb/PRC 39/32 (1613–15), ff. 12ᵛ–15; PRC 39/33, ff. 19–19ᵛ.

[61] C. L'Estrange Ewen, *Witchcraft in the Star Chamber* (n.p., 1938), p. 9; Macfarlane, *Witchcraft*, pp. 16, 60.

[62] In general, see Douglas Hay, 'Prosecution and power. Malicious prosecution in the English courts, 1750–1850', in Douglas Hay and Francis Snyder, eds., *Prosecution and Policing in Britain 1750–1850* (Oxford, 1989), pp. 343–95. See also G. R. Quaife, *Godly Zeal and Furious Rage. The Witch in Early Modern Europe* (London, 1987), ch. 10; Gaskill, 'Witches and witchcraft accusations', pp. 70–3.

[63] Gábor Klaniczay, 'Hungary: the accusations and the universe of popular magic', in Ankarloo and Henningsen, eds., *Early Modern European Witchcraft*, pp. 238–9.

[64] Scot, *Discoverie of Witchcraft*, pp. 15, 17; Stearne, *Confirmation and Discovery*, p. 34. See also Bernard, *Guide to Grand-Jury Men*, pp. 77, 194–6; Fuller, *Profane State*, p. 351; John Webster, *The Displaying of Supposed Witchcraft* (London, 1677), ch. 14. Regarding the decline of witchcraft prosecutions, 'Transparently malicious charges were frequent enough to call into doubt a crime that was easy to suspect and very hard to prove': Michael MacDonald, *Witchcraft and Hysteria in Elizabethan London* (London, 1991), p. 52.

[65] Thomas, *Religion and the Decline of Magic*, p. 646.

There are a number of cases which might be explained in this way. At the Faversham trial in 1586, described above, Joan Cason vainly asserted her innocence, and instead blamed 'diverse matters and instances of the malicious dealings of hir adversaries against hir, reciting also certeine controversies betwixt hir and them, wherein they had doone hir open wrong'. As for maleficent magic using ivy-gum, she protested sadly, it was no more than a cure for toothache. At least one contemporary observed that the evidence was weak and justice was miscarried, and perhaps the most striking indication of fraud was the regret later shown by her enemies, some of whom 'wished her alive after she was hanged, that cried out for the hangman when she was alive'. In other cases the malicious streak seems even more evident. In 1651 twenty-five parishioners at River testified against Helen Dadd of Hougham for bewitching children and livestock. The grand jury threw out all the charges against her – including one for entertaining familiar spirits – except those brought by Thomas Hogbin, yeoman, for killing his horse and his three-year-old son. She was convicted and executed, but within a matter of weeks six persons came forward to testify against Hogbin for murder. Alice Hogbin deposed that the boy had 'told herr that his Father did drive him out of his House to worke and hee sayd that hee was not well able to goe by reason of his lamenes in his backe'; another witness saw the boy struck down with a rake, whereupon his father 'did give him a kicke and a spurne with his Foote such as this inform[an]t sayth shee wold have bine loath to have given to a dogg'. Two women who secretly examined the corpse deposed that Hogbin had denied anyone access to it so as to conceal the injuries he had inflicted. If this was indeed what happened, presumably Hogbin decided to capitalise on current opinion against Helen Dadd by indicting her for murder by witchcraft.[66]

V

Overall, one can see that whilst interpersonal disputes were often the source of witchcraft accusations, the feeling of guilt following the refusal of alms, as stressed in the model accusation, need not have played so

---

[66] Holinshed, *Chronicles*, III, pp. 1560–1; KAO, Q/SRc E3, ff. 62–3, 69–71, 75–6; E4, ff. 64, 70; Q/SB 2, f. 3; Q/SRc E4, ff. 3, 107. Despite the apparent weight of evidence against him, Hogbin was acquitted at Canterbury in 1652. In 1581 a syphilitic Kentish vicar prosecuted a woman for witchcraft against whom he was 'enviouslie bent', by which means he 'was cured or rather excused the shame of his disease': Scot, *Discoverie of Witchcraft*, pp. 5–6.

great a part. Resentment and a vengeful spirit between conflicting and competing parties of similar social status could suffice. When William Godfrey was accused, proceedings apparently followed the classic course of events: hostility and suspicion followed by misfortune, personal conviction, and, finally, by accusation. But Godfrey's social position relative to his accusers makes an explanation based on guilt seem implausible. Similar to William Lawse, tried for witchcraft in the same year, he was a middling self-sufficient landlord and householder with a family and servants. He certainly had no cause to demand anything from his neighbours and therefore gave them no reason to feel uneasy at not having fulfilled their charitable responsibilities towards him. Cases such as these seem to suggest two things: first, the operative existence of a broad scope of persons who could plausibly be accused as witches; second, the conscious or unconscious utilisation of witchcraft prosecutions by evenly matched opponents in order to break situations of deadlock, especially where patriarchal authority or superior rank could not be deployed. Accusations may also have occasionally served to redirect, even reverse, the direction in which power normally flowed in communities – between competing households as much as between feuding individuals – thereby enabling the weak to undermine the position of social superiors when conflicts arose.

In a summary of his argument, Macfarlane notes that his generalis-ations regarding strain placed upon neighbourly bonds, and the resulting accusation of witches as a reversal of guilt, are 'purely speculative and cannot be substantiated until detailed studies of the treatment of the poor and old . . . have been undertaken'.[67] Subsequently, however, the Macfarlane/Thomas framework has too often been uncritically accepted and the theoretical stereotype treated as in some way a definitive state-ment about witchcraft accusations in England. Method and result have accordingly been allowed to justify and reinforce one another, as one historian demonstrates when he unquestioningly advocates the export of 'well-established anthropological methods' to the study of witchcraft and praises the 'conceptual clarity' they produce, whilst referring to 'the now familiar generalisation that the vast majority of witches were poor, elderly women'.[68] It is clear that the experience of witchcraft in early

---

[67] Macfarlane, *Witchcraft*, pp. 204–7, 207n.
[68] Richard A. Horsley, 'Who were the witches? The social roles of the accused in the European witch trials', *Journal of Interdisciplinary History*, 9 (1979), 689, 694, 699–700.

modern Kent was not *necessarily* conditioned by status or gender, that accusers frequently might disregard familiar typologies, and that the prosecution of witches could reflect every sort of communal disturbance. Perhaps then, in a way, men like Godfrey and Lawse should be viewed as ordinary victims of the Witchcraft Act, rather than the exceptions to some artificially imposed rule.

In general, the value of comparative models of witchcraft prosecutions is open to question if they are used to provide ready-made answers rather than as sources of imaginative stimulation.[69] Some historians now favour a multicausal approach to the study of continental witchcraft because experience and circumstances were in fact so varied – and often the applicability of the stereotype so doubtful – even within the general 'European pattern'.[70] With this diversity in mind, there is a strong case for viewing English witchcraft as a variant of the European model rather than an exception to it – an approach which calls for comparative analysis within an early modern (as opposed to anthropological) context. The validity of Macfarlane and Thomas' comparisons to patterns of African witchcraft accusations is questionable anyway, due to differences in the economic, intellectual and legal structures of early modern European societies and their modern primitive counterparts – something Thomas himself has accepted. The final part of Macfarlane's study, moreover, in fact does more to illustrate the diversity of primitive beliefs in African countries than it does to justify the preceding interpretation of the English material.[71]

But perhaps African beliefs do have something to teach the student of

---

69 See E. P. Thompson, 'Anthropology and the discipline of historical context', *Midland History*, 1 (1972), 43; T. G. Ashplant and Adrian Wilson, 'Present-centred history and the problem of historical knowledge', *Historical Journal*, 31 (1988), 257–60.

70 Robin Briggs, *Communities of Belief. Cultural and Social Tension in Early Modern France* (Oxford, 1989), p. 396; Levack, *Witch-Hunt*, pp. 2–3; Marijke Gijswijt-Hofstra, 'The European witchcraft debate and the Dutch variant', *Social History*, 15 (1990), 181–94.

71 Thompson, 'Anthropology and the discipline of historical context', 46–8; Rowland, 'Fantasticall and devilishe persons', pp. 172–6, 189; Levack, *Witch-Hunt*, pp. 234–5; Midelfort, *Witch Hunting*, p. 4; William P. Monter, *Witchcraft in France and Switzerland. The Borderlands during the Reformation* (London, 1976), pp. 10–11; Ankarloo and Henningsen, eds., *Early Modern European Witchcraft*, 'Introduction', pp. 1–2; Ginzburg, *Ecstasies*, p. 4; Keith Thomas, 'An anthropology of religion and magic, II', *Journal of Interdisciplinary History*, 6 (1975), 92–3, 108; Thomas, 'The relevance of social anthropology to the historical study of English witchcraft', in Mary Douglas, ed., *Witchcraft Confessions and Accusations* (London, 1970), pp. 55–7, 71; J. A. Sharpe, 'Witches and persecuting societies', *Journal of Historical Sociology*, 3 (1990), 78; Macfarlane, *Witchcraft*, pp. 211–36.

English witchcraft, precisely because of this very diversity. It has been argued that instead of the model accusation which tends to formularise the experience of witchcraft, evidence from Kent in the sixteenth and seventeenth centuries favours a less reductionist method of inquiry. Witches were frequently integrated and productive men and women in the local community with occupations to pursue and families to support and be supportive. At the same time, the law which enabled individuals to prosecute witches did not circumscribe who could be accused and upon what grounds. In the light of this, perhaps there can be seen a maverick principle at work, producing patterns of activity as irregular and unpredictable as human nature itself. Accordingly, one might conclude that the versatility of codes of beliefs and behaviour visible in the communities of south-east England, as much as in the tribes of Africa, have been obscured by a process of theorisation and categorisation, and that the desire to understand and predict events has sometimes compromised the ability to observe and describe them.

If one general conclusion can be drawn from this randomness, perhaps it is that the early modern mind was different not only in the belief that witches possessed occult powers, but also in that people were willing to pursue personal quarrels with a degree of persistence and ruthlessness which, though appalling to us, may have fallen within the accepted mores of the period. One can easily imagine the potentially, and even essentially, hostile character of communities in which individuals or groups might harass an enemy even unto death, and in which harmony was constantly being broken and remade.[72] As other recent studies of European witchcraft have suggested, the Kent material shows that accusations resulted from a broader range of tensions than has commonly been allowed; and yet although traumatic social and economic change in the later sixteenth century may have exacerbated these tensions, it did not necessarily lead directly to an increase in witchcraft accusations from below. The appeal of such an idea is enhanced by Macfarlane's historical relocation of the onset of individualism, referred to in the first

---

[72] On endemic malice, see Lawrence Stone, *The Family, Sex and Marriage in England* (London, 1977), pp. 95–9; J. S. Morrill and J. D. Walter, 'Order and disorder in the English Revolution', in Fletcher and Stevenson, eds., *Order and Disorder*, p. 154; Peter Burke, *Popular Culture in Early Modern Europe* (London, 1978), pp. 176–7; Sabean, *Power in the Blood*, pp. 31–2, 53–4. 'Hatred, jealousy, and conflicts of interest ran through peasant society. The village was no happy and harmonious *Gemeinschaft*': Robert Darnton, *The Great Cat Massacre and Other Episodes in French Cultural History* (London, 1984), p. 33.

section of this chapter. Perhaps, then, the enmity and breaches of charity that could lead to such accusations should be seen less as a product of declining standards of neighbourliness, and more as a perennial aspect of relationships within neighbourhoods.[73]

To conclude, it is conceivable that such a strong emphasis was placed upon 'neighbourliness' in the period because in reality social relations were so commonly characterised by its dark reverse side: malice – an enduring, but often latent, prickly hostility which could be channelled consciously or unconsciously into prosecutions for witchcraft. Under these circumstances it is logical to suppose that the integrated and, above all, competitive person would be as vulnerable to such a charge as would a more marginal figure in the community. This leaves many questions unanswered about exactly why there was a rise of witchcraft prosecutions in the sixteenth and seventeenth centuries, and why regional variations appear to have been so marked. But for the moment it is sufficient to observe that, in the eighteenth century, endemic hostility of the sort described here did not cease to manifest itself in the form of witchcraft trials because enlightened or humanitarian opinion prevailed at village level, still less because this hostility abated. Rather, it was that the double-edged sword of the law, which had at least made possible the rise of prosecutions in the first place, no longer permitted the physical expression of malice through this outlet.

---

[73] On the relationship of endemic malice to witchcraft accusations, see Levack, *Witch-Hunt*, pp. 118–19; Robin Briggs, 'Witchcraft and popular mentality in Lorraine, 1580–1630', in Brian Vickers, ed., *Occult and Scientific Mentalities in the Renaissance* (Cambridge, 1984), p. 342. 'Hatred, fear and violence were endemic in rural England before the Industrial Revolution, and many witchcraft accusations were simply extensions of personal hatreds and family feuds': Michael MacDonald, *Mystical Bedlam. Madness, Anxiety and Healing in Seventeenth-Century England* (Cambridge, 1981), pp. 107–11, quotation at p. 109.

I am grateful to Keith Wrightson and Cynthia Herrup for comments on an earlier draft of this chapter, and to Patrick Collinson for providing me with a number of references.

11. *Patriarchal reconstruction and witch hunting*

MARIANNE HESTER

One of the most consistent yet least understood aspects of the early modern witch hunts is how accusation and persecution for witchcraft came to be largely directed against women, throughout Europe and the so-called New World.[1] In an attempt to question why the greater proportion of those accused of witchcraft were women, this chapter seeks to move beyond Keith Thomas' analysis in *Religion and the Decline of Magic* (1971) and also beyond the dichotomy of 'sex-related versus sex-specific' set up by Christina Larner's work.[2] Focusing mainly on English material, it argues that in our quest to understand the phenomenon of the witch hunts we have to see male–female conflictual relations as an integral part of the process of accusation and persecution. The accusation of women was not merely a reflection of an age-old stereotype, nor merely the by-product of a patriarchal society; the witch hunts were a part of, and one example of,[3] the ongoing mechanisms for

---

[1] Monter has, for instance, pointed out that sex remains the most important, because most consistent, feature of most witchcraft accusations: E. W. Monter, *Witchcraft in France and Switzerland* (Cornell, 1976), p. 119; and Demos has stressed that the one most consistent feature both transnationally and cross-culturally of the witches was their female sex: J. Demos, *Entertaining Satan* (New York, 1982), p. 63. A few places such as Finland and parts of France saw greater numbers of men, or equal numbers of men and women, accused for using witchcraft: A. Heikkinen and T. Kervinen, 'Finland: the male domination', in B. Ankerloo and B. Henningsen, *Early Modern European Witchcraft* (Oxford, 1990), pp. 319–38. This does not, however, detract from the argument presented in this chapter regarding the history of the construction of the witch. Where traditionally the witch had been perceived as male, as was the case in Finland, during the period of the early modern witch hunts the number of women accused of witchcraft rose, thus indicating the influence of the construction of the witch as female elsewhere.

[2] C. Larner, *Enemies of God* (Oxford, 1983).

[3] Monter suggests that acts such as infanticide were also a focus for prosecution of women in the early modern period to a greater extent than had been the case previously. It thus appears that during the sixteenth and seventeenth centuries there were a variety

social control of women within a general context of social change and the reconstruction of a patriarchal society. It is generally recognised that Europe in the early modern period experienced a variety of major changes in terms of demography, ideology, economy, religions and political systems. Levack has rightly pointed out that change is not a feature unique to this period, and that 'change' alone cannot explain the witch hunts at this time.[4] None the less, during the sixteenth and seventeenth centuries, Europe experienced changes and a restructuring of society which created many uncertainties, ambiguities, tensions and conflicts – not least with regard to male–female relations.[5] Within this context witch persecution served – in a dynamic rather than functional sense – as a means of recreating the male status quo in the emerging social order. This chapter examines some of the evidence for the relationship between witchcraft and patriarchal reconstruction, in particular links between 'the female' and the witch, the gendering of expectations and meanings and male–female conflict with regard to resources.

Keith Thomas, talking of course primarily about the English context, states that 'the judicial records reveal two essential facts about accused witches: they were poor, and they were usually women' (p. 520). He places witchcraft within its social environment, arguing that the answer to who the witches were can be found at the village level where allegations arose. Essentially,[6] Thomas argues that witchcraft accusation was related to failure to carry out some hitherto recognised social obligation; a poor woman would ask for charity or to borrow essential supplies (often from another, slightly better off, woman), but would be

---

of attempts to control female sexual behaviour in particular, and women specifically, through both formal witchcraft accusation and by legal retribution against other sexual 'deviance'. The accusation of witchcraft was only one of the formal means serving to control women socially at the time.

4 B. Levack, *The Witch-hunt in Early Modern Europe* (London, 1987), pp. 139–42.
5 S. D. Amussen, *An Ordered Society* (Oxford, 1988); J. Klaits, *Servants of Satan* (Bloomington, 1985). Taking Amussen's evidence concerning the threat to the gender hierarchy as his starting point, Sharpe suggests affirmatively that: 'the notion that the Elizabethan and Jacobean periods experienced a crisis in gender relations, one facet of a more general concern for social hierarchy and social order, seems worth pursuing, and might well have a bearing on the frequency with which women, and women of a certain type, were accused of witchcraft', J. Sharpe, 'Witchcraft and women in seventeenth-century England: some Northern evidence', *Continuity and Change*, 6 (1991), 183.
6 And echoing Macfarlane's work: *Witchcraft in Tudor and Stuart England* (London, 1970).

denied and eventually, if misfortune happened to the one who had denied her, would be accused of using witchcraft to cause the misfortune. This classic model of witchcraft accusation has since been shown to have a wider application than merely for England,[7] although one might question whether it actually explains why it was women who predominated amongst the accused. For Thomas, this scenario of social relations in a context of changing, conflictual, moral obligations does explain why the accused were older, poor and often widowed women. He points out that during the late Tudor and early Stuart period, when formal witchcraft accusation was at its height, village conflicts around neighbourliness grew especially acute. The erosion of the manorial system with loss of customary tenancies and common land created poverty while at the same time breaking up old cooperative village communities. Widows were particularly adversely affected by these changes leaving them vulnerable to witchcraft accusation. As he concludes:

> This deterioration in the position of the dependent and elderly helps to explain why witches were primarily women, and probably old ones, many of them widowed . . . Their names appear among the witchcraft indictments, just as they do among the recipients of parochial relief. For they were the persons most dependent upon neighbourly support. (p. 562)

Thomas (like Macfarlane) clearly shies away from seeing this outcome for women as in any way related to male–female conflict. He argues that because the misogynistic or 'blatantly sexual aspects' of witchcraft common in continental literature such as the *Malleus Maleficarum* were not a feature of English trials, and especially because the accusations were often from one woman to another rather than between women and men, 'the idea that witch-prosecutions reflected a war between the sexes must be discounted' (p. 568). Thomas thus presents a complex analysis of possible links between early modern social relations at the village level, beliefs about witchcraft and neighbourliness, and social change which incorporates women's position as dependent poor and especially as poor widows. But, despite his claims to the contrary, he does not actually manage to explain why it should be women rather than men who are in this position of vulnerability, of dependency and poverty. This

---

[7] Demos, *Entertaining Satan*; A. M. Walker and E. H. Dickerman, ' "A woman under the influence": a case of alleged possession in sixteenth-century France', *Sixteenth-Century Journal*, 22 (1991), 534–54. Thomas' outline also bears a close resemblance to the recent witchcraft accusations Favret-Saada discusses in relation to the Bocage in France: *Deadly Words* (Cambridge, 1980).

is because his somewhat positivistic approach to the material detailing the accused and victims of witchcraft does not allow him to examine the process of gendering of the social relations he otherwise so eloquently describes.

Since *Religion and the Decline of Magic* was first published in the early 1970s the work of Christina Larner has probably had the greatest impact on historians' perceptions of why it was largely women who were accused of witchcraft during the early modern period. Larner argued that the witch hunts in early modern Europe (and especially in Scotland – the area of her researches) were sex-*related* with regard to women but not sex-*specific*.[8] Larner did not give precise definitions for these terms, but indicated that the term 'sex-related' meant that the witch hunts were 'one degree removed from an attack on women as such' (p. 92). 'Sex-specific' would only be applied if all the characteristics of the witch were attributable to women, and in practice, she argued, this is not the case because 'the two principal characteristics of the witch, that is malice and alleged supernatural power, are human rather than female character-istics' (p. 92). She concludes that while the vast majority of those accused of and those prosecuted for witchcraft were women, the witch hunts were not actually about women hunting, but were more to do with the imposition of a Christian political ideology. It was the age-old gender stereotype of the witch that made them sex-related. There are, however, some problems with Larner's dichotomy of sex-related versus sex-specific. For a start, Larner's own work is actually more ambiguous than the dichotomy that has arisen from it suggests. As she says when discussing the link between witchcraft and the type of person accused, there is some evidence to suggest that the relationship is direct: 'Witch-hunting is woman-hunting or at least it is the hunting of women who do not fulfill the male view of how women ought to conduct themselves' (p. 100).

Secondly, defining 'sex-specific' by reference to a set of character-istics which can seemingly only apply to one sex ignores the possibility of change in the perception and interpretation of any characteristics attributable to men or women. Neither sex has a monopoly on any characteristics or behaviour – except as constructed and specified at any particular time. With regard to the early modern period there is some evidence to suggest that the principal characteristics of the witch were being perceived increasingly as female characteristics,[9] including a

---

[8] Larner, *Enemies of God*.   [9] Klaits, *Servants*, pp. 58–9.

perception of malice and use of supernatural power as more likely to be female characteristics.

This leads us to another related problem, that of placing as central to witch hunting the imposition of a Christian political ideology and the argument that the sex-relatedness of accusations is separate from this and merely to do with the age-old stereotype of the witch. This misses the point (otherwise implicit in the quotation from Larner) that gender relations are an integral part of Christian political ideology, constructing and being constructed by this.[10] It is not enough, to use Scarre's words, 'to say that more women than men were tried for witchcraft because the stereotypical witch was a woman'.[11] Finally, Larner's use of the dichotomy of sex-related versus sex-specific has unfortunately set up a dualism which it is often difficult to look beyond – where historians tend to concur emphatically with her argument of sex-relatedness, while not thinking beyond this and merely ridiculing and marginalising the argument that the witch-hunts were indeed sex-specific.

If we *are* to use the terms 'sex-related' and 'sex-specific' at all, then we should use the terms to reflect a more complex situation. I would suggest that the witch hunts were not merely sex-related or merely sex-specific, but – at different times and at different levels – both related to and specific to women. We may, for instance, consider beliefs amongst the learned elite and the development of a legal framework for dealing with witchcraft, especially prior to the witch hunts, as sex-related; while at a local level, amongst the peasantry, beliefs and activities against witches were – in most European countries – sex-specific. If we focus on the development of the witchcraft construct amongst the learned elite in the centuries leading up to the witch hunts, we see that unequal male–female social relations were also reflected in and constructed by the emerging notion of the witch. One of the results, a sexual double standard with female sexuality presented as inferior to that of men, is obvious in texts such as the *Malleus Maleficarum*.[12]

But in this pre-witch-hunt period the focus of persecution was those persons considered by the Catholic church as 'heretics', including both

---

[10] And see Briggs, chapter 2 in this book, for a critique of Larner's focus on one central reason, rather than many reasons, for the witch hunts.

[11] G. Scarre, *Witchcraft and Magic in Sixteenth and Seventeenth Century Europe* (London, 1987), p. 51.

[12] H. Kramer and J. Sprenger, *Malleus Maleficarum* (Nuremberg, 1496). See also C. Merchant, *The Death of Nature* (London, 1980).

men and women;[13] although at a local and informal level, persecution of those deemed to be witches was probably more specific to women even then. Cohn, for example, documents instances of local lynchings, supposedly of witches, that all appear to be of women.[14] In most of the countries affected by witch hunts we see an orientation of persecution away from men, and also away from the elite, towards women and in particular poorer, older and often widowed women during the sixteenth and seventeenth centuries. Formal witch accusation changes from being merely sex-related to being more sex-specific at this time.[15]

We need to move beyond the dichotomy set up by Larner's work so that we may develop a more sophisticated analysis of why the majority of those accused of witchcraft during the sixteenth and seventeenth centuries were women, and this requires a deeper look at male–female relations (or gender relations) during this period than most historians have so far attempted.[16] If we are to understand how a *female* witch stereotype developed, and how and why witch hunting was directly linked to sex/gender, we must take into account that European society prior to, as well as during, the witch hunts was male dominated or patriarchal, with a resultant gendering of social relations, social structures and discourses at many different levels. We need in particular to take into account the dynamic nature of patriarchy, where continuity of inequality between men and women relies on changing forms of oppression over time. As I have pointed out elsewhere, societies that are male dominated rely on constructions of 'the female' which present women as both different and inferior to men; and sexualisation, or eroticisation, of 'the female' in a variety of ways over time, is particularly important in constructing, and thereby maintaining, this difference.[17] Where the early modern witch hunts are concerned we have much evidence of this sexualising process, where it was particularly female sexuality that was perceived to make women different from men.

[13] Levack, *Witch-hunt*; Klaits, *Servants*. Klaits suggests that in earlier witch trials 'men had comprised close to half of the accused' (p. 52).

[14] N. Cohn, *Europe's Inner Demons* (London, 1975).

[15] Klaits also appears to document this change from sex-related to sex-specific, although without using these terms. He attributes the increased focus on women as the accused during the early modern period to 'a dramatic rise in fear and hatred of women during the era of the Reformation', p. 52.

[16] For a good example of an approach to the witch-hunts that takes male–female relations into account at the heart of the discussion see C. Karlsen, *The Devil in the Shape of a Woman* (New York, 1988).

[17] M. Hester, *Lewd Women and Wicked Witches* (London, 1992).

Male sexuality was not discussed in a similarly negative manner.[18] Thomas also provides evidence of this for England from Robert Burton who wrote 'of women's unnatural, unsatiable lust'.[19] Women were considered sexually insatiable and prone therefore to sinful and deviant behaviour, by contrast to the 'norm' which was construed as heterosexual, procreative sex under male control.[20]

In recent years there has been a tremendous development in the theorising of the processes involved in what Thomas terms the 'war between the sexes', that is the oppressive relations, structures and discourses that characterise patriarchy for women. Hobby, talking specifically about women's activities within the patriarchal context of seventeenth-century England, has outlined the many ways women's lives were curtailed by comparison to those of men, but also how women acted within this context as subjects making choices, albeit limited ones: 'Women find ways of coping with their oppression and ways of resisting it, but this capitulation or resistance is not free or self-determined: it can normally only occur within the limits and on the terms of the framework set by the dominant group, men.'[21]

During the period of the witch-hunts the patriarchal ideal for women was that they should be quiet (not scolds) and subservient to their husbands (not cuckolding the latter). Marriage, as the site of a heterosexual, procreative sexuality under the control of men, was – as expressed in many sermons, pamphlets and other literature at the time – deemed the only appropriate place for any sexual activity to take place.[22] These ideas were expressed most obviously by the middle and upper classes, but they were also reflected in attitudes towards and decisions about the behaviour of women from the lower classes as exemplified by church court cases: many women were punished through these courts for bearing an illegitimate child and for fornication, that is, heterosexual

---

[18] Sexuality is socially constructed and we should more appropriately talk about 'sexualities' if we are to take individuals' experiences into account. I am using the terms 'female sexuality' and 'male sexuality' to convey the dominant gender ideology of the time. See also discussion about men's fears concerning women's sexuality, in Roberts, chapter 7 in this volume.

[19] In K. Thomas, *Religion and the Decline of Magic* (London, 1971), p. 568.

[20] See Amussen, *An Ordered Society*; M. Hester, 'The dynamics of male domination using the witchcraze in sixteenth and seventeenth century England as case study', *Women's Studies International Forum*, 13 (1990); Hester, *Lewd Women*.

[21] E. Hobby, *Virtue of Necessity* (London, 1988), p. 8.

[22] See Amussen, *An Ordered Society*; S. Shepherd, *The Women's Sharpe Revenge* (London, 1985); L. Woodbridge, *Women and the English Renaissance* (Urbana, 1986); L. B. Wright, *Middle Class Culture in Elizabethan England* (Chapel Hill, 1935).

intercourse outside marriage.[23] Witchcraft accusation must be seen in this context of widespread fears that women were by no means complying with the ideal of the quiet compliant wife.[24]

The women accused of witchcraft may be seen as victims of the witch hunts, but the construct of the female as an actively sexual, hence sinful being, upon which accusation of witchcraft relied, shows us that women were by no means considered passive or compliant. Women were perceived to be morally weak by comparison with men, but this could also make them appear ultimately stronger than men.[25] Women's supposedly insatiable and immoral sexuality was likely to lead them into allegiance with the devil who could fulfil their sexual desires even better, so it was feared, than mere mortal men. In the English trial material this allegiance was explicit within some of the later trials such as the 1645 trials in Essex involving Matthew Hopkins, but also implicit through the symbolism of the familiar and witches' marks in other trials.[26] Clive Holmes notes that Thomas Cooper, in a text of

---

[23] M. Ingram provides extensive examples and interpretations of such cases from the church courts: *Church Courts, Sex and Marriage in England 1570–1640* (Cambridge, 1987); and P. E. H. Hair lists many original indictments and outcomes: *Before the Bawdy Court* (London, 1972). It is important to note how often women ended up accused of fornication and illegitimacy without having intended either. Precisely because the penalties were high, both legally and socially, for women who had committed either of these offences, it may be expected that women did not commit them willingly. See Amussen, *An Ordered Society*, p. 116.

[24] This general view of 'the female' was to remain dominant until the end of the witch persecution, as indicated by John Sprint's *The Bride-Woman's Councellor*, a sermon preached towards the end of the seventeenth century. Arguing, in a typical way, that woman was responsible for the original sin and led men into damnation through association with the female body, Spring suggests that: 'tis but fair and just, that she, who hath been so greatly instrumental of so much Mischief and Misery to Man, should be actively engaged to please and comfort him', J. Sprint, *The Bride-Woman's Councellor* (London, 1709, first published 1699), pp. 6–7. The quote from Sprint also indicates the change that was to take place over the sixteenth and seventeenth centuries towards a greater emphasis on women's role as chaste as well as dutiful wife. Indeed the change in (ruling class) gender ideology, which devalued women in a different but equally oppressive way, appears to have played a very important role in facilitating the eventual decline of the formal witch-hunts. The 'new ideology' changed the perception of women from that of 'powerful and threatening witch' to that of 'hysterical woman', thereby re-emphasising women's (subordinate) place in marriage. Keith Thomas makes a similar point: *Religion and the Decline of Magic*, p. 569.

[25] For the role of demonic possession in the construction of women as the weaker sex see C. Holmes, 'Women: witnesses and witches', *Past and Present*, 140 (1993), 45–78; and Karlsen, *The Devil in the Shape of a Woman*. For further discussion of sexualisation and witchcraft accusation in a number of different countries see A. Barstow, *Witchcraze* (London, 1994).

[26] See Sharpe, ch. 9, this volume; Klaits, *Servants*, p. 56.

1617,[27] 'made an explicit attempt to conflate the familiar's sucking blood from the witch with the continental discussion of the coven and the witch's relationship with Satan'.[28] Bernard's *Guide to Grand-Jury Men*, a decade later, provided a fully argued theory of this link. And *sexualisation* of the witches' mark was made especially apparent after 1630s, with the publication of the fourth edition of *The Country Justice* by lawyer and JP, Michael Dalton. In this, Dalton cites Bernard 'with enthusiastic approval', but also changes Bernard's insistence that witches' marks may be found anywhere – although in 'very hidden places' – to a more explicit focus on the genitals. Thereafter, magistrates recommended that the pre-trial body search for witch's marks be 'focused upon the genital area'.[29]

In the circular, self-fulfilling, gender discourse of the witch hunt period women were perceived as more likely to be sexually deviant than men because women were by definition (like Eve in the Garden of Eden) sexually deviant. And deviance, in a God-fearing and deeply super-stitious society, was construed as witchcraft. James VI of Scotland (later also James I of England) wrote, for example, in his *Daemonologie*:

> The reason is easie: for as that sexe is frailer than men is, so it is eas-ier to be intrapped in these grosse snares of the Devill, as was well proved to be true, by the Serpents deceiving of Eve at the beginning, which makes him the homelier with that sex ever since.[30]

Here we have a direct example of the link between the construction of 'the female' as different and inferior to men and 'the witch'. It was men who stood to gain by the linking of witchcraft and 'the female' because it provided them with a greater moral and social status than women, and also, as I shall discuss further below, because it probably allowed them greater access to resources and potentially lucrative crafts and trades than women. The belief in witchcraft, as found during the sixteenth and seventeenth centuries, must be seen as a gendered ideology serving the material interests of men within patriarchal relations, and not merely, as

---

[27] T. Cooper, *The Mystery of Witch-craft: Discovering the Truth, Nature, Occasion, Growth and Power Thereof, with the Detection and Punishment of the Same, as also the Several Strategems of Sathan* (1617), pp. 88–92.

[28] Holmes, 'Women: witnesses and witches', 67 n. 57.

[29] Holmes points out how Dalton in his summary shifts the language of Bernard's argument: the teats, 'these the Devil marks . . . be often in their secretest parts, and therefore require diligent and careful search'. Holmes, "Women: witnesses and witches', 70–1.

[30] Cited in Larner, *Enemies of God*, p. 93.

Thomas suggests, as a means of dealing with guilt after 'unneighbourly' behaviour.

The age-old female stereotype of the witch does not, as both Thomas and Larner indicate, in itself explain why women predominated amongst the accused during the early modern period. We have to look to the general context of male–female relations, conflict and discourse to gain a better understanding of how the construct of 'the female' became synonymous with the witch. The process of gendering is of central importance: that is, the process of construction and positioning of women (by themselves, other women and men) as inferior and subordinate to men, and the many subtle or not so subtle pressures underlying such constructions and positioning. General beliefs about witchcraft in the early modern period were linked to sex/gender in such a way that it was expected that women and not men would use witchcraft for retribution and to cause harm – that is, there was a gendering of expectations and meanings.

Delphy has pointed out, with regard to social relations in French peasant society, that it is the sex of the individual that determines how a task is perceived rather than the nature of the task itself.[31] We can see this process clearly in trial material from England, Europe and New England, where men and women might carry out similar activities but only women end up accused of witchcraft, or where it is women who end up accused of men's misdemeanours. One pattern we are all familiar with from the trial material involves the suspect asking someone from another household, usually a woman, for food, other household items and even money. When refused this, the refuser or her/his family subsequently suffers death or illness. The woman making the demand is then accused of witchcraft. But if a man makes demands of a woman then it still the woman who is accused of witchcraft – as in the case of John Chaundeler and Elleine Smithe at the 1579 trial in Chelmsford. The pamphlet for the trial tells us that Elleine Smithe inherited some money from Alice, her mother, which Alice's widowed husband, John Chaundeler, then demanded for himself. It transpires that John and Elleine have fallen out over his demand for the money. Subsequently John Chaundeler dies, and before his death states that Elleine bewitched him so that he was unable to eat or digest meat. The result is that she ends up as the accused.

In another instance, from the same trial, it is Thomas Prat who takes

---

[31] C. Delphy, *The Main Enemy: A Materialist Analysis of Women's Oppression* (London, 1977).

Mother Staunton's grain but it is Mother Staunton who ends up accused of witchcraft. The pamphlet for the trial describes Mother Staunton walking past Thomas Prat's house with some grain. He wants some for his chickens and takes it from her. He has previously equivocated about whether or not she is a witch, stating at one time that she is not but having on another occasion 'raced her face with a Nedle' and subsequently believed himself bewitched.[32] When his chickens eat Mother Staunton's grain three or four dozen of them die, supposedly providing evidence that *she* has bewitched them.

I have already indicated that Thomas in *Religion and the Decline of Magic*, amongst others, does not agree that the witch-hunts may be linked directly to male–female conflict or sex struggle. Since we find from the trial material, both English and other European, that women who were accused of witchcraft largely used witchcraft against other women, and that accusations were often directed by women against women, Thomas argues that this shows there was a conflict *between women* rather than a struggle between the sexes. Others have more convincingly attributed this situation to women's position and general lack of power in a patriarchal society, where apparent use of witchcraft became an alternative for women 'incapable of using the more normal or socially approved means of revenge such as physical violence . . . or recourse to law courts', that is, unable to use the means usually employed by men.[33]

Larner echoed by Sharpe has also suggested that while men use physical violence, women are more likely to use verbal violence as represented by cursing. Thomas gives numerous examples of cursing leading to an accusation of witchcraft, but, although his examples are almost exclusively of women, he makes no mention of this fact. He quotes Thomas Cooper's 'stock pattern' of the link between cursing and witchcraft accusation: 'When a bad-tongued woman shall curse a party, and death shall shortly follow, this is a shrewd token that she is a witch.'[34] Yet while Cooper clearly takes a gendered view of the curser,

---

[32] Hester, *Lewd Women*, pp. 173–40. Laura Gowing, in her discussion of women's slander litigation in early modern London, describes how scratching the face and especially the nose of a woman was a punishment indicating that she was a whore. See 'Language, power and the law', in J. Kermode and G. Walker, (eds.), *Women, Crime and the Courts* (London, 1994). We can speculate that to 'race [Mother Staunton's] face with a nedle' similarly symbolised that she was being presented in sexualised terms; women accused as witches were often presented as sexually deviant.

[33] Monter, *Witchcraft in France and Switzerland*, p. 124, and see Sharpe, 'Witchcraft and women'.

[34] Thomas, *Religion and the Decline of Magic*, p. 512.

Thomas does not take this up, instead concluding in gender-neutral terms that cursing 'was a means by which the weak and defenceless tried to avenge themselves upon their enemies' (p. 512).[35]

Seeing witchcraft as a form of negative power available to women in a particular inegalitarian context is an important part of the overall picture of the witch hunts, but we must also be careful not to lose sight of the complexity of male–female relations that such use of witchcraft by women entails. It is too easy to end up[36] by focusing on women's use of witchcraft and women's accusations against one another as a problem related largely to women and women's communities, that is as women's problem, rather than as an outcome of a wider patriarchal context. Holmes provides some interesting evidence of men's and women's relative social positioning and the process of formal witchcraft accusation suggesting that women's accusations against each other were indeed secondary to men bringing the cases to court. Using data from the English home circuit, he argues that it was primarily men who brought charges of witchcraft, while women played a more ancillary role:

> men, usually those of some status in their communities, were the more engaged participants. It was they who brought charges and who orchestrated the prosecution . . . Women, though active in the creation of local suspicions through gossip, and in the deployment of the traditional protective therapies and techniques that ratified accusation, were ancillaries in the formal procedures of quarter sessions and assizes.

We need to consider that women's social position made them vulnerable to becoming witches, but also vulnerable to 'possession' and to

---

[35] See M. Ingram, 'Scolding women cucked or washed', in Kermode and Walker, *Women, Crime and the Courts*, p. 48 for discussion of cursing and in particular scolding as a specifically female offence. Ingram points out that in Tudor and Stuart times ' "scold" was a strongly negative term, in destructive impact only second to "whore" . . . as a pejorative label applied to women. Yet it was also redolent of female strength and power, since it was traditionally supposed that a scold was capable of outfacing the devil.' (Ibid.)

The punishment of women convicted specifically of scolding appears to parallel witchcraft accusation in that it became more severe in the same period as witchcraft became a major female crime, that is, from the mid-sixteenth to the mid-seventeenth century. See ibid., p. 57; D. Underdown, 'The taming of the scold: the enforcement of patriarchal authority in early modern England', in A. Fletcher and J. Stevenson, eds., *Order and Disorder in Early Modern England* (Cambridge, 1985), pp. 116–36.

[36] As Sharpe does to some extent in 'Witchcraft and women'.

becoming bewitched.[37] Furthermore, women were often the ones in charge of the domestic goods the witch requested, and it was between women that the related transactions of lending and borrowing were likely to take place. Material from other societies and periods also gives us some important clues about the role women may have in relation to other women. We find that within patriarchal societies, women are often placed in the position of moral gatekeepers who socially control other women, and that there are various ideological, material and psychological pressures on them to do so. By acting as moral gatekeepers they may feel valued or at least have some power, even if their actions at the same time place both themselves and other women more firmly within patriarchy. The role women have in contemporary and historical Middle Eastern and North African societies, for instance, of carrying out cliterodectomies on other women is a case in point. Nawal El Sadawi explains how older female relatives (mothers, grandmothers) are the ones who have the 'privilege' to carry out these operations, which reinforce women's inferiority and sexual servitude to men.[38]

Within the particular patriarchal context of early modern Europe, then, use of witchcraft was a means (albeit negative) by which women could increase their power. There are examples in the trial pamphlets and records of women using witchcraft to better their situation in many different ways. When we look more closely at witch trial material, it is also apparent, however, that witchcraft beliefs were by no means hegemonic among the women accused of witchcraft, or those providing evidence. In the trial pamphlets from Essex we find that, while some of the women probably did believe that they had or could have used witchcraft, others are described as not sharing this belief and appeared to be much more sceptical about witchcraft. For example, at the 1566 trial at Chelmsford one of the accused, Elizabeth Frauncis, appears to believe that she could and did use witchcraft to procure, amongst other things,

---

[37] Holmes, 'Women: witnesses and witches', p. 76; Demos, *Entertaining Satan*; Karlsen, *The Devil in the Shape of a Woman*; R. C. Sawyer, ' "Strangely handled in all her lyms": witchcraft and healing in Jacobean England', *Journal of Social History*, 22 (1989), 461–85.

　　In other socio-historical contexts some of the parameters may of course be different. For example, in the present-day notion of witchcraft on Santa Catarina island, Southern Brazil, it is still the case that women are deemed witches but they use their witchcraft exclusively against children and men rather than against other women: S. Weidner Maluf, 'Witches and witchcraft: a study about representations of female power on Santa Catarina island', *International Sociology* 7 (1992), 225–34.

[38] N. El Sadawi, *The Hidden Face of Eve* (London, 1981).

sheep and a wealthy husband via the cat-familiar Satan. By contrast, in a 1582 trial at St Osyth, Elizabeth Bennet (who is said to deny that she herself used witchcraft) is shown to attempt to explain how she thinks an accusation against another woman, Ales Newman, can be understood in more 'rational' terms without recourse to witchcraft. She is recorded as saying that Ales was merely angry at Johnson, the collector for the poor, because he did not give her the handout she required, although what she says ends up being tied into the evidence against Ales, because the words she uses to signify anger – 'harded speeches' – are at the same time construed as a sign of women's misdemeanour, as cursing, and hence witchcraft. We see here an example of the gendering not only of language and meanings, but of expectations about women's behaviour.[39]

At a local level we thus see women using the means available to them to improve their condition, but we also see how the constructs which led them to use witch-like behaviour at the same time construed them as witches – whether they wanted this or not. At a local level, use of witchcraft can be seen as a part of the day to day activities of the 'women's community' but – crucially – relying on wider patriarchal gendered notions of the witch, and elite ideas about the unruliness of women and the need to control them. Witchcraft accusations may therefore, to a large extent, be situated (as Thomas situates them) within the women's community, but they were integrally linked to and served to reinforce – or reconstruct – the male status quo.

Finally I want to look at the male–female conflict around resources that formed a part of the contextual background to the early modern witch hunts, as already hinted at by the case of Elleine Smithe's inheritance and John Chaundeler's claims on it. There appears to be a link between male–female relations, economic change and witchcraft accusation – even if we cannot always establish a direct link between individuals accused of witchcraft and specific instances of male–female conflict around resources and livelihoods.

In taking early modern England as our example, we have to think of a society with a rapid increase in population, and resultant pressure on resources;[40] with women outnumbering men, yet with decreasing means of livelihood for women. Convents had been closed during the

---

[39] Hester, *Lewd Women*, pp. 166–7, 183–4. It is of course problematic to take the pamphlets as representing the views of the women themselves as the pamphlets were not written by the women but by others, and always men, usually present at the trials.

[40] Thomas, *Religion and the Decline of Magic*; R. A. Houlbrooke, *The English Family* (London, 1984); Macfarlane, *Witchcraft in Tudor and Stuart England*.

Reformation, and women were being excluded from crafts and trades such as weaving and brewing as well as from the guilds; enclosure of common land (already happening in Essex at this time) exacerbated the difficulties of a growing mass of landless peasants, amongst other effects removing the space for grazing for women's livestock.[41] Thomas, as indicated earlier, does link some of these economic changes to the impoverishment and dependence of certain lower-class women, and especially widows. This may also be understood by the more widely acknowledged concept of the 'feminisation of poverty' – a concept that also applies within the present global economic context.[42]

A number of historians have documented how the period of pre-capitalism and early capitalism, that is, the early modern period, saw a deterioration of women's role in production.[43] Moreover, Chris Middleton indicates that it was specifically men who became predominant in the occupations which were foremost in the development of the emergent capitalist production (as had also been the case in the development of the earlier feudal production). He argues that capitalist production developed at the expense of 'sexual equality', that is, at the expense of women.[44] Sylvia Walby suggests in addition that when there are changes in the economic sphere, such as changes in production methods, conflict around male–female power relations takes place in order to ensure male dominance.[45] We can indeed find some evidence of a realignment of male–female power relations in the sixteenth and seventeenth centuries due to the major changes taking place in the economy at that time. Evidence of women's work, in areas such as brewing and weaving, suggests that there was a struggle between the sexes around making a living, which also had the effect of ensuring that men rather than women obtained the better positions in, and thus control of, the emerging capitalist economic structure. Overall, patriarchy was maintained within the developing economy, and women's relative dependence on men ensured.

---

[41] See Amussen, *An Ordered Society*.

[42] H. Scott, *The Feminisation of Poverty* (London, 1984).

[43] See L. Charles and L. Duffin, eds., *Women and Work in Pre-Industrial England* (London, 1985); J. Kelly, *Women, History and Theory* (Chicago, 1986); A. Clark, *Working Life of Women in the Seventeenth Century* (London [1919], 1982).

[44] C. Middleton, 'The sexual division of labour in feudal England', *New Left Review*, 113–14 (1979), 147–68; and 'Women's labour and the transition to pre-industrial capitalism', in Charles and Duffin, eds., *Women and Work*, pp. 181–206.

[45] S. Walby, *Patriarchy at Work* (Cambridge, 1986).

The case of brewing provides an interesting example. Brewing is acknowledged as an important industry in the early modern period, because beer, and in particular ale (brewed without hops), was the staple drink of men, women and children at most meals. Women did the brewing of ale needed for immediate consumption by the household, and prior to the sixteenth and seventeenth centuries women also brewed ale for sale. Judith Bennett has documented how the exclusion of women from brewing took place over a considerable period, but it was during the sixteenth and seventeenth centuries that brewing finally changed from a female to a male occupation. Excluding women from brewing occurred alongside the separation of brewing (by men) from the sale (by women) of beer, a policy pursued by the government with the aim of imposing stricter regulation and supposedly simplifying the collection of taxes, as well as improving the quality of the beer brewed. Bennett concludes:

> All of these changes were very slow and uneven, proceeding over the course of several centuries and affecting different regions of the country at different times and in different ways. But their overall effect was clear; by 1700, brewing, which had been a home-based trade dominated by women four centuries earlier, was becoming a factory-based industry controlled by a steadily shrinking group of wealthy males.[46]

Alongside the other economic changes mentioned by Thomas, the changes to the brewing industry must seriously have reduced the earning capacities of village women.[47] It was only widows who retained access to brewing through inheritance from their husbands. Michael Roberts documents how the *selling* of ale became an occupation informally reserved for poor widows during this period.[48] Sue Wright similarly points out that in the urban environment of Tudor and Stuart Salisbury there were numerous women, especially widows, who were licensed as alehousekeepers (the poor end of the market) but few as innkeepers (the richer part of the market).[49]

---

[46] J. M. Bennett, 'Misogyny, popular culture, and women's work', *History Workshop Journal*, 31 (1991), 166–88, quotation at 169.

[47] Clark, *Working Life*, p. 228.

[48] M. Roberts, '"Words they are women, and deeds they are men": images of work and gender in early modern England', in Charles and Duffin, eds., *Women and Work*, pp. 122–80.

[49] S. Wright, '"Churmaids, huswyfes and hucksters": the employment of women in Tudor and Stuart Salisbury', in Charles and Duffin, eds., *Women and Work*, pp. 100–21.

With regard to the discussion in this chapter there are a number of important issues which arise from the example of the brewing industry. These include: the construction of women as incapable of brewing; the link of this construction to the witch; and the position of widows as both brewers and ale-sellers.

Bennett shows convincingly how the popular and also negative representation of the alewife, in 'prose, poetry, ballads, drama, carvings, sculpture, and drawings' (p. 169) was linked to her demise. For instance, the early sixteenth-century poem, *The Tunning of Elynor Rummyng* depicts the alewife Elynor Rummyng as a grotesque and ridiculous old woman, who is of dubious religious and sexual virtue, and a highly unscrupulous tradeswoman (p. 170). She 'is almost a stock figure in misogynistic literature: a grotesque, old witch-like woman', but also 'a corrupt tradeswoman who sells her customers adulterated drink at hard-driven prices in a disgusting atmosphere' (p. 171). Bennett argues that such popular representations undermined the position of the alewife by questioning her general trustworthiness, while at the same time allowing men to be seen in a much more positive light. The construction of the alewife as different and inferior to the male brewer often relied, like the construction of the witch, on her sexualisation or eroticisation, and we find, in the example of Elynor Rummyng, allusions to her also being associated with witchcraft: she entertained a customer who 'seemed to be a witch', she dressed up 'after the Saracen's guise' and 'like an Egyptian', and 'the devil and she be sib' (p. 170). It is difficult to tell whether alewives or women who brewed beer were accused of witchcraft directly.[50] Yet the construction of the alewife and the witch relied on similar terms, and both served to justify the social control of women and the maintenance or reconstruction of the patriarchal status quo – securing men's dominant position within the social order, and also opening up new areas for male control.

For women during the early modern period financial independence was generally linked to their marital status. Women on their own, particularly widows, were more likely to be financially independent than married women because married women were deemed subordinate to their husbands (as reflected in the law) and under their husbands' control financially. Widows might inherit their husbands' land, property and/or craft or trade, and unmarried women might occasionally inherit their

---

[50] Macfarlane gives the occupation of one husband of an accused witch (out of forty-nine known for Essex) as a beer brewer. See Hester, *Lewd Women*, p. 162.

fathers' land and property or engage in other productive activities.[51] Thus during the period of the witch hunts women's work was largely defined by the institution of marriage. For example, a woman could only practise a craft alongside her husband, taking on his craft, or in her own right as a widow or as a single woman living in her father's household.[52] Where the example of brewing is concerned, Bennett suggests that the masculinisation of the brewing trade had the effect of changing the economic balance between husbands and wives, the wife becoming more dependent on her husband. Unmarried women were also very badly affected: 'they became less and less able to compete with men or married couples for customers, licences, and economic legitimation'.[53] The women, likely to be widows, who were still able to be brewers might therefore pose a threat to the increasingly male monopoly of the trade. They were vulnerable to misogynistic attack or possibly witchcraft accusation as a result.

By looking at material concerning socio-economic changes in the sixteenth and seventeenth centuries we find that the picture regarding witchcraft accusation and women becomes more complex. On the one hand, women accused of witchcraft tended to be those, as identified by Thomas, who were among the most vulnerable in the economy, that is, labouring women, widowed and possibly older, and poor. But they might also be amongst those in competition with men for work in lucrative areas such as brewing, that is, women carrying out a craft or trade, and more specifically, widows, who were more able to do so. Dependent or in competition, either way they might be seen to pose a threat. Women were generally in a less advantageous situation than men within the changing economy, especially within the peasantry and amongst artisans and traders – the areas that were particularly relevant to the emerging capitalist economy and also the group amongst whom witchcraft accusations predominated.

To conclude, by examining the processes involving gendering of social relations, expectations and discourses concerning the witch in the early modern period we may surmise that witch hunting became sex-specific at this time, serving as one means of maintaining and reconstructing male dominance and male power *vis-à-vis* women.

---

[51] See S. L. Watkins, 'Spinsters', *Journal of Family History*, 9 (1984); Charles and Duffin, eds., *Women and Work*.
[52] See Amussen, *An Ordered Society*, chapter 3.
[53] Bennett, 'Misogyny', 182.

Patriarchy, potentially under threat in the rapidly changing society, was merely reconstructed to maintain the status quo. Our understanding is enhanced by consideration of the conflictual and dynamic male–female relations at the time, and by taking a deeper look at the context of male–female relations than historians have often tended to pursue with regard to this period and topic.

Part 5

Decline

12. Witchcraft repealed

IAN BOSTRIDGE

I

For a long time now, the study of witchcraft has been afflicted with a tenacious and commonsensical historical assumption: that some time around 1700, probably before, and almost certainly in league with something like 'rationality', 'science' or 'rationalisation', witchcraft disappeared off the intellectual map.[1] The period between widespread educated credulity around 1670 and the triumph of confident jeering scepticism some time in the eighteenth century has been largely ignored.[2]

---

[1] For example, W. E. H. Lecky, *A History of England in the Eighteenth Century*, 7 vols. (1878), I, pp. 266–7; Lecky, *History of the Rise and Influence of the Spirit of Rationalism in Europe*, 2nd edn, 2 vols. (1865), I, pp. 1–150; H. T. Buckle, *The History of Civilisation in England*, new edn, 3 vols. (1871), III, p. 363; H. C. Lea, *A History of the Inquisition of the Middle Ages* (New York, 1955); Lea, *Materials Towards a History of Witchcraft*, ed., A. C. Howland, 3 vols. (New York, 1957); Wallace Notestein, *A History of Witchcraft in England from 1558 to 1718* (Washington, 1911), especially pp. 313–33, and tribute to Lecky, p. ix; G. L. Burr, ed., *The Witch-persecutions* . . . (Philadelphia, 1897); K. V. Thomas, *Religion and the Decline of Magic* (Harmondsworth, 1973), especially chs. 18, 22; Brian Easlea, *Witch Hunting, Magic and the New Philosophy* (Brighton, 1980); Barbara Shapiro, *Probability and Certainty in Seventeenth-Century England* (Princeton, 1983), ch. 6; Brian Levack, *The Witch-hunt in Early Modern Europe* (1987), esp. pp. 217–24; E. W. Monter, 'The historiography of European witchcraft: progress and prospects', *Journal of Interdisciplinary History*, 2 (1972), and his more recent brief review article, 'European witchcraft: a moment of synthesis?', *Historical Journal*, 31 (1988).

[2] For the 1670s see, for example, Henry More, Joseph Glanvill and Robert Boyle, shoring up religion with authenticated supernatural narratives. See Joseph Glanvill, *Some Philosophical Considerations touching Witchcraft* (1676); Robert Boyle to Joseph Glanvill in *The Works of the Honourable Robert Boyle*, ed., Birch, 6 vols. (1772), VI, p. 58 (18 Sept. 1677) and pp. 59–60 (10 Feb. 1678). For confident ridicule see, for example, Robert Halsband, ed., *The Complete Letters of Lady Mary Wortley Montagu* (Oxford, 1967), III, pp. 187–9, letters to Lady Bute and Sir James Steuart, 8 Nov. and 14 Nov. 1758.

Elsewhere I have tried to present a history of belief in this period which goes beyond joining the dots.[3] But any account, provisionally entitled 'The Decline of the Belief in Witchcraft in England', is beset with problems of definition and conceptual confusion (for instance, how is a belief historically manifested?). A few pointers must suffice in this brief chapter, which is not to say that the grander effort is not worth making. If we can understand the relationship between writing, action and belief in a marginal but defining area like witchcraft, we will have achieved a great deal both in terms of reassessing historical monsters like 'the Enlightenment' and in providing a model for understanding similar problems in other periods.

The relationship between these variables – writing, action and belief – is, however, complex. We should not confuse the business of the prosecution of witches in England – the history of persecution – with either the 'discourse of witchcraft' (narrowly and unproblematically defined as a body of texts) or the belief in witchcraft (often parlously psychologistic, individualistic and awkwardly placed for historical analysis). There is no universally valid connection between these three, although they can overlap: for instance, the belief of an individual is often if not always conditioned by the discursive resources available to that individual.

Peaks of prosecuting zeal in the late sixteenth and mid-seventeenth centuries were extraordinary events, perhaps 'epidemics' (which we might indeed want to treat psychologistically) and were followed by long periods of piecemeal, or routine, 'endemic' prosecution of witches at a lower 'sustainable' rate. From the viewpoint of 1700, the possibility of another bout of witchcraft persecution was not safely dead and buried as those with hindsight may assume. Moreover, the discourse of witchcraft – the public elaboration of witchcraft's place in the order of things – has no self-evident dependence on the intensity of prosecution. That this discourse needed a high, or even a moderate level of active participation, prosecution or conviction to thrive or survive is not self-evident. It may be so. It may not be so. It cannot simply be assumed.

This chapter tried to do its work without these assumptions. If we start by refusing to take the fact or chronology of 'the decline of witchcraft' for granted we can look afresh at the eighteenth-century evidence. That evidence does not point to witchcraft retaining its seventeenth-century virulence into the eighteenth century, but it does indicate a different story from the familiar tale of intellectual redundancy. Witchcraft theory was startlingly persistent. The body of ideas built around the threat of the witch was remarkably resilient. There are no new eighteenth-century witch-finder generals to be unearthed, but we can find strongly held beliefs and strong commitments operating even in an ideologically inauspicious climate. As a body of ideas, witchcraft had a currency and a certain viability in the eighteenth century, despite the absence of widespread or legitimate persecution. By 1736, the year of the repeal of the British witchcraft legislation, witchcraft theory was isolated and much ridiculed in print and, doubtless, coffee-house. But behind closed doors, we cannot be so sure; and witchcraft theory was certainly *not*, to borrow a phrase from Dr Johnson, 'beyond the need for rational confutation'. That it is today should not mislead us into assuming that this sweeping brand of modern scepticism came into the world confident and fully armed.

By showing the political and religious crannies in which witchcraft theory could lurk in 1736, I hope to give credence to two related notions: that the demise of the witchcraft debate between members of the elite who wanted to be taken seriously had political and ideological rather than purely intellectual occasions; and that the ideological colouring which witchcraft acquired in the early eighteenth century was a double-edged affair, both ensuring the demise of witchcraft as a mainstream discourse, and paradoxically ensuring its survival and occasional reemergence at the fringes, as long as the ideological framework of the *ancien régime* remained in force.

This exploration of the repeal of witchcraft legislation in the British parliament will eventually form part of an attempt to write a synoptic account of the decline or transformation of witchcraft as an intellectual category; but it also stands as a simple exercise in historical reclamation. The repeal of the witchcraft legislation of England and Scotland in 1736 is still seen as an afterthought;[4] it has never been deemed worthy of explanation. This chapter will start by asking why repeal happened, and why it happened in March 1736. It will then look at the opposition to repeal and identify the interests – political, religious and national – which motivated the admittedly small number of outright opponents. But any account of 1736 needs to start with a brief sketch of the seventeenth- and

---

[4] See, for example, Paul Langford, *A Polite and Commercial People: England 1727–1783* (Oxford, 1989), p. 282.

eighteenth-century background and an inoculation against the familiar answers of the prevailing historical model.

II

In the seventeenth century, witchcraft was a handy ideological tool with a real intellectual appeal, a wide constituency and a capacity to be moulded to serve new and varied interests. During the 1640s, to be sure, witchcraft prosecution had acquired a dangerous association with disorder, notably through the witch 'craze' initiated and sustained by the 'witch-finder general' Matthew Hopkins. Consequently, at the Restoration it was easy to ridicule the persecution of witches as the chosen pursuit of lunatic sectaries.[5] Nevertheless, witchcraft was not easily to be marginalised or driven to the fanatical fringe. The discourse of witchcraft had not spent its force by 1660, and a wide range of intellectuals subsequently maintained its necessity as a piece of Christian orthodoxy. One author among them even placed it at the centre of a response to fanaticism. The excluded Laudian cleric, Meric Casaubon, writing after his own restoration, saw the virtues of preserving traditional supernatural beliefs, bringing them to the aid of the whole process of a miraculously guaranteed and sacred Restoration. The supernatural elements of the old intellectual order – including witchcraft – had to be respected if the restored social, political and ecclesiastical order was to capture hearts and minds. Moreover, supernatural aspects of the orthodox world view, from royal divinity to miracles and diabolical intercourse with human beings were all of a piece. There could be no picking and choosing. All had to be retained and refurbished.[6]

Of course, the late-seventeenth-century affinity between witchcraft belief and dissent or religious radicalism cannot be entirely gainsaid. Witch hunting, the gruesome practical instantiation of the belief in witch-craft, is a feature mainly of dissenting circles by the 1690s, from Salem to the affair of the 'Surey Demoniack'. Men like Casaubon were not, as far as is known, great witch-finders, but witchcraft remained an entrenched part of their intellectual agenda for reasons of religion and statecraft combined. This only confirms the point made in opening, that

---

[5] Samuel Butler, *Hudibras*, ed., J. Wilders (Oxford, 1967), part 2, canto 3.

[6] Meric Casaubon, *Of Credulity and Incredulity in Things Natural and Civil*, 2nd edn (1672), for example, pp. 7, 29, 36, 164–5, 186–7, 199. See Bostridge, 'Debates', pp. 114–25.

belief and discourse have to be methodologically disentangled from the process of persecution.

This is not to say that there were not established clerics in the British Isles busy persecuting witches – but many of them were Scottish. To these activists, witchcraft was more than a theoretical buttress of church and state. The campaign against witchcraft, with all its heady rhetoric, played a symbolic role in Scottish opposition to English intellectual and religious colonisation of their kingdom. This is particularly evident in covenanting attacks on the variety of English infidelities, religious and political, from the 1650s on. For many Scots, the English were both leaguers with the devil and an impediment to godly resistance to witchcraft, makers of diabolical pacts and breakers of solemn leagues and covenants.[7] The Renfrew witch trial of 1696–7 was an occasion for Scots to worry about English interference in Scottish concerns. As one individual put it: 'the proceeding of the Government in another Nation', Scotland, is not to be 'Judged and Censured' by English *Esprits forts.* English responses to Scottish prosecution of witches in fact show no rising tide of scepticism south of the border.[8] Indeed, publication of Francis Hutchinson's major sceptical work on witchcraft, *An Historical Essay concerning Witchcraft* (1718), first planned in the first decade of the eighteenth century, was delayed over ten years by the English ecclesiastical hierarchy's reluctance to offend Scottish sensibilities around the time of the union of the two kingdoms.[9] The belief in the validity of laws against witches remained a feature of Scottish intellectual life long after the union.[10] As we shall see, the slight parliamentary resistance to the repeal of 1736 derived from Scottish opposition to Walpole. In itself, the Scottish example demonstrates the continuing and

[7] *The Scotch Presbyterian Eloquence* (1692), for example, pp. 45–6, 50, 55, 58–9, 66, 100, 107; Alexander Shields, *A Hind Let Loose* (n.p., 1687), pp. 324, 368; Edward Gee, *The Divine Right and Original of the Civill Magistrate from God* (1658), pp. 220–4; Bostridge, 'Debates', pp. 141–5.

[8] Bodleian MSS Locke b4 d107, Robert Wylie to William Hamilton, 16 June 1697; see also the sermon preached by James Hutchisone before the Commissioners of Justiciary appointed for the trial of the Renfrew witches in 1697, printed in *Scottish Historical Review* (1910); reports in *The Flying Post* (266, 267, 283, 285, 297, 308), *Lloyd's News* (64), *The Protestant Mercury* (130, 131, 134, 137, 141, 149, 150, 153, 154, 162), *The Post Boy* (275), and *The Foreign Post* (9).

[9] See BL Sloane MS 4040, f. 302, Francis Hutchinson to Hans Sloane, 4 Feb. 1706.

[10] Alexander Carlyle, *Autobiography* (1800), ed., J. H. Burton (1910), introduction, for the Associate Presbytery's judgement in 1743; David Hume to William Mure, MP for Renfrewshire, 14 Nov. 1742 in *The Letters of David Hume*, ed., J. Y. T. Greig, 2 vols. (Oxford, 1932), I, p. 44.

powerful appeal of the rhetoric of witchcraft as a means of organising political and religious perceptions.

There was no one historical moment at which witchcraft ceased to be a serious subject of educated concern in England, but neither is there a single perspective from which we can trace the 'decline of witchcraft belief' as if it were a piece of natural history. The reason for concentrating on the repeal of the laws about witchcraft in this essay is partly formal and partly a matter of perspective. We seek to explain an undoubted event in the history of witchcraft, and to do so without all the unwarranted assumptions we have unpicked hitherto. But focusing on one historical moment between the 1690s and 1736 can help us prepare for repeal by letting us understand how and why the climate of the debate had frozen out those who were zealous for prosecution. My necessarily brief account of that moment is particularly schematised because it pivots about one individual, Daniel Defoe. The intention is not to privilege Defoe's point of view, as if he were some sort of historical world soul, but rather to show the process of discursive transformation through the history of an individual, and to explain a conundrum. Supernaturalism and the occult are important features of Defoe's work, fictional, quasi-fictional and non-fictional alike. He was a man educated firmly within a dissenting tradition which treasured supernaturalism in its heart.[11] The conundrum is Defoe's apparent volte-fact on the issue of the existence of witchcraft. In 1711, at the height of the 'rage of party', and as a writer in the interest of Harley's moderate and eirenic Tory ministry, Defoe wrote an article in his *Review* which thoroughly endorsed belief in witchcraft as a piece of Christian orthodoxy. Yet in the 1720s he produced works pursuing a far more ambiguous line.[12] Analysis suggests that in 1711 support for witchcraft belief was calculated to appeal to the sort of cross-party coalition which Harley and,

---

[11] For example, Daniel Defoe, *Robinson Crusoe* (1719) (Oxford, 1981), esp. pp. 133, 78–9, 153–5; Defoe, 'A vision of the angelick world', in *Serious Reflections of Robinson Crusoe, Romances and Narratives by Daniel Defoe*, ed., Aitken (1899); Defoe, *A Journal of the Plague Year* (1722) (Harmondsworth, 1966), esp. pp. 124, 204, 205, 252; Defoe, *The Storm* (1704); Defoe, *The Fortunate Mistress* (1724) (Oxford, 1981), esp. pp. 220, 289; Defoe, *Moll Flanders* (1722) (Penguin, 1989), esp. pp. 65, 257–8, 268. Defoe was educated at Newington Green Academy under the supervision of Charles Morton, later cosignatory to the preface to Cotton Mather, *Memorable Providences Relating to Witchcraft* (1689). See also Charles Morton, *Compendium Physicae*, ed., S. E. Morison (Boston, 1940), esp. pp. 4, 161, 87, 195.

[12] *Review*, VIII: 90, 20 Oct. 1711; Daniel Defoe, *A Political History of the Devil, As Well Ancient as Modern* (1726); Defoe, *A System of Magick* (1727); Defoe, *Essay on the History and Reality of Apparitions* (1727).

by extension, Defoe, his agent, were trying to construct. In October 1711, it was a non-party issue, secular cum religious, which could embody a vision of a broad Christian commonwealth defined negatively against the image of depravity and deviance, the witch. This is a role the diabolical trafficker had played in Meric Casaubon's world view, and it was to form part of the medical controversialist Richard Boulton's stillborn defence of traditional belief in the 1720s.[13]

However, in 1712, during the contentious trial and pardon of the supposed witch, Jane Wenham, the issue of witchcraft itself became politicised in a welter of pamphlets for and against the conviction, pamphlets which revelled in the rhetoric of party conflict; yet again the Whig and Tory hobbyhorses of priestcraft and the church in danger were trotted out. What is more, during the course of the period between Defoe's *Review* article and the works on the occult he published in the 1720s, his Harleian vision of non-party Christian government evaporated. Party rule triumphed in Defoe's eyes. Witchcraft thus lost much of its use in Defoe's scheme of things. It reemerged, parodically inverted, as a metaphor for party conflict and party rule themselves. In Defoe's history of the devil, witches properly speaking were no longer needed because diabolism (factional rule incarnate) reigned at the very seat of power.[14]

This analysis of witchcraft during and after the 'rage of party', focused on discursive transformation – indeed, *inversion* in a very strict sense – in the work of one individual, Daniel Defoe, could be extended. Initially the bipartisan theory of witchcraft was an intellectual resource for all. Then, seized upon in the party struggle, it became increasingly perceived as the intellectual property of a discredited clique of highflyers and Tory extremists. The witch had been a focal point for a quasi-religious conception of political authority, a mixture of the anti-sacerdotal and anti-regal qualities analogous to and a diabolical inversion of that paramount exemplum of the mixed person, the king himself. The crime of witchcraft embodied the amphibian nature of political authority in the highflying scheme of things, as an offence which blended together civil and religious apostasy. The belief in it was beginning to be perceived as wrongheaded, and as having a dangerous potential for raising

---

[13] Richard Boulton, . . . *A Vindication of a Compleat History of Magick* . . . (1722).

[14] For example, Francis Bragge, *A Full and Impartial Account of the Discovery of Sorcery and Witchcraft, Practis'd by Jane Wenham* (1712); *A Full Confutation of Witchcraft* . . . (1712); Defoe, *A Political History of the Devil*, pp. 388–9.

uncomfortable issues and civil disturbance. Having then become associated with the losers in the political struggle, belief in witchcraft came to be seen as fit matter for ridicule.[15] What might be called the last witchcraft debate took place in the years around 1720 between the future bishop of Down and Connor, Francis Hutchinson, and the eccentric physician, Richard Boulton. Hutchinson pointed out the dangerous religious factionalism and potential for popular ferment which witchcraft belief involved. Boulton's forlorn attempt to resurrect the vision of a unified Christian community defining itself against the enemies of society harks back to Defoe and Casaubon. In retrospect, it was a plain anachronism.[16]

By the 1720s the ideological foundations of witchcraft had slipped. The metaphysical underpinnings and an ontology alive with spiritual activity remained intact but irrelevant or at most mildly embarrassing for sceptics like Hutchinson who wriggled out of the contradictions which the rejection of witchcraft and the necessity of spirits at work in the world seemed to entail. One need only consider John Locke's remarks on spirits, scattered through a variety of his works, to see that witchcraft was not ruled out by the new epistemology. Locke's conception of human understanding could be used, as Boulton used it, in support of belief in witches.[17] In general it was not. The reasons were ideological. Witchcraft belief was not exterminated by new forms of reasoning about the material world. The metaphysics and the epistemology to support such beliefs remained intact. But in political terms, we can see why witchcraft theory could have had little appeal for those wedded to Lockean

[15] See, for example, Anthony Collins, *A Discourse of Free-Thinking* (1713), p. 30; White Kennett, *The Witchcraft of the present Rebellion* (1715); Joseph Addison, *The Drummer* (1716), prologue and p. 47; *A Seasonable Apology for Father Dominick, Chaplain to Prince Prettyman the Catholick . . . In which are occasionally inserted some weighty Arguments for calling a General Council of the Nonjuring Doctors, for the further Propagation of Ceremonies, Unity, Dissention, and Anathemas; and for the better improvement of Exorcism and March-Beer* (1723), pp. 7ff., 14, 28; Thomas Gordon, *The Humourist* (1725), dedication and p. 74.

[16] Francis Hutchinson, *An Historical Essay Concerning Witchcraft* (1718), esp. p. 181; Boulton, *Vindication*, pp. 117, 155, ix, v, xii, 82.

[17] See Richard Boulton, *A Complete History of Magick, Sorcery, and Witchcraft* (1715), frontispiece and preface; Philip van Limborch to John Locke, *Correspondence of John Locke*, ed., de Beer (Oxford, 1976–), IV, pp. 295–8, 17/27 and 21/31 July 1691; John Locke to Nicolas Thoinard, *Correspondence . . .* , II, p. 454, 14 Oct. 1681; John Locke, *An Essay Concerning Human Understanding*, Bohn's edn (1885), I, p. 425, sect. 5; p. 443, sect. 31; II, p. 124, sect. 23; Locke, 'Some thoughts concerning education', in *The Works of John Locke*, 10 vols. (1823), IX, pp. 6, 205, 182–3; Locke, 'A discourse of miracles', in *Works* (1823), IX, p. 264.

ideals such as the confirmed separation between secular and religious jurisdiction.[18]

Having reassessed the credibility of witchcraft theory up to 1736, we can turn to the question of repeal. The circumstances of repeal can tell us how much further the marginalisation of witchcraft had gone by 1736; an analysis of those circumstances can tell us how marginalisation was occurring and amplify the ideological tale we have already told.

III

Religious controversy broke out with renewed vigour in the 1730s after a decade of relative stability presided over by Walpole's 'Pope', Edmund Gibson, bishop of London. Gibson himself sensed in parliament 'an evil spirit . . . working against Churchmen and Church matters'. He had wished to revive the jurisdiction of ecclesiastical courts, and commit the execution of laws against vice and irreligion to the ecclesiastical hierarchy, and spoke in a letter to Walpole of being 'tossed about and insulted by people of almost all denominations, many of whom were known to stand very well with the Court'. As Hervey noted in his *Memoirs*, the 1735–6 session of the new parliament devoted its chief discussions to 'Church matters'. An attempt to repeal the Test and Corporation Acts was followed, most disastrously for Edmund Gibson, by the furore over the Mortmain and Quakers' Tithe Bills, which led to his final break with Robert Walpole. As in the years preceding the Hanoverian succession, accusations of priestcraft and irreligion were bandied and anathemas hurled.[19]

This anti-clerical temper was not a mere whim of elements within the House of Commons. It extended throughout the elite, with the hubbub surrounding the nomination of the supposedly deistical Dr Rundle to the see of Gloucester; the abuse and criticism newly directed at Bishop Gibson's own magnum opus, the *Codex Juris Ecclesiae Anglicanae* of 1713 which had given theoretical form to attacks on ecclesiastical jurisdiction; and the controversy on the nature of heresy between James Foster, a dissenting lecturer, and Henry Stebbing, a high church divine.

---

[18] On which see Richard Ashcraft, *Revolutionary Politics and Locke's 'Two Treatises of Government'* (Princeton, 1986), pp. 496–7.

[19] Norman Sykes, *Edmund Gibson* (Oxford, 1926), pp. 122–82 and esp. 148–9; J. Hervey, *Memoirs of the Reign of George II*, ed., J. W. Croker, 2 vols. (1848), II, p. 87; see also Stephen Taylor, 'Sir Robert Walpole, the Church of England, and the Quakers' Tithe Bill of 1736', *Historical Journal*, 28 (1985).

All this added to the sense of religious ferment. The uproar ended in the political arena with Gibson's withdrawal from the charmed circle of power, and in the contemplative realm with William Warburton's *Alliance between Church and State* of 1736 which set out new rules of engagement.[20]

Witchcraft disappeared from serious discourse in the period following the extinction of the rage of party; and it is my contention that a period of parallel and intense religious controversy two decades later revived the issue, in attenuated form. The context for the repeal of the witchcraft legislation is not a putative judicial spirit of reform, but rather a half-decade or more of ecclesiastical upset.[21] The religious set-tos just outlined were exactly the sort of thing which Walpole had sought to avoid through Gibson's management of the church. Having wanted to move away from the sectarianism of the last years of Anne, Walpole had ended up with a prelate who some saw as being bent upon imitating William Laud. The repeal of the witchcraft act in early 1736 might have been seen as an indication that such high-church pretensions were being expelled from the body politic in their most absurd form. But can we get any further than this in relating the measure to the hither and thither of political manoeuvre?

The problem with the 1736 repeal is that it seems to emerge out of nowhere. The ideology of witchcraft lost credibility and usefulness in the wake of its adoption by Tory factionalism, and the ensuing Whig ascendancy, but the process by which this ideological transformation became a root-and-branch change in mentality is more difficult to judge. By the time of the Jew Bill, in 1753, when images of witchcraft were

[20] M. Foster, *Examination of the Scheme of Church Power laid down in the Codex* (1735). See, for example, H. Stebbing, *A letter to Mr Foster on the subject of Heresy* (1735); J. Foster, *An answer to Dr Stebbing's Letter on the subject of Heresy, a letter* (1735). Stebbing possibly contributed *The Case of the Hertfordshire Witchcraft Considered* to the Wenham debate, but see Notestein, *A History of Witchcraft*, p. 374; J. C. D. Clark, *English Society 1688–1832* (Cambridge, 1985), pp. 137–41; Langford, *A Polite and Commercial People*, pp. 38–44. But, for a caveat as to Warburton's significance see Stephen Taylor, 'William Warburton and the alliance of church and state', *Journal of Ecclesiastical History*, 43 (1992).

[21] Although the House of Lords, agreeing on 24 Feb. 1735/6 to meet in committee on the 26th to discuss the bill for the repeal of the witchcraft act, did suggest 'that the Judges do then attend', *Journal of the House of Lords*, 9 Geo II, 1735/6. On motives and means for eighteenth-century legislation see Joanna Innes, 'Parliament and the shaping of eighteenth-century English social policy', *Transactions of the Royal Historical Society*, 5th ser., 40 (1990), esp. 77–8 (on the role of judges and law officers); 82 (on anti-Walpolean moves for law reform); 89 (on the role of the executive in generating or directing legislation).

deployed in the satirical print (whether as an implicit condemnation of the absurd highflying fanaticism of those who opposed Jewish naturalisation, or as a reminder of the diabolical motivation of the Jewish lobby, we cannot be sure) we know that belief in witchcraft was eccentric, its use in propaganda a reworking of the rhetorical deposits of the generations.[22] The year 1736 is a different matter. What is more, the precise purpose of the bill is unclear because of the paucity of surviving parliamentary evidence. There are no official records of any parliamentary debate beyond the bare outline provided by the journals of the houses. Government involvement in the initiation of the bill is, as so often, difficult to fathom.[23] Any account must be tentative and rely on the accumulation of anecdote or the extrapolation of motive. Despite all these problems, it certainly seems worth asking why the witchcraft act was repealed in 1736, whether there was opposition, and from whom.

The bill's sponsors included John Crosse, described by Horace Walpole as 'a very good friend to my brother' and a fairly representative Old Whig, and John Conduitt, who served as master of the mint from 1727 until his death ten years later. A frequent speaker for the government in the house, he opposed the repeal of the Septennial Act, that coping stone of Whig stability, in the 1735/6 session. What makes Conduitt's sponsorship of repeal more interesting is that he was Sir Isaac Newton's nephew by marriage, his chosen successor at the Mint, and the guardian of the Newtonian tradition. Conduitt's involvement in the repeal of the witchcraft act may well have enhanced the identification of Newtonianism as the ideology of a sound and rational Whig settlement which purged the nation of antique superstition. The bill was presented to the Commons and delivered to the Lords by Conduitt; Crosse chaired the committee of the whole house which considered the bill before third reading.

The third and final sponsor, Alderman George Heathcote, was 'one of the most frequent and violent speakers for the opposition'. Heathcote was, according to Lord Egmont, 'a republican Whig', who in March

---

22 See *Catalogue of Prints and Drawings in the British Museum*, Division 1, 'Political and personal satires', 3 vols. (1870–), for example, 3270, 'All the world in a hurry, or the road from London to Oxford' (1753), 3214, 'The gypsy's triumph' (1753). But cf. [Adam Fitz-Adam], *The World*, 34, 23 Aug. 1753: 'it is shrewdly suspected that the same people who imagined their religion to be at stake by the repeal of the one [the Witchcraft Act], are at present under the most terrible consternation at the passing of the other [the Jew Bill]'.

23 See Innes, 'Parliament and the shaping of eighteenth-century English social policy', p. 85, on paucity of records; p. 89, on obscurity of motive.

1731 participated in the anti-clerical assault by moving the motion to prevent the translation of bishops. Even more significantly, in the year of the repeal of the witchcraft act, he spoke in favour of the repeal of the Test Act. He did not oppose the government out of sheer spite, and on several occasions voted with the ministry.[24]

These are a mixed lot, but if we are looking for a common thread, the sponsors of repeal might be seen as representative of an emerging 'coalition' between some ministerial and opposition whigs in reaction to the revived highflying favoured by Gibson, and his attempts to advance ecclesiastical influence. The same groups formulated and supported the schemes concerning Quaker tithes and mortmain which drove Gibson from influence. The Quaker tithes bill was read for the first time in the Commons a week before the new Witchcraft Act received royal assent; and the day after the third reading of the witch bill, a motion for the repeal of the test laws was lost in the Commons. According to Stephen Taylor, at this stage in his career 'Walpole probably hoped that debate on religious issues, by appealing to ideology, would emphasize the differences between opposition whigs [who supported some measure of relief for the Quakers] and Tories [who did not]'.[25] Repeal of the witchcraft legislation may have played a symbolic role in indicating the increasingly, though not definitively, secular nature of the state, legislation less liable to offend or inconvenience than the repeal of the test and corporation acts. It is striking that when those latter measures were under threat again, in the 1820s, witchcraft emerged once more as an issue.[26] But while repeal of the witchcraft legislation may have formed a fairly uncontentious part of the response to feelings that the state was in danger – no-one was suggesting that Gibson was a proselytising believer in witchcraft – there was some opposition, and it is important to analyse its motivation.

The historian chancing upon a stray parliamentary opponent of the

---

[24] Romney Sedgwick, *The House of Commons 1715–1754*, 2 vols. (1970), under name of member; *Journal of the House of Commons*, 9 Geo II, 1735/6. For the continued association between the Newtonian tradition and the rout of superstition and witch beliefs in particular, see Hogarth's execrably punning 'Frontis-Piss' of 1763, engraved by LaCave; Samuel Ireland, *Graphic Illustrations of Hogarth* (1794–99), 2 vols., I, pp. 175–6.

[25] Taylor, 'Sir Robert Walpole', 58.

[26] Within the framework of the *ancien régime*, the test and witchcraft continued to be somehow perceived as bound together, see *Antipas: a solemn appeal to the Archbishops and Bishops with reference to several Bills . . . especially that concerning Witchcraft and Sorcery* (1821), opposing the repeal of the Irish witchcraft legislation.

witchcraft repeal in 1736 might be forgiven for experiencing incredulity closely followed by a conviction that the individual concerned must have been singularly eccentric. For the traditionalist, who sees repeal as the progressive and inevitable result of a communal 'loss of belief' in the late seventeenth century, this is self-evidently so. Any opposition was, in the event, wide of the mark. The contemporary mood suggests the same: two parliamentary journals, Edward Harley's and Thomas Wilson's, allude to repeal with no hint of real controversy.[27] In a historical account which charts a different course, the loner could instead be a key to unlock yet more of the ideological secret history of the expulsion of witchcraft from public affairs. Unusual certainly, in his willingness to raise the issue in parliament, he is a man with a history and with interests which, however marginalised, might be profitably analysed rather than rejected out of hand as mere lunacy. The eccentric in question was the brother of the earl of Mar, rebel leader of 1715 – James Erskine, Lord Grange.

The received account of Erskine's stand on sorcery is utterly contemptuous and dismissive:

[Erskine] contracted such a violent aversion at Sir Robert Walpole, that having, by intrigue and hypocrisy, secured a majority of the district of burghs of which Stirling is the chief, he threw up his seat as a Judge in the Court of Session, was elected member for that district, and went to London to attend Parliament, and to overturn Sir Robert Walpole, not merely in his own opinion, but also in the opinion of many who were dupes to his cunning, and his pretensions to abilities that he had not. But his first appearance in the House of Commons undeceived his sanguine friends, and silenced him for ever. He chose to make his maiden speech on the Witches Bill, as it was called; and being learned in daemonologia, with books on which subject his library was filled, he made a long canting speech that set the House in a titter of laughter, and convinced Sir Robert that he had no need of any extraordinary armour against this champion of the house of Mar. The truth was, that the man had neither learning nor ability. He was no lawyer, and he was a bad speaker. He had been raised on the shoulders of his brother, the Earl of Mar, in the end of the Queen's reign, but had never distinguished himself. In the General Assembly, which many

---

[27] C. L. S. Linnell, ed., *The Diaries of Thomas Wilson, D.D., 1731–7 and 1750, son of Bishop Wilson of Sodor and Man* (1964), entry for Thursday, 26 Feb. 1735/6; Edward Harley, Cambridge University Library MS Add. 6851 (Parliamentary Journal for 1734–51), entry for 22 Jan. 1735/6, f. 30.

gentlemen afterwards made a school of popular eloquence, and where he took the high-flying side that he might annoy Government, his appearances were but rare and unimpressive; but as he was understood to be a great plotter, he was supposed to reserve himself for some greater occasions.[28]

This anecdote is alluded to in Keith Thomas' *Religion and the Decline of Magic*, setting a seal on the accepted model of the decline of witchcraft; but by unpicking it in detail we can build up a very different picture of Erskine.[29] To view the 1736 repeal as a dotting of i's evades the need for explanation; in the same way, to label Erskine's opposition as mere eccentricity is to dismiss his actions as inexplicably bizarre. They may have been, but they deserve a rational examination first. We need to explore the motivation of his stand in this particular instance, to relate it to his other political actions, unwinding the tangled mess of his political career to understand why Erskine, undoubtedly capable of shrewd behaviour, could have been so spectacularly off course.

We can start by reconstructing Erskine's intellectual formation and milieu. Only thus can his opposition to the 'Witches Bill' be understood. His desire to 'overturn Sir Robert Walpole' and 'annoy Government', his relationship to the earl of Mar and his reputation as a 'great plotter' will all have their part to play. For the purposes of this chapter, however, the vital recognition is that Erskine's ideological affiliations in the years between 1715 and 1745 are a link between two important features of the discourse of witchcraft up to 1715 as outlined above. A Scot and a 'highflyer', it will emerge that Erskine's opposition to the repeal was indeed part of a more general attack on Walpole; but one which drew its consistency from a concern for Scottish rights and Scottish religion, and a related anxiety about the spiritual standing of the 'Robinocracy'.

Erskine's diary reveals that in his youth he was far from being the sort of convinced Presbyterian we have earlier implicated in the defence of witchcraft belief and prosecution. In the late 1690s he had condemned Scots Calvinists as 'narrow spirited and prejudiced creatures' and affected 'a great esteem for John le Clerc at Amsterdam' reckoning him 'one who had shook off these prejudices and thought freely'.[30] In

---

[28] Carlyle, *Autobiography*, p. 10.

[29] Thomas, *Religion and the Decline of Magic*, p. 694.

[30] James Erskine, Lord Grange, *Extracts from the Diary of a Senator of the College of Justice* (Edinburgh, 1843), p. 83. These are extracts from the MS listed in HMC, *Report on the Manuscripts of the Earl of Mar and Kellie* (1904), marked 'Memoirs VI'. Most of it relates to Erskine's religious experiences.

1708, Erskine might have been over such youthful freethinking, but remained ironically dismissive of the supposed virtues of clerical government: 'It is a good thing that now both Church and high Kirk join in their principles as to screwing up the power of the clergy; which I hope will teach people that Church and Kirk are at the bottom of the same kidney, and that neither ought to be too much indulged or trusted to.'[31]

By this time Erskine was a successful lawyer, well on the way to influence. Snugly ensconced in the bosom of the Stuart establishment he was successively member of the faculty of advocates (1705), lord of session (1707) and, finally, lord justice clerk (1710). In the years around 1707 he was as keen on the union as any Scotsman on the make, despite the caveats:

> I'm much affraid that there may still be a great deall of uneasyness about it. [But] I'm sure it is in the power of the Government and Parliament of Brittain to make the Union not only durable, but most acceptable and advantagious to this country, *as I expect it shall*. [my emphasis]

An ardent pragmatist, he was full of scorn for the 'fury and impertinence of biggots on either side'.[32]

The death of Queen Anne and the ensuing rebellion were turning points in Erskine's career. In 1714 he was dismissed from his post. In 1715 his brother Mar led the Jacobite uprising, and the family estates were consequently sequestered. In subsequent decades Erskine did his best, in his own words, 'to preserve from ruine the forfeited famillys of my friends and relations'. Having been a student companion of Walpole's Scottish agent, Islay, Erskine thought he had a sure route back into the confidence of the government. He had been disappointed, his family slighted, as he made clear in a letter of 1733:

> Such has long been their way, to profess great friendship to me and the familly . . . and much readyness to do us good, and seemingly to propose better for us than we do for ourselves; but when it came to the execution, to prevent the doing of it by shifts, tricks, and lies . . . Why should we sit still and let them trick us into poverty, contempt, and insignificancy?[33]

---

[31] Letter to his brother Mar, 29 Jan. 1708 in HMC, *Mar and Kellie*, p. 426.
[32] Ibid.
[33] 'Letters of Lord Grange', in *The Miscellany of the Spalding Club*, III (Aberdeen, 1846), pp. 1–71.

In the same period, after 1715, Erskine's religious leanings were transformed. By the 1720s he was the very model of a Kirk man, active in the affairs of the General Assembly, well-known for 'strengthening the hands of the zealous orthodox ministers'. 'It verie much refreshes me', wrote one correspondent, 'to find any, especially of your high station, that often live at the greatest distance from God, fill'd with just and clear apprehensions of true religion, and the decayed and languishing state thereof in this dead and withered time.' Indeed, the decayed and languishing state of religion, in its broad and narrow senses, became a theme of Erskine's opposition to Walpole's regime. He complained of the great man's 'openly rediculing all vertue and uprightness'; of the 'geddyness and corruption of our age'; and an addiction to 'lewd and idle Diversions'. He gave his friend Robert Wodrow a picture of Queen Caroline continually 'bantering and scolding the narrou principles of the Church of Scotland'.[34]

This last remark alerts us to the framework within which this spleen and religious anxiety were exercised. From 1715 on Erskine was moving towards a thoroughgoing defence of Scots rights and Scots particularity, in both politics and religion. We need not, as so many of Erskine's enemies did, stoop to accusations of hypocrisy.[35] To start with, family and personal honour were legitimately bound up with national honour in the case of a family as prominent as Erskine's: 'poverty, contempt, and insignificancy' was the threatened fate not only of the Erskines, but of the whole kingdom under the new dispensation. Walpole and his crew were 'these oppressors of the familly we belong to, *and* enemys of Britain'. Religion and politics were bound up together, too, as Erskine's attitude to the Simson affair acutely demonstrates.[36]

John Simson was a notorious Scottish theologian, prosecuted in the General Assembly of the Kirk for teaching unsound doctrine. The case created uproar and became one of the *causes célèbres* of eighteenth-century Scottish ecclesiastical politics. Erskine, deeply involved in the prosecution of the deistical Simson, was convinced that the affair was being used by the Walpole administration as part of an attack on Scottish rights and integrity:

---

[34] John Wylie to Erskine, pp. 1–71, 8 May 1721, HMC, *Mar and Kellie*, p. 521; Andrew Darling, minister at Kintoul, to Erskine, 3 Feb. 1724; HMC, *Mar and Kellie*, p. 525; 'Letters of Lord Grange', pp. 56, 57; *The History and Proceedings of the House of Commons . . .* , 1742, IX, p. 93, 5 Mar. 1735; Robert Wodrow, *Analecta*, ed., M. Leishman, 4 vols. (Glasgow, 1842), IV, p. 146.

[35] See Wodrow, *Analecta*, III, pp. 510, 306.   [36] 'Letters of Lord Grange', p. 47.

ther seems to be a designe, at some Assembly, to throu up him [Simson], or some other bone of contention, to break and divide us: That when our Assemblys break upon this or other points, they will be prohibited by the King, and either Commissions, or some other select meetings, called by the King's writ, will have the management of Church affairs.[37]

For Erskine, as for so many others before the '45, the religious and state affairs of Scotland were of a piece, and seemed increasingly under threat from English interference. The unionist careerist, sceptical of temperament, came to believe, under the pressure of a variety of events, that the balance of the 1707 settlement was being unbalanced by the actions of a corrupt and irreligious ministry. It is within this context that we have to locate Erskine's opposition to the witch bill, taking him as seriously as his friend Robert Wodrow did:

> that person hath made a bold appearance for the truth; and if any suspect him as forming a designe to manage a party among the Ministry, and to affect leading and dictating to them, such, in my opinion, have acted a very imprudent part at this time in supporting Mr Simson so much, since by this method they have given that eminent person a handle (wer he seeking one) to recommend himself to the affections of all in Scotland, who have a concern for the purity of doctrine, and preventing error in this Church.[38]

Before outlining the sequence of events which may have led to Erskine's speech of 1736, Erskine's relation to the discourses of witchcraft outlined in the first part of this chapter needs to be charted. First of all, Erskine's personal beliefs, his inner and inaccessible convictions, are debatable; but it is worth noting that from the 1720s to his death he was unambiguously supernaturalist in religion, both in matters of the operation of divine grace and the ministrations of the devil and his agents.[39] Secondly, Erskine's early if temperate enthusiasm for the Anglo-Scottish union does place him initially outside the orbit of the Presbyterian knot who saw true witchcraft belief as a mark of Scottish rectitude as against English infidelity; but, his increasing suspicion of the English government and concern for Scottish identity and honour make his visible support for the Jacobean witchcraft

---

[37] For Simson see *DNB*; *Analecta*, IV, p. 144.

[38] *Analecta*, III, p. 511.

[39] See, for example, *Analecta*, III, pp. 207, 410; II, pp. 47, 86–7, 171, 255, 323, 379.

legislation an ideological manoeuvre within an identifiable tradition.[40] Finally, Erskine was, as our opening anecdote has it, a 'highflyer': hot for the rights of the Kirk; for the power of the General Assembly; for the restriction of lay intrusion into clerical privileges. His refusal to distinguish between the religious and political well-being of his nation has been noted. Despite the doctrinal chasm which separated such Calvinist highflyers north of the border from highflyers and non-jurors in England, there is an affinity in their common attitude to the proper relationship between the sacred and secular domains, an affinity which was reflected in the resilience of the discourse of witchcraft within both groups. This makes it all the more striking that Erskine was, in his latter years, an associate of John Wesley, whose public condemnation of the repeal of the witchcraft act reflected his own highflying roots as well as his Scriptural fundamentalism.[41]

The attack on Scottish rights reached its apogee in 1734 during the election of the representative Scottish peers; troops were used to overawe the electors. Members of the Whig opposition – Chesterfield and Carteret – approached the dismissed peers in the wake of the election, and proposed that steps should be taken to force the ministry to account for the apparent malpractice. The peers engaged two men as their chief advisers, Dundas and the lawyer, James Erskine of Grange. Erskine was heavily involved in opposition manoeuvres, and the government started to move against him, introducing a bill to prevent Scottish lords of session like himself from being elected to the House of Commons. He quit his employment to secure his seat.[42]

Having been alienated from the mainstream of Westminster politics, 'represented as a hypocrite, and pretender to religion . . . as divisive and factious', in anger of 'lossing his friends at London', political crisis now pushed Erskine back into the centre of affairs.[43] The period which

[40] For the distance between the pre-1715 Erskine and, for example, Robert Wylie, an opponent of union and proponent of legislation against witches (see n. 8 above), see HMC, *Mar and Kellie*, p. 273, Erskine to Mar, 20 Aug. 1706.

[41] HMC, *Report on the Laing Manuscripts*, 2 vols. (1914, 1925), II, p. 348. For Wesley see, for example, Henry Moore, *The Life of the Reverend John Wesley* (Leeds, 1825), p. 323 and *The Journal of the Reverend John Wesley*, Everyman edn, iii, p. 412, entry for 4 July 1770.

[42] See *Arniston Memoirs: Three Centuries of a Scottish House 1571–1838*, ed., G. W. T. Omond (Edinburgh, 1887), pp. 82–3; Erskine's speech against the manipulated election in *The History and Proceedings of the House of Commons*, IX, pp. 69–71; Pulteney to Erskine, 24 Feb. and 22 Mar. 1734 and Earl of Stair to Erskine, 20 Mar. 1734, all in HMC, *Mar and Kellie*, pp. 531–4.

[43] *Analecta*, III, pp. 306, 510.

followed the failure of Walpole's Excise scheme was one of threatening instability for the ministry, in its relations with Scotland as elsewhere. In 1735 Dundas, Erskine's colleague, gave his son an apocalyptic vision of a 'struggle for the sinking liberty of our country [Scotland] till God in his providence interpose to save us'. Erskine himself declared that 'the opposition to Sir Robert Walpole and Ilay is stronger and more rooted than, perhaps, it was to any ministry since the Revolution . . . high church, whig and dissenter, closely united in it, and all their own disputes buryed in this common pressure'.[44] It was in the midst of this turmoil that Erskine chose to speak against the new witchcraft legislation. We have seen how in 1711 the Harleyite Daniel Defoe sought to bury disputes and appeal to 'high church, whig and dissenter' by writing in support of an orthodox belief in witchcraft. Whatever Erskine's hopes as to the likely appeal of witchcraft belief to disaffected Tories, his speech against repeal must be seen primarily as that of a Scottish member, concerned for Scottish particularity in government and religion, and for the maintenance of orthodoxy in the kingdom as a whole (a favourite Scottish theme since the 1630s).[45] In the 1730s Erskine was still a supporter of the union between England and 'North Britain', joining with the Whig opposition to espouse the complaints of England as well as his own nation. He used English grievances as a lever to effect common relief: '[Walpole] makes bold schemes against our libertys, as was most certainly his excyse scheme which he pushed like a mad man after England.' But he had a particular concern for English invasion of Scottish prerogatives, complaining that 'in England, nothing is made of our Act of Settlement, and all pouer is undoubtedly in the hands of the Supream Court [sc. Parliament]'. Religion could be a target for an irreligious, scheming, Anglicising ministry, with Walpole and Islay seeking 'our breaking in pieces' and making 'Mr S[imson] an instrument to tear and rent us'.[46] In the year following repeal, Erskine was still pursuing Scottish interests, speaking in the debate on the Porteous riots, and opposing the bill of pains and penalties against the city of Edinburgh.

Erskine's behaviour seems less eccentric in such a context. His behaviour shows a specifically Scottish tradition trying to operate in an

---

[44] *Arniston Memoirs*, p. 81, Dundas to his son at Utrecht, 6 Feb. 1735; 'Letters of Lord Grange', p. 44. By late 1736, Thomas Wilson was convinced that 'Scotland and England are ripe for Rebellion', see his journal p. 178, entry for 24 Oct. 1736.

[45] See Conrad Russell, *The Causes of the English Civil War* (Oxford, 1990), pp. 118–22 on 'Scottish imperial' policy in the 1630s and 1640s.

[46] *Analecta*, IV, p. 144.

English arena. What is more, Erskine was no dolt. The worthy Wodrow eulogised him; Pulteney and other members of the opposition wooed him; Walpole feared him enough to frame legislation to exclude him from the House of Commons. What remains to be explained is the chasm between the sponsors of repeal, with their negative manoeuvre to paper over the cracks in the Whig coalition; and Erskine, with his positive gesture, via witchcraft, to the ranks of outraged Scottish and, perhaps, English orthodoxy. The chronology is unfortunately lost to us – we cannot know precisely when Erskine spoke, in response to what, or whether his intervention elicited or followed the amendment which extended the new legislation to Scotland. But Erskine's decision to speak against the 'Witches Bill' was a miscalculation because he mistook the complexion of the House of Commons, and the shift in the status of English discourse about witchcraft which had followed 1712–14. He was playing by Scottish rules. That anecdotal 'titter of laughter' may indeed have ended Erskine's career as a serious politician, but it did not silence him nor can it be denied that Erskine had his reasons for responding to the repeal. The development of his religious and political stance pushed him closer to a position which earlier Scots had adopted, where belief in witchcraft became for Erskine, as it had been for them, a matter of national pride, a symbol of independence, and an act of resistance to a deistical and irreligious English ministry. It may well be that repeal, calculated from one angle to define a common whiggish rationalism, was also intended to split the opposition, or at least to expose the likes of Erskine to a salutary dose of ridicule. It may be that Erskine hoped to carry disaffected Tories and dissenters with him.[47] We can be sure that 'his sanguine friends', the anti-Walpolean Whigs with whom he had joined forces, were disappointed. The paucity of opposition to repeal within the House of Commons does not tell us much about the beliefs of individual members, the residual prejudices and sentiments of Tory or Scottish members. But the fact that only Erskine was bold enough, or misguided enough, to brave the giggling and scorn of the house, tells us something about the triumph of polite and 'rational' discourse, and the rising blushes which must have stifled any budding expressions of a belief in the power of witches. Nursing for so long his Scottish resentments, smarting from English abuse, Erskine confused the English and Scottish contexts of opposition and his attacks were brushed aside as uncouth nonsense.

[47] Cf. Stephen Taylor at n. 25.

IV

James Erskine evidently saw the repeal of the witchcraft act as part of a more general assault upon the citadels of fidelity. He worried about the credentials of English bishops, 'none of them being firm to any set of doctrinall principles, they are much dispised'. One of his particular *bêtes noirs* was Benjamin Hoadly: 'Bangor, nou Sarum, is sunk into a hackney writer.'[48] Hoadly's reputedly deistical *Plain Account of the Nature and End of the Sacrament of the Lord's Supper*, appeared in 1735. The issue of Hoadly's freethinking in the *Plain Account* was the starting point for the only extant pamphlet straightforwardly opposing the repeal of the witchcraft act, written in the form of an address to the sponsoring members, and attached to a reissue of an anonymous work, *The Witch of Endor: Or a Plea for the Divine Administration by the Agency of Good and Evil Spirits* (original date uncertain, but some time in the early years of the century). It manifested many of the same concerns as Erskine and may help us to understand latent prejudices which remained, for the most part, unexpressed.

This *Address* recapitulates many of the old arguments about witchcraft, but it focuses on the threat of freethinking which the repeal of the witchcraft legislation represented: 'the design being to secure some of the *Outworks* of *Religion*, and to regain a Parcel of Ground, which *bold* Infidelity hath invaded'. The author uses heavy sarcasm and addresses the House of Commons with heavy irony: 'I dare not entertain the least Thought, Gentlemen, that you have any of the *Freethinking* Qualities, that are so prevalent, at this Time of Day . . . ' While implying that the arguments against a proper belief in witchcraft are irredeemably vulgar, the product of ignorance and raillery, the author wryly exempts his distinguished audience: 'It would be inexcusable to trouble you any longer, *Gentlemen*, with this Way and Manner of *decrying Witchcraft*; and I'll venture of Prophesy [!], *such* sort of Arguing will not be made use of in your *own Learned Debates* upon the same subject.'[49]

It is Francis Hutchinson, now bishop of Down and Connor, author of

---

[48] *Analecta*, IV, p. 146.
[49] *The Witch of Endor* (1736), pp. xlv, xliii. Cf. footnote on p. v which mocks the Commons' contempt for the authority of Coke's *Pleas of the Crown*, 'which I don't doubt, but your Worships have consulted, and pity'd *his* Understanding and Knowledge too'. At one point the mockery verges on the insulting: 'When the *Gospel* of Christ was Preaching, (which ever condemns Witchcraft, and *Sorcery* . . . however you, our *Representatives*, shall please to determine the Affair *within Doors* . . . '), p. xi.

the definitive sceptical work, *An Historical Essay concerning Witchcraft* (1718), whom the pamphleteer wants to discredit. He paints him as a vulgarian, free and easy with fantastical stories about the contortions and wonders which may be achieved (implausibly) by nature alone, without the intrusion of the supernatural. Hutchinson's book bandies tales about showmen and charlatans, so many indeed that his opponent, with a nod and a wink, can 'profess . . . [that] I am perfectly Ignorant whence our Right Reverend, got all this KNOWLEDGE, or where his SOBER AUTHORS are to be met with'. The pamphleteer shows his opponents playing with dangerous vulgarity and outrageous freethinking, mounting a disturbingly plebeian, if episcopal, threat to traditional orthodoxy. It is to the service of this scheme that the author of the *Address* bends his urbane and witty tone, punning and cracking jokes about the Gin Act, the other 'spiritual' crisis of 1736.[50]

The intellectual and theological argument pursued in tandem with this drollery is one which unmasks the central contradiction in Hutchinson's discourse, between the denial of witchcraft on the one hand, and the assertion, on the other, that, as Hutchinson put it, 'the sober belief of good and bad Spirits is an Essential Part of every good Christian's Faith'. How can this assertion and this denial be squared? Or, as our author has it: '[it is] inconsistent with such a Belief, that all Communications should be reckoned Imaginary, and that the Intellectual World should not serve the Purposes of an Almighty Being, in rewarding or punishing according to the Divine Appointment'. The author is keen in associating the 'Fundamental Part of the Statute' with the 'Protestant Religion and Interest', which 'as 'tis grounded on the Holy Scriptures, so it stands, and I hope, will ever stand, supported by the Legislature'. His definition of witchcraft is a broad one – 'any sort of Communication with, or Operations upon the Intellectual, and Corporeal World' – and having cited the Bible, and Hutchinson himself, on the necessity of spiritual ministration and depredation, he asks how the legislature can possibly be considering what he calls an 'absolute Repeal'. This last phrase suggests the possibility that the witchcraft legislation could have been revised so as to minimise prosecution, while retaining its ideological and defining function, in both religion and statecraft; a contemporary nod to the conceptual distinction between ideology and persecution. But then, the author is adamant that, as 'an Offence capital immediately against the Divine Majesty', witchcraft deserves to be punished. The association

---

[50] *The Witch of Endor*, pp. xxv–xxvi, xxxiii. Cf. *The Hyp-Doctor*, no. 285, 23 Mar. 1736.

between orthodox belief in witchcraft and the maintenance of true religion culminates in this passage:

> [I] must believe, that, in the *Preamble* of your Bill (which I have not seen) you have taken all possible Care to guard against the Suggestions of a *censorious* Age; by *supporting* the *Christian Doctrine*, and declaring to the World, (as Bishop *Hutchinson* does) *That the* sober *Belief of Good and Bad Spirits is an* essential *Part of every good Christian's Faith*.[51]

There is also a social threat lurking behind this legislation, which points back to the condemnation of Hutchinson as a dangerous truckler with plebeians and freethinkers: 'However, it must be said, the *contrary* Temper [i.e. freethinking] is too obvious amongst us *without Doors*; and this has induc'd me to trouble you in such a Manner . . . ' The author poses as a hard-nosed realist who can tell the honourable members about affairs in the outside world, 'however *merry* you may have made yourselves about SPIRITS in St *Stephen's* Chapel'. Witchcraft belief is an important buttress of orthodox religion, which parliament neglects at its peril.

The postscript alludes to a very different sort of pressure from without doors, 'your *Electors* . . . [and] *Thousands* besides' who require an answer to these objections. There is a tension, between this manipulation of public opinion, and the author's almost paranoid fear of the licentious mob: 'I now hear what I have to offer, comes *too late*, and there seems no other *Reason* possibly to be assign'd for it, but, that my unknown *Printer sides* with the *Majority*, in *procrastinating* the birth of this little Pamphlet.' That this charge reached the light of day hardly indicates particular interest on the part of the threateningly *anonymous* artisan; but fear of the plebeian is in evidence, in both mysterious particularity (the printer) and threatening mass (the '*Majority*').[52]

Earlier, however, the author makes an assessment of the balance of clerical opinion which is very different:

> [witchcraft can be considered as] an Affair purely of a *Religious Nature*, abstracted from the *Civil Punishment* [again the distinction between persecution and ideology]; and, if I might ask; what, if the *Concurrence* of an *English Convocation* had been had, in making such a *General Repeal*?

Witchcraft is evidently a Tory issue, and the cherished belief of a silent majority of the English clergy. The author manages to bind up witchcraft

---

[51] *The Witch of Endor*, pp. viii, xxviii, v.   [52] Ibid., pp. xliii, xlix–l, xliii.

with another recognisably Tory grievance, the disappearance of a sitting convocation. This involved the entrusting of the nation's spiritual interest to parliament. In the pamphlet as a whole, the author asks the legislators to exercise their spiritual responsibilities with care. In this particular passage, he asserts that were the clergy to have a say, as would be proper in a consideration 'abstracted from the *Civil Punishment*', the matter would stand very differently.[53]

So we can identify this address as thoroughly Tory in ideology: siding with the ordinary clergy, as against two bishops, but fearing the mob; crying out that the church is in danger, and condemning the licence of the modern majority. This reading of the text allows us to define the sense in which those who supported the old witchcraft legislation felt embattled; and to catch the authentic but silent meaning of the constituency – marginalised, embarrassed, ridiculed – from which its author emerged. It was a constituency Erskine's 'long canting speech' in the Commons failed either to find or arouse.

V

It is misleading, therefore, to make the repeal of the Jacobean legislation against witchcraft a mere footnote to the history of rationalism. Repeal did not emerge from out of nowhere as an afterthought, a process of mopping-up in a struggle against superstition that had been won some time 'between the Restoration and the Revolution'. It had a context and a meaning, both to some extent recoverable. Erskine and our anonymous pamphleteer represent an identifiable nexus of concerns which can be seen at work long before 1736, and did not suddenly die a death either on the stroke of midnight, 31 December 1699, or when George II put his signature to the act of repeal.[54]

Neither was repeal an undifferentiated and simple, nor a solely English process. The parliamentary procedure of discussion and amendment resulted not in a simple repeal as had been envisaged by the bill's

---

[53] Ibid., p. xxvii. Compare the pamphleteer's concern for convocation, with that of Erskine and his predecessors – like Robert Wylie – for the continued existence and dignity of the General Assembly of the Scottish church. Highflying in Scotland and England was being bound up with the issue of witchcraft.

[54] Buckle, *The History of Civilisation*, III, p. 363: 'the destruction of the old notions respecting witchcraft . . . was effected, so far as the educated classes are concerned, between the Restoration and the Revolution'.

sponsors, but in a new witchcraft act which punished imposture, the pretended 'use or exercise [of] any kind of Witchcraft, Sorcery, Inchantment, or Conjuration'. The Lords' consideration of the bill also ensured the extension of the new legislation to Scotland; an afterthought which is a neat example of the insensitivity to the affairs of North Britain about which the likes of Erskine complained. The late measures against imposture had an ideological function, serving to underline the new reading of the Old Testament injunctions against witchcraft which those who wished to ditch the prosecution of witches had long favoured.[55]

The 1736 legislation was itself repealed in the 1950–1 session of parliament with the intention of preventing possible prosecutions of well-meaning spiritualists. Chuter Ede, home secretary, was whiggish in every sense, asserting that 'this Measure is a considerable advance in the direction of religious Toleration'. Another member, Lieutenant-Commander Thompson, saw the measure in a more engagingly eccentric light, making a speech which encapsulates many of the false conceptions besetting the historian of witchcraft:

> If, as I hope, the House gives a Second Reading to this Bill today we shall be doing rather a remarkable thing. I do not speak as a Spiritualist, but in my view we shall be reaffirming an outlook and a point of view very necessary in an increasingly material age. In 1735 [*sic*] the Witchcraft Act brought to an end officially what had, in fact, been at an end for some years – the belief in the reality of witchcraft. Witchcraft had been practised from the very beginning of time; during the 16th and 17th centuries there was tremendous activity in England and on the Continent, but with the dawn of the 'age of reason', so called, belief in the reality of witchcraft faded . . . By 1735 the official view was that these powers no longer existed, whether they were good or evil, and we have been committed to a sort of official scepticism ever since that day . . . [this bill will] reaffirm that we honestly admit that there are powers given to some people in the community which enable them to do things which, for 215 years, we have not believed were physically possible.

This passage sums up many historical misconceptions, unwittingly hints

---

55 For amendments see *Journal of the House of Lords*, 26 Feb. 1735/6 and *Journal of the House of Commons*, 4 Mar. 1735/6. On the 'proper' reading of the scriptural injunctions against witchcraft, see *The Witchcraft of the Scriptures: A Sermon Preach'd on a Special Occasion. By Ph.S LL.D* (1736), esp. pp. 19, 22, 24, and Joseph Juxon, *A Sermon upon Witchcraft* (1736).

at a truer perspective, and suggests unexpected continuities in the history of witchcraft legislation.[56]

This chapter set out by questioning the cogency of vague notions according to which belief in the reality of witchcraft 'faded' in the wake of a nebulous 'age of reason', some time around 1700. As an intellectual assumption about the genealogy of our own beliefs, this position runs very deep, as Lieutenant-Commander Thompson's remarks show. Once the assumption has been questioned, and we ask whether witchcraft might not have been a serious issue in 1700 and beyond, our whole perspective on this issue shifts radically.

As we have seen, the 1735–6 act did not commit everyone to scepticism as regards the existence of these powers, 'good or evil'. Even after 1736, apologists for the old attitudes continued to speak out; but their fate was increasingly to be marginalised and ridiculed. The repeal of the Jacobean legislation set the seal on an elite consensus that convictions of witches for real sorcery were unsafe. This was, then, a confirmation of an 'official view' in force since the end of the 'rage of party'. It is here that Thompson's remarks point towards the perspective canvassed in this essay: the history of the fate of the elite discourse of witchcraft is largely the history of an official point of view and its transformations, transformations effected both by specific, and contingent, political events, and by longer-term shifts in the structure of ideology.

Finally, of course, 215 years on, witchcraft legislation was once more being used to fight bigger battles to defend spiritual values 'in an increasingly material age'. The witchcraft issue had its various uses in the seventeenth, the eighteenth, the nineteenth, and even the twentieth centuries. And writing about witchcraft today, no doubt, has its uses too.[57]

---

[56] *Hansard*, 5th ser., vol. 481, session 1950–51, cols. 1486, 1467 (1 Dec. 1950). On 20 June 1950, Charles Botham had been convicted on three counts of false pretences. He had also been charged with two counts of conjuration under the 1735/6 act, but these were not considered by the court.

[57] 14 and 15 Geo. 6. ch. 33. *Fraudulent Mediums Act, 1951*. (An Act to repeal the Witchcraft Act, 1735, and to make in substitution for certain provisions of section four of the Vagrancy Act, 1824, express provision for the punishment of persons who fraudulently purport to act as spiritualistic mediums or to exercise powers of telepathy, clairvoyance, or other similar powers. 22 June 1951.) For recent, non-historical, debate about witchcraft see 'Propaganda, fantasy and lies blur reports of ritual abuse', *The Guardian*, 10 Sept. 1990; 'Save poor little witch girl; drugged child rape victim's nightmare in lair of Satan', *News of the World*, 6 May 1990; 'I sacrificed my babies to Satan', *Sunday Mirror*, 25 Mar. 1990; 'Witch story to believe?', *The Spectator*, 24 Mar. 1990; 'Root out Satanists . . . Mrs Thatcher last night vowed to rid Britain of devil worship orgies involving the sexual abuse of children', *The Sun*, 14 Mar. 1990.

13. *On the continuation of witchcraft*

WILLEM DE BLÉCOURT

In this chapter, I will combine some general points of critique on Thomas' *Religion and the Decline of Magic* with specific refutations of his remarks on the 'survival' of traditional witchcraft into the twentieth century. While my overall criticism is mainly of a theoretical nature, the specific comments are illustrated with material taken from my research on Dutch witchcraft. Although a comparison of witchcraft in England with that in the Netherlands might yield some salient differences, here it is above all meant to provide further possibilities for the study of 'witchcraft' – that is, labelling people as 'witches' – in historical European contexts. Among other things, I will argue that, at least in some situations, the opposition of 'magic' and religion prohibits the recognition of the latter as a legitimising category that also encapsulated witchcraft.

I

When commenting upon a book more than twenty years old, as *Religion and the Decline of Magic* is,[1] one has to take into account that it has already been criticised and that its author will have had the time to reconsider some of his hypotheses and conclusions. However, that should not deter one from criticism, especially when the book is still referred to (the Dutch translation was published only a few years ago) and even constitutes the starting point for most students of early modern

---

[1] References are to the Penguin University Books edition: Keith Thomas, *Religion and the Decline of Magic. Studies in Popular Beliefs in Sixteenth- and Seventeenth-Century England* (Harmondsworth, 1973).

witchcraft. Also, I think it is possible to uncover some problems that have, at least partly, escaped attention so far.[2]

One of the concepts that figures predominantly in Thomas' book is 'magic'. In 1975 it was the subject of a well-known discussion between the author and the anthropologist Hildred Geertz. According to her, 'magic' was a concept which was not very suitable to build a book on. Thomas should have been more aware of the emergence of 'magic' as a labelling activity: 'the categories which he uses when attempting to develop causal hypotheses are those of *some* of the subjects themselves'.[3] In his reply, Thomas admitted that he should have paid more attention to 'the changing vocabulary in which magical practitioners and magical activities were described'. He nevertheless insisted on maintaining the term. While the use of European concepts for the description of non-European societies could indeed be seen as 'ethnocentric', it escaped such a classification when applied to European history. 'But though unsuitable for export they may well be good enough for home', Thomas countered. 'In *Religion and the Decline of Magic*, I was attempting to write English history, not to engage in cross-cultural analysis and I must plead guilty to having used language which contemporaries themselves, or most of them, would have understood.'[4] By implication, every inhabitant of Renaissance England was more or less agreed on the meaning of a term like 'magic'.

As we have, since this discussion took place, witnessed the rise of 'popular culture' studies,[5] we should at least be observant of the possibility that the people who were said to practise 'magic', might

---

[2] Cf. my critique of another classic in witchcraft studies, Carlo Ginzburg's *The Night Battles*: Willem de Blécourt, 'Spuren einer Volkskultur oder Dämonisierung? Kritische Bemerkungen zu Ginzburgs "Die Benandanti"', *Kea. Zeitschrift für Kulturwissenschaften*, 5 (1993), 17-29.

[3] Hildred Geertz, 'An anthropology of religion and magic, I', *Journal of Interdisciplinary History*, 6 (1975), 71–89, citation: 76–7, emphasis added.

[4] Keith Thomas, 'An anthropology of religion and magic, II', *Journal of Interdisciplinary History*, 6 (1975), 91–100, citations: 97, 94.

[5] The concept 'popular culture' is problematic. It is first and foremost an overall label under which the attacks by different 'educated' groups on practices and conceptions of other, not necessarily 'uneducated' groups can be gathered. Its subject matter, however, has been reified to indicate the culture of the lower classes. This not only presupposes rigid class societies but also neglects the communicability of cultural features and the debates on these. Cf. Stuart Hall, 'Notes on deconstructing "the popular"', in Raphael Samuel, ed., *People's History and Socialist Theory* (London, 1981), pp. 227–40; Wolfgang Brückner, 'Popular culture. Konstrukt, Interpretament, Realität. Anfragen zur historischen Methodologie und Theoriebildung aus der Sicht der mitteleuropäischen Forschung', *Ethnologia Europaea*, 14 (1984), 14–24.

themselves have classified their activities differently from those who described them.[6] Thomas, I am convinced, must have reached this conclusion as well, for he recently stated that a historian's approach to the past must be similar to the anthropologist's approach to another, 'alien', society. 'This involves a state of complete open-mindedness, a decision to take nothing for granted, a recognition that the investigator has to begin by working out all the basic categories and silent assumptions implicit in the behaviour of the people he is studying.'[7] If one studies cultural concepts in a socially multilayered European society, their meanings might differ from one group of people to another. This implies that, though 'magic' (like 'superstition') can be taken as an indigenous concept, it first has to be identified as a concept that was employed by some people in an attempt to control the activities and thoughts of *others*, even within the same administrative boundaries. Furthermore, in the case of 'magic', it would be wrong to use it *a priori* as a classificatory principle in modern research, at least if the practices of those others that were ranked under 'magic' are to be fully comprehended. Adopting the anthropologist's relativistic outlook, the historian of 'magic' should either limit him- or herself to the (manifold) groups that adhered to the concept and to its changing traditions, or break it down to its various components and study (one of) those in relation to other, *non-*'magical' concepts.

I would not advocate, as Geertz did in 1975, that any particular notion (one of these 'magical' components, for instance) is embedded in 'covert, closed systems of ideas about reality'.[8] In this, I agree with Thomas, when he wrote that 'it remains to be established whether the charms and rituals always constituted a coherent system'.[9] But whereas it is indeed doubtful that the people who felt bewitched, talked about fairies, saw ghosts, consulted an astrologer, or whatever, would, even unconsciously,[10] have resorted to some encompassing framework, to a special 'world-view',[11] it would also be rash to assume that they did not

---

[6] Cf. the review by Randal Keynes, *Journal of the Anthropological Society of Oxford*, 3 (1972), 149–57.

[7] Keith Thomas, 'Ways of doing cultural history', in Rik Sanders et al., eds., *De verleiding van de overvloed. Reflecties op de eigenheid van de cultuurgeschiedenis* (Amsterdam, 1991), pp. 65–81, citation: p. 74.

[8] Geertz, 'An anthropology', 84.

[9] Thomas, 'An anthropology', 106.

[10] Geertz, 'An anthropology', 88.

[11] On the now rather obsolete concept of 'world view', see, for example, Orvar Löfgren, 'World-views: a research perspective', *Ethnologia Scandinavia*, 11 (1981), 21–36.

use any classification at all. One of the tasks of the historian of culture is to reconstruct 'the various cultural codes present in early modern society'.[12] As Thomas himself put it: 'we can only make sense of a particular object, practice or belief by identifying its place in the system as a whole'.[13] That 'system', however, might not be as 'whole' or 'closed' as we would presume it to be. As, in practice, classifications would only acquire meaning in specific situations and settings, a reconstruction of those is needed *before* we jump to general conclusions. People in seventeenth-century England who felt that they had fallen victim to bewitchment, might very well have confided in their local minister that they were harbouring 'superstitious' thoughts, while to their neighbours they stressed the 'reality' of their experiences. They might have consulted official doctors, as well as cunning men, astrologers or quacks. Indeed, the notion of 'shopping around the medical market'[14] implies that there could have been different solutions, and consequently different classifications, to the same practical problems by the same people.

The study of 'magic' as an historical-anthropological problem, that is to say, as an attempt to understand the ideas and practices of concrete, historical *others*, should, in my view, always begin with the wish to reconstruct indigenous meanings. It would, therefore, be more relevant (and also more practical) to start with specific notions of specific people, instead of broad categories, as the latter compel the researcher to tackle all the cultural (and also social and economic) features of a society. In *Religion and the Decline of Magic*, Thomas has only covered a small part of historical English culture, the boundaries of which are mainly defined by dominant categories (whether those of present-day academics or past elites). I would not be surprised if, when studied separately, astrology, ghosts, witchcraft, fairies, or whatever 'magical' phenomenon, should prove to be restricted to different social situations and to belong to different traditions and even to different trends (a certain amount of overlap notwithstanding). When in the following paragraphs I limit the discussion to witchcraft, it is not only because of the huge amount of

---

12 Michael MacDonald, 'Anthropological perspectives on the history of science and medicine', in P. Corsi and P. Weindling, eds., *Information Sources in the History of Science and Medicine* (London, 1983), pp. 61–80, citation 66. MacDonald attributes this notion to Geertz, 'An anthropology', but as 'code' is not similar to 'system', it is rather an elaboration of her perspective.

13 Thomas, 'Ways', p. 75.

14 Cf. Dorothy Porter and Roy Porter, *Patient's Progress. Doctors and Doctoring in Eighteenth-century England* (Cambridge, 1989).

work needed to collect systematically all instances of 'magic' within a given region, but also because it is theoretically problematic to join them all together within a single frame.[15]

II

In his chapter 'Witchcraft: decline', Thomas devoted most of his attention to the decline of witch trials. He documented a growing scepticism in intellectual circles, together with an increasing demand for proof at the judicial level. Whether similar doubts gained popularity among those who thought themselves the victims of witchcraft remains in the dark. 'The dwindling number of prosecutions is not evidence that allegations were no longer levied. It only shows that they were no longer seriously entertained by the courts.' He went on: 'But although popular feeling against witches *survived* the repeal of the Act in 1736, it is *possible* that the volume of accusations had begun to dwindle.'[16] By suggesting the possibility of a change in 'popular' opinion, Thomas in fact admitted that the continuation of informal witchcraft accusations, the tradition of witchcraft in the stricter sense, did not form part of his investigations.[17] He also expressed his view on the later examples he came across: to him they were merely 'survivals', thereby implicitly accepting a general decline of witchcraft. During the last twenty years this idea has not been refuted.

For present-day European witchcraft research is mainly restricted to the period of the hunts. The student's interest evaporates together with the smoke of the last pyre. The reason for this undoubtedly has much to do with the dominant rationalistic historiographic tradition, in which witchcraft was considered an aberration and in which the witch trials were seen as a blot on the development of human (that is, white male) enlightenment. Witchcraft was a fantasy, its prosecution a craze. Essentially, witchcraft was a sure sign of otherness, a chimera that was defined by distance, whether in space or in time. It was assigned to

---

[15] As the Wagenborgen tailor Staal said in 1944 (to quote but one example): 'Witches and ghosts are nonsense, but omens exist', see Willem de Blécourt, 'Het Groninger veldwerk van Tjaard W. R. de Haan', *Driemaandelijkse bladen*, 37 (1985), 95–117, esp. 108. See also the more general discussion in Linda Dégh and Andrew Vázsonyi, 'Legend and belief', in Dan Ben-Amos, ed., *Folklore Genres* (Austin, 1976), pp. 93–123.

[16] Thomas, *Religion*, pp. 694–5, emphasis added.

[17] Cf. William Monter, 'European witchcraft: a moment of synthesis?', *The Historical Journal*, 31 (1988), 183–5, esp. 185.

'primitive' cultures and 'backward' or even 'sick' societies. As the anthropologist Mayer declared: 'We all feel that a society that gives excessive prominence to witchcraft must be a sick society, rather as a witch-ridden personality is a sick personality.'[18] As far as the presentation is concerned, modern students of witchcraft seem to have emancipated themselves from those presentist and sociocentric notions. On closer inspection, however, the varnish proves rather thin and flaking. Witch trials still form the main focus of the historian's attention and it still has to be explained why so many women were killed for crimes which 'in reality' they did not commit.[19]

Although the insertion of anthropological insights in the historian's toolkit has improved the situation a little during the last two decades, it has not led to a critical reconsideration of the object of research. In fact, there is still considerable confusion, especially when the object is labelled 'witchcraft' but actually proves to be 'witch hunts'. Even if it is admitted that 'witch beliefs' lingered on after the abolition of the trials, they are not found suitable for systematic scrutinisation. 'Unfortunately, nobody has yet attempted a thorough study of magic in the eighteenth century', Malcolmson remarked more than ten years ago, and his remark, which also applies to the nineteenth and early twentieth century, still holds today.[20]

There is, of course, the problem of sources. At least some criminal prosecutions produced depositions of witnesses which facilitate the case studies that are needed to reconstruct local participants' rationales.[21] But even the Church courts, which, in England and the Netherlands at least, were acting fairly independently from the secular institutions which conducted the criminal investigations, lost their interest in witchcraft

---

[18] Philip Mayer, 'Witches', in Max Marwick, ed., *Witchcraft and Sorcery: Selected Readings* (Harmondsworth, 1970), pp. 45–65, citation, p. 58.

[19] See, for example, Brian P. Levack, *The Witch-hunt in Early Modern Europe* (London and New York, 1987).

[20] Robert W. Malcolmson, *Life and Labour in England 1700–1800* (London/Melbourne, 1981), p. 86. See also, Donald Nugent, 'Witchcraft studies, 1959–1971: a bibliographical survey', *Journal of Popular Culture*, 5 (1971), 710–25, esp. 721; Joachim Friedrich Baumhauer, *Johan Kruse und der 'neuzeitliche Hexenwahn'* (Neumünster, 1984), p. 195.

[21] See, for example, David Warren Sabean, 'The sacred bond of unity: community through the eyes of a thirteen-year-old witch (1683)', in Sabean, *Power in the Blood. Popular Culture and Village Discourse in Early Modern Germany* (Cambridge, 1984), pp. 94–112; R. W. Scribner, 'Sorcery, superstition and society: the witch of Urach, 1529', in Scribner, *Popular Culture and Popular Movement in Reformation Germany* (London/Roncevalle, 1987), pp. 257–75.

(as well as in other moral offences) at the beginning of the eighteenth century.[22] Would it be worthwhile to search for traces of witchcraft in eighteenth- and nineteenth-century documents, when the usual sources cease to provide information? For one thing, it can be argued that, even within the classic paradigm of witch-hunting research it would be relevant to study the decline of local witchcraft, if only to ascertain the relative importance of the various elements that contributed to the cessation of the judicial murder of witches. That would, however, leave the question of why in some places and among some people witchcraft continued to be a way to comprehend some of the facts of daily existence. A more theoretically valuable argument would be that the scientific premises that underlie most historical witchcraft research are strongly biased towards rationalistic presuppositions, as well as towards contemporary 'elitist' views.

In any reissue of Thomas' *Religion and the Decline of Magic*, I would suggest that all references to 'primitive' societies and to 'survivals' should be edited out (unfortunately, these concepts are not incorporated in the index).[23] Such notions are, after all, too much connected to evolutionistic discourse to be academically viable today.[24] Surely, Thomas did not adhere to the nineteenth-century metaphor that equated immaterial 'survivals' with the material relics that constituted the object of archaeology ('to survive' can sometimes just be read as a synonym for 'to last').[25] But while Thomas clearly did not see seventeenth-century

[22] Thomas, *Religion*, pp. 309–10; Willem de Blécourt, 'Four centuries of Frisian witch doctors', in Marijke Gijswijt-Hofstra and Willem Frijhoff, eds., *Witchcraft in the Netherlands from the Fourteenth to the Twentieth Century* (Rijswijk, 1991), pp. 157–66, esp. pp. 160–1. See also, Marijke Gijswijt-Hofstra, 'Witchcraft before Zeeland magistrates and church courts, sixteenth to twentieth century', *ibid.*, pp. 103–18; Willem de Blécourt and Freek Perebook, 'Insult and admonition: witchcraft in the Land of Vollenhove, seventeenth century', *ibid.*, pp. 119–31. On northern England: Philip Tyler, 'The church courts at York and witchcraft prosecutions, 1567–1640', *Northern History*, 4 (1969), 84–109; Peter Rushton, 'Women, witchcraft, and slander in early modern England: cases from the church courts at Durham, 1560–1675', *Northern History*, 28 (1982), 116–32.

[23] Thomas certainly has noticed the patronising aspects of the adjective 'primitive', with 'its condescending evolutionary overtones', see Thomas, 'An anthropology', 93.

[24] On evolutionism in anthropology and folklore, see, for example, Marvin Harris, *The Rise of Anthropological Theory* (New York, 1968); Richard M. Dorson, *The British Folklorists. A History* (Chicago, 1968); Simon J. Bronner, 'The early movements of anthropology and their folkloristic relationships', *Folklore*, 95 (1984), 57–73.

[25] This development seems to have passed Ginzburg by; see, for example, his recent book *Ecstasies. Deciphering the Witch's Sabbat* (London, 1990); cf. Perry Anderson, 'Witchcraft', *London Review of Books*, 8 November 1990, 6–11.

witchcraft as a remnant of pre-Christian times, he seems nevertheless to have depicted nineteenth-century witchcraft as a 'survival' of the seventeenth-century variant, to mention but one example.[26] For the evolutionists, the meaning of survivals was to be constructed so that it fitted their ideas of ancient mythology, and it was certainly not to be related to contemporary contexts.[27] Likewise, for Thomas, the meaning of nineteenth-century witchcraft was the same as he had constructed for its seventeenth-century predecessor. 'The majority of . . . informal witch accusations recorded in the eighteenth, nineteenth and even twentieth centuries conform to the same old special pattern of charity evaded, followed by misfortune incurred', he wrote.[28] Thomas' analysis of witchcraft is linked, albeit rather crudely, to his description of the social and economic context in which the uttering of accusations apparently took place. 'Poverty, sickness, and sudden disaster were thus familiar features of the social environment of this period', he concludes about the seventeenth century in the beginning of his book.[29] Accordingly, 'survivals' are to be found in the same milieu: 'By the nineteenth century traditional magical beliefs were largely restricted to the more intimate communities of the English countryside.'[30]

Statements like this are not only problematic because of their evolutionistic bias that links 'primitive' environment to 'primitive' thought, they also lack the evidence of the absence of witchcraft in more accessible places like cities. The nineteenth-century folklorists, on whose writings Thomas mainly relies, were so convinced of their hypotheses about peasant survivals, that they did not look elsewhere. Apart from the folklorists' materials, which after careful assessment can still be of some use, what kind of sources could count as a reliable entrance into the world of the witches from the eighteenth century onwards? I shall consider two.[31]

After the authorities had brought the criminal trials against maleficial

---

[26] On earlier 'catholic survivals', see Thomas, *Religion*, pp. 82, 85, 214.

[27] Cf. Georgina Bowes, 'Cultural survivals theory and traditional customs', *Folklife*, 26 (1988), 5-11.

[28] Thomas, *Religion*, p. 696.

[29] *Ibid.*, p. 20.

[30] *Ibid.*, p. 797.

[31] See also Gustav Henningsen, 'Witch persecution after the era of the witch trials. A contribution to Danish ethnohistory', *ARC. Scandinavian Yearbook of Folklore 1988*, 44 (1989), 103–53; Judith Devlin, *The Superstitious Mind. French Peasants and the Supernatural in the Nineteenth Century* (New Haven/London, 1987).

witches to a stop,[32] they still conducted trials in which witchcraft was involved. Up until the twentieth century, people were prosecuted for crimes of violence against alleged witches. Also, cunning men and women were liable to prosecution, for instance as unlicensed practitioners of medicine. In practical terms, though, it is almost impossible to retrieve these cases from the huge quantity of court records, since the indexes (if any) were compiled on the basis of other denominators. (But one could always start with one jurisdiction, work in teams, or, which is the most rewarding, search for witchcraft as part of a study into physical and verbal violence.)

The second source, which has the advantage that it often includes references to the first, is the newspaper. It may at first seem ironic that precisely the 'general improvement in communications', which, according to Thomas, contributed to the decline of 'magic',[33] should turn out to provide the most important source for the documentation of its continuation. On second thoughts, it is hardly surprising, since the attack on 'superstition' was the main reason why early journalists reported the occurrence of witchcraft.[34]

III

Going through nineteenth- and early twentieth-century newspapers, I have unearthed around 300 witchcraft cases, scattered all over the Netherlands. Given the regional bias of the newspapers I consulted,[35] this number hardly differs from the number of sixteenth- or seventeenth-century cases.[36] Folklore research during the 1960s has resulted in

---

[32] Debates on correct judicial procedures and on the (in)ability to prove witchcraft predate the refutation of the underlying concept of devil worship; see, for example, Thomas, *Religion*, pp. 538, 685, 688; Wolfgang Behringer, *Hexenverfolgung in Bayern. Volksmagie, Glaubenseifer und Staatsräson in der Frühen Neuzeit* (Munich, 1987), pp. 224–331; Robin Briggs, *Communities of Belief. Cultural and Social Tension in Early Modern France* (Oxford, 1989), p. 45.

[33] Thomas, *Religion*, p. 778.

[34] For English and Canadian newspaper accounts on witchcraft, see R. Trevor Davies, *Four Centuries of Witch-Beliefs* (London, 1947), pp. 188–200; Robert-Lionel Séguin, *La sorcellerie au Québec du XVIIe au XIXe siècle* (Ottawa, 1978).

[35] The main search was of newspapers from Drenthe, Overijssel and Friesland. They did, however, contain reports of witchcraft elsewhere in the Netherlands, if only to counter accusations of backwardness.

[36] See for a tentative overview the list in Marijke Gijswijt-Hofstra and Willem Frijhoff, eds., *Nederland betoverd. Toverij en hekserij van de veertiende tot in de twintigste eeuw* (Amsterdam, 1987), pp. 332–9.

approximately 6,000 witchcraft legends.[37] Was there really a decline in witchcraft accusations? The answer is, of course, positive, if only because of the vast population increase. Furthermore, at least one general development can be discerned: witchcraft became mainly prevalent among women of the lower social classes.[38] True to their vocation, folklorists only interviewed the aged in the countryside; journalists, however, reported several cases from the cities. Broadly speaking, witchcraft has indeed declined, though not along the lines Thomas proposed. Yet to focus on the general decline might blind the researcher to the fluctuations in different kinds of witchcraft.

Some years ago, there was a discussion about the value and trustworthiness of newspaper accounts of witchcraft. The French ethnologist Favret-Saada, for instance, stressed that they did not throw any light on the local system of bewitchment and unbewitchment, but rather, by presenting sensational and isolated cases, provided a front behind which the real witch believers could hide.[39] In this she is supported by her Danish colleague Schiffmann, who investigated Polish witchcraft. 'The interviewer', the latter writes about the students of witchcraft, 'is put on a sort of trial, to see whether his interest is connected with the "scandalous" bits or with real information; the first category of intruder is well known in the countryside'.[40]

In present-day witchcraft research newspapers clearly are an insufficient source. For the nineteenth and early twentieth century, they are often the only source. If they are to be used, it has to be established whether their sense of the sensational was similar to that existing today. Although nineteenth-century articles on witchcraft were obviously meant to ridicule the 'stupid superstitions' that ought not to be part of

---

[37] Ton Dekker, 'Witches and sorcerers in twentieth[-]century legends', in Gijswijt-Hofstra and Frijhoff, eds., *Witchcraft in the Netherlands*, pp. 183–95.

[38] The overall decline of male involvement in witchcraft accusations (in Holland from around 1600 onwards and in Drenthe since the beginning of the eighteenth century) deserves more attention. So far, it has been related to the increasing separation between male and female domains, as well as to the rationalisation of the former. See Willem de Blécourt, *Termen van toverij. De veranderende betekenis van toverij in Noordoost-Nederland tussen de 16de en 20ste eeuw* (Nijmegen, 1900); Hans de Waardt, *Toverij en samenleving. Holland 1500–1800* (Den Haag, 1991).

[39] Jeanne Favret-Saada, *Deadly Words. Witchcraft in the Bocage* (Cambridge/Paris, 1980), pp. 31–8.

[40] Aldona Christina Schiffmann, 'The witch and the crime: the persecution of witches in twentieth-century Poland', *ARV. Scandinavian Yearbook of Folklore 1987*, 43 (1988), 147–65, citation 153.

'our enlightened era', it has to be assumed that they do not only contain exceptional cases. To the reporters (often locals, albeit of a different class), any eruption of witchcraft was itself an excess. Comparison of the accounts with each other, as well as with the later folklore records,[41] also leads to the conclusion that the last century's newspapers present 'normal' witchcraft, if not in all the desired detail. They also 'have an advantage over the current folklore records in always showing us the tradition in a concrete social context and also always providing us with definite chronological bases'.[42] The disadvantage is that they usually lack the names of the participants, as do many legends.[43]

Like any corpus of texts that has been compiled systematically, newspaper articles on witchcraft can be analysed on several different levels. One can look, for instance, to the social, economic or religious aspects. Above all, the mutual relations and interdependence of the several analytical aspects of witchcraft should be emphasised, especially when reconstructing indigenous meanings.[44] In doing so, one may start by considering each instance of witchcraft labelling on its own and proceed to differentiate its several communicative elements before interrelating them into broader patterns. In dealing with witchcraft texts, I found it most rewarding to start with *content*, to proceed with *participants* and *genre* and to round off with looking at *spatial* and *temporal* distribution. This set of points of special attention has been derived from anthropological and folklore methodology. Folklorists, having left the concept of the *Kulturkreis* behind, now use mapping as a means to trace contemporary contexts.[45] Anthropologists, by taking the linguistic turn, have, among others, developed action and evaluation

---

[41] In the Netherlands, the systematic collection of legends only started in the twentieth century. See for an overview of articles on witchcraft in books and periodicals Fred Matter, Willem de Blécourt, Ton Dekker, Willem Frijhoff, Marijke Gijswijt-Hofstra, eds., *Toverij in Nederland, 1795–1985. Bibliografie* (Amsterdam, 1990).

[42] Henningsen, 'Witch persecution', 148.

[43] Cf. Heinrich J. Dingeldein, 'Spuren fortlebenden Hexenglaubens. Zu einer Geschichte aus dem hessischen Odenwald und ihrer Hintergründen', *Hessische Blätter für Volks- und Kulturforschung*, 14/15 (1983), 18–30.

[44] This approach seeks to move beyond that in which several aspects of witchcraft are only discussed one by one, cf. Alan Macfarlane, *Witchcraft in Tudor and Stuart England: A Regional and Comparative Study* (London, 1970); Adrian Pollock, 'Social and economic characteristics of witchcraft accusations in sixteenth- and seventeenth-century Kent', *Archaeologia Cantiana*, 95 (1979), 37–48. See also the chapter on the social context in Levack's synthesis, *The Witch-Hunt*.

[45] See, for example, J. J. Voskuil, 'Les limites de la méthode cartographique', *Technologies, idéologies, pratiques*, 4 (1982/3), 105–16.

concepts, as well as the notion of person categories.[46] In witchcraft discourse, we now are able to ask in which broader category (i.e. *genre*) specific notions were placed and what sort of persons were involved. It has been found that a minimal set of person categories would contain three roles: the bewitched, the witch and the unwitchment expert, 'each of them is defined by the place that is consigned to him by the two others'.[47]

The sequence in which the points are applied is not compulsory; patterns and trends can be revealed by considering distribution before genre. But it remains vital first to break witchcraft down into its various manifestations, to consider, for example, the different processes or persons that were thought to be bewitched and the different techniques that were employed to lift a charm. In nineteenth-century Drenthe (a province in the eastern Netherlands), to mention but one example, the bewitching of butterchurns was restricted to the cattle-breeding areas. It was not attributed to specific persons and was therefore fought with general counter-measures (like a cross on the churn or a page from the Bible in it). The number of occurrences increased with the increase in dairy farming; it decreased to virtual non-existence with the establishment of butter factories.[48] Apart from the impersonality of this kind of witchcraft,[49] the findings seem pretty obvious. They show, however, that a specific form of witchcraft could exhibit its own pattern and could, in that way, differ from other forms. An overall decline of witchcraft can be better understood when the different traditions and their fluctuations are taken into account. In the next paragraph I elucidate several different components of analysis, but this set can, of course, be extended.

IV

In June 1877, several Dutch newspapers reported a witchcraft case from Oude Wetering, a hamlet in the province of Zuid-Holland, near Leiden.

---

[46] Malcolm Crick, 'Recasting witchcraft', in Crick, *Explorations in Language and Meaning. Towards a Semantic Anthropology* (London, 1976), pp. 109–27; see also Crick, 'Anthropologists' witchcraft: symbolically defined or analytically undone?', *Journal of the Anthropological Society of Oxford*, 10 (1979), 139–46.

[47] Patrick Gaboriau, *La pensée ensorcellée: la sorcellerie actuelle en Anjou et en Vendée* (Les Sables-d'Olonne, 1987), p. 105, translation mine. See also Inge Schöck, *Hexenglaube in der Gegenwart, Empirische Untersuchungen in Südwestdeutschland* (Tübingen, 1978), p. 16.

[48] De Blécourt, *Termen van toverij*, pp. 192–4, 256.

[49] Cf. James Obelkevich, *Religion and Rural Society: South Lindsey 1825–1875* (Oxford, 1976), p. 285.

The story ran as follows. One of the children of a certain peat-bargee had died. When soon after a second child fell ill, suffering from severe intestinal pains and nervous fits, the father consulted the Scriptures and discovered that his children were under the spell of his nextdoor neighbour – a chaste girl, about 20 years of age, whose name and reputation were beyond reproach. Subsequently, the young woman was lured into the house and threatened in order to compel her to unwitch the child. She was luckily saved from her predicament by the other neighbours. Thereupon the bargee resorted to boiling a black chicken alive, which should have forced the witch to reenter his home. This also failing, he embarked to Amsterdam, to pay a visit to a soothsayer.[50]

This 'true account' can, of course, be seen as a story which does not refer to any concrete historical event and is only circulated in newspapers.[51] After all, the claim for 'truth' could be part of the story as a legend. In this special instance, I have not looked for independent sources; there are, nevertheless several court records that deal with similar cases.[52] But if the account is true, if the events it describes actually took place, should it be seen as an exceptional case (which would also need explanation)? I suggest this case is not unique. By commenting upon it I will show how it fits into contemporary witchcraft discourse.

First, there is the interpretation of illness as a result of witchcraft. It would be irrelevant to try to identify the kind of disease in medical terms, to translate it into official medical discourse. (Of course, if a doctor's comment had been transmitted, it would show how he reacted to witchcraft.) For even if there were sufficient indicators to reach a medical diagnosis in this case, other cases will show different illnesses (stomach aches, however, appear to have been attributed to witchcraft more often).[53] What counts here is the sequence. It was only after the second child took ill that the conclusion about the cause was reached. Sometimes

---

[50] *Provinciale Drentsche en Asser courant*, 14 June 1877, taken from the *Nieuwe Rotterdamsche Courant*, translation mine.

[51] Cf. Gillian Bennett and Paul Smith, eds., *The Questing Beast* (Sheffield, 1989); Jan Harold Brunvand, *The Mexican Pet. More 'New' Urban Legends and Some Old Favorites* (New York/London, 1988).

[52] On the divergence and convergence of newspaper accounts and court records, see de Blécourt, *Termen van toverij*, pp. 89–90. See for a conviction in a case of maltreatment of a (black) hen, Willem de Blécourt, 'Wie was de duivelbanner en andere vragen; het toverijgeval te Opheusden in 1918', *Volkscultuur*, 4: 2 (1987), 26–35.

[53] Cf. de Blécourt, *Termen van toverij*, pp. 151, 177.

disaster had to strike twice before it was recognised as witchcraft. As Devlin remarked in her collection of nineteenth-century French 'magical' customs: 'Only when the individual felt his bad luck to be unnatural and excessive did he start to think of witchcraft as the possible source of his troubles.'[54] How precisely the man (his wife is not mentioned, so he might have been a widower) divined who was to blame, remains unclear. He might have used divination by key and book,[55] in which case he must already have suspected his neighbour – she was certainly not generally known as a witch. He could not, however, have applied this method before he ascribed his child's illness to a human agent, so it is possible that to find the cause he just leafed through the Bible and stumbled upon a passage about witches.

The traditional way to counteract a bewitchment was to compel the witch to remove the charm by blessing her victim.[56] In this case, it was impossible for the suspected woman to escape the accusation, as witchcraft discourse left no way out. Either she pronounced the blessing, in which case any improvement of the sufferer was taken as a proof of her guilt, or she refused, which also counted as a sure indication of her involvement.[57] The only thing she could hope for was that no improvement set in, which would hardly have been probable given the effect the ceremony would have had on its participants. Confronted with the demand to cure a bewitched person on the spot, most women still tried to escape, by refusing, or by pretending that they did not know the right words. In both cases, physical persuasion was called for.

The trick with the black hen was also known in former times; it seems to have been typically Dutch[58] (as the use of witch bottles, for example, appears to have been confined to England).[59] By boiling the creature, one

---

[54] Devlin, *The Superstitious Mind*, p. 100.

[55] This technique was also found in nineteenth-century England, see Thomas, *Religion*, p. 255.

[56] Cf. Thomas, *Religion*, pp. 611, 648, 657; Briggs, *Communities*, pp. 26, 93; Devlin, *The Superstitious Mind*, p. 114. From this it should not be concluded that a witch could also lift the spells of others and therefore publicly practised healing, cf. Richard A. Horsley, 'Who were the witches? The social roles of the accused in the European witch trials', *Journal of Interdisciplinary History*, 9 (1979), 689–715.

[57] Cf. Briggs, *Communities*, 94. See also Schöck, *Hexenglaube in der Gegenwart*.

[58] Cf. de Waardt, *Toverij en samenleving*; in France poultry was boiled for this purpose too: see Devlin, *The Superstitious Mind*, p. 111.

[59] Thomas, *Religion*, pp. 648–9; Eric Maple, 'Cunning Murrel. A study of a nineteenth-century cunning man in Hadleigh, Essex', *Folklore*, 71 (1960), 37–43; Ernest W. Baughman, *Type and Motif Index of the Folktales of England and North America* ('s-Gravenhage, 1966), G271.4.7.

would irresistibly draw the witch to it.[60] As such, it could also be used to identify witches: the first one to step over the threshold while the rite was performed was taken for the culprit. Geographically, this 'chicken-test' was concentrated in the centre of the Netherlands, mainly in the provinces Zuid-Holland and Utrecht. In the northern provinces only the sick person's urine was boiled; in the predominantly Catholic areas in the south such techniques were absent.[61] Luring and identification methods underline the need to counteract witchcraft by dealing with the witch in person. They will mostly have been transmitted orally, between neighbours and family members, but also by specialists.

The use of Holy Writ, however, is the most striking feature of the 1877 case. It shows a direct relation between religion (as it was interpreted by the flock) and witchcraft. We may also surmise that the peat-bargee was of an orthodox Calvinist conviction. Since a relationship of this kind does not fit academic boundaries, it has, so far, not been generally acknowledged. Writers on Protestantism and on orthodox communities considered witchcraft as belonging to 'superstition' and not to religion proper, and thus to be out of their scope. Folklorists, by defining non-religious 'superstition' as the principal ingredient of legends, did not think it proper to inquire about religious opinions. The spatial distribution pattern of techniques like the chicken-test and others that were meant to lure witches nevertheless points to a general connection between an aggressive kind of witchcraft and orthodox Calvinism: they occupied the same area. The 'black belt', as this area is called, extends from the islands of Zeeland in the south-west of the Netherlands, across the region between the great rivers and the lowlands of Utrecht towards

---

[60] An ostensive connection between witches and black chickens is mentioned nowhere and remains speculative. In other cases nails or the victim's urine was boiled, sometimes together with the chicken. Since nails were thought to have been vomited in cases of witchcraft, the use of them, as well of the urine, could be interpreted as an instance of 'sympathetic magic' (cf. Baughman, *Type and Motif Index*, G257.1, G271.1). Performers of these rites though, are not known to resort to this classification and it is also doubtful whether they would reveal this way of thinking in other situations.

[61] In the 1930s folklorists conducted a survey in which they asked how witches could be recognised in general and specifically if the informants knew if divination with key and Bible and the chicken test had taken place in their village. Checked against newspaper accounts and later folklore fieldwork, the answers provide a fair view of the occurrence of these practices at the beginning of the century. See Willem de Blécourt, 'Heksengeloof: toverij en religie in Nederland tussen 1890 en 1940', *Sociologische gids*, 36 (1986), 245–66. On the folklore surveys, see A. J. Dekker (introduction) and J. J. Schell (index), *De volkskundevragenlijsten 1–58 (1934–1988) van het P. J. Meertens-Instituut* (Amsterdam, 1989).

the borders of the former Zuiderzee and the island of Urk and from there up to the north-east of Friesland.[62] If one region is put into focus, the pattern might even be seen in more detail. In the north-eastern province of Drenthe, bewitchments of people mainly occurred in the peat districts, that also harboured the orthodox Calvinists of the province.[63] It would hardly be reasonable to accept that the close-knit communities of the orthodox Calvinists were divided into a group of 'superstitious' non-believers and a group of ardent adherents to the Calvinist creed.

Concrete, though scarce, evidence of the relation is also present. We see a deacon of the church in Dantumadeel (Friesland) performing divination with Bible and key, an orthodox farmer at Smilde (Drenthe) consulting a witch doctor, a labourer of the same persuasion in Nijeveen (Drenthe) having a bewitched child. We come across almost endemic witchcraft in typical orthodox communities like Staphorst (Overijssel) and Urk. In Nunspeet (Gelderland) a strong believer even tried to commit suicide after he had carried out the chicken-test (it was later said that he hanged himself, not because of the sermon his minister had delivered on the prohibition for true Christians to believe in witches, but because of the consternation the case had caused and to escape prison). From nearby Lunteren, a woman was reported to have said that it was written in the Bible that witches existed; another woman in Bennekom (south-west Gelderland) never went into the church, as she feared a certain family of witches, so she listened to the sermon while sitting in the consistory. Finally, on the south-western islands of Zuid-Holland and Zeeland it was noted on several occasions that places in the Scriptures were cited to underpin ideas about witchcraft.[64] The connection was surely not only to be found in Oude Wetering. But how is it to be explained?

V

'The boundaries of "magical" activity', Thomas concluded, 'were thus determined by the attitude of the Church to its own formulae and to the potentialities of nature.'[65] With the Reformation 'magic' was taken out

---

[62] For a general characterisation, see, for example, Niek Miedema, 'The orthodox protestants and enforced marriage', in Jeremy Boissevain and Jojada Verrips, eds., *Dutch Dilemmas. Anthropologists Look at the Netherlands* (Assen/Maastricht, 1989), pp. 5–23.

[63] De Blécourt, *Termen van toverij*, pp. 204–5.

[64] De Blécourt, 'Heksengeloof', pp. 258–60.   [65] Thomas, *Religion*, p. 304.

of the church. 'The protestants were helping to make a distinction in kind between magic and religion, the one a coercive ritual, the other an intercessionary one'.[66] They 'attacked not only folk magic, but also large part of the old ecclesiastical magic as well'.[67] Their campaign seems to have succeeded in the end, in so far as Thomas himself submitted to Protestant theology by portraying 'magic' and religion in terms of rivalry.[68] In this view, witchcraft as part of a Protestant religious system will appear to be an anomaly, which can only be resolved by taking refuge in the theory of 'survivals'.

So far I have concentrated on some of the more questionable aspects of *Religion and the Decline of Magic*. There is, of course, much that will remain beyond criticism, for example the author's insights into the praxis of paradoxes.[69] If Protestantism promoted self-help and presented it as an alternative to superstition, accordingly it left some room for dealing with witchcraft. 'Protestantism', Thomas notes, 'forced its adherents into the intolerable position of asserting the reality of witchcraft, yet denying the existence of an effective and legitimate form of protection or cure.'[70] This was exactly the dilemma that faced nineteenth-century orthodox believers. Their leaders did not teach that witchcraft was unreal or some kind of nonsense, they classified it as devilish, thereby legitimising its existence.[71] To the flock, both the catechism and the Bible, by endorsing the reality of witchcraft, corresponded with their experiences and even helped to sustain their explanations. But, unlike Catholicism, their official bodies did not provide general and practical counter-measures.

Catholics could easily obtain blessed items to protect their houses, persons and livestock from evil influences. If needed, they could call in the local pastor or consult a specialist in one of the monasteries. For Protestants these ways were officially closed, although some did visit Catholic priests. Their orthodox Calvinist brethren however, who were caught between the official creed and the need for practical cures, placed self-help above superstition. In their milieu bewitchments called for a violent reaction. Yet in all the cases in which unwitchment had to be forced, violence was only a means. In specific settings it might have been the only way to secure a desired aim, but it was hardly seen as the ultimate solution.

[66] *Ibid.*, p. 88.   [67] *Ibid.*, p. 305.
[68] See, for example, *ibid.*, pp. 206, 763.
[69] See, for instance, *ibid.*, p. 687 on the paradox of demonology.
[70] *Ibid.*, p. 590.   [71] De Blécourt, 'Heksengeloof', p. 260.

By discussing content in relation to genre and spatial distribution, I hope to have shown one of the possibilities of future witchcraft research. It is, of course, not the whole story. Speaking in terms of witchcraft can be considered as a way those intimately involved tried to comprehend developments that were initially beyond their control. While the manner in which they conducted the witchcraft discourse was closely linked to their religious outlook, the diseases and disturbances they reacted to had much to do with social, demographic and economic trends. To trace the interrelations between these trends and witchcraft accusations, the latter will have to be differentiated, as well as localised and temporalised. Thomas' study, though a product of its time, has, by taking witchcraft beyond the confines of the trials, very much initiated this line of approach. No doubt he regrets the fact that he has had so few critical followers during the last twenty years or so.

Index

Past and Present Publications

General Editor; JOANNA INNES, *Somerville College, Oxford*

Family and Inheritance: Rural Society in Western Europe 1200–1800, edited by Jack Goody, Joan Thirsk and E. P. Thompson*

French Society and the Revolution, edited by Douglas Johnson

Peasants, Knights and Heretics: Studies in Medieval English Social History, edited by R. H. Hilton*

Town in Societies: Essays in Economic History and Historical Sociology, edited by Philip Abrams and E. A. Wrigley*

Desolation of a City: Coventry and the Urban Crisis of the Late Middle Ages, Charles Phythian-Adams

Puritanism and Theatre: Thomas Middleton and Opposition Drama under the Early Stuarts, Margot Heinemann*

Lords and Peasants in a Changing Society: The Estates of the Bishopric of Worcester 680–1450, Christopher Dyer

Life, Marriage and Death in a Medieval Parish: Economy, Society and Demography in Halesowen 1270–1400, Ziv Razi

Biology, Medicine and Society 1740–1940, edited by Charles Webster

The Invention of Tradition, edited by Eric Hobsbawm and Terence Ranger*

Industrialization before Industrialization: Rural Industry and the Genesis of Capitalism, Peter Kriedte, Hans Medick and Jürgen Schlumbohm*

The Republic in the Village: The People of the Var from the French Revolution to the Second Republic, Maurice Agulhon†

Social Relations and Ideas: Essays in Honour of R. H. Hilton, edited by T. H. Aston, P. R. Coss, Christopher Dyer and Joan Thirsk

A Medieval Society: The West Midlands at the End of the Thirteenth Century, R. H. Hilton

Winstanley: 'The Law of Freedom' and Other Writings, edited by Christopher Hill

Crime in Seventeenth-Century England: A County Study, J. A. Sharpe†

The Crisis of Feudalism: Economy and Society in Eastern Normandy c. 1300–1500, Guy Bois†

The Development of the Family and Marriage in Europe, Jack Goody*

Disputes and Settlements: Law and Human Relations in the West, edited by John Bossy

Rebellion, Popular Protest and the Social Order in Early Modern England, edited by Paul Slack

Epidemics and Ideas: Essays on the Historical Perception of Pestilence, edited by Terence Ranger and Paul Slack

The Political Economy of Shopkeeping in Milan, 1886–1922, Jonathan Morris

After Chartism: Class and Nation in English Radical Politics, 1848–1874, Margot C. Finn

Commoners: Common Right, Enclosure and Social Change in England, 1700–1820, J. M. Neeson

Land and Popular Politics in Ireland: County Mayo from the Plantation to the Land War, Donald E. Jordan Jr.

The Castilian Crisis of the Seventeenth Century: New Perspectives on the Economic and Social History of Seventeenth Century Spain, I. A. A. Thompson and Bartolome Yun

The Culture of Clothing: Dress and Fashion in the Ancien Régime, Daniel Roche†

The Sense of the People: Politics, Culture and Imperialism in England, 1715–1785, Kathleen Wilson

Witchcraft in Early Modern Europe: Studies in Culture and Belief, edited by Jonathan Barry, Marianne Hester and Gareth Roberts

* Also published in paperback

† Co-published with the Maison des Sciences de l'Homme, Paris